A Long Way from Tipperary

A Memoir
by
Lloyd Mullen

Bound Biographies

Produced in association with

Bound Biographies

10 Pipits Croft, Bicester, OX26 6XW

www.boundbiographies.com

Typeset in Garamond by www.wordsbydesign.co.uk

09 08 07 06 05 04 03 8 7 6 5 4 3 2 1

British Library Cataloguing in Publication Data.
A catalogue record for this book is available from the British Library

ISBN: 978-1-905178-62-9

For

The family who tolerated
and Valerie who typed.

Introit

This is not an attempt at an accurate record, it is simply how I remember, after eighty years, some of the things that I saw, heard about and did over those years. They, of course, are coloured by my feelings at the time and my feelings now. They are also coloured by the fact that I am constantly remembering little bits and pieces that I've left out and also that I'm trying to leave out the names of many people because it would be just too confusing for everybody who read this later on to try to remember whose name belonged to whom. However, I'm convinced that I have made an honest attempt to reproduce, for family who come after, the happiness of life that I have had so far.

I hope I've included some of the guilt feelings that I have at being so happy in the midst of a period of history which was quite dreadful for millions, particularly in the countries where I lived – North and South of Ireland, Pakistan, India, Sri Lanka, Uganda – all these places have had dreadful turmoil in the eighty years that I'm talking about. I can only say that the people in those countries, as I met them, have all been extremely kind and pleasant and quite different from the sort of people we read about in the newspapers, who apparently make the history in these places.

There is also, of course, the guilt feeling that one hasn't been able to prevent some of the dreadful things that have happened, but one simply has to go on struggling to bring about new attitudes in people when they may have very good reasons for having the bad attitudes which come out.

So I hope you will forgive any sense of judgement that you come across here because I don't mean it to be a sense of judgement; I mean it to be just simply the facts as I saw them at the time, and indeed maybe not even the facts but just the events as they presented themselves to me.

Anybody who is going to read to the end has my gratitude.

Christmas 2012

Begin at the beginning

Younger sister Pearl, self, Mother and twin-sister Ruby, as we looked when we left school

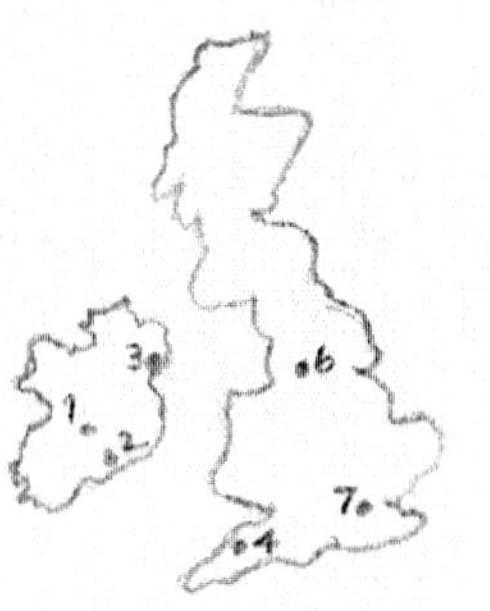

1.	TIPPERARY	Ireland
2.	WATERFORD	Ireland
3.	CO. DOWN	Northern Ireland
4.	DEVONSHIRE	England
5.	LAHORE	Pakistan
6.	MANCHESTER	England
7.	LONDON	England
8.	BANGALORE	India
9.	COLOMBO	Sri Lanka
10.	KARACHI	Pakistan
11.	KAMPALA	Uganda

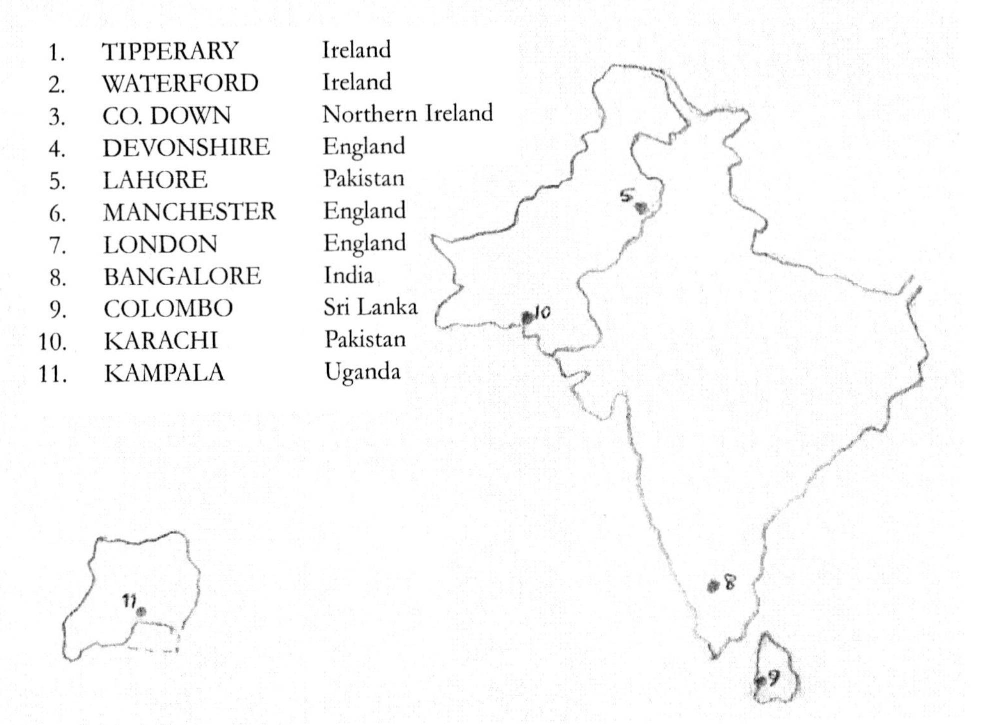

Places and Dates

		Chapters
Tipperary	1931 – 1940	1 – 2
Waterford	1940 – 1948	2 – 3
Co. Down	1948 – 1956	3 – 5
Devon	1956 – 1959	5
Pakistan	1959 – 1968	5 – 10
Manchester	1968 – 1970	10 – 11
London	1970 – 1972	12
India	1972 – 1974	13
Sri Lanka	1974 – 1978	14
Pakistan	1978 – 1982	15 – 16
London	1982 – 1987	16 – 17
Uganda	1987 – 1991	18
Retirement	1991 – Present	19

CHAPTERS

1
Till Daddy Died

My toy horse jogged across the kitchen flagstones towards my nanny – Mum-Mum we called her – and she raised her feet in mock fear. How kind, I thought, she's not really afraid but she's pretending to be in order to make me happy. I was three years of age and this was my first realisation that someone outside the family loved me. My parents and twin sister automatically loved me – we were all part of one unit – but Mum-Mum was outside that unit; as was Henry, our gardener, who had had to bury some dead puppies only the day before. Our nanny was called 'Mum-Mum' because her daughter, Nellie, also worked in our house and called her 'Mother', which we couldn't pronounce.

Mum-Mum and Henry came from Holycross in Tipperary. Mum-Mum's house was a one-roomed thatched cottage. Henry's was similar but had a slate roof. Both were only half a mile away. The land in between was owned by farmers, great hurlers or Gaelic football players – two Irish games organised by the Gaelic Athletic Association, which had been founded in nearby Thurles, where my father had his solicitor's office.

My father was greatly respected because he was a Protestant solicitor who would defend Catholics in court, even IRA men if he was convinced that their case was just. The First World War had ended only twelve years before and many of our neighbours were Protestant landed gentry retired from that conflict, with my father as their solicitor and another world conflict beginning to brew up.

Our house was called Springfield. We moved from it when I was three to a large old rectory called Glenree. The move was the first time in my life I had been able to see out of the windows of our Fiat motorcar, the back of which was filled with pillows and blankets, on top of which my sister, Ruby, and I sat looking out. We wobbled a bit but managed with Hannah holding us. Hannah was the younger of two sisters who would work with us in our new home. They were nieces of the gardener and had to be trained as maids. They turned out to be very good maids, although I do remember my mother complaining about dirty wainscots from time to time!

The family outside Glenree – September 1939

We had great fun in this new house, running up and down the front stairs and up and down the back stairs, and down a very long corridor from the back of the main house to the kitchen wing. We were able to ride our little tricycles up and down this corridor, crashing into walls and each other. A lot of work was being done. The house had no running water when we moved in and a huge tank was being built out in the middle of the yard – pipes and new lavatories and bathrooms being installed. This was, of course, great fun to us but we must have been a frightful nuisance to all the other people who were trying to get the place into shape. Things were not easy right out in the country – we were four miles from the nearest town.

Twin tricyclists

We came to love both Maggie and Hannah, and a lady called Mrs Collins who used to come in, would you believe it, at five o'clock in the morning to light the big range because there was no heating or lighting. Henry had a little oil house out at the far end of the yard where he lit twenty-seven oil lamps for a full house in the evening. We had the smell of paraffin, the dust of coal, and bits of wood lying around where people had tried to start the fires.

There was the complication of animals. One of our curates asked my father to look after his Alsatian while he went on holiday... without telling my father that the dog occasionally had fits! An unfortunate carpenter was chased by the dog and had to jump in through a low window just as the dog nipped off the back of his trousers! There were mice and cats, and rats out in the yard; and there were foxes that used to come in and kill the chickens. They were a great nuisance; you couldn't keep out a fox even with the best wire netting – it would find a way of getting around it, or through it, or over it. A little beyond that we had a local farmer's cows coming in each evening to be milked and we loved going along to watch this. Some were very good milkers and some weren't. Slowly we learned that different people had different skills.

Perhaps the most interesting connection we had with animals was with the local hunt. The whipper-in used to take the dogs, or hounds as we were taught to call them, up and down the road outside our main avenue and boundary once or twice a week, and we would see her going by, sitting up on her horse. She got to know my mother very well and she would give a toot on the hunting horn and whenever that toot came, we would all rush out to see her. Later on we were actually taken to 'The Hunt' in the car with Daddy and driven from place to place. We would see the horses and the hounds and occasionally, very occasionally, we actually saw Reynard himself... although he was usually much too clever to get caught.

That hunt was the beginning of a lifelong friendship with the huntsman's family, for their son went to the same school I did. I followed him, about twenty years behind, in a career that took him right across the North-West-Frontier and back again, and we remained friends until he died aged ninety-seven.

That girl who we saw tooting the horn married another friend and went off to Northern Rhodesia.

Just as we children had great fun exploring the inside of the house and exploring the old outbuildings around the yard, which had a pump right in the centre, we also had fun exploring the very large orchard which had been left behind by those who lived in the house before – plenty of trees, gooseberry bushes, and ploughed-up land where we grew potatoes and vegetables. We even grew figs along the back wall of a cowshed, which was one of the walls of the garden. Beyond that there were fields in which we had wonderful fun, running about wherever we liked. Some of these fields had dells: long, wide, deep hollows full of bushes, trees and mystery spots where you might find a fox or a badger. We never did, but we were always afraid we would because they were supposed to be able to give you a bad bite if you got in their way.

So we ran about the place; in fact, the commonest expression we used to hear from both our mother and Nanny was, "Now, off you go – run out and play."

Running out and playing consisted mainly of first a dash through the flowerbeds, over some of the paths and the avenue, on to the little fence and under a huge tree where there was a swing. We would jump onto the swing, sit on it and get going – whichever of us got there first, Ruby or myself, pushing the other, shouting and laughing. In the distance, Hannah or maybe Mum-Mum or Nelly would appear to make quite sure we weren't damaging ourselves, although really I think they were more worried about the flowerbeds and the nice things that Henry had planted for my mother. My mother was very keen on gardening, and very good at it. Then we'd dash down through the pathways under the trees until we came to an old house hidden among the trees where we could get inside and play ghosts. And then on down to the end where two pieces of wire stopped us from going into the field.

My father didn't farm the land; he let it out to different local farmers. One field just outside that wire was often used to grow wheat and sometimes beet (sugar beet), because at that time sugar beet was quite a big thing in Ireland. Some sugar beet factories had been built, one right close to us on the way into our local town of Thurles.

Another thing we loved to do was to follow the local farmers when they were ploughing. I remember the expression, 'Opening a headland'. Now opening a headland was a great skill because it meant you went into a rugged, rough-shaped field, full of nothing but grass, weeds and remnants of last year's crops. The ploughman who opened the headland had the job of getting down to one end, near enough to the ditch to make full use of the rest of the land, but not so close in as to get every future implement entangled in the hedge, and from that point on, with his horse and his plough, plough a straight furrow right up to the other end of the field. Very difficult – but when he had succeeded he then had to turn around and come back down, parallel to that headland opening furrow, usually about, say, seven or eight feet across from it because, of course, he couldn't turn the animal and the plough in such a narrow space as to come right beside it. So he had to come down parallel to it – that was a skill – and then turn round and go up alongside the first one! Two little children capable of running under the plough or under the horse's hooves or the ploughman's feet and making a great nuisance of themselves were no help, but we enjoyed it immensely. Then, later on was the sowing of the seed and harrowing, and ultimately reaping.

It was a splendid experience and gave us a great practical understanding of what seasons are about, what horses are about and what hard work is about.

One of our favourite ploughmen was the eldest of four sons of a farmer who lived up the road. I remember he once put me up on the horse when they were unshackling at the end of the day and gave me a ride on it. I recall being quite frightened when the horse ran away with me jogging about on its back like a tiny sack of potatoes and Johnny saying, "All right, all right! Whoa! Whoa!" and me trying not to fall off; I didn't fall off, but I was pretty relieved when we came to a halt and he was able to come and lift me down.

Especially I remember the sheep and how quickly they would crop the grass down low. If you really wanted to get your lawn done quickly you'd get some sheep in on it and then get them off before they did too much damage. We watched the man come in with his sheepdog and stand at the gate. To our amazement, the dog would go off around in a circle and very gently shepherd the sheep out onto the road and back to the farm where he wanted them to go. There were competitions for this.

A son of one of our local family friends became famous as the Irish Champion Sheepdog Handler, while a cousin of ours married a girl (a neighbour of his up in County Kildare) who became the Ploughing Champion of Ireland and was specially commended for being able to open the straightest, firmest, most even headland in the whole country.

So these things had a kind of fall-back effect on our lives in a way that we could never have expected.

In the centre of the lawn, right opposite our house, there was a very old oak tree. It had one of those stumps of a base – a trunk about six or seven feet across going up only about six feet and then breaking out into three enormous trunks, each of them bigger than an average tree, going off in different directions. The result of this trio of trunks meant that there was a hollow into which you could climb and sit and become monarch of all you surveyed.

On a warm summer day, there was nothing better than to get a copy of a comic – the Beano or the Dandy – and sit in there. When people came shouting for you to come in to lunch or tea, or to get washed or go to bed, you just stayed there quietly and didn't say anything, but, of course, the household quickly learned where you were and would creep across and suddenly you would find Maggie or Hannah jumping up and saying, "Ah! Caught you. Now come on," and then you had to go in and do whatever they wanted you to do.

There was a small thorn tree halfway down the avenue where a pigeon would come and make a nest every year. Now whether it was the same pigeon or not I don't know, but certainly a pigeon would sit there and not be frightened. I used to climb up when I discovered the nest and get quite close to it, looking to see if there were eggs. Sometimes there were and sometimes there weren't. We had been taught never to touch eggs in the nest... and we didn't. I would sometimes get up and the pigeon might be there, but it didn't fly away – it just looked at me and I turned round and went away.

And it was the same with the orchard – there was one particular apple tree where a thrush used to come year by year and make a nest. I went in and looked at it, and there was the little thrush on the nest but it didn't fly away either.

These were permanent fixtures in our lives – the pigeon, the thrush and even the crows. There weren't too many crows or jackdaws; actually it took us a very long time to distinguish between a jackdaw and a crow, but birds did play a part in our lives.

Another thing that we got used to was damaging ourselves; we were always falling out of trees or scraping our knees on the ground, or generally cutting ourselves with some knife that we shouldn't have picked up, or scratching ourselves as we tried to push our way through some barbed wire fence, but it became a habit not to worry about those things – they were just a part of life. I'm glad they were because later on when unfortunate things happened we weren't bothered about it too much.

Further afield our lives were restricted to visits to friends of our parents or the local church; for instance, we had great fun going to the Master of Hounds' place because we saw all the hounds in their kennels and we watched them being fed – all the meat being thrown in and you heard their howling – and then the latest story from the Master about where they had hunted last week and where they were going to hunt next week. We also saw some of the horses in their stables, and he explained to us why this one could jump and that one couldn't and what happened when somebody fell off.

And then there was another family who had a house down on the river. We used to go to them, and there was a story of how one evening when they came back from a party, they left the car in the drive without putting on the brake and came out next morning to find it had gently rolled down headfirst into the river! Fortunately, at that point the river wasn't too deep and there was enough of the car sticking up for it to be dragged out, but engines in those days didn't dry off too quickly and this became a celebrated story around the place.

Another family lived in the wonderfully named Castlefogarty. It was the remnant of a small castle, half of it turned into a modern house, but it did have to us the great advantage of being accessible only through about an acre of trees. You wound your way in and out of these trees and finally came out onto very well kept lawns where invariably you saw six or seven Red Setters, beautiful animals, running about the place. When they saw you, as a stranger, coming, they came bounding across and looked marvellous, with the auburn, feathery effect of their coats against the well-cut green lawns.

There were two children in this family, a boy and a girl. The boy was very quiet, well mannered, gentle and well behaved, while the girl was a tremendous tomboy – well-behaved but a real tomboy, and she was the only one in the whole countryside around who was able to climb their monkey-puzzle tree! She actually used to go in underneath and climb up close to the trunk. Now, anyone who has seen a monkey-puzzle tree with harsh prickles at every point will understand why a monkey can be puzzled, but this young lady was not puzzled – she managed it!

Once when we went to an Easter egg hunt at their place, she was the one who had set it out, and one of the Easter eggs, wrapped in silver paper, was to be seen halfway up the trunk of this monkey-puzzle tree. Well, there wasn't a single person wanting to even attempt to go and get that, but she did; she climbed up and brought it back down.

On the way to their place there was a particular piece of road, a little winding incline up to a turn to the left, with small trees and bushes on either side, which always comes to mind when I meet those lines by Katharine Tynan:

> All in an April evening April airs were abroad,
> A sheep with her little lambs passed me by on the road,
> A sheep with her little lambs passed me by on the road,
> All in an April evening I thought on the Lamb of God.

That little piece of road wound its way to Mum-Mum's house where we sometimes went to see whether she would give us sweets to eat. Then we would come back again, after what was considered by the maid who was with us to be a proper outing for the children that afternoon – make their legs sufficiently tired for them to be quiet when they got back to the house! I still see that piece of road as one of the most peaceful things in the universe.

And so it was that against this very peaceful background my sister and I were given a birthday present on our fourth birthday – a special present… and that was to start going to school!

We set off with Daddy in his car. He drove down the road, past the church, round the corner, down over the river, up the other side, past the sugar-beet factory which was new and shining (they even had new railway lines bringing the trains laden with sugar-beet into it) and then on into the first houses on the outskirts of Thurles, and finally to our little 'National School' as it was called.

With Nellie outside Mum-Mum's house

There were about, I think, between thirteen to sixteen children in all; it was a really comfortable, small house whose original large front drawing room had been turned into a classroom and the gardens around had been turned into a playground. That was where we met Mrs Walshe, whom I now look back on as a wonderful teacher, though at the time I just thought she was a nice, kind lady who had been given the job of looking after us for a while.

From the very start, school was for us an enlarging experience. First there were many more children than we were used to meeting; we had really not met other children en-masse before and therefore we just played with each other; now here were about a dozen other children to talk to, mix with, run with, play with, sit beside in class, listen to their answers, see them putting up their hands. We discovered we had to put up our hands if we knew the answer. That was one kind of enlargement.

Another kind of enlargement was quite different. Mrs Walshe had, along one side of the classroom wall, a huge map of the world and I remember she showed us also a globe of the world and told us that the world was round, like a ball, so we believed it because she was a teacher and she said so. Then she showed us, in a funny way, how you could take this ball and take the map that was on it and try to pull it out straight into one piece, from the back, so that you only saw the front, and that front was in fact like the big map on the wall beside us. So we looked and she asked, "Does anyone know anybody in Australia?" Somebody did; "...in America?" Somebody did. Mrs Walshe put her pointer, which was like a billiard cue, right on Australia or right on America. Slowly we learned about the continents.

Then we learned about countries, and all the time she was coming back down to where we were because I remember she finally showed three maps in turn, one of Europe, one of the British Isles and one of Ireland. Then she pointed to Ireland in the whole big map of the world and we all said, "Oooh! So small, oooh! oooh!" We were really disappointed, dejected almost, that Ireland, which we thought was a wonderful place, should be such a tiny speck just on the edge of all these other big countries.

Anyway, she went on and made matters more interesting by showing us maps of Ireland, then maps of the county of Tipperary, then a plan of the town of Thurles. She was even able to show the spot where our school was, where we were just at that moment, and she said, "Now that's where we are in the world." We said, "Oh! Miss, we don't quite understand that," but we did understand, funnily – we knew that she was telling the truth, and we believed her because she was the teacher.

Then she talked about the school and how big it was compared with houses nearby and how small it was compared with the big cinema just opposite to it across the road. Then she showed us a plan of the school and our classroom and asked, "Are we able to keep the whole world clean and tidy?" Of course we weren't; that was a silly question. And, "Are we able to keep Ireland clean and tidy?" "Oh, no, how can we? Other people have to do that." And gradually she worked back to the simple fact that we had a classroom of our own and that by keeping that clean and tidy we were making our contribution to keeping the world clean and tidy and we couldn't expect other people to do so if we didn't keep our little bit clean and tidy! That was the second kind of enlargement.

The third kind was a rather odd one. I think probably after one or maybe two years there, by the time we were about five or six, for some reason we started to learn French. Now, I do remember one thing which stuck in my mind, and that was how the word 'now' in English (three little letters), in French is 'maintenant' – or, as we pronounced it the moment we saw it, main-ten-ant... such a long word. So that was a kind of third enlarging.

It was a very useful lesson because somehow or other we felt part of the world and Mrs Walshe managed to make us feel that we had some interest in the world. It altered our ideas about things because when we saw the train coming to the sugar-beet factory on our way home, we knew that train had come from somewhere else where they grew beet.

And so the world began to make sense for us after about our fifth birthday. It was a great year that, a great year of widening experience.

One incident took place on these journeys with Daddy to school in the morning, which gave me a jolt. It happened like this: we were driving down the road, this narrow, Irish country road, past our church. Turning to the right we discovered a small queue of motorcars and lorries – actually one was moving away. There was a lorry and another car, and Daddy had to stop and wait behind that car. We watched a policeman who walked across the road to each driver, who would then lean out and hand his driving licence to the policeman. I asked Daddy what was happening and he said, "He's just checking peoples' driving licences, that's all," and he leant across me and took something from the glove box – I think it was his driving licence. Anyway, the policeman dealt with the motorcar in front of us and that was satisfactory and then Daddy drove up a little bit and leant towards the window and said, "Good morning, Officer." The policeman took a step back and saluted and said, "Good morning, Sir – sorry, I didn't mean to stop you... that's all right, Sir, you go straight on." Daddy said, "Thank you very much," handed me back the piece of paper, which I put into the glove box, and we went on. But I had the feeling that there was some unfairness here which I wasn't too happy about, because the driver of the lorry and the driver of the car in front of us had had to stop and hand the thing over and wait while the policeman inspected it, but because my father appeared to be well-known the policeman didn't bother to check. I felt, and still feel, uneasy about it, even to this day.

One day in school, another boy and I crashed into each other as we tried to jump over the small cock of hay in the middle of the playground at the same time from opposite directions. His forehead came up in an enormous bump, and my eyebrow was split open and blood went everywhere. I was taken into Mrs Walshe, who got her son, an eighteen-year-old boy, to take me up the road to the doctor, who looked at it, mopped it up and then began to put in two or three stitches.

Mrs Walshe's son was watching all this and as the doctor was putting in a stitch – literally it seemed to me, with almost a needle and thread the way you would do some sewing – the poor unfortunate youth went green, absolutely green, not grey, not white but green, and he fainted and fell onto the floor of the surgery. The doctor said to me, "Stay there, don't move," and left a needle and thread just above my eye while he went to deal with this boy. He called a nurse from another room to look after him, then came back to me and finished stitching my wound. About ten minutes later I had the task of bringing this eighteen-year-old safely back to his mother in the school, with my own eye well patched up.

Can you imagine, too, in those days, in the little shop next to the school, where we were allowed to go in break time – just one at a time if we stayed on the pavement and went straight into the shop –

we were able to get forty aniseed balls for a penny, so, naturally, even if we had a ha'penny we went along and bought twenty.

Another place where we went fairly regularly with Daddy was to the Golf Club. I am surprised now, looking back, that we children were allowed to be there at all, but we had to obey very strict rules, such as always standing in particular places, always staying quiet and not moving and only following after the golfers once they had started to move along. We were never allowed to pick a ball out of the long grass (which was called the rough) and so on. While it was a nuisance at the time, it was actually a very good discipline because it taught us that if other people want to enjoy themselves in a way that you can't, then you must simply stand by and watch and let them enjoy themselves. My father was a good golfer with a scratch handicap.

He also liked his game of tennis. He was a good tennis player and I think it was from him that I developed my love of sport – different kinds of sport.

One thing I didn't pick up from him, unfortunately, was his music. He was very musical and a good pianist – he always had a grand piano in the drawing room and played away. He was also a good singer and sang in a Methodist choir in Dublin when he was in the Boys' Brigade, where he was a captain. Music was a great part of his life. It never became such a full part of mine and I sometimes wonder what I have missed because music is a very great unsolved mystery.

Of course, to all these comings and goings there was a very steady background. My mother was not with us on many of these outings but somehow or other we knew that she was there back at home with the rest of the people in the house, making things right, as we used to think of it, so that whenever we came back there was either a meal for us or the place was clean and tidy or there was something to be done or not done.

I remember one most interesting time; she was a bit excited one day and she said that there was going to be a showing of the Aurora Borealis – can you imagine that word for us little ones! We were to go and have a good rest after our tea, and then she would get us up and let us come to a certain good window where we would look out and see this Aurora Borealis.

Now I have no idea how she knew there was going to be an Aurora Borealis because it is the last thing you would expect in Tipperary – it's not anywhere near the North Pole or any place where this is supposed to happen but, sure enough, it did happen and it was the most splendid sight. I have never seen one like it since, even though we've been up near the Pole and seen the Green Aurora Borealis that occurs nowadays. We were under seven years of age, and our mother held our heads against the glass of the window to make sure we could see it from inside the house – I suppose it was too cold to go outside. It had literally every colour of the rainbow, like the whole spectrum you see in a really good rainbow, waving, wibbling and wobbling, growing big and growing small, and growing bright and growing, not dark, but faint, right across the whole sky. It was an absolute kaleidoscope of marvellous colours, happening, happening, happening. I've forgotten how it ended but anyway, we went to bed extremely pleased and even to this day I remain extremely pleased about that lovely feeling.

The other spectacle of colour which this memory reminds me of was my mother and father setting out for a fancy-dress ball dressed in Pierrot costumes. We looked at them and thought they were half clowns or something, but we were allowed to be brought down from our beds by the maids to see them before they went off to this fancy-dress ball. They really did look like marvellous fairies or clowns in their costumes – just as bright but in a very limited way compared with the Aurora Borealis.

We said goodbye to them in the hall, at the foot of a huge grandfather clock, where I was always getting into trouble because I used to love to open the door of this grandfather clock, step inside and hide from my sister or anyone else that we were playing with, maybe Mum-Mum or Nellie. Of course, I disturbed the weights and the chains and everything else in the works, and my father would then be very angry and I would be told never to do it again. Finally, I think the stage came when I didn't ever do it again, but in between there were one or two contretemps I can remember very well when my father was most displeased. I have to say in fairness that my sister was very much better behaved; she never got inside the grandfather clock nor did any of those bad things that I seemed to always be doing.

In those days the hall stairs, as we called them, which went up to the first floor, were very important in our lives; also the windows out of which we could look at the countryside. Occasionally, we used to come to the top of the stairs and if anything was going on down in the hall and we were supposed to be in bed – maybe it was, say, nine o'clock at night and we were meant to be asleep – we would try to peep by coming down one or two steps and look through the upper banisters to see if we could see what was going on.

The most exciting thing that we ever saw was the IRA men who came. We had seen them from our upstairs windows because they had switched off their headlamps as they came over the bridge about half a mile down the road – the bridge over the main railway line between Dublin and Cork. They then coasted down in the dark, very carefully drove into our place, got out of their cars as quietly as they could and came into the hall. My father would meet them and insist on them leaving their guns in the hall, standing upright against the wall on the other side of the grandfather clock. My mother, of course, was sometimes with us, sometimes down in the hall, but always terrified as these men, usually in tweed or in raincoats or overcoats depending on the weather, went into the drawing room with my father – he didn't have an office in his house. They would be there for perhaps up to an hour or two, talking, then out they would come, take their guns, get into their cars and drive away quietly.

There was a kind of understood deal between him defending the fair ones in Court and refusing to defend them if he thought that they were not straight. Imagine, therefore, years later when my father died, a policeman coming to my mother and saying, "Excuse me, madam, but what would you like us to do with the twenty-four guns that we have in the police barracks in your husband's name?" Imagine my poor mother! Well, what had happened was that Daddy had taken such guns as he was unhappy about, deposited them in the police station so that they could be retrieved, maybe after a Court case where they had been successful, or maybe where he had actually acted against his clients, and said they were not getting back their guns, or something equally as dangerous. I don't know exactly what my mother meant, but I do remember her saying, "Oh, just do what you like with them." Imagine the poor policeman then trying to account for what happened!

Much more friendly were the bridge parties and other parties that took place downstairs. We would be looking at them and seeing what they were doing, because, as children, we hated to be left out of anything, way out there in the country where such things as the arrival of another human being was a great occasion!

In our bedroom we slept in two little cots parallel to each other with an armchair in between. Sometimes Daddy sat in that armchair, sometimes Mummy, or it could be one of the maids, but usually Daddy, and he read to us for a little while. I suppose we fell off to sleep because, while I can remember him reading, I can't actually remember saying goodnight to him, whereas I can remember saying goodnight to Mummy. She would tuck us up and go off and leave us, and we would be asleep very quickly, of course, because we were so tired out after the day.

My twin sister and I, naturally, had areas of play which were quite private to ourselves; she with her dolls and her prams and her houses. I didn't play with her that way at all; nor did she come with me when I sat on the stone flags beside that long corridor from the main house down to the kitchen and rummaged in an old cupboard. I would pull out the newspapers where they were stored after my father and mother had finished with them, and try to read them.

I remember distinctly being able to read about Tommy Farr and Joe Louis having an international boxing match, a World Championship fight. I remember, of course, a lot about Hitler and Jesse Owens, the athlete, and Hitler refusing to stay in the stadium and give him his medal. And I do remember, too, a lot about Mahatma Gandhi and Indians. I didn't understand precisely what all these people were doing, but I knew their names and I could see photographs of them. Even nowadays photographs are reproduced of some of the great athletics moments that I saw in the original newspaper while sitting on the cold stone floor.

When my mother or someone saw me they would say, "Come on, get up from there, you'll catch a cold," and then I would get up onto my knees and carry on reading and think that that satisfied them, but it was something for me that gave me the beginnings of breaking away from the limits of life in the Irish countryside. I didn't *feel* I was breaking away; I just began to be aware that in America people had boxing matches and in Germany people had races. In other parts of the world there were different things. In India I knew one of our nearby local friends was in the British Army – in the Royal Army Veterinary Corps. All this led to my expectation that the world was a place that you would go out into.

That expectation crystallised very clearly one afternoon when the lady who tooted the hunting horn held my sister's hand on one side, and my hand on the other. We stood looking down into a stream where a paper chase in which we were all engaged had been halted because the people laying the paper had jumped across the stream – you could see the paper on the other side but the paper on the stream had been somewhat swept away. While we stood there it clearly formed in my mind a picture of a life that was to be lived.

I knew this lady was getting married and going off to Rhodesia at that point, and the vision I had of life – I suppose I was aged six or seven – was that first you went to school, then there was something, I didn't know what that was, then you had to go and work in Southern Rhodesia or South Africa or India or the North-West-Frontier, and then you had to come back and work near Big Ben because that was the centre of it all. After another stint somewhere else, maybe Malaya, you then retired and lived in the country. That feeling, I think, was caused by the fact that the retired Indian Army Colonel who read the lesson in our Church, and the retired Major who took the collection, had stories of their times in different parts of Africa and Asia.

I had no idea then that the pattern my life would later follow would fulfil quite a deal of that expectation and that I would be able to share it with those who had gone before. For example, the clergyman who baptised our younger sister was one of a family of four who had gone to the same school that I attended long afterwards, and he had become the Bishop of Gambia. A brother had become the Chief Secretary of Tanganyika, another brother had become Chaplain to the Royal Air Force and the other had become Governor of Seychelles – it seemed to be quite normal to us that people would go away and come back.

Every morning one of the local clergymen used to come into the school and say some prayers and sing a hymn, which only took about five or ten minutes, and then he went away. We met him once again as one of the curates when he came to our church, Holycross, Sunday School. We all sat inside the pews – which were high above our heads and our legs couldn't reach the floor from the benches – and he sat alongside us and talked to us.

An image that he gave us has stayed with me to this day: he was telling us that we shouldn't be proud. We should never be proud and when we saw other people doing bad things we shouldn't think that we were better because if we thought we *were* better, that was an even bigger sin than the bad things they were doing. I don't know that he used the word 'pride' but he certainly got us to see that we shouldn't think well of ourselves and badly of others and he gave us this funny image – well, interesting image. He said, "…and you know that horrible old man, dirty in his clothes and rags, lying in the gutter, probably because he is drunk or something, and your Mummy takes you by the hand and leads you away around him and on you go – never feel superior to anybody like that because he might be Jesus in disguise." I've often thought of that sentence when meeting people later on in life... 'he might be Jesus in disguise'. It has stopped me in my tracks from time to time.

And then my parents went to New York for the World Fair in 1939. It took a long time because they had to go by boat in those days. I think we were sent off to be with Aunt Flo, who was my father's nearest sister. She was very close to him in a family of eleven (thirteen children really, but two had died). When they came back from America of course we had this wonderful series of memories that they brought with them and all sorts of little artefacts around the house, with the Statue of Liberty prominent in the designs on them all. It certainly made America a real place to me at that time.

Then my father died – quite suddenly, unexpectedly – of a heart attack.

All this time our dear little sister was no more than a bundle in the background of our lives, cared for by Nanny – indeed protected by Nanny from my treating her pram as a racing car, even when she was in it!

Holycross Abbey – 1936

2
A Different School

We children were sent to stay with friends in a house called Gaile House. We used to have pillow fights with a boy my own age, and indeed I'm afraid we broke some jugs in the washbasin and his father put his head through the door and said, "Did I hear some breaking crockery in here?" I haven't heard the word 'crockery' very often, but whenever I do I think of that event.

And then my Uncle Eddie came to pick us up and bring us back home. He came one night in January; it must have been very early January as my father had died just before Christmas but we didn't know, we just knew Uncle Eddie had come to bring us back home. It was quite late at night and the countryside was very dark, absolutely black, no light at all really, and I remember we were taken out to his motorcar which had an engine in the back and that was of great interest to us – that the engine should be in the back of the car and not in the front. We liked Uncle Eddie because he was a funny fellow, rather silly. I remember he once jumped on a cow's back in our field and tried to ride it but fell off, of course, and we thought it was very funny although everyone else thought it was very silly.

Anyhow, we got into the car; my sister got into the back. I was sitting in the front in the passenger seat, and he got in and said goodbye to our hosts. We were just getting ready to set off when I asked, "Where's Daddy?" He said, "Oh, Daddy's gone to Heaven," and I thought, 'Why is he a coward? Why can't he just say 'Daddy's dead' and leave it like that. Daddy might have gone to heaven, might have gone to hell, we don't know; why is Uncle Eddie a coward?' I was so upset that he was a coward because he was such fun; he did so many fun things with us.

While sitting in the silence thinking like that, suddenly, from outer space, a white laser beam, thin, straight, strong, came down in a long line like lightning, out of the dark sky and touched the ground just in front of the wheel of the motorcar and somehow I knew that God was going to lead me on as it were, from that point. I knew a dreadful thing had happened – Daddy was dead – but I knew at the same moment that there was nothing to worry about, just to go straight ahead. An amazing experience. That white laser beam went away, though it stayed in my memory.

We drove on in the darkness and I remember – probably it was about eight o'clock at night when we got home – being brought into the house. We turned right in the hall and went into the drawing room and there was my mother, sitting alone in the middle of a sofa crosswise in front of the fire looking very small and hunched with her elbows on her knees and her hands clasped together, and the rest of the family standing about the room looking at us as we came in. I remember her turning her head slightly towards us and saying, "Ah, my children."

I'm fairly sure that Aunt Flo was one of those people in the room and was staying in the house at the time because, years later, my mother told me how she and Aunt Flo had had to share a bed because there were so many people in the house after Daddy's death. One night Aunt Flo was actually in bed and Mummy got into bed beside her and Aunt Flo said, "Fanny, I noticed you didn't say your prayers." My mother told me how she had said to Aunt Flo, "No! I'm not going to say them ever again; I'm just so angry with God for having taken George away, I'm not saying them any more." My aunt said, "Mmmm, all the same, Fanny, I think you should." So my mother said that in a rather grumpy mood she got out of bed, got down on her knees, put her head in her hands, said something and got back into bed. She told me that as her head hit the pillow, she had a powerful sense that Jesus was standing just behind her, almost in the wall, and said, "Don't worry, Fanny, everything's going to be all right."

During those years leading up to the outbreak of war before my father died, we children had idyllic holidays at a place called

Ballybunion, down on the south-west corner of Kerry, and there we would spend two months, July and August, in cottages that Daddy rented, right on the cliff top. All we had to do was run out, go down about one hundred and twenty rather uncertain clay and stone steps to the beach, and there we were, in the water swimming. The water was quite warm in those days – still is I suppose because of the Gulf Stream and the North Atlantic Drift and, of course, it was summer time. My mother used to come down with us, and one of the maids would spend a while, then change and the other one, Maggie, would come down.

My father stayed back in the house in Tipperary because he had his office in Thurles and he had to work. He would come down at weekends and his keen golf was very satisfied by the famous golf links at Ballybunion where there was plenty of scutch grass and sand, and a strong sea wind to blow the ball all over the place. Playing golf there was a tremendously challenging exercise.

We loved our time there – we ran about down the steps to the beach; we ran about on the beach in nothing but a little pair of trousers or shorts or bathing togs, and explored all the local caves, gullies and inlets. Once I went too far and an on-rush of water from the sea came in and hit me, knocked me down and when I tried to stand up again another wave hit me and knocked me down. I got really worried for a second until somebody, a total stranger, came and lifted me out on his shoulders and put me down on dry land.

I also remember up on the cliff top, a little further over towards the town from where our cottages were, there was a funfair. The great thing for us was the dodgems; I loved the dodgems but I also loved the little girl who was the daughter of the man who owned the whole funfair. I think it was the first time in my life I had fallen in love, so I had two reasons for wanting to go there – one was to see her and the other was to get in the dodgem car and go round as fast as possible. I couldn't tell you now which was more interesting, I think the girl, but I know that one night I behaved very badly because when Mummy and Daddy were with us and they said we must go home now, I wanted to stay for one more ride in the dodgems and I was so thwarted and angry that I actually hit Mummy. I'm not quite sure whether Mummy pretended to be hurt or really was hurt, but I must say it rather blighted my reputation and my own opinion of myself for some time; I suppose the fact that I'm recording it now means it's pretty permanent in my memory.

Another dent in my own opinion of myself comes from a day when I was asked to go and collect some eggs. I went to the place and collected the eggs, about a dozen, which were given to me in a rather thin paper bag. As I walked back home I found that the bag occasionally bumped against the side of my knee and I remember saying to myself: if I'm not careful these eggs will break. Well, I wasn't careful and some of the eggs did break and when I handed over the bag to Maggie she found rather a mess with only about nine of the twelve okay. I later heard Mummy telling Maggie that people shouldn't give small boys paper bags in which to carry eggs, but I felt guilty myself – it was me who had done it. I could have stopped it; it wasn't the person who gave me the paper bag.

A much more light-hearted occasion which dented my reputation was the day we were invited to a rather nice lady's house to have afternoon tea. We children were specially invited because they were old and long established clients of my father. So we went along and behaved very well, took the piece of cake or biscuit that was nearest to us and didn't speak until we were spoken to, and sat up. Alas! When we were in the motorcar outside the house, just leaving, everybody said goodbye and thank you very much, but I apparently said in a loud voice, "Mummy, will we get our *real* tea when we go home?"

Just as the war closed in on Europe so my father's death closed in on our family. It would be quite impossible for my mother to live in the country when there was no coal for the range and no petrol for the car – even to get oil for the lamps was difficult. Life was going to be impossible and one could see that something had to be done. I didn't see it until one night when Mummy and I were sitting in the dining room after dinner; my two sisters had gone to bed and the servants had gone off duty. We were sitting there in silence when my mother, who was a very beautiful woman, moved a little uneasily in her chair and said, "Oh, Lloyd, we've got to leave this old place, I can't stand it any longer," and suddenly I realised that she was thinking I was Daddy.

I said to myself, 'my goodness, I've got to start making decisions round here, something has to be done', and at the same time there went through my mind the clear thought that there was no need to worry. She knew I was only a child and had to go through school; she knew that I would grow up, but all the same that sudden sense of being responsible for other peoples' future, and my own, changed me from a little boy running round in a pair of shorts to a little boy looking at a large world.

It was a salutary experience indeed because that same little boy who had always wanted to be included in the adult world and do all the things that the adults did and run along with them, suddenly wasn't quite so sure that this adult world was the thing to get into. One simple example was how we were excluded from the tennis court and tennis parties because we used to run onto the court and pick up the ball; or used to get tangled up in the net, or when the court was damp or wet, we would run on it and make holes in it with our feet and, generally speaking, be a nuisance rather than a help. We used to hide behind Henry in those days; he was the one who had the job of marking out the court, putting up the net and making sure the wire surrounding the court was high enough to prevent the balls going off into the cow field or down into the wood as the game would have to stop until the ball was found. One job I was sometimes given was to sit outside this wire surround and if a ball did go over, or manage to wiggle its way underneath, I was supposed to find it and throw it back, but I found myself very much in a secondary position and didn't enjoy it too much.

One last person I do remember before we leave that house was a man called Don Craig; he was blind. He lived about half a mile up the road, but in the evening he used to come down to talk to my father and they would listen to the eight o'clock (or maybe nine o'clock) BBC news on our wireless set. In those days this was made of three or four big batteries all joined together by wires; it looked like a big box, made crackling noises and so on, but you could hear the voice quite clearly.

Don Craig used to sit in a big armchair by the fire and try to start his pipe; now my sister and I loved to watch this because it took him about fifteen or sixteen matches to light this pipe. He would get it and puff it and then it would go out and he would do it all again. We were always caught between being amused by the fact that he took so many matches to get this going, and on the other hand he was blind so we didn't want to laugh at him. Although the blindness and the lighting of the pipe were not connected, there was a kind of happy unease in the middle of it all.

My father and he were obviously great friends and I remember very well that Don was there the day that Chamberlain declared war on Germany. It was a very odd experience; my sister and I were underneath the dining table – a big old-fashioned table with heavy legs – we were actually sitting in a rocking chair that folded down into a kind of boat and you could sit in this semi-boat which, if you pushed it properly, would make movements along the carpet and go forwards and backwards and that's what we were doing when Britain declared war on Germany. Indeed, the boat was rocked in many more ways than one!

While the whole of Europe rocked, the two months of January and February 1940 passed very quickly for us. I can't really remember what happened in them, but I know when they were over I was in Bishop Foy boarding school in Waterford. My two sisters were in a boarding school in Dublin and my mother was in Dublin staying with an uncle of ours, a brother of my father's. This was while she found a place for us, which she did fairly soon and for the next several years we lived in a flat in the centre of Dublin town.

My sisters and I had quite different experiences in boarding schools. I can't speak for them, except that they seemed to have had a good education down the years. I can only speak for myself and say that, maybe I shouldn't have been, but I really was very happy from the day I arrived in school.

In those days boarding schools were very rough, tough places. I can best give anybody reading this an idea of what they were like when I tell them that years after, when I went to see a film called 'A Clockwork Orange' in Leicester Square in London (because that film

Bishop Foy School

had a reputation for showing a dreadful side of the human character), I came out into the broad daylight – I had gone to the matinee – saying to myself, 'My goodness, what was all the fuss about; anybody who had been to a decent boys' boarding school would know jolly well that that sort of thing is just the way life is; it's nothing to write about or get het up about, that's it.'

Fortunately for me our boarding school experience was altered quite dramatically just one year after I'd started – it must have been 1941, I can't be sure. What happened was this:

We returned from the summer holidays to find that the school had been literally transformed into a fully co-educational boarding school and that the girls who had lived separate lives in a separate part of the world (but who did come down to the same classroom), were now mingled up with us boys and we were all together in one large school – it was an old bishop's palace actually. It was a tremendous experience and they had painted it all light colours, pastel shades. All the old brown woodwork and ugly floorboards had gone; we even had carpets on the floors if I remember, and couldn't believe it!

But I'm jumping a bit forward – let's go back to the first day I arrived in school. My first memory is of a boy with an unusual name, Herbert Babbage. I don't think I had heard the names 'Herbert' or 'Babbage' before, either as a surname or a Christian name. This was really my first experience of the newness of it all, this unusual name. Then I remember him showing me a big portrait in the main Hall of Lord Roberts of Kandahar, Pretoria and Waterford, the most famous 'old boy' of the school. I think his family had been on the Board of Governors for some time, but there he was, a great hero of the Mutiny in India, who had won the V.C. on the ridge in Delhi by holding out against the enemy.

This made me feel that this was a very important place. It was important because it was on the way, through the Hall, to where there were showers and bathrooms and that was my first experience of what to do when you came back from playing games. You went in there, took off all your clothes and had a shower! I had never had a shower in my life until then – always a bath. Then there were the dormitories and classes and so on. Dormitories and classes all fitted in but games were a new experience. They were a new experience because I had never, nor had my sisters, engaged in team games before; we had never been members of one team against another team, playing with a ball or that sort of thing.

On my second day I discovered that I was part of the junior rugby practice; I was on the Stripes side and the other team was the Blues. We had these two jerseys; ours was stripes, light blue, and the other side was dark blue because the school colours were royal blue, navy and white. I arrived late for the game because I didn't yet have a bicycle like all the other boys, and even getting on my boots was a problem in those days because they were so hard to get your feet into, let alone tie up the laces. I ran out onto the pitch while the game was on – it had been going for I suppose fifteen minutes – and I can still see the master who was in charge, acting as referee and coach, waving to me and telling me to join in. I had been watching and noticed that this game consisted of one group throwing the ball to each other and the other group trying to knock them on the ground. This wasn't easy, but I had to find out all about it so I ran out and then, to my alarm, a very large boy in blue, with red hair, came charging towards me holding the ball. Now I knew that my business was to stop him, but he was so big. Anyway. I charged at him and grabbed him round the knees – I can still feel the impact of his knee on my shoulder! We both shot up in the air, the ball went off sideways somewhere and our team managed to get back, pick up the ball and go on. Somebody said to go after the ball, so I went after it and played until the game ended.

I went back into the changing room, a little wooden pavilion, to change, take off my boots and put on my shoes in order to walk back to the school. While I was there, I was rather slow, because I didn't know my way around things, and I overheard two other boys talking. One said to the other, "Goodness, did you see that little new boy – the way he tackled Harry Ham?" "Yeah, very brave," and they went.

There I was left in this pavilion, all by myself, having heard two other boys, bigger than me, saying I had done something very brave. Now, you'd think you'd be pleased – well, I suppose I was pleased but also, again, it burdened me with the fact that from now on I was going to have to do that. This was not such an easy thing, especially when I saw Harry Ham in real life – he was an enormous boy, although only aged about fifteen or sixteen and a very decent boy – but I have no happy reflection that it was a good thing to have to remember to do for the rest of my life!

Anyway, I did it and I'm glad that I did because, if you don't play rugby whole-heartedly you really do get hurt, whereas if you do play it whole-heartedly you don't get hurt and you get on with it; and I think that's true of most things in life.

Another rather unusual growing-up experience occurred in between Daddy's death and my actual arrival in school. I had been sent to stay with a family in Templemore who looked after me very well and gave me Picture Posts to look at. The Picture Post was a great magazine at the time of the early years of the war. I remember one morning sitting on the floor in a window niche looking at the Picture Post – there was a picture of a train coming from the distance into a building site where there was a large, strong navvy sitting on a girder holding something and waiting for the train to bring bricks for the building site. It was obviously an advertisement, a very good advertisement, but the thought that went through my mind (and where it came from I can't imagine) was this: 'Goodness, look at this; isn't it disgusting. I'm only a child and I play with bricks and trains and have great fun with them; these are adults and they are trying to make money out of them, that's terrible'. What a dreadfully priggish attitude to have aged eight! I don't know where it came from, but even to day I am not happy with commercial advertising, even though I've been fairly fortunate because of it.

Mrs Walshe had taught us well in our little National School so I was able to manage my lessons fairly well and keep going and that side of life didn't have any great worries for me, fortunately. Nor did games, which I was able to pick up, though again I remember seeing the girls playing hockey, which was an interesting experience because I didn't know girls could play with sticks and balls so hard as they did. I even remember the name of one girl, Daphne Ferguson (well, perhaps I liked her because of her appearance). She played very well, and indeed became an Irish hockey player later on.

Our playing fields were not just for boys or just for girls, they were for both and we used the same pavilion – I expect there were masters and mistresses on duty to make sure we all changed our clothes properly and behaved in a decorous manner.

What I do remember is a tiny shop on the corner just inside the gate as we went into our playing fields and this was where you could buy some sweets and bars of chocolate; mind you, not many of us had any money to buy them but we did occasionally when we could and eat them on the way back, holding onto the bicycle with one hand and eating the bar of chocolate with the other.

It's fair to say that the next nine years were spent in this pattern of school, in the Bishop Foy School. Our boarding experience in what we called 'The Palace', and our games out at this playing field called 'Grantstown', sometimes cycling, sometimes walking, and that small shop which was called 'Ma Ryans', was a sort of relief from all the serious stuff. Nothing changed over those nine years... except that a war was won and lost and all our lives were turned upside down.

During these years I passed my time in the relatively peaceful and safe atmosphere of Bishop Foy School, down at the mouth of the River Suir, which passed by our house where I lived in Tipperary and into the sea at Waterford. In that school I did my ordinary lessons, played games and had great fun in free time… with the rest of the world, unfortunately, killing each other!

As we grew older it did impinge on us a little more and we were reminded of people like our famous 'old boy', Lord Roberts, and the family who still lived nearby, and also we looked at the photographs which were on the wall of the dining hall just behind us as we sat and ate our meals. These photographs looked down on us. I remember distinctly a family of four, all of whom played rugby football for Ireland; a different family of four, all of whom played hockey for Ireland; a single person who became Regius Professor of Greek in Trinity College, and another man who became the first top 'passer out' of the Veterinary College in Dublin – all these people made us feel we had to do the same when we grew up. The hockey players went to India, two of them into the Indian Army and two into the Indian Civil Service, which was called the I.C.S. and was considered to be the best possible job that one could have in those days.

The actual life of the school was really conducted by two people who had been there from 1920, just after the First World War – Nick was the butler in the dining hall and Tommy Gorbey was the caretaker. The reason that they were so prominent in our lives was that they had both come to the school with the officer under whom they had served in the Army, a man called the Reverend Seymour, an Army Chaplain, who became the headmaster. When he died they stayed on and their military attitude of obedience to authority imparted itself to us.

The headmaster when I was there was a man who had had a Welsh Rugby Football trial – he didn't actually play for Wales but had a trial for the international team and this put him up in our esteem. He had also fought in the war and been, unfortunately, damaged in one lung, which meant that he wasn't as physically fit as he wanted to be for our sake, but he was very keen on our games. I look back to his influence with much gratitude, even though I know he was unpopular with one or two people because he wasn't sufficiently harsh on our discipline. I didn't mind that!

Another great, solid figure in our lives was the science master. He was always called Pa Watson because he looked big and old and a very steady man. I remember him meeting me on my way to the laboratory for his science lesson. He saw me carrying my books and stopped and said, "Ah, Mullen, all your knowledge under your arm." He said it in fun but it was quite a good reminder that the business of life was to get knowledge into your head, not carry it about under your arm. We can carry it about nowadays in little machines of all kinds.

I recall two rather daring episodes by two boys which reflected Pa Watson's attitude in a very good light. There was a boy with a terrible stammer and when he was asked a question one day he got it perfectly right so that Pa Watson said to him, "Oh my goodness, Baldwin, that's very good indeed. How did you manage to do that?" Baldwin said, "E-e-elementary my dear Watson," and Pa Watson replied, "Ah, very good… the joke seems to be on me."

On another occasion, a different boy asked him if he could leave class early because he had permission from the headmaster to go to a dental appointment in the town. Pa Watson's son was the leading dentist in the town at this time and he said to this boy, "Are you going to my son, the dentist, because I'm the one who taught Ronald how to draw teeth?" This boy very rudely replied, "Yes Sir, I know you did, that's why I don't go to him." Again, after an initial pause of silence, while the rest of us waited in horror, he said, "Well done, Baxter, the joke seems to be on me. Off you go, boy, off you go."

Pa Watson gave me one piece of very good advice when I met him after I had left school. He said, "Ah, I hear you are going to be a schoolmaster; well, if you ever become a housemaster or headmaster take my advice and go into every room in the school once a month… you'll be amazed at what you find." I did follow that advice and I think the most amazing thing I ever found in any room was a live goat, tethered, quietly munching its grass and other things in the back room of a boys' boarding school!

A legendary figure in our growing-up at that time was a boy called Dick Easton. Now Dick Easton had done pretty well everything that one ought not to do as a boarder in a school and all these things were remembered by Nick the butler. Nick used to tell us what Dick did. I can only here recount the most amazing and perhaps disgraceful thing he ever did which was to creep into the bedroom of the then headmaster, the Reverend Seymour, and climb on top of his very old, wide wardrobe, lie down flat on it and spend the whole night there. In the morning when the coast was clear again, he came down and went out! How on earth he got away with accounting for where he had been one doesn't know, but this Dick Easton was famous for being able to do almost anything.

Something which kept me busy in my last couple of years was being games secretary. Now I look back, it seems somewhat extraordinary that I was given this position; just a boy at school to be the one who arranged all the football, hockey and cricket matches with other schools. I found myself dealing with their sports masters, even sometimes with the headmasters, making agreements about which ground we would choose to play on, which day, what we would do if the weather was bad, what the age of the teams to play would be, who would mark out the pitch, what kind of tea would be served, when and where, etc.

I now look back on it as being wonderful training for the responsibilities of later life, but how on earth anybody risked allowing me to do it in those days I really wonder. I either got on my bike and went and talked about it (we didn't have the use of a telephone, we just had to go and call on the school and make arrangements) or they came and called on me. Occasionally I was dragged away from something I was doing to find out that a game had to be cancelled due to illness at the other school, chicken pox or something, and then I had to tell everybody. It did somehow force me to think of other things beyond just the game itself. For instance, I remember one of the problems was putting up the flags along the side of the touchline, measuring the distance they should be from the touchline, and making sure the ones in the corner were right in the corner and not out from the touchline.

Quite the opposite was the daily regularity of worship in the Cathedral in the morning. Our school prayers took the form of a visit to the choir stalls of the Cathedral where we would calmly and quietly go through a prayer, a psalm, a lesson, a hymn and then leave. This regularity of morning worship, only about ten minutes, laid a kind of foundation for the rest of my life and I have been able, at times of crisis and at times of happiness, to remember bits and pieces of psalms, hymns and prayers without anything serious in my mind except that this is just a normal thing in life, not something extra. So many people try to think that religion is an extra thing whereas for us, certainly in those days, it was just a normal bit of life. To keep it going we had a chunk of it in the morning, just as we had a chunk of mathematics in the later morning, a chunk of games in the afternoon and a chunk of homework in the evening – just ordinary life. But some things were not ordinary and I remember one which seems to me extraordinary.

There was a boy with whom I was friendly and, as always happens between boys who are friendly, we did occasionally have a fight. During one of these fights I managed to get his head under my arm and hold it tight against my side, pulling him round and round and round. He wasn't able to do much, but as I was doing this something suddenly inside me said, 'Hey, you're enjoying hurting him, that's wrong'. Instantly I let go and I can honestly say that from that day to this I have tried to avoid deliberately hurting people. But where did it come from? I'd never heard of the words 'sadism' or 'masochism' but, at ten or eleven years of age at the time, it was quite plain to me that this was wrong, it was not right. I was very glad of that discovery because in a way it was like a free gift out of nothing.

More serious was the fact that another red-headed boy, Charlie Develin, with whom I played rugby, left school early in order to join the Royal Air Force and we learned only about ten months later that he had been killed on his first flight. It lives with me to this day because he was out-half; I was scrum-half and it was my business in rugby to pass the ball to him, make sure he was there or find out where he was and pass the ball to him in such a way that he could take it easily at full speed while he was running – and there he was…

dead! Killed! He had been the rear gunner in a Lancaster Bomber. One didn't know what to think then, and certainly one didn't know what to think when, about a month later, there was a memorial service for him at Tramore, where he lived. He had been a dayboy and we all wore our Boy Scout uniforms as we stood around the grave. It is not possible for me to go through an Armistice Day all these years later without thinking of him.

Far right middle row – Charlie Develin
Far right on the ground – Lloyd Mullen

A side of the school that I think was rather weak was that somewhere along the line I picked up, and I think others picked up, too, a sort of Philistine attitude to Music, French and Art. We somehow didn't think that those three subjects were as serious as the others, even though we sang in choirs and knew that the French had been central to the whole war, run over on both sides, so we ought to at least know the language, but we didn't. Perhaps there was a reason for art – our art teachers were always very amusing men. For example, one told us how when he had been a young art student he went to Spain to learn more about painting and had no money, so he walked up to a policeman in the street and hit him on the jaw, as a result of which he had to spend some time in jail where he got free food and lodging! Perhaps one is bound to take a light-hearted view of art after that… though maybe not of law and order!

Another event I remember was that each Sunday evening letters were collected which the boys had written to their parents at home – we had to write one letter a week home – and it was my job at one stage to collect these letters and take them to the Post Office, which was on the quayside of the river, and put them in the post box. I often enjoyed looking at the addresses on them, as long words fascinated me. One of the towns in nearby Cork was called Castletownroche, and I still regard it with pleasure to this day because it rolls off the tongue so nicely. Also, perhaps because it was a Sunday evening, when I was putting the letters in the post box I used to look across the river and up the hill on the far side where I could see the house where our local bishop lived, Bishop Harvey, and because he and his wife were both Governors of the school we used to go there and have tea some afternoons. He was very much regarded as one of the good ones because not only had he played rugby for Ireland, he had at one stage played cricket and caught and bowled W.G. Grace. This, of course, puts him in the pantheon of the greats – if you bowl and catch the most famous cricketer ever then little boys will be glad to look across the river at the house where you live.

The school made us enter for scripture examinations every year, for which we studied for about half an hour three days a week; the examination was sat by all the Protestant schools in Ireland. I was very pleased one evening; I had left what we called our 'Prep Room' for a while and when I came back in everybody started clapping and I stopped and went sheepishly to my place. The headmaster had come in and was holding a piece of paper and said he was glad to say that I had come first in Ireland in the particular year I was in. That was a great joy. Imagine my amazement when, many years later, the young lady who I married was able to tell me that she had come first in India in the same examination in the same year! Maybe there is something in currents that blow across the world… one doesn't know.

Then there is what the artists call the 'blessed accident'. Another boy and I once had a very blessed accident. While we were fooling around near the billiard table, he aimed a kick at me with his slipper, which shot off and went right up, hitting the ceiling flat on and leaving a very clear footmark. Thereafter that footmark was pointed out to every trembling new boy as 'the foot mark of the ghost of Bishop Foy'. Some of them did tremble because they looked up and thought it couldn't have got there any other way except by a ghost, and we traded on it for quite a long time.

Serious things did not escape us entirely. I can remember when I was the most junior boy on the most junior table. It was my job at breakfast time to fill up the mugs with tea and milk from an urn and pass them up the table to the other boys – there were about twelve on this long table. They were always eager for their drink so I was a little worried when one morning I arrived late... perhaps I couldn't find my tie or something! I rushed into the dining room, sat down quickly, started filling the mugs up and passing them along when another boy hissed across the table to me (we weren't allowed to talk until our porridge was finished), "Hitler has attacked Russia." Through my mind went the absolute clear thought, 'Ah! that's finished him, now he's done for,' because somewhere we had been taught about Napoleon and the vast areas of Russia that had foiled him – it's probably true to say that Russia did play an enormous part in finishing Hitler, or rather in letting Hitler finish himself; but how tiny boys in Ireland realised it still remains a little source of wonder to me in the way in which education and up-bringing works.

Then there were the holidays and what I did in them. One of the great advantages of living in Dublin was that at that time, during the war, the two most famous theatres in Dublin – indeed, two of the most famous theatres in the world, the Dublin Gate Theatre and the Dublin Abbey Theatre – were working all the time because they were not engaged in the war. The Gate Theatre produced plays alternately throughout the season, week by week... modern plays, traditional plays, modern plays, traditional plays. The Abbey Theatre produced only plays with an Irish background and the result was that I was able to go and sit in the back row of the Gate for a shilling and see the most up-to-date versions of all the great traditional plays, like School for Scandal, and all the very modern ones which were being written by Christopher Fry and others at that time. Also I could go to the Abbey Theatre, suitably located in Abbey Street, and see the Irish acting which at that time was a very high standard and rather focused on the life of Ireland under W.B. Yeats, our great traditional poet and lover of independence.

Our lives were in many ways limited, but one of the ways in which they opened out was in the fact that Ireland has four provinces and two of these, Munster and Leinster, are very close to each other. We lived in Munster and the school was also in Munster, but one of the boys with whom I went to the little National School later left and went to a school just across the border in Leinster. Consequently, years afterwards, when he'd become a brilliant hockey player – and good rugby player, although he was really too small to be effective at rugby, but was a brilliant games player generally – he became captain of the Leinster Schoolboys Hockey team. In the same year (this was many years afterwards) I became captain of the Munster Schoolboys Hockey team and I remember four boys from our school were in the team and the school hired a taxi for us and drove us to Dublin. I stayed in my own house with another boy, and we had to play this inter-provincial match against Leinster.

The Leinster team was generally considered to be more likely to win because it had a larger number of schools, especially around the Dublin area, and had very good coaches, etc. It was amusing for the two of us, being captains of the opposing teams and yet had both been in the same school together a long, long time ago. Anyway, a few minutes from the end of the game, when it was one-all, our centre forward found their goalkeeper out of position and put in a very good shot. The ball was going about a foot off the ground, straight into the net as I thought – I actually began to turn round and say to myself, 'that's good, we've done it, we've won, there's only a minute left' – but, from nowhere this old friend of mine came literally flying through the air like some sort of swallow with his hockey stick turned the wrong way round and he actually hit that ball in the air right over my head back into the field of play before it could get into their goal. I've never forgotten that and I never will.

A staff member whom I remember with particular gratitude from those days in school was my gym instructor, Mr Fraser. He really did a great deal for all of us. He taught us almost everything in the gym – parallel bars, wall bars, horse, horizontal bars, swinging clubs, groundwork, boxing, and ju-jitsu – a wonderful array of things. He even did the building of tableaux and criss-cross marching for displays. He was a man of sixty or so and had been a gym instructor in the British Navy, so he was pretty fit.

One of the things we used to say to him when we were arrogant little boys of thirteen or fourteen, was, "Sir, but what use is all this? Why should we have to do these exercises?" and he would say, "Well, you never know, one day you might need them and you might be glad to have them – you never know what might happen." We had a dramatic example of that from him himself.

One day, another boy, called Spearman, and I were fooling about in the yard in front of the gymnasium – a fine, big, new gym which had been built when the school was turned into a co-ed school. This yard was big enough to throw things around in, and during our fooling around Spearman took a hockey stick and, from a long distance, flung it at me. It went low, about a foot off the ground, so I was able to jump up and let it go underneath my feet. Just at that moment, Mr Fraser cycled into the yard and the hockey stick went straight through the front spokes of his bike, which stopped dead. He shot up into the air, landing way out in front, but he didn't land awkwardly – he just put his hands down on the ground, tucked his head in and did the neatest little neck-flick you've ever seen. He landed on his feet, turned round, pointed to the unfortunate Spearman and said, "Spearman, come here, come here!" After that there was no more questioning about what use gym might be or when it might be any good to us – we had had really clear evidence.

3
Holiday Time

Another part of our lives was holidays and when we were in school the holidays were very long. The Easter holiday was short, only about eight or nine days, but the summer holiday was anything between twelve and sixteen weeks and the Christmas holiday was about three, maybe four weeks. They were *real* holidays. We weren't given projects to do in them, we were just let loose; you went home and that was it and you went back the next term and hadn't had to do anything in between.

During the Christmas holidays, when I went back to Dublin, one of the happy things I recall was that Lansdowne Rugby Club ran a holiday scheme for schoolboys where anybody between the age of fourteen and eighteen could go down to the club, give in their name and then become part of a training scheme to play against groups of schoolboys from other places in the holidays. This way the club picked up talent for the future, and I've no doubt that they did get some good players that way.

We enjoyed it very much because the man in charge was a responsible and caring individual who looked after us and later became an international referee, which thrilled us, especially when he sent off one of the dirtiest players I've ever known in an international match. He just blew the whistle, stood there, pointed to the pavilion, and though there was a long, long pause, because this was quite a famous player in his day, that man had to walk the whole length of the diagonal of the pitch just because a man, whom we greatly respected, would stand no nonsense. He had very high standards both of behaviour and of technical rugby.

So, between visits to the theatre, pantomimes and playing rugby in the afternoons, Christmas holidays were fairly well occupied.

Easter included the 'Easter holidays' as they were called because there was the usual set of services from the end of Lent: Maundy Thursday, Good Friday, Easter Sunday and Easter Monday. Also around that time of year, the finals were being played of different rugby and football competitions as the winter began to come to an end, some time usually in April, and then we went back to school.

The summer holidays were a different matter altogether. I spent most of them with my cousin, Bertie, on his farm down in County Kildare, and some of them camping with a group, then called Varsities and Public Schools Camps (V.P.S.C., pronounced 'Veeps' for short). These camps were organised by the Children's Special Service Mission (C.S.S.M.) in Ireland, who had a roving clergyman who spent the year visiting different Protestant schools, talking to the pupils about the importance of Jesus in our lives. The response, as you can imagine, was very varied from those who were extremely interested to those who weren't in the least bit interested. In the summer holidays this group of people ran these camps for anyone who was interested.

The camps were organised by university students (that's where the word 'Varsity' fits in). They looked after the food, the tents, digging the latrines (we all had to do it, but they made sure it was done properly), the arrangements when we went climbing mountains, swimming in rivers and tracking our way through forests; they were in charge and we were boys, and that's where the 'Public Schools' bit came in. We were probably about fifty or sixty in perhaps fifteen to twenty tents on any campsite. One camp was on the estate of a family who had been friends of my father, way down in Tipperary; this was in County Wicklow. They had two estates, one in Tipperary and one in Wicklow – and so I felt slightly at home. The theme throughout the camps was physical enjoyment, and hard work, too, keeping the place tidy, going collecting food, washing-up and many other chores. It was really 'religious evangelism'. An international rugby player, who, at the time, was playing for Ireland, said one or two sentences that interested me because I wondered whether they would prove to be true: "You may if you're lucky score twenty tries for Ireland at rugby, or score two or three centuries at cricket. You may go into business and become a millionaire, or you may become a film star or actor and have your picture everywhere and lots of people applauding you. You may even sleep with a thousand girls, but I can tell you that if you do not have Jesus in your life you will never, ever be satisfied."

This took us aback because, after all, we were only about fifteen or sixteen and hadn't actually done any of those things (though, mind you, we might have imagined that we were going to do them one day!), and to have this put up front in your face to think about was really quite something. Although I haven't become a millionaire or done any of those other things, I would guess that the statement is true. But it's a very selfish way of looking at things, asking the question, 'do they satisfy you?' The question really is, 'does what you do satisfy other people – those around you? Do they become bigger, happier people as a result of your interaction with them?'

The officers all had nick-names, for example, the Commandant, who was the boss of the whole thing, was called 'Commy' and the Adjutant, who was responsible for seeing everything was there, food, games equipment, etc., was called 'Adjy'. The one who was responsible for seeing that we washed and kept ourselves clean was called 'K.C.B.', Knight Commander of the Bath.

One summer I was asked to go with the Commandant to the campsite early to help unload a lot of necessary goods from a trailer which he towed behind his car, so off we set. As we got on to the more country roads near the campsite things began to bump about a bit, and even though he drove carefully, a large bin, full of rice, jumped out of the trailer, landed on the road and we actually saw it skating along, passing by the car and stopping, leaning sideways against a bank. Fortunately it didn't overturn and the rice remained in the container, so we were able to stop, get out and put it back on the trailer.

These camps were a great help towards building up our strength and keeping us fit. We climbed nearly all the mountains in the Wicklow range, not far from Dublin, swam in rivers and lakes, climbed all sorts of trees, played all kinds of games on both rough and smooth ground and, generally speaking, we developed quite good physical strength. This, I think, gave rise to the expression 'Muscular Christianity', not an expression I like but it's not one that can be made fun of because I have come across many good Christians in my time who have had to stand up to all kinds of problems and were jolly glad to have had all that physical training as well as mental and spiritual training in their background.

An added bonus from this experience of camping with boys from all sorts of other schools and all types of families, and under more or less the same conditions (I expect it would be the same if one was in an army), was that we learned to notice the different types of characters of people. I have one very sad memory of one boy who was plainly very ruthless, very cruel and none of us could make out why that was. It came as a sadness but not really a great surprise when we learnt that he had been found guilty of seriously maltreating many people in another country and I think he had to go to prison. This has often left me wondering about the nature of human beings and I wonder whether it's fair to completely blame that boy; he certainly had something about him that was definitely evil, but whether that came into him from his ancestry or whether he was really responsible for it himself, I don't know. The one thing is that in this life each one of us has to be held responsible for our own actions – there is no way of avoiding that – but there is no question in my mind that people do have different personalities to begin with and some of us may have rather more problems to deal with inside ourselves than others.

However, life in the rest of my summer holidays, which was mainly with my cousin Bertie on his farm, was so physical, active and alive in many ways that I didn't think about these problems at all. The countryside was very hilly and full of weeds. Thistle, ragwort and dock were so common that if you were found with a lot of them on your land you could be fined by the local authorities because you were spreading bad things into other farms. Farming was no idyllic life in those days.

I did enjoy going down from the village, where the house and yard was, to the field where the cows were and driving them back up the road where they would turn into the yard through the gate by themselves, then turn right of their own accord into the cowshed. They walked along to different stalls where Bertie or Uncle Norman would put them in the stall and get ready to milk them. Then, after they had been milked, there was the business of doing the whole thing again backwards, except this time you had to get them out of the cowshed and the yard as quickly as possible otherwise they would begin to splatter all kinds of dirt all over the place.

I remember, too, Bertie telling me about bad grass because of some dry period and they had to feed the cattle with a lot of turnips. He said, and I noticed, that you could taste the turnips in the milk but, of course, this is not something that comes through to the town dweller because before the milk reaches the town it goes through various creameries and dairies and is purified and so forth. The other factor to take into account is that cows do not go on holiday, so a farmer can't take a holiday! He just has to stay there to milk his cows in the mornings and evenings. It has to be done; there is no let up and it is not easy to find anyone else to help you.

When the cows had been milked, the milk was carried in buckets into the creamery or dairy at the back of the house where there were machines for separating the cream from the milk. Uncle Norman and cousin Bertie had actually built this extension where all these machines were; it was very large, in very plain concrete. I often wondered how on earth they managed to fit in so much building work with their normal farming work. I can remember pouring the milk into the top of these machines and then winding a handle. After some time the skimmed milk came out on one side and the cream began to drip out rather slowly on the other. The cream would be passed to Aunt Flo who, in her own time, would take it to another machine – she used to make butter from this cream, very good butter. We used it in the house, naturally, but she was able to make plenty to sell to other people in the village, too.

On the more recreational side, we used to go hunting rabbits with a shotgun and even with a ferret. If you put the ferret in one hole, the rabbits would be chased out of another hole and run away. You then had a chance of shooting them; sometimes you were successful, sometimes you weren't, but there was a place nearby, a sort of warren down in a dell, where there were no other people about, so it was fairly safe to take pot-shots at rabbits as they ran by. We weren't really very successful. We had to take much more care with the ferrets because they have very sharp teeth and unless you're very careful they give you a nip. Even if you carry them beside you in a bag (through which they can breathe because it's very thinly woven), they can sometimes nip the side of your leg, more by accident than design, as you walk along.

I remember once suggesting to Bertie that he might try to shoot a few pigeons. He stopped and looked at me pityingly and said, "Pigeons! My goodness, pigeons can tell you what type of gun you're carrying." It was his way of saying that pigeons are very clever birds and very difficult indeed to shoot. They are!

Another excitement was taking one of the cows to the bull. We didn't have a bull in our own herd and some other farmer about four or five miles away, had a good bull, and when the cow was ready we used to have to take her over there. I remember, as a boy, learning how to recognise when the cow was ready for the bull. This was simply done by noticing that the other cattle in the herd, both male and female, would jump up on this cow's back and if she stayed there, and let them stay there, then you knew that she was ready for the bull to jump on her back. We used to tell Uncle Norman and he would make arrangements with the owner of the bull and on a certain morning we would have to walk the cow very slowly along the road so that she could meet her paramour! There was always a fear, of course, that it might not work and that she might not have a calf as a result of their meeting, but so far as I can remember, there was always a successful outcome.

However, one thing definitely didn't work. My uncle loved horses and he had very good ones, big strong shire horses – one could pull a plough by itself – and he had mares for breeding. If you had a good shire horse mare, heavy in build, and you took her to a racing stallion, the resulting foal would be what we call the Irish Hunter; that is to say, a horse, very strong, not too heavy, able to gallop fast (not like a racehorse, of course) and able to carry perhaps quite a heavy man when he was out hunting. That was very important in

Ireland because hunting horses was really the central growth point for our whole horse industry. Even then, hundreds of horses used to cross from Ireland to England every week by boat, with jockey, owner, trainer and head groom – about six or seven people with each horse. Those horses were either hunters or real racehorses bred in some of our best racing studs, or they could be just ordinary ponies, all crossing for the English market where there were so many more people ready to buy. Ireland didn't have that huge number of people ready to buy horses or with sufficient money to pay for them, but the entire country was focused on horses. The two commonest and most important races in the Irish year, then and now, were the Grand National at Aintree and the Derby at Epsom.

I remember an occasion when the planned arrangements went wrong. My cousin told my uncle that one of the mares was ready for the stallion, so arrangements were made. One morning all three of us got into the pony and trap with this mare between the shafts. We went six or seven miles, quite slowly, along the road to where the stallion was in the other farmer's stables. We arrived and there was the usual 'Good morning, how are you'. I think we also had a cup of tea. I was just a spectator, aged about thirteen or fourteen. They untackled the mare from the trap and put her out into the edge of the yard with some men around, because it is a very dangerous business introducing a stallion and a mare: (a) they haven't seen each other, (b) the mare is not quite sure what is going to happen, and (c) the stallion is absolutely certain what's going to happen, but he's such a big fellow and so strong and heavy and determined to have his way that all sorts of things can go wrong.

I watched from a safe distance while this was being prepared. There was the mare out by the edge of the yard, and then they opened the door of the stable where the stallion was. You could already hear him, neighing inside the stable because he knew there was excitement for him outside. As the door was opened, he literally jumped out, with a man on either side clinging onto the ropes attached to his bridle trying in some way to control him while he found his 'lady'. Gradually they managed to calm things down, but there he was, snorting and sniffing and looking immensely large – far bigger than any animal in the rest of the farm. Unfortunately, the mare didn't show any signs of interest. Normally she would stiffen, quiver a little and pass water, but, no… no reaction. The men were a bit worried, but there was no stopping the stallion now, so they let him come over towards the mare. She made it plain that she didn't want his attentions by simply bucking and kicking out with her hind legs any time he came near her, even raising her head and turning round, trying to get away.

The men in charge managed to hold this massive animal and get him back to the stable while the rest of us got the mare out of the yard. My uncle was very upset and blamed my cousin for not having judged the situation correctly, but such animal delicacies are not always easy to detect.

In the midst of all this hard work on the farm and all the different things that had to be remembered, Sundays used to come as a regular heart of the week. Peace would descend and people would put on their best suits and nice dresses and go to church carrying their prayer books, as we did in those days. The clergyman would usually give a very homely sermon and traditional hymns would be sung. The harmonium would be played and after the service the small number of people, probably about twenty, would foregather outside in front of the church and chat for a little while before going back to their respective motorcars and thence to their homes. In our case it was very simple because the church was on one side of the village street. In fact, it was the only building on that side, and we just had to walk back across the road and up the hill a short distance to our house.

This reminds me of a wonderful story concerning the police barracks which was at the very top of the hill. The policeman in charge had a tradition of walking down the street at ten o'clock at night, when pubs were supposed to close. There was only one pub down on the bottom corner. He would walk down, and as he did so the lights in the pub would go out and all talking and noise would stop. He would pause at the crossroads at the bottom where the pub was (the other three sides just had fields), then turn round and slowly walk back up the hill. When he was about three-quarters of the way back to the barracks the lights would come on again in the pub, and by the time he got to the top of the hill, if you listened carefully, you would hear the singing beginning again inside.

This was a noble tradition carried out from generation to generation, but the story goes that one night the sergeant in the barracks had some guests and he asked his son to go down to the pub at about five minutes to ten to get some alcohol – I think it was about ten bottles of Guinness. So his son went down, but to everybody's sadness, about a quarter-of-an-hour later he came back and said to his father in front of the guests, "Father, they wouldn't give me anything because they said I was under age and it was after hours." The sergeant turned to his friends and said, "There's Ireland for you... no respect for the law!"

Another feature of my summer holiday in County Kildare was that my cousin ran a small dance band. Although he had never learned music and couldn't read it, he could play the piano and quite a number of instruments. They used to go around to different dance halls and spend the evening playing while people danced. It was very interesting because he showed me – and the word is 'showed' – what music was. If a member of the band was sick or couldn't come for some reason, my cousin would fill in. One time he had to play a piccolo, which he hadn't played before, so he said to a man who knew how to play, "How do you blow?" Having been shown, he experimented by putting his fingers over different holes, working out the note progression. After a little while he was able to play, not well, but competently enough.

Watching him, I realised that the music was in his head and he saw it, as it were, out in the space in the sky. These instruments – pianos, violins (we call them fiddles) etc – were only a means of getting the music out of your head into the air where other people could hear it, and that was a great revelation for me as a child.

Another revelation, when I was about fifteen or sixteen, was when I went to a dance in a very rural spot. I noticed while we were dancing that the door at one end of the hall was open (it was summer) and occasionally couples would disappear outside. It didn't strike me as unusual or usual; it just happened. However, I was a little taken aback when the girl I was dancing with – who was older than me and I didn't even know her name but she was nice and friendly – actually led me out through this door and danced down a little path behind some bushes, where she began to make advances towards me!

Even though I had been to a co-educational boarding school and we all knew about boys and girls, this sort of, shall we say, 'open approach to love making' was not something that I was used to and not something I could quite cope with. I felt uneasy that, (a) I was going to do something wrong and (b) that if I didn't do it, the girl might be offended or hurt. Anyway, I managed to talk my way out of it; I think but am not sure, she was disappointed, and we went back into the dance hall. However, later on I heard two girls talking and one asking the other the question, "Who were you out with?" and I realised then the naturalness of physical activity in some communities.

This was all part of the process of growing up but it was at variance with the ethos that prevailed in our boarding schools where boys were expected to protect girls from the depredations of others and look after them. Boys who tried to play fast and loose with girls were not regarded with any favour at all. Indeed, I can remember boys being warned severely by others that if they behaved badly they would get it in the neck.

Life was uncertain and complicated, and of course it was further complicated by the part religion played in the Irish psyche – the confusions which later arose, especially with difficulties in the Roman Catholic Church, were easily understood by those of us who had grown up in that period.

The war had ended as all these things happened and a new outlook on life was beginning to come back into us Irish. Things that had not been available before began to come back, English products. A very simple thing, I remember, razor blades – we did not make good razor blades in Ireland but in England they did and they hadn't been available for some time because the war was on; biscuits – we didn't make very good biscuits at that time, biscuits made in England were better.

Life changed in that we began to get back to a system of standards and what standards were. Of course, those people who had come to Ireland as refugees from the war were now able to leave and go back to their countries. I remember one or two who had gone to that other boarding school in Waterford who were Quakers – they had been brought over by the international Quaker attempt to save so many people from European terrorism. They were now leaving, which was a pity because the foreigners added spice and opened our eyes to the fact that English and Irish were not the only two languages to be spoken.

This probably is the best place to mention that my twin sister was much better than me at Irish, and our younger sister was very good indeed. In many ways I'm sorry, but when I look back at the way life went, I don't see that it would have been of much practical use to me. Practical use aside, however, there is a lot of Irish poetry which is very moving if you can get into it, good love poetry, dirges and descriptions of the countryside – when you don't know them in your own language there are always a few areas of understanding that go missing.

These holidays in the country showed me how warmly, carefully and sensibly my relations cared for me. They knew my mother was a widow and that she lived in a flat in the city and that children in a flat in a city during long holidays can be the most frightful burden and nuisance. They certainly did all they could to relieve her of that and I gained greatly by living in a society which I still regard as normal. You had to go to the pump to get water and then carry it in and boil it on a range, and you had to light the lamps. Mind you, electricity had just arrived and cars were beginning to be more commonly seen now that the war was over and petrol more freely available. Other things that could be imported were coming back and clothes were of a different fashion. All that sort of thing was taking off at the end of the 1940s coming up to 1947, and the Irish horse, cattle and pig industries (the latter was always in great competition with the Danish bacon industry) were beginning to look up, but fundamentally we were still a very rural society not yet linked into the great strides being made in the world outside.

This was the time when I was coming up to my final examinations in school. I did in fact get a minor scholarship to Trinity College, Dublin, but it was not sufficient in money terms for me to be able to go to the University so, despite the scholarship, I was not able to do that and had to go and look for a job. The only easy job for me to take which would allow me to go on studying and attempt to get my degree outside of university would be to become a junior teacher and since I liked teaching (I'd always liked helping the more junior boys with their work) that didn't worry me at all. I also liked the idea of coaching games, especially hockey and rugby that I enjoyed playing myself, and also indoor games like table tennis and billiards.

This is probably the place to make an aside about billiards. Billiards had no official part at all in our school life but in our boarding house there was a billiard table on a large landing through which we often passed on our way to various classrooms and, if you wanted to, you could just play a game of billiards, which we often did. There wasn't a great rush for the table – it was a very leisurely activity, and after I left school I realised that I had been most relaxed when playing billiards. There was nothing competitive about it – we didn't have the honour of the school at stake; we didn't have the history of the people who played billiards before us pressurising us to do better; we didn't have anything except to have fun with the person with whom we were playing, and since none of us was really very good, we could enjoy it immensely. It didn't matter if the bell went, all you did was simply stop, put away the cues and balls, put the cover over the table and go to your meal, prep or whatever it was the bell was calling you to do.

The bell absolutely governed your activities, with one slight exception – for meals in the boarding house it wasn't the bell, it was the gong. Somebody rang a gong because that would have been the tradition when it had been a bishop's palace.

This feeling of total relaxation while playing billiards threw up a contrast, which shows that the rest of our lives must have had some tension in them, waiting for the bell to tell us to do this or waiting for an activity in which there would be some tension, but I have to say that I was never conscious of it in either my work or play – it's simply comparing it with the total lack of tension in playing billiards.

The other indoor game which took up a good deal of our time and had a lot of tension attached to it was table tennis. The tension was caused by the fact that there were two members of staff who were excellent players; in fact, I think they took part in the national championships. We could watch them and see how they played. One or two of the boys in our time were excellent and able to keep up with them and play well and the rest of us had the ambition to do as well. I tried very hard to be a good table tennis player, not very successfully, but I could play adequately. This added a further interest to life because sometimes you would be standing beside three people and they would ask you to make up a four, or there was just one person very keen for a game who would ask you to play. There is no doubt it makes you very quick in reaction because the ball comes to you very fast and you haven't got much time to think. Also it was a useful thing to have indoors on a wet day.

The gymnasium was wonderful and we had gymnastics two days a week; we also had rugby and hockey two days a week. This meant that the six afternoons of every week were fully occupied in a sufficiently physical manner to make you tired enough to sleep at night. I sometimes saw a boy falling asleep during prep with his head going down slowly onto his arm, even while still writing! I don't think it ever happened to me but perhaps it did. Certainly once you got out of prep and went upstairs, by the time you got into bed you really did sleep, right through to the next morning.

One thing I remember very clearly from that period of my life in school was a history lesson in which our very quiet but highly amusing history master was telling us about the Battle of Aughrim in Ireland. He explained that this battle was part of the great contest between France and England for control of the Empire across the world because there was India where they fought a battle at Plassey, Canada where they fought a battle at Quebec and Ireland where they fought a battle at Aughrim. He told us that the Irish forces in Aughrim had a French General, whose name was St. Ruth. As he walked around the room dictating notes, he told us the story of the battle in this way:

The battle was going well for the Irish until a stray cannon ball carried off the head of St. Ruth. This head contained the plans for the rest of the battle! Hoots of laughter went up around the room and drowned out whatever words he said next, but for absolute clarity about why a battle might be lost to one single cannon ball, it was the best example I can imagine. It was said in a calm matter-of-fact way without any note of fun or cynicism or interest, just a plain statement of fact. He was actually a very good teacher and taught us English some of the time and his history was excellent, as I've since discovered, because he didn't get into too much theory – he dealt with very plain, straightforward facts which had as much relevance to the real result in the world as the cannon ball had to the battle of Aughrim.

One of the less satisfactory aspects of our life was our two concrete tennis courts. They were just made of plain, rough concrete, well marked out of course, but the ball bounced so high on them that it didn't matter where you were, you could almost always get to it because the high bounce kept it in the air for so long. The game that we called tennis was really quite different and not as attractive as lawn tennis or even clay court tennis, although to this day I think that lawn tennis is far more pleasant a game than either on concrete or clay.

There are those moments that we remember from our school days when we were thoroughly embarrassed. One such incident for me occurred when I was crossing the street between the school building and the palace. A group of four of five of us were talking and laughing, all telling stories about what had happened that day with one master or another, and I was telling them how I had said something derogatory about the headmaster. His name was Mr Fleming and I had called him 'old Flem' or something like that. I was telling the others but hadn't realised that he was right behind me when I spoke, so he must have heard and suddenly, from behind came the voice: "And here I am, Mullen, right behind you again, hearing it all." We fled in several directions with, "Sorry, Sir… Sorry,

Sir!' coming out of our mouths sideways as we let him go past, and then came together to mull over our bruised egos. He was very pleasant about it, laughed it off and went about his business.

On another occasion he called four or five of us senior boys into his study to tell us that he wasn't totally satisfied with the way the senior boys and girls were behaving towards each other and the example they were setting to the other children. Apparently I looked at him as though I didn't understand what he was talking about. He walked across, put his arm around me and gave me a sort of hug and tickle and said, "Go on, Mullen, you know perfectly well what I'm talking about," whereupon all the others broke into laughter and I did, too, so we all got the point in a very pleasant and happy way.

One grave disappointment occurred when a member of the Board of Governors took four of us down to Cork to see the very first New Zealand rugby team that came to Ireland after the war. They played against Munster. We were appalled at the tricks they got up to in the game – we would have been sent off the pitch for them – like catching the other fellow's jersey when the referee was not looking, deliberately obstructing and doing all sorts of things in the scrum. Then an incident occurred when each of the Munster forwards, standing in a lineout, instead of jumping for the ball turned and hit his opposite number so that there were about four chaps lying on the ground and four others looking askance at the referee blowing his whistle. I can still hear the Munster captain's words, shouted quite loudly, "Ref, you take charge of this game, or we will!"

My school career ended with the annual summer dance in 1948. One of our group made some derogatory remark about a rather portly guest sitting at a side table and was shut up very quickly by somebody else saying, "Shhh, that fellow won a V.C. at Dunkirk." So it seems that on my very first day in Bishop Foy School I was shown a V.C., Lord Roberts of Kandahar, Pretoria and Waterford, and on my very last day I was shown another V.C., although all I could see was the back of his head. This seems to me to reflect in some way the then unusual relationship between the Protestants of Southern Ireland and the British Empire, and to presage the next stage of my life, which was a job in Northern Ireland.

4
My First Job

It came about this way: I had won a scholarship to Trinity College, Dublin but it was not sufficient to enable me to take up a place in the University; I had to find a job, so I replied to an advertisement in the Irish Times for a Junior Master at a preparatory school. It was a Box Number advertisement so I was taken by surprise about two or three weeks later when somebody called to see me in Dublin and explained that the headmaster of the school to which I had applied had asked him to come and give me a preliminary interview to see whether it would be worthwhile my going for a fuller interview at Mourne Grange School itself, which turned out to be in Northern Ireland.

Mourne Grange School

The interviewer was a very pleasant fellow who expressed himself amusingly but directly, by saying that the headmaster had asked him to come and have a look at me and if I was out of the question, to tell me so! He felt I wasn't quite out of the question and arrangements were duly made for me to travel up to Northern Ireland to have an interview with the headmaster.

The school was situated at the foot of the Mourne Mountains, which required a train and bus journey. I arrived to find the place rather deserted, because it was summer time and everybody was away except the few people who stayed on to keep the school going during the holidays. When I actually got to the building I saw a man mowing the grass with a very large motor mower way down on the bottom terrace – there were three terraces down from the main building to the very bottom field. He was wearing only brown corduroys, which had been cut into shorts from longs, held up with a tie for a belt, and he saw me and stopped. The maid who had opened the door to me went down and spoke to him and he came up... this was the headmaster!

Thus the interview began with him looking for his shirt, and introducing me to the deputy headmaster. He told me that he had previously had a teacher from my school, one named Dick Easton, who was etched in my mind as the naughtiest boy I had ever heard about. He even told me that Dick Easton's tutor at Trinity College had recommended him for many reasons, but ended with the remark that he was not averse to a party and had for some time been a fortune teller with a travelling circus!

And so it was that after a few more exchanges about classroom activities, games in the afternoon, evening prep and other out-of-school activities, including the fact that I would of course be full-time resident for the entire term, I found myself appointed Junior Master.

About three weeks later, I was standing on the station platform in Dublin assembling around me a party of eleven or twelve boys, with all their luggage, to take to the school for the first term of the new school year. We had to change trains at Goraghwood because there was at that time a type of Customs check between Southern Ireland

and Northern Ireland. This was not very serious, but every boy had to get out at the station and find his own trunk, tuck box and bicycle, if he had one with him, plus other bits and pieces, and then we had to get them across onto the other train. All this was done fairly easily but it did mean that I had to go up and down the platform because some of the goods were at one end of the train and some at the other. I also had to make sure that all the boys – who by this time had either lost their scarves or lost their caps or were telling me that another boy had taken his cap and thrown it out of the window – were on the correct train.

I managed to sort all that out and was standing halfway down the train thinking what a good job I had done and how a lesser man might not have been able to keep his calm in such confusion, when a tall gentleman approached from behind. Wearing the de rigeuer grey double-breasted suit and brown trilby hat that was worn in those days, he put his hand on my shoulder very gently and said, "Isn't there anybody in charge of all you little boys?" Actually there wasn't, but for the next eight years, three times a year I repeated this performance without losing a boy, a tuck box, a bicycle, or any of the little pieces of carpentry which he may have made and was bringing back to his parents for Christmas.

The school was a good one, beautifully set in the Mourne Mountains and with plenty of space for the boys to run about outside and a lovely little chapel which set off a kind of quadrangle between it, the main building and the playing fields. It had just the right atmosphere for the bringing up of children and the introduction to their later schools – public schools in England mainly. The dormitories had been given the names of Public Schools, like Haileybury and Oundle, and the classrooms were called after universities: Cambridge, Oxford, Durham I remember. One or two other rooms had obvious specific names, like the Study.

One feature that most schools would not have had was a very large Hall with a fine stage and very modern gadgetry in the way of lights and stage fittings. This was because the headmaster had been stage manager of the Oxford University Dramatic Society, O.U.D.S., when he had been up with such people as Hugh Hunt and others

The School Chapel

who became famous afterwards in their own field of drama. The reason he had come back and not gone on the stage was that he was his father's only son and this was his father's school, so he more or less had to come back and run it.

He had very generous ideas. I remember once the senior master saying to him that they would have to put up the price of music lessons. His reply was that he wanted to avoid this as much as possible because, (1) neither he nor the rest of the staff were actually starving, (2) some of the parents of these boys made immense sacrifices to send their children there and (3) he felt that every boy should leave the school, whatever his circumstances, able to swim, ride a horse, use a dark room, sing in a choir, play an instrument, paint a reasonable picture, fire a rifle, act in a play, and all those things that most of us would take for granted. He was determined that these boys should learn how to do them and go on to their next schools capable of taking a full part in the life of that school, which they would attend when they were about twelve or thirteen, having come into his school aged seven or eight.

My introduction to the rest of the staff was very interesting in that I arrived at the afternoon teatime and joined the staff around the table. As the most junior and new member (and they didn't even know my name), I sat at the very end of the table. I had a cup of tea but all the sandwiches, biscuits, cake, etc., were out of reach. I had sufficient sense not to either ask or stretch, so there I sat, drinking my tea, while the others had plenty to eat and enjoyed themselves, talking and laughing. Someone did say, "Hello" to me and asked my name. Finally, one of the senior members of staff up near the head of the table, I think second from the top, noticed that the rest of them had omitted to pass me anything to eat. He leant out into the middle of the table, half standing up, and took a slice of bread (with butter on it) in his fingers, and reached right down across all the others and put it on my plate with the words, "I'm so sorry, excuse my fingers, my toes are sore."

There is a way in which that incident, together with my original interview, summed up the whole of the life of the school as I lived it over the next eight years. It was a happy place where you just got on in a happy way no matter what situation arose. All the proprieties were adhered to and the serious matters were looked after in a very correct and balanced manner. I can remember in our Armistice Day service in the chapel when the headmaster quoted the British Ambassador to Southern Ireland at that time, in the following words, "A bugle sounds through the hills and glens of Ireland calling its men to the battlefields of the world and weaving a green thread into the tapestry of history." A most economical way of combining all the shades of meaning of Southern Ireland, Northern Ireland, the British Empire, people who died in battle and people who fought in battles that ought never to have been brought upon them, all beautifully done.

Tom Robinson, another boy from the same school as me, joined the staff and figured in an incident that reminded us all very much of the inimitable Dick Easton. There was a dance at the golf club just across the road from the school. I couldn't go because I was on duty that particular day; the headmaster did not like dancing so he didn't go but all the rest of the staff went.

The story as it came back to us afterwards was: The motorcar in which four or five of the resident members of staff went, was driven back very carefully and slowly because of the consumption of alcohol at the dance. There had been no room for Tom, so he went on his bicycle… in his tops and tails! On the way home it seems he cycled beside the car, down the hill towards the marvellous gate (which was always open), where it swung in off the road, down to the school. The car was going so slowly that Tom, on his bicycle, was able to go on ahead and wave to them, shouting and laughing, and turn in through the gate, but alas!... for some reason the gate had been closed that evening and when the motorcar arrived they found a mixture of gate, bicycle and Tom, which they were able to sort out!

However, by the time morning came and the headmaster and I were in chapel with all the boys, no other member of staff was seen to be present. The headmaster, having taken the service, went out through the vestry door; I went out through the main back door entrance to the chapel and stood talking to him as the boys filed out in their regular well-behaved manner off to their various classrooms. The headmaster said to me, "Lloyd, I'm raging not to have been in on it myself; what a night! It must have been wonderful, but do go and get those chaps and make sure they're out of bed to take their classes. You go and look at Cambridge, Durham (and he named one other place) and I'll go to the others." So off I went and I did find them all. One of them, a great fun-loving chap, was eating an onion with one hand and putting on his gown with the other and saying, "Lloyd, does my breath smell?"

The school did not have a swimming pool but in the summer we cycled two miles down to the sea and saw that the boys got plenty of salt seawater in which to practise their swimming. However, teaching them to swim was not at all easy because there were waves and no organised place where you could take them into calm water. I remember having to carry quite small boys in my arms out into the water where they were just about out of their depth, and holding them while they tried to move their legs and arms in a way that would cause them to swim. Now you can imagine some of these children were very frightened indeed and I still hear the cries, "Oh! Sir, please don't let me go, please hold me, please, please…" and then the delight when they discovered that they were swimming and I had taken my hands away, put them back and taken them away again. It was quite revealing to me, and a great relief, how many boys learned to swim without being too stressed by the whole matter.

Of course, occasionally the unexpected happened, like a seriously disturbed boy running away from the school, aged eleven. He found his way back to his home in the south of Ireland where his mother, a rather old widow, had problems dealing with him and asked for a member of staff to go down to her house to bring the boy back. A member of staff duly went, but the next thing we had was a phone call from the mother to say that matters had been held up and they might be late returning to school because the boy had managed to lock the master into their bathroom and he couldn't get out!

A lot of our time was spent acting with the Newpoint Dramatic Society when we were not actually teaching or on duty in school. In a production of Hamlet in Newry Town Hall, I played the small part of Horatio. One night, standing in the wings, the stage manager grabbed me and pushed the book under my nose and said, "Read that." It turned out that the actor playing the ghost had not turned up and his voice was supposed to come out of the wings at Hamlet, "…but look, amazement on thy mother sits." So, in a totally different accent, I attempted to be the ghost, but the amazement that should have sat on his mother's face sat on Hamlet's face when he heard my unexpected voice from the wings! He did *not* burst out laughing, I will say that; he carried on and I don't think the audience realised that anything odd had happened.

The ghost was in fact being played by a splendid actor whom we all regarded as the most amusing man with connections all over the world. These connections became very useful in our actual production of Hamlet because we had had two 6' 6" sentries taken from the local army unit who stood as sentinels at the foot of the throne and were very impressive. Now it happened that their army unit was shifted just about a week before the show began. When the actor who played the ghost heard about this he said, "Nonsense, I'll ring my friend at the War Office and get all that stopped." The rest of us smiled knowingly, as much as to say, "There he goes again… he won't be able to do it," but in fact he did. A signal came through from London to say that when unit *so-and-so* of the army was shifted, Privates XYZ and PQR were to remain at base until the production of Hamlet was over.

A more dramatic event for me in the theatre – when Hamlet runs Laertes through with his sword – was the sense of excitement because out of the corner of my eye I saw all the hands in the audience rush up to their throats. In the darkness their hands were white and you had this white band going up to peoples' throats right across the theatre as if to prove just how effective the production was.

Acting in Ian Hay's 'Housemaster'

Altogether we had great fun with our dramatic productions, taking them all over Northern Ireland into various drama festivals, sometimes winning the first or second prize or sometimes none at all.

The small quadrangle between the chapel, main building and the sports field played quite an important part in the life of school. One evening, when I was standing looking out over the playing field at a beautiful sunset down across Carlingford Loch, the headmaster's mother came up behind me and very quietly said, "I see, Mr Mullen, that you are enjoying the sunset and very beautiful it is." I replied, "Yes, Mrs Carey, I am." She replied, "You know, these are the eternal things; that sunset you and I are looking at now will never be the same again; this wonderful moment is just here for now and then it's gone. But it's eternal." She continued, "People make a great mistake when they think that the eternal things are those that last forever... no, they can be the most beautiful things that will never, ever be the same again and we remember them." Well, it certainly added to my concept of eternity.

Another experience I had in that quadrangle was quite unexpected. One morning as I was crossing it slowly, thinking of nothing in particular, on my way to a classroom, there came into my head a vision of all the girls in the world – those I knew and those I didn't – but they weren't standing upright like girls, they were like sheep, all moving in one direction very slowly, all with white wool, a great field of sheep. I didn't know they were girls at first until, as I was looking at them, they stood upright, became girls, all different in appearance, turned towards me and looked way past me over my head. It dawned on me that instead of thinking of girls as fully individual human beings all with their own hopes, fears, ambitions, mistakes and successes, I had somehow been thinking of them as a collective group without individualities of their own. This was a growing experience for me because I had realised it in the case of the children I was teaching – all these children were different – and I naturally realised it in the case of the men with whom I played rugby, hockey and cricket. All had their own strengths and weaknesses, but I had not really come to terms with the reality of these individual differences in the lives of girls, even though I had two sisters and a mother of my own and had been to a co-educational boarding school.

A feature of life in the chapel was that the school had, by tradition, used the same six psalms for the six days of the week from the beginning, and still did, and these psalms were to be learned by heart by all new boys without looking at them in the book. In other words, everybody came into chapel, joined in the service but did not open the book to sing the psalm. We all picked it up from those who were already present and knew it. After some time this tradition worked and we did get to know the psalms, but one amusing result was in the case of the headmaster himself. He had been to the school when he was very young and had always wondered why 'Good Mrs Murphy would follow him all the days of his life'. He had been unable to sort out the fact that the words really were 'Goodness and Mercy will follow me all the days of my life', so there he was, for a long time, singing away happily and probably every Wednesday, that Good Mrs Murphy would follow him all the days of his life!

I do think that Good Mrs Murphy followed me all the days in my life for I enjoyed my time in that school immensely. If you ask me, 'Did Goodness and Mercy follow me all the time I was there?' I would say 'Yes,' partly because I was, at the start, one of the most junior and had perhaps the least responsibility and got carried along by the others and didn't have the business of making all the arrangements for the fun that we had. I even learned to teach first year Greek, something I would never have thought of doing before I went to that place.

5
Wider Horizons

In the long summer holidays of 1949 I had the good fortune to go on a tour of Europe. This began under the clock at Victoria Station with one of those parties of about a dozen people who meet and go off together, never having met before. We went down to Dover, crossed the Channel, went through France and Switzerland, into Italy to Milan, where our holiday really began, but I did discover on the way down the different values of currencies. I changed too much money into Swiss Francs and so when I got into Italy I had Swiss Francs to get rid of. I bought Lire and got so many that I made a profit. Indeed, I temporarily thought of going round and round in circles from France to Switzerland to Italy, making a profit on every circle!

We went to Milan (this was my first time in Europe) to see La Scala, the great Cathedral and all the wonderful architecture, which I found exciting. We went down to the Riviera and along to Rapallo and stayed in a place called San Michele di Pagano.

The twelve of us went for a walk one evening to a small village called Portofino. Although unheard of at that time, it did become famous for the marble dance floors that were on three levels up the side of the cliff overlooking the sea. You and your partner could dance on the top level, lights shining on it, then go down the steps and dance on the second level in front of the band (who played in a grotto formed under the upper level). Down yet more steps to the bottom level, you could dance around out under the palm trees in the balmy evening, then sit down at a table and have a drink. It was the most romantic place ever. In fact, so romantic that I even remember the name of the girl I danced with that night, Betty Benson. (I hope she has had as happy a life as I've had.)

We walked back about a quarter of a mile to where we were staying and because we were in such good humour we decided to get into a fisherman's boat and row out onto the very calm sea. I still remember Betty saying, "Let me row, I want to row." She was a little bit tipsy, so we let her row and she rowed and rowed and then let go of one of the oars. It gently floated out of reach and she said, "Oh, look, look at that oar, it's floating." We said, "Yes, it's floating!" Well, we managed with a sort of punting action to get back, but had to go down next morning to give the fisherman some money for his oar. I expect he had found it and made a profit on the deal, but it wasn't very convenient for him.

Then we went back to Milan and over to Venice, where I found myself locked out on the balcony of St. Mark's with the original horses there, the real bronze ones (or whatever they are made of). I was locked out at lunchtime because a dear old lady, in very furry slippers came along and closed the latticework behind me. I couldn't get back in so had to call to her – thankfully, she returned and let me back in. When I see photographs of Venice now and the huge crowds, I think back to that time, when there were only about ten to twenty of us in the whole of St. Mark's Square. We were shown everywhere: Murano, Burano, Torcello, the islands and even the Lido, and also went swimming; it was a wonderful experience to see that beautiful city without people, just gondolas. Even the gondoliers had to tout for custom, as there were so few people. They gave us a marvellous ride, sang, and all the romance was there.

We then went on to Assisi and Florence to see the Ufizzi Gallery. I understand you have to queue now; we just walked in and looked around. Indeed, I stood in one room, an octagonal room of Botticelli's and was the only person in that room. While I was looking at these wonderful paintings I saw the blue-coated shoulder of one of the attendants peep in and go away and that was all. When I've told my friends about this experience they say, "Good heavens, Lloyd, not even the Queen of England or the President of America will ever stand in that room alone again – even their bodyguards will crowd them out… you were very fortunate." And I was, it was a glorious time.

A little less glorious a few days later was when we were down in Rome. The British Government devalued the pound and the £22 I had remaining suddenly became £11! But even in Rome I had a good experience. I got a slight touch of sunstroke and had to sit down near the Forum, and while there a street photographer came across to take my photograph. Now street photographers were very poor and they wanted to take your photograph and get some money. I weakly waved my hand and said, "No, no, I can't." He said, "Ah, you are sick, I get you taxi, one moment," and he got a taxi. I was able to give him my hotel card from my pocket and he told the taxi driver to take me to the hotel. As I got in, I struggled to get some money out to give him and he said, "No, no, you sick, you go, you get better, go, go, go." That's had a wonderful effect on me where Italians are concerned ever since. When I got back home to Ireland I realised what a difference there is between the British Isles and the Continent.

There were many family connections in Mourne Grange School – fathers who were sending their sons, and sets of brothers, but one family was larger than all the others. They had five sons and one daughter and they all went through the school at some time or another, even the girl – I think she was the only girl ever to have studied in the school, however temporarily. They lived not too far away and their father was leader in Ireland of the Oxford Group, as it was called in those days. He had two sons who had been through the school, one son on the staff teaching, two boys in the classroom learning, and they formed a very important part of the school connection.

I remember someone commenting on the serious Christianity of the Oxford Group and their adherence to absolute standards. This was summed up by the headmaster who invited the father, the Reverend Hannon, to present the prizes at Sports Day because, as he said, "They may have their peculiarities but they are house trained." That remark more or less summed up the establishment attitude to the Oxford Group in those days. It was just being renamed Moral Re-Armament, and indeed, as a result of that connection I went to the headquarters of Moral Re-Armament in Caux, Switzerland a few years later and found it a very worthwhile experience, giving me a vastly wider understanding of the possible outreach of Christian living in the world than I had had before.

It was on this visit that I saw something which altered my whole perception of life. I arrived early for a full morning meeting in the main Conference Hall. As others arrived and sat down, but before the panel of speakers appeared on the platform, an immaculately dressed American in his late twenties ran up onto the stage and with the nimblest, clearest expression, said laughingly, "They say that Confusion comes from Compromise and Clarity comes from Change. Well, I come from Kentucky, where our chief exports are tobacco and whiskey. My father thought I was becoming too good an advertisement for our exports, so he sent me to Paris to study Foreign Affairs. In Paris I had so many foreign affairs that I had to come down here to Switzerland and the cool of the mountains for a rest. I arrived here a month ago and I have decided to stay with what I found here for the rest of my life," and he ran off the platform just as the main speakers walked sedately on.

Amused and interested, I sat on through the meeting. Shortly, a tough hard-boiled Italian Communist, who had been a bodyguard to the leader of his party, took the stage. He spoke no English and was translated by an Englishman almost twice his height in a sort of 'Mutt and Jeff' performance. He told how, after the war, when poor Italians were very poor indeed, he had organised action in a large factory in Sesto San Giovanni in the north of Italy. Outraged workers burst into their bosses' offices, caught the bosses, dragged them down into the factory and threw them head-first alive into their own furnaces. Some bosses were out at lunch, but they were caught on their return and put up against the factory wall, then run down with their own trucks. Once on the ground, they were driven over. As a result of meeting Moral Re-Armament men in Italy (one of them an Irishman whom I knew) this man had changed his attitudes entirely, even going back to his Roman Catholic Church. He was now committed to a new kind of revolution, a new way of changing the world.

I sat in my chair stunned, saying to myself, "You were on The Grand Tour, in Portofino, Genoa, Milan, Venice, Florence, Rome, when this man was murdering his bosses. You saw Italy in ruins. You enjoyed your holiday. You went back to your comfortable job in Ireland. Since then you have not said one prayer for Italy, let alone given a penny to help. Yet you call yourself a Christian. What have you been doing?" The answer came at once.

I suddenly saw, spread across the whole side of that conference hall, a map of our rich western world, covered in pine trees, with each man climbing to the top of his own tree, me among them. I felt that this would continue until the day the rest of the world gets so frustrated at our selfishness that they come, chop down our trees and throw us in the furnace. All I could think was – "By God, you deserve it!"

I found my way out of that meeting, stunned and startled, on to the mountainside looking down over Lake Geneva far below, and decided to try to listen to God and find what He wanted to do with the rest of my life.

I was sure that I had heard, out of the mouth of one rich, laughing, ex-Capitalist American, and one poor, snarling ex-Communist Italian, a way forward for people everywhere, a way we could all go together, no matter what our background or upbringing.

Back to Mourne Grange, two other families I remember because I was asked by them to go and tutor one of their sons in the holidays. In one case the family had the problem that their young boy became a friend of the gardener's boy on their estate and didn't think it a good thing that he should go to Eton when the gardener's boy couldn't, so he decided to fail his examination deliberately. This wasn't really the right way to bring in a tutor to help but I was asked both by the parents and headmaster to go along and see what I could do, and I did. I am happy to say that the boy did go to Eton, because he wasn't at all backward – he was just an ordinary boy who needed a chance to let off steam.

They had a golf course on their estate and the people from the local town used to come out and play golf. In the afternoon, when we had finished our work, I used to take him round the estate doing various things, one of which was to teach him how to use a shotgun properly. On one occasion I found him trying to get through one of those rotating gates with the shotgun loaded, pointing under his chin; I had the fright of my life! Anyway, we got through and I said to him, "Now look, if you come through here quietly and wait a moment, you should be able to get one of those rabbits that are out underneath the trees. Then go for a long walk right around the golf course and by the time you get back here the rabbits will be out again and you'll get another... but do please be careful because there's a tee just up there near a tree behind the warren and golfers may be driving off, so make sure you don't take a pot shot when there's anyone there." He replied, "Oh no, Sir. It's quite all right, it's our golf course."

The other family that I spent some time with were absolutely straightforward and I only mention them because they gave me the chance to do something very interesting. They wanted to sow some special seed in one of their fields by using the old-fashioned fiddle. Now I don't know whether the reader will understand how that's done, but you have a sort of sack in front of you, stretched out tightly. You put it over your neck and hold it out front and all this seed is in this sack, swaying to and fro in front of you as you walk along. You have a fiddle – or shall we call it a stick with a string attached to it like a fiddle – and by moving this across and back, across and back, you spray the seed out over the land and it settles very evenly and smoothly.

All the years that I was at that school I was working for my degree at London University where I was able to take an external Honours Degree. I was fortunate to be able to do it through Wolsey Hall, Oxford, which was at that time a very well-established and experienced correspondence college, and I managed to get a 2.1. I felt that I hadn't quite wasted my evenings or holidays, when I might have been out doing something else, but had spent my time sitting in studying after I'd corrected all my exercise books and so on. In that remote school at the foot of the mountains, there weren't too many distractions so once I had done my stint of work and play with the boys and other members of staff, there was sufficient time to get on with my degree course.

Somebody had once said to me that a degree was a kind of 'passport' and indeed, this proved true, because while I had gained a great deal studying English, History and Latin as different sections of my degree work, the fact that I simply had a degree (and a 2.1) meant that I was able to ring people and make applications, which were taken more seriously than they would have been if I hadn't had that degree, simply because the 'passport' was attached to the letter.

Two characters of a very different kind had a deep effect on me while I was at that school. The first was the elderly professional cricket coach who used to come for the summer term to coach cricket. Being the cricket master, I was half over him, half under him. He was a very good coach, and made sure that these small boys would be able to go into the very competitive world of public school cricket and show themselves to good effect. I am forever grateful to him for all the simple truths he taught me, especially about batting.

The second life-long friend it was my good fortune to meet via cricket came back from National Service in Hong Kong and spent one term with us as assistant cricket master and general teacher. Peter Everington then took up his scholarship at Cambridge and we have remained friends ever since.

The other unusual person who had an effect on me was a small boy who was discovered by his mother's best friend when she came to Ireland to see her friend. She went to their rather grand house in the country and found to her horror that her friend had died and the father, who was a busy man with a business that took him all over the place, had left the boy, their only child, in the care of the servants. She found him more or less in a cot in a corner of the kitchen. I won't bother you with the details but she took an immense amount of trouble and finally brought him to the school where we were able to fit him in.

Now, one ought not to have favourites as a schoolmaster and one should not give one boy more attention than another, but I'm afraid I did give this little fellow a bit more attention. In fact, we were all told to because it helped him to come into the school with some sense of warmth, acceptance and love. He did quite well and went on to a good public school afterwards, but before that a strange thing happened. When I left that school and, of course, said goodbye to everybody, for some reason he wasn't around so I didn't see him before I went. Then about six months later, during one of my breaks, I called in to the school to see them for a while. This boy saw me and more or less emotionally attacked me with tears to say that I had gone away without saying goodbye and that was not fair, that was terrible. Of course we were able to put everything right but it did give me a grim warning about letting oneself become too meaningful to others without taking full care for the consequences.

An unexpected bonus of having been in a school myself as a pupil for eight years and then having taught in a school for eight years, was that I realised education is a slow business – it's a growth inside a person and there is no way you can suddenly switch and twist and make it go faster. It has to develop inside and won't do so unless that person is, for want of a better expression, loved, cared for and nurtured. That is why I think many theories of education fall a little bit dead because they don't take into account the learner's need for warm acceptance.

The manner of my leaving that school and going on to my next post was quite normal. I just got in touch with Gabbitas Thring, the education agents in Sackville Street, London. They sent me various notes about schools that had positions in which I might be interested and suggested I call when I was in London. Well, I was in London and I called in and had sufficient sense to talk fairly straight, because at that time there were many prep schools in England, some of which were excellent and some of which were far from excellent. The person who was in charge asked to see what they'd been sending me and I gave him all the chits of paper that I'd received. He swept them all off his desk with one swing of his arm and said, "Ah, no, I think we can do something better; excuse me for a moment," and he got up and left the room. He came back with one piece of paper in his hand, saying, "Well now, this is a good school; I know the headmaster personally. He doesn't send all the boys to Eton but a large number of them go and others go to very good schools; it has a good reputation and from what I have seen of you so far, I'm prepared to at least recommend that he gives you an interview. What would you like to do?" So I said, "Let's wait a minute," and I found out more about this school, St. Michael's... that it had been at Uckfield in Sussex and had been evacuated during the war down to the West Country, near Barnstaple in Devon, and that after the war it had not come back but stayed down there and consequently the ethos of the school had changed only very slightly. It sounded to me to be just the right kind of thing after the two schools I had been in myself, both as pupil and teacher. So I said, "All right, I'll have a go at this; let's get in touch with the headmaster," which he did. The headmaster gave me an appointment at his London Club.

St Michael's School

I was staying with some Moral Re-Armament friends at that time and they asked me what I was doing. I told them I was changing jobs and was hoping to get a position in a school down in Devon. When I mentioned the name of the school, a full-time MRA worker piped up, "Goodness, that's my old school," and he told me how he had gone to it when it was in Sussex. He was able to give me some of the history of the school and I said I would let him know the result of the interview. To my surprise he called on me the next morning with the up-to-date review of the school's activities – something that they published at the end of every summer term – and he said, "Now you can read it before you go for your interview," which I did. It was full of photographs and told which team had won and which had lost, who had passed what exam and who had gone to what school and so on, which at that time was very relevant and interesting to me. It became so relevant that in the middle of my interview, which I went to the following day, the headmaster who was interviewing me suddenly broke off and said, "My goodness, you seem to know more about my school than I do!" It was a good laugh with which to begin and I was fortunate enough to be given the post to start the following September.

The school was set well back from the Devon coast and overlooked where the rivers Taw and Torridge met. It was celebrated country because Henry Williamson had chosen it for his well-known book, Tarka the Otter.

The school did not have its own chapel but it looked down over a very fine lawn towards the river and on the left-hand side there was an old Saxon church. On the right-hand side opposite, about a hundred yards across, there was a famous Saxon Oak, which had been mentioned in the Domesday Book.

It was about the same size as my previous school: some eighty-five boys boarding, with the resident staff of about six or seven and the usual retinue of matrons, assistant matrons and cooks, all of whom were very important figures in the life of the school because we were a community out in the Combes. Those who know the Devon Combes will know the very close type of unity life which develops among the people who live and work there.

Some friends had given me an introduction to a local potter, Michael Leach, son of the very famous Bernard Leach, and I got to know him and his wife and family (four children all at school) and was delighted to see his pottery. It was the first time I had ever been close to a real artist producing pots of all different kinds and selling them, literally, at the roadside on the North Devon coast and also from the showroom in his pottery. A small fingerboard sign on the road from Barnstaple to Bideford simply said, "Yelland Pottery" and many motorists would turn into that small lane and visit the showroom.

The school's academic standards were high and I began to develop an ulcer worrying about whether I could keep up the level of work which my predecessor had achieved with the pupils. This worry was further accentuated by the new type of work and people I met. In this school the teaching was very clearly compartmentalised. For example, the mathematics master got on with his mathematics and if he were to take one game of hockey, cricket or tennis, he took that and that was all – he more or less then disappeared. This seemed to work for all sections of the school, even music, where the music mistress appeared, took her classes and went away. This was different from the kind of life that I had been used to; I found myself to a certain degree alone in my own work for the first time in my life and I had to learn how to deal with this.

I learnt to accept that this was how English people worked; they each did their own particular job (and did it well) and let other people get on with their jobs. This was somewhat different from the way we had operated in Ireland, both in learning and teaching, where there was a certain amount of intermingling of effort and, I wouldn't say exactly 'team spirit' but a certain collection or cohesion of effort.

A great help in my settling down to solve this problem was my friendship with the Leach family who were only about a quarter of an hour's bus drive down the road and with whom I began to spend some of my days off and some Sundays. They had very interesting tales to tell of Michael's background in the Oxford Group and in St. Ives amongst all the artists his father mingled with, Barbara Hepworth, Cardew and many others. His wife's background had been in Uganda, where her family had been very long-standing and well-known coffee planters; I think one of her uncles had been a bishop, rejoicing in the title of Bishop Upper Nile.

Also, as you can imagine, the four children, because of their parents' backgrounds, were all very interesting themselves and had many and varied opinions about what should and should not be done while they lived the perfectly normal school life of coming and going with their satchels each day.

The Leaches gave me an introduction to a family in Bristol because when I went back to Dublin it was convenient to take the train from Barnstaple to Bristol, from where I could take the plane across to Dublin – in those days it was a very small plane and going over the Welsh mountains one could easily get sick with the turbulence! My meeting with this family and staying with them only one night was very helpful, because the following thing happened.

They used to sit around the breakfast table after they had finished eating and for a few moments share with each other the various thoughts that had come to them in their time of prayer in the morning. I'm not sure which type of Christianity they had, but it was just normal religion as far as I could see, so I sat with them and listened. With them was an older lady – I believe she was an aunt – who said, "There was once a thing I had in my life that I wanted desperately to get rid of and I couldn't; I prayed to God that He would take it away, but He didn't. So after some time I said to myself, 'Oh well, I'm just like that, nothing can be done about it.' Then I suddenly realised that actually I was clinging on to this very thing that I was asking God to take away, sub-consciously grasping it to myself, at the same time as I was asking Him to take it away, so once I realised that, I was able to stand still and give it to Him and just say, 'There it is, God,' and throw it away."

When she said this I realised that I was, in a strange way, grasping the ulcer in my stomach with fear and clinging on to it. So after breakfast I went to my bedroom and remember standing in the middle of the room, putting my hands in front of me and saying, "There it is, I'm giving it to you, God, this ulcer, this pain." I can only say that I felt a kind of 'whoosh!' and thereafter I was not conscious of any more pain – it just literally did seem to go away.

All this time my sisters were working in Dublin – my older sister at one of Dublin's leading accountants and my younger sister in the Guinness offices. When I came home on holiday they were still working all day so we didn't really see very much of each other, but my mother, in our flat in Dublin, was a kind of 'centre' who kept the whole family together as it were, even though we were quite separate from each other in our individual lives. I spent a lot of my holiday time with the family in Kildare and other places. Also at this time I used to go up to London to work in the books department of Moral Re-Armament. It was as a result of this work that I met some people who would later play a part in my move to my next job.

I only stayed in Devon for three years, but there are one or two very interesting things I should say about it. Against a background of absolute normality the following are a few things that I remember very clearly:

The school had a rule that after lunch the boys could collect as much tuck as they liked from their tuck boxes and take it up with them to their dormitories, where they should lie on their beds for the next half- or three-quarters of an hour and either sleep or read a book, but they had to stay quiet. The result of this was that small new boys would carry up to their dormitory huge numbers of bars of chocolate, bags of sweets and so on and start eating them… and they were allowed to. They went on eating until either they fell asleep or became sick, when matron had to come and deal with them. The result of this complete freedom was that after as little as half a term, even the newest boys would be going to the dormitory after lunch with just one or two sweets or half a bar of chocolate because they had learned that the best way to enjoy life was to be moderate!

Another unusual feature of this school was what was called 'The Gun Room'. It had indeed been the room where the guns were kept when it had been a private residence, but in this room, which was quite small, the boys were allowed to do anything they liked as long as they wore Wellington boots and rugby jerseys over their normal clothes. The Gun Room was actually on the way from the corridor which led from outside, through to the centre of the school, so that while the boys were in there – and they were throwing balls and doing all sorts of things – people were passing through. Nobody knew or cared what the boys were doing but they were allowed to do it. However, as soon as they came out they had to put on their house shoes because inside the building only house shoes were allowed. I was always fearful of some terrific accident happening when I was on duty and having to get the doctor to stitch up some boy's head or something, but it never did happen, thank goodness!

There was a strict rule that when the boys were out in break time in the playground they were not allowed to sit down on cold stone steps because this was regarded as the easiest way to catch a cold. One day when I saw a very small boy absolutely engrossed in a book, sitting on the very cold stone, I walked around the other side of the playground and came down towards him to give him a chance to see me and get up but he was so immersed in his book that he didn't see me. I went behind him and looked over his shoulder and saw that he was reading a music score. He was entirely absorbed with this music score, following it down the page. That was to me a very great surprise.

Another very good idea the headmaster had was that the boys should go out into the woods and collect sufficient wood for the boilers to heat the water for their baths and showers. They were allowed the full run of the estate so they were able to bring back plenty and, of course, it taught them to choose the size they could carry and the size that would be suitable for going into the boiler. They were very good at it as a rule, but I do remember once there were cold baths for some of them because they hadn't been able to collect enough wood early in the week.

Another event which brought the whole school together in a very close way was an epidemic of Asian Flu, resulting in something like seventy-eight of the boys being in bed at one time with the illness. We on the staff were pressed into service to act as semi nurses and doctors, to go up and down carrying water and juices to keep them from becoming dehydrated. I am happy to say that it worked out well in the end, but while it lasted I had the greatest respect for the matron who was able to keep control of the whole of this operation. The parents, too, were very long-suffering because they must have known what was going on and worried about the teaching staff looking after their children in a medical way.

Once a week an elderly and most charming Austrian lady would come to the school. She had been a violinist in the Austrian State Orchestra and got out of the country in time to escape from Hitler and was now working in Devon visiting various schools, teaching the violin. Some of the stories she had to tell – and she was a most cheerful person – were really enough to make me realise what a charmed life I had led living in Ireland throughout the war.

Another unexpected experience was to find a new boy, aged only seven, sitting in the classroom; I had been asked to take this class of seven-year-olds because their teacher was sick. I wasn't used to teaching such young children but I discovered to my amazement that after half the class had gone through and I was going round looking at the books and what the children had written, this one new boy had actually begun to make quite well organised notes of everything I had said from the beginning of the class to the end. This astonished me because they were the kind of notes a university student would make in a lecture, so I was not surprised years afterwards to learn that he had become a world authority on ancient manuscripts from Central European languages.

Another experience was to come downstairs from my room one Sunday morning when all the rest of the school had gone to church and find a small boy wandering about near the table tennis table. I asked him if he was all right and why he wasn't at church with the others and he told me that he was a Jew. I hadn't known this so we talked a bit and played table tennis and then chess; he was quite a brilliant boy and beat me at chess every time without any problem at all. I later heard an amusing tale from his parents (they lived in India where his father, I believe, was a director of Unilever and his mother a Manchester Guardian correspondent) of how he had, to their great embarrassment, seen a leading Indian politician in an aeroplane talking to his parents and later, when they were all back in their respective seats and lunch was being served, this boy apparently seized one of the knives and rushed down to attack this politician. As the mother said to me afterwards, "He must have overheard some of my remarks about the politician!"

Another story, which I think reflects the importance of being careful about what one says and does, and a story which took longer to mature, concerned a boy who was in my English class. Apparently I got the class to move the desks away from the middle of the room to leave a space, where we acted different scenes from Shakespeare's plays. He reminded me of using rulers as swords in a fight in

Macbeth. He also told me that his mother had sent him a letter while he was in school at that time telling him they were going to spend part of their holidays in Stratford-upon-Avon. There were three Shakespeare plays on and she suggested that he ask his English master which of these he should attend. The boy showed me the letter and I apparently said he must go and see all three! The mother took him to see all three and he told me later that from that day on he had simply one ambition and that was to become an actor. I'm pleased to say that he did, and to do that he gave up a promising career with the British Council to give his all to the stage. The sad thing is that I heard he had died of some disease not too long after.

He did meet me once in the corridors of the British Council and we were joking and laughing and he said, "Of course, you are to blame – you made us act those Shakespeare plays and then my mother took me to Stratford-upon-Avon and from then on I never wanted to do anything else."

It was a connection with acting that led to my leaving that school and going on to another job. I read a letter in The Times by Michael Redgrave who had come back from Russia with his team of actors. He told how they had been accepted and received in Russia very warmly and appreciatively and that while he was there he had come across several Russians who spoke perfectly fluent English without ever having been outside Russia. This had impressed him and he had enquired why. The answer given was that the Russians had the intention of giving lots of teachers of English to the new schools in the newly independent countries of Asia and Africa. Remember this was in the 1950s and '60s and these teachers would teach history and English, at Russian expense, in the leading schools in these countries. What clicked in my mind was that these teachers would have been sent with the intention of spreading a Communist ideology through the future leadership of these nations because that was the English-speaking elite, and so I wondered whether there was anything I could possibly do to redress the balance and counteract this.

I heard at the time of a school in Pakistan called Aitchison College; it was said to be the leading school and was looking for a new teacher of English. I was ambivalent in my reaction. On the one hand I thought, if nobody goes and helps spread an ordinary ideology of freedom then Communism will take over one day – on the other hand I thought of Pakistan as a hot, sandy place, ruled by Martial law… perhaps I would just disappear from view and never be seen again! So I didn't really know what to do. I was surprised when I looked at the next edition of The Times Educational Supplement to find the very first advertisement in the overseas section, beginning with the letter 'A': Aitchison College, Lahore, asking for applicants for a teacher of English in their senior school. I sent off an application to the British Council, who were acting as recruiting agents in Britain, and did not particularly worry what kind of reply I received. I did have one and was asked to go to London for an interview.

Some friends invited me to stay with them in London and asked me to come to afternoon tea the day before the interview, so I took a train from Barnstaple to Paddington. Despite realising that I was going to be late for tea and wanting to rush and take a taxi to get there on time, inside my head somehow there was this persistent suggestion: take it easy, don't rush, go slow, no need to hurry, all that kind of thing. This troubled me because it was at the very least bad manners to arrive late and also it was rather odd.

Anyway, I did go along rather slowly and arrived at about five minutes to five when some other guests were actually beginning to leave. Feeling embarrassed, I sat alone on a rather nice sofa watching a very fine lady pouring out tea from a glorious teapot and thought I had rather let things get out of control. However, there I sat and she graciously gave me tea and offered me cakes, which I duly accepted.

While I was there a man bustled in; he obviously knew the hostess very well. He apologised for being late and explained why, and this very warm-hearted kind of fellow then came straight across and sat beside me, saying "Good afternoon, my name is Roger Hicks, what's yours?" I told him and he then said, "What do you do?" When I replied that I was a schoolmaster, he said, "I used to lecture long ago but don't do it any more – what's your subject?" So I told him and he said his had been History and he asked where I taught. I said I was currently teaching in Devon but was thinking of leaving and had just applied for another post. He asked where and I said, "You probably wouldn't know it, but it's in Pakistan, a city called Lahore and the name of the institution is Aitchison College." "Oh," he said, "I know the Principal very well, he's a friend of mine; I've often been there." I really felt as if I might sink through the sofa! Anyway, he said, "Yes, yes, you will find him a very erudite man and he understands European needs, so you'll be very well looked after if you do take this job, I can assure you. It will be a very interesting life – you know about the college I suppose?" I said I didn't and then he proceeded to tell me that it had been founded in 1884 in order to educate the sons of the princes of the various states of India in an attempt to bring them into the modern world. They were being left behind and were being rather misled, he said, by some of their own chamberlains, who made a useful business out of controlling the young princes as they grew up and getting their own welfare looked after rather than the welfare of the people of the state.

By the time our conversation ended I felt I knew almost as much about the College as I had known about my last school in Devon before I went for the interview for that post. It was a surprising experience. Anyway, he asked me to let him know how I got on and I promised to do that and didn't see any more of him for some time.

I spent the night with my friends and shared a room on the top floor of their three-storey house. In the morning I said my prayers in the usual way but as I got up from my knees the most extraordinary thing happened. There came clearly through my mind like a streaming laser beam, the following sentence: 'Tell them that you would prefer the job in the senior school, but say that you will take the job in the junior school if it's offered to you'. You can imagine how this left me wondering. I duly got dressed and went to my interview at eleven o'clock in the British Council building.

The interview was normal for those days; there was a panel of about five people: one from the university, one from the Foreign Office, one from the British Council, and two others – I can't recall where they came from. They talked about this and that and asked me questions which I answered as best I could and explained why I wanted to go, and then a hiatus occurred... The chairperson said, "Mr Mullen, we are so sorry that we may have brought you here this morning under false pretences; we had a signal from Pakistan only yesterday and it almost seems that the post which we advertised and for which you applied does not in fact exist! We haven't been able to sort it all out yet but what we have discovered meanwhile is that there is a post in the English language teaching section of the junior school there. We don't exactly imagine that you will be interested in it but we feel bound to tell you since we have brought you here in these circumstances." I heard my own voice in that strange emptiness saying, "Well, if you are thinking of offering me the post in the junior school I'm certainly willing to consider it, but I would prefer the post in the senior school for which I have originally applied. Can you tell me anything more about this post in the junior school?"

Suddenly they were all on the back foot and I was interviewing them and they couldn't answer any of my questions. We went on talking a little more and then another extraordinary thing happened. The chairperson said, "Mr Mullen, have you been trained in Moral Re-Armament?" There was a pause because I was surprised at this question and I said, "Yes, I have actually." The response from the chairperson was, "Oh, thank goodness... the Principal has told us that he wanted people if possible trained in Moral Re-Armament, or at least people who believed in God because he has had so much trouble from members of staff who don't." This exchange left me wondering what was going to happen next. Anyway, we parted on good terms and I went back to my work in Devon.

About three weeks later I received a letter, which I didn't keep, unfortunately, but it went something like this:

Dear Mr Mullen,
When you receive this letter you may well think that the British Council is such a confused organisation that you don't wish to have anything more to do with it! It now seems that the post for which you originally applied in Pakistan, does indeed exist and because time is short we would be very grateful to know if you would be willing to take the post in the senior

school in order that we may begin to make the necessary arrangements for the term which begins in September.

I now found myself needing to find out more about the British Council, Aitchison College, Pakistan, teaching English to foreigners in their own country and kitting myself out for a tropical climate. All these things were fascinating and quite straightforward as I came to them step by step. I also had the task of saying goodbye to the school in Devon, where I had been offered a partnership, and also saying goodbye to my family at home in Ireland.

Thus life was very busy but, fortunately, owing to the British Council running a very good course for new arrivals and a very good conference on Moral Re-Armament being held in Switzerland, I was able to get over two of the difficulties. I also had the good fortune to meet Roger Hicks, the Principal's friend, again and he gave me some very useful information and advice because he had spent years in the sub-continent and was a friend of many of the leaders of both India and Pakistan. A story he told me is well worth recording here.

Pakistan was really founded by Qaid-i-Azam Mohammad Ali Jinnah, a Muslim lawyer married to a Parsee, who was a friend of Roger and went to the House of Commons with him when Churchill, after the war, was out of office and Sir Stafford Cripps was a great figure on the Labour benches. The following exchange took place while they were in the House:

Winston Churchill referred to his "...Honourable friend opposite, whose massive intellect, boundless energy, great integrity, and immense learning, have for so long been used to the great detriment of this state." Of course, the whole House exploded in laughter and Stafford Cripps himself put his head back and roared with laughter. Qaid-i-Azam leant over and touched Roger on the arm and said to him, "When we can do that in Pakistan then we will be really free."

6
INTERPLAY OF CULTURES

I arrived in Lahore in early August and the weather was still so hot that when I got out of the plane and stepped onto the tarmac, for one moment I thought I was in the exhaust from the aeroplane engine and took five or six quick steps to get out of the burning heat. Of course, the burning heat stayed there and I realised with amazement that this was what the heat was like all around the place. I also noticed that the only people on the tarmac were one or two necessary airline officials. Everyone waiting was way back in the small building at Walton Airport, standing underneath the shade of the building and the trees around it, and it was very noticeable when we did get across to the building that the temperature went down

Entering Aitchison College

several degrees. It was a wake-up call to the reality of the heat which I had heard about, but the reality is quite beyond imagination.

My first view of the college, where I was to spend the next nine years, was very straightforward in an impressive sort of way. The college had indeed been built for the Princes, Nawabs and Maharajahs of India. The gardens had been laid out spaciously and graciously, and right across the entire compound no plant was allowed to grow taller than four feet. Also the branches and leaves from many of the flowering trees were not allowed to come down more than eight feet from the ground. This meant that wherever you stood in the three hundred and seventy five acres which formed the entire college, you could look across a most beautiful panorama of flowers up to four feet high, underneath another panorama of many different kind of trees all coming down to eight feet above ground level!

To keep this arrangement at its best throughout all the seasons, seventy-five gardeners (who were called malis) were employed. They were busy all the time. One of their main tasks was to keep this very level ground, for we are in the middle of the Punjab plain remember, well irrigated. This was achieved via small mounds of earth, called bunds, surrounding each area of tennis court, cricket pitch, hockey pitch or flowerbed, up to a few inches high. Water would be allowed to pass into this and would stay for a day and night, by which time it would have evaporated or soaked away, but another opening would be cut into the bund and if there was any excess water it could flow out.

The buildings themselves were magnificent. They really did look like maharajahs' palaces. They were very well built, airy and spacious, and in modern times some ceiling fans had been put in which kept the air circulating, but they had already been designed to allow air to pass through both sideways and lengthwise in all of the buildings.

There were three boarding houses: one for the Sikh princes, one for the Hindu princes, and one for the Muslim princes. These were in order down one side of the main avenue, while a little beyond there was a mosque for the Muslims and at the other end there was a temple for the Hindus and a separate temple for the Sikhs. There was a main assembly building a little farther away at the end of which was 'Cypress Avenue', because it was indeed an avenue of cypresses.

This arrangement gave an air of great stillness to the college. It also helped immensely in the sense of discipline, because one would have to be very vulgar or ill-bred to misbehave in such surroundings. I was quietly surprised in my early days by the respectful nature of the boys. If I walked past boys sitting on a bench under the trees or knocking a hockey ball about to each other, because I was a member of staff they would stand up or would stop knocking the ball around and put their foot on it and wait until I had gone by, before carrying on again. This would have seemed rather odd to Europeans, but it was the sort of behaviour which made possible the discipline which prevailed in the old princely states of India with which the British Government had to deal when they took over from the Moghul Emperors.

That take-over had been made comparatively easy due to the fact that the Moghuls had introduced a language called Urdu (which means army camp) throughout their stay in the sub-continent – a stay of about two hundred and fifty years. When the British arrived in the form of The East India Company and later more direct Government intervention, they found that this language was a very useful lingua franca right across the entire sub-continent.

I obviously had to set about learning Urdu and found that, in addition to a tutor who came to teach me, the members of staff, the boys and the servants in the various capacities as I met them, were very helpful, too. Indeed, it wasn't long before I realised that the quality of these people, staff members, boys, pupils and servants in the college, was really the very best it could have possibly been. This extended to their families and friends as I met them, so I found myself in the extremely fortunate position of landing in a foreign country in a continent where I had never been before, but amongst some of the most delightful people that I could have hoped to meet. This, naturally, made my life fairly easy and enabled me to deal with any difficulties I met. For example, every European who went to the sub-continent in those days suffered immediately from stomach trouble – tummy pains of every kind. This is because we Europeans carry bugs in our tummies here which come alive when they meet certain kinds of water in the Asian sub-continent and it is a very painful experience. I used to feel that somebody was wringing my intestines inside me, winding them up, and this went on for a whole year, on and off. I can remember distinctly the very day in September, a year after I arrived, when suddenly I felt different; my reaction was that I wanted to pick up a tennis racquet and go out and play a vigorous game of tennis, which I had not wanted to do all that first year. This was the experience of becoming what the old ones used to call 'acclimatised'. I had become acclimatised and was very glad of it, too!

Becoming acclimatised to the social norms of this new society into which I had stepped was not quite so straightforward, but can be perhaps indicated by a remark made to me by one of the brightest boys I taught at that time. He stopped me as I left the classroom one morning and said, "Excuse me, Sir, but may I say something to you?" I said, "Of course, please." He replied, "Sir, when you are talking to us about anything I get the impression that in your country people feel responsible to those below them. It is not the case here; in our country people only feel responsible to those above them." He later took a course in International Law at Cambridge and ended up as the president of his country's Bar Association. I discovered that, by coincidence, one of his fellow students on that same course was a Nigerian boy I had taught in Devon.

The Principal, Shah Sahib, proved to be charming and erudite, a real Renaissance man. He played cricket and tennis to the highest standard; he was a swimming champion and his knowledge of world affairs as well as of local affairs was extraordinarily generous and detailed. I was not surprised to discover that he had been his country's first ambassador to Afghanistan and to Ceylon after Pakistan got Independence. Indeed, when he was in Afghanistan his job was to convince the American ambassador that, without their ever publicly saying so, Pakistan was on the side of the West in the Cold War; he achieved this by learning to play bridge because the American ambassador was really only interested in bridge! He achieved the same success in Ceylon where he had exactly the same task, to ensure the American ambassador reported back that Pakistan was on the side of the West, and he did this by learning to play golf because the American ambassador to Ceylon was more interested in golf than anything else. By becoming a close friend of his fellow ambassadors, he was able to achieve his country's objective in the most polished, pleasant and inexpensive manner.

Shah Sahib's first action as far as I was concerned was to invite me to a tennis party at his house, which was very pleasant. After spending the day playing tennis, he took us to the theatre in the evening. This was at his old Government College and he had arranged very good seats for us. The play was called 'The Queen and the Rebels', and I have to say that when the queen walked on the stage everything else disappeared and all the rest of my life, interesting though it was at the time, disappeared also. I could think of nothing else for a while except this queen – she was beautiful. Imagine my delight, amazement and joy when I discovered at church on Sunday, in the Cathedral (we went to Lahore Cathedral), there she was, sitting about three seats in front of me with her family. I was told her name was Promilla. She was a Christian girl, not a Muslim or Hindu, which would have made things very complicated.

Alas, I have to report that after a very short while she disappeared and it was some time later that I discovered that the British Council had given her a scholarship to Manchester, where she was able to specialise in linguistics and language teaching techniques. She was effectively off the radar for the next three years, because while her course lasted two years, India and Pakistan went to war during the third year and travelling back home was too difficult. She spent a further year in Manchester where she had great success at the university.

The Principal had warned me that in view of the change of climate I should not attempt to do more than teach the thirty-two classes which I had in the week, and take the three games. He said I would find that this would use up all my energy. After some time we could change the arrangement, but I was not to feel I had do anything more.

I discovered more about this man. He was in charge of the detail of the gardens, and I saw the plans that he made of the different

Promilla

kinds of flowers. He was also in very close touch with the heads of his departments, to whom he allowed great freedom. They were all rather distinguished people in their own right: science, mathematics, theology, etc., and the art section of the school was good, too.

So I took his advice, did as he said and discovered very quickly that the teaching needed to be straightforward and to some degree old-fashioned and pedantic, because the boys came up from essentially old-fashioned, pedantic and, one might almost say, rural backgrounds. They expected things to be done formally and correctly and did not respond to casual asides and attitudes, partly because, even if they did understand them and follow them, it set them somewhat at odds with their elders and they were always very anxious to be respectful to those above them. This made teaching in one way very easy because the pupils gave tremendous respect to the teachers and behaved very well. On the other hand, when they were off duty and in their free time and not supposed to be under the eye of anybody, they could, like boys anywhere in the world, get up to all sorts of things!

Another thing I discovered very quickly was their immense physicality. They played hockey, squash, tennis and cricket with an enthusiasm and aggression that I was not used to. I also noted that when they rode horses or fired rifles or did anything practical they were extremely effective.

Even though the country's sporting facilities were very poor, in the succeeding years Pakistan became world champions at hockey, squash and cricket. When I look back now it seems extraordinary because the facilities available to other countries, such as Germany, Australia and India, were very much greater indeed.

A good example of the Principal's grasp of present situations can be seen from the remark he made about a boy knocking a cricket ball around near the roller while we were watching a major match on the main cricket ground at Aitchison College in front of the magnificent pavilion. It happened as follows:

A boy called Majid Jahanghir (who later played for Pakistan) played a beautiful shot right across the ground, a cover-drive, which

Aitchison College Cricket Ground

hit the bottom step of the pavilion and bounced back into the field of play. I said to Shah Sahib, "You know, I think Majid may become as good a player as his father, Jahanghir," (who played for undivided India and was famous for being the only one to bring down a bird at Lord's with a ball he bowled). The reply was, "Oh yes, he will certainly be as good as his father, he may even be better, but his young cousin, Imran, will be better still." In saying this, he pointed down to an eleven-year-old boy fooling about with others off the field of play near the roller. Probably everybody has heard of Imran Khan by now, but for the Principal to have spotted the future greatness of this cricketer when the boy was only eleven really says something remarkable about the man.

Another remarkable thing about Shah Sahib was the way in which he made use of the curious history of British administrators in undivided India, using them as an example of loyalty to a central Crown in London in an attempt to inspire the same sort of loyalty from the different tribes to which the boys belonged, to a new centre of power in Karachi, which was then the capital of Pakistan. This was not at all easy. Some boys were from Sunni backgrounds, some from Shia, others from Sufi backgrounds – some boys were decidedly cosmopolitan in their background having perhaps come from India at the time of the Partition of the sub-continent, others having come from distinctly tribal backgrounds along the North-West-Frontier or Baluchistan.

All these boys were different from each other and their attitudes to each other could only be best described as simple – they didn't get into any kind of complicated discussions or conflicts or intellectual disputes about the differences between them, which were obvious. They did concentrate on their one simple allegiance, which was to the Muslim religion. This was very useful and very binding, but it was not the same as a loyalty to one country, Pakistan. The Principal certainly saw it as one of his important responsibilities to try and get these boys to understand that while they were loyal to a religion, which was worldwide, they ought also to be loyal to a nation which was only Pakistan-wide.

I could see that this was why he had called in the British Council to try to get a wider leaning of members of staff and why he was turning to Moral Re-Armament because he saw in it a way in which people of goodwill but of different basic beliefs could in fact work together for the good of their own family, their own tribe, their own country and the world, without resorting to the conflicts which he had seen in the Partition of his own country, India, and of course the dreadful holocausts across Europe in the two world wars earlier.

This understanding of the political and social realities of his own sub-continent came to an end with great sadness in a very short while. When he had been a junior master at Aitchison, many years before, he had, quite correctly, chastised a boy at the school. That boy was promoted through political processes to a position where, now a man of about fifty, he was in a position to take revenge… and he did. His first action on being elevated to his post was to summarily dismiss Shah Sahib from his post as Principal of Aitchison College. You can imagine the hullabaloo that this caused throughout the entire society, but our Principal refused to take any action which 'would make matters worse', as he put it. Indeed, he said that he had tried to turn down his appointment originally because he felt that something might one day happen which would, in his words 'Not redound to the credit of the college.' Certainly this behaviour did not redound to the credit of anybody, and so for a short while we lived in a kind of limbo until a new Principal was appointed.

So excellently had the Principal arranged the work of the college that even though he was no longer present, it was able to run both as an academic institution and as an administrative unit quite well, and we were able to carry on with our lessons, games and bringing up the boys almost as if nothing had happened, even though everybody knew that the ultimate sanction of a final authority did not exist.

The new Principal had one thing going for him which proved to be a tremendous help. He really did know how to deal with building contractors, and since the college was building a new junior school – because the numbers were going up from about three hundred, which had been the number when I arrived, through six hundred up to nearer one thousand – he saw to it that the buildings, boarding houses, new road layouts, etc., all happened on time, which was an extraordinary achievement for a man who was also running a college.

The other large building project was the new Principal's own idea entirely. He decided to erect new, good, modern servants' quarters because of the really quite dreadful, near hovel-like conditions in which all the servants had been living up to that time. He designed it himself, a courtyard with two rooms and a bathroom and kitchen around it, and a sufficiently high wall for the Muslim ladies to regard it as Purdah. There were eighty of these neat, tidy dwelling places built around a wide open space, in the centre of which he built a community hall with a doctor's surgery attached. He also saw to it that the same doctor who looked after the children in the school – and remember they were the children of the richest people in the country – looked after the servants and also their children.

This was something approaching a revolution in society at that time. Because he came from a powerful political family but did not share his family's views, he was always under the eye of either the Intelligence of the Central Government or the Intelligence of those who supported his own family, who were opposed to the Central Government. So in addition to being Principal of the country's leading college, he had to look over both shoulders at different groups of people who wanted to do him down in one way or another.

He had plenty of experience in dealing with those who tried to do him down! He happened to be a student up at Balliol at a time when the students of other Oxford colleges would gather in front of Balliol, knowing it housed many foreign students, and shout, "Bring out your blacks!" This is *not* something we expect to happen today, but it did then. His way of dealing with this was – because he was 6' 4" and twenty stone – to come out with some African students on either side of him, who were almost as big, and walk towards these abusive people… to their great alarm and also that of the policemen watching. He rather rejoiced in the fact that the police didn't have to intervene because those who had been shouting so loudly beat a hasty retreat when they saw what was approaching them!

He also had the dubious experience, as a boy, of having lost his temper when playing in a school cricket match. He had picked up a stump, run down to the other end and attacked the umpire for having given him 'out'! After the match he was called by his family to their great friend, Mahatma Gandhi, the advocate of non-violence, who suggested to him that he should not be violent, whereupon this small boy replied to the Mahatma, "When I'm as old as you, I will be non-violent!"

Alongside this Principal's somewhat aggressive behaviour, there was a great adherence to traditional values – to respect for authority, for older people and for family friends. I remember seeing him as host to Sir Olaf Caroe, a former Governor of the North-West-Frontier Province, who visited Aitchison College. He showed him around and then asked, "What is the thing you notice about Lahore now which is so different from when you were here last?" Olaf Caroe replied, "There are no Sikhs... Lahore was always full of Sikhs."

Another occasion when I saw him in this 'respect' mode was when I was with him in his office and a messenger came from outside to say that one of his uncles had called to see him. This uncle was an old man, but he was illiterate and was of no particular significance in the world in which the Principal moved. Nonetheless, he quickly rose from his desk and rushed round his office trying to find his turban. He found it behind the door and hastily put it on his head. He made sure his gown was on properly and straightened it out, then waited quietly inside the door so that when the messenger brought in the uncle, this enormous man knelt down on the floor and put his two hands on his uncle's feet and stayed there until his uncle put his hand down on his shoulder and said something. Then the Principal stood up and they began to talk.

Such a personality has, of course, one great drawback. Other people are unable to grow and develop in its shade, and this meant that while he was there as Principal the other members of staff and administration always felt in some slight fear of what was going to happen next. They knew he was fair, particularly from the discovery that he had paid the fees for a boy who had fallen on hard times and who would have lost his place as an entrant to the Pakistan Air Force, just by not having enough money to get through the various medical and other examinations he had to undertake. When the boy finally got through them all and joined the Air Force, it came to light that it was the Principal who had paid for these things out of his own pocket, without saying a word to anybody, and indeed the whole thing came out by accident.

So this very complex character replaced a very different kind of Principal, and I suppose I can say honestly that my time was enjoyable because I was in some way protected from the fall-out of this kind of inter-tribal in-fighting which went on all the time in the sub-continent.

I did, however, run into it once head-on when the Principal had expelled from the college a very bad boy who had caused a lot of trouble. I came back to the college after the long holidays to discover that this boy was going to return and come into my house of about fifty-two boys. I thought the only thing to do was to refuse this, so I went straight to the Principal in his office and told him that I couldn't accept this and that if the boy came back I would have to resign. I explained to him that I knew perfectly well that my position was different from his – that I would go home and not be subject to problems that would follow, whereas, if he were to do the same he might be shot dead. He accepted this and asked me quite reasonably whether I would meet the boy's parents, relations, friends and so on. I said, "Yes, of course I will meet anybody, but the answer will still be 'No'. I will not have this boy back because it will be a sign to everybody else that they can do what they like and get away with it." He said he understood that.

Finally, about three or four of the boy's relations came to see me, many not speaking English and we had to use an interpreter. It was quite heart-rending for me in one way to see these older people trying to persuade this young foreigner to take their relation, this young boy aged about eighteen or nineteen, back into the school, in a country that was now free and from which these foreigners had been expelled some years ago. However, I had to stand by the principle of it and the Principal stood by me; he kept saying, "Whatever Mr Mullen says I will do… you will have to ask him." It meant that he was putting the onus, the burden, fully and squarely on me and that he would at least have some 'out' when the end came and he would be able to say, "Well, it wasn't really me; I had to stand by what my member of staff said."

In fact, what happened was very interesting. There came a kind of secret signal from somewhere that this boy's family had got the President's secretary to send a message suggesting, not actually saying, that he ought to be brought back to the school. This was worded in such a way that it seemed like a diktat. However, when this was refused and the diktat went back, a message returned to the college that 'Oh, no, that wasn't what was meant at all, it was just an enquiry to see whether anything could be done. No, the boy mustn't go back under any circumstances.' The Principal and I looked at each other with some kind of smile on our faces, which had not been there when we started, because we didn't know then what the real story was.

Our long vacation from the second half of June to the second half of September used to be spent in the cool of the mountains, the valleys of Swat, Dir, Chitral, Hunza and, of course, across the border in Kashmir where we used to stay on the houseboats on either the Dal Lake or Lake Nagin.

It was on the Dal Lake that I saw the British Memsahib in real life; the widow of a British Army Officer. She had kept her home in Scotland and her houseboat in Kashmir and went from one to the other throughout the year. She spent the British summer in Kashmir and the Kashmir winter in Britain. While we were with her she called the owner of a houseboat on Lake Nagin to her houseboat on the Dal Lake, introducing us to him and making sure that 'the deal', as she called it, was a good deal, a good 'bandobast'. This was the word used – a kind of agreement about everything. It was a good one and we spent two or three weeks a year on that houseboat on Lake Nagin. It meant you could go from there to any part of the Kashmir valley you liked, either on foot, by pony or, if you had one, by small jeep or go by shikara on the lake itself.

Kashmir certainly is very beautiful indeed. The Moghul Emperor, Jahangir, said of it, "If there be paradise on earth this is it, this is it, this is it." Most of the celebrities of the world would appear to agree, because when I read the remarks in the Visitors' Book on the houseboat, made by presidents, famous film stars and different characters from all over the world, they all agreed that Kashmir was the most beautiful place imaginable.

I also had evidence much closer to hand. A very brilliant geography master, John Matthews, came to Aitchison College whilst I was there. He made his own teaching material by having about £3,000s' worth of cameras slung around his neck and a small, short-wheel-based Jeep, which he drove anywhere he possibly could. He used to take me along, I think for safety really, rather more than company, because I wasn't in his class as a geographer at all. He was a bachelor and had been all over Europe and many parts of the world, and I think he intended to go all over the world before he died. I remember standing with him on the top of a small knoll looking right around 360 degrees; there was the lake and around it some green, then the trees, then slightly darker brown, then blue sky and white clouds, more blue sky and white mountain tops in the distance, on all sides. I heard him say, more or less under his breath to himself, "No, there isn't any view in Switzerland or Austria as good as this – this is tremendous."

At this time I was also learning the value of two networks into which I seemed to have strayed. One was the British Council and the other was Moral Re-Armament. Wherever I went throughout the world, I found that these two groups were accepted and respected. Additionally, they seemed to have supporters in most parts of the world, so I was often given an address from one place to another or told who to speak to in such a British Council office when I got there.

These two, what you might call 'unseen cobwebs', spread around the world and were a tremendous strength. They seemed to be replacing the old missionary networks that had existed courtesy of the European empires, and I could see, too, why they were actually trusted more. The original missionary groups had people who were loyal to their particular group – whether Protestant, Catholic, Muslim Shia or Muslim Sunni – and the original diplomatic ways were always (in the past and still in the present) loyal to only their own country. However, the British Council and Moral Re-Armament seemed to be free of these shackles and able to give honest, impartial assistance and advice without pushing any of their own agenda. In fact, part of their agenda was to include everybody, whatever their religion, political background or social status, in an attempt to keep the world on an even keel.

The British Council's English language teaching programme was a particularly good example of this throughout the continents, especially Asia and Africa, but Latin America, too. The more English those people learnt the more socially mobile they became, the more economically powerful and the more politically free, so it was not possible to accuse the British Council of any sort of neo-colonialism because the person who knew the English language could use it either for or against Britain, just as the original letter to The Times by Michael Redgrave had suggested. Their activities and attitudes both suited my own feelings about what a Christian life should do in the world, that it should be lived for the better interest of everybody, wherever, and not for the specific good of any particular group from where the original Christian came.

This naturally made my life extremely easy in one way, no matter which part of the world I found myself in. It is a fact that in Pakistan the Muslims greatly respected any Christian who said quite openly that he was there because he believed in Jesus and the various truths of the Bible that they happened to know, too. They were also equally open in their attitudes. I well remember a small group of about six boys, aged between twelve and fourteen, explaining to me very deferentially how, when their Muslim Umma came into the world, they would most unwillingly have to kill me because I was an infidel. They wouldn't *want* to kill me. I was their teacher and they respected me and were grateful for how I helped them, but, nonetheless, that was what would have to happen because I wasn't a Muslim. I can still see them in their college blazers, very well creased grey trousers, shining black shoes, white shirts, house ties and rather sheepish looks on their faces as they admitted that they didn't want to carry out what their religion told them to do.

Both groups came into formal action in the second half of the 1930s and by the oddest of coincidences the very first paragraph of an early personal account of the British Council contains a reference to a member of the Oxford Group (as it was in those days before it became Moral Re-Armament), who more or less saved the bacon of one of the British Council Officers on tour in the Middle East. This officer was having difficulty crossing a frontier when someone else spoke up and said, "...but I know the local man and he's my friend." The local man was indeed in the British Council office and a member of the Oxford Group. This strange coming together of interests, of course, has to admit to almost hiding another interest.

The British Council was undoubtedly a propaganda organisation in an attempt to counter the propaganda of the Axis powers, Hitler especially, in the run up to the Second World War. The nations were re-arming and the very name 'Moral Re-Armament' meant that the group of people in it were trying to re-arm anyone they met, morally, rather than materially or militarily. Both organisations share the common view that material betterment does not lead, in the long run, to the kind of world that we need – it leads ultimately to a conflict based on greed. I am happy to say that all the time I was in the British Council and have known Moral Re-Armament, the people in both those groups have been far less greedy than others that I have come across in different and similar groups in other parts of the world.

Another advantage of the linkage between different members of these two groups was that there was an automatic assumption of confidentiality between people about what they would say to each other and there was no question of having to take time to find out who was responsible and who wasn't – one just believed it and I have two strange examples of this which convinced me.

One was in Pakistan, which was then called West Pakistan – East Pakistan was on the other side of India. In this West Pakistan, an old

Pakistani who was a faithful Muslim and quite keen to have Pakistan, nonetheless lamented the fact that the sub-continent of India had been divided with such dreadfully divisive consequences for the future as well as the past. He actually said to me, "I could go to Britain now, today," (this was 1960) "...and find four or five men and bring them back here and, through their knowledge of and friendship with some leaders of our two nations, they would be able to almost put these two nations back together again and undo it." Now this, to some of his friends would have been treason.

Equally, when I visited a friend in Calcutta on the other side of India, and we were having afternoon tea, about an hour after tea began a high ranking Indian Civil Servant rushed in and said, "I'm so sorry I'm late, please forgive me but I couldn't get away. It was my duty to sit there and listen to Galbraith telling us how much money the Americans have given India in the last three or four years – awfully boring. Look at the British; they did nothing but take the money out of India and we like them, yet the Americans tell us how much money they put in and we can't stand them!"

This type of conversation was certainly not made public in those days amongst the normal diplomatic channels and if it was no one would repeat it – this was just lingua franca between us in the Council and Moral Re-Armament across the whole sub-continent. Through our links with the students, the trade unions and the people who worked in key sections of the society, and also because we were not diplomats – we were not running around with diplomatic number plates on our cars – they really did trust us and they knew we were not going to grind an axe *against* them but maybe even grind one *for* them.

The physical advantages of a posting to Lahore, which used to be called 'the Paris of the East', were immense. I remember a flight from Lahore right across the sub-continent to Dacca in East Pakistan – I think it took about five hours and just long enough to allow me to read an entire Shakespeare play on the way and also to look out of the window to my left as we went along to see in the distance the full length and stretch of the Himalayas. These high Himalayas are impossible to imagine unless you get up there above them and look down and say to yourself, 'Goodness, they start over at Peshawar or Hindu Kush and go right across for three or four thousand miles into China and there is only one pass through and that is the Khyber Pass at this end'. An incredible experience and so absolutely beautiful. Then you touch down in Calcutta where you find an old city, which used to be the capital of the British Empire in India for a short while, and it is so different. The Bengali people are very different from all the others, highly intellectual, musical, talented, quick and slick in all their doings and they really are a wonderful people and they have a city which is organised tightly, neatly, tidily and with very small streets. They are not particularly interested in great public appearances as, say, were the Moghuls who put up magnificent buildings like the Taj Mahal in Agra and the Red Fort in Delhi.

Mention of the Red Fort in Delhi reminds me of an interesting afternoon I had with a colleague when he took me there because he felt we could go in and see Pandit Nehru receiving the Russian Leaders, Bulganin and Kruschev. I was surprised when we simply took a taxi to near the building and walked right up to the main entrance where a 6' 6" sentry stood and put up his hand, apparently to stop us. However, when we walked straight on firmly, he turned the hand that might have stopped us into a salute and we walked past him into the auditorium where there were fine red chairs laid out in an unusual way. We went in and sat down two rows behind Bulganin and Kruschev. I remember thinking that if I had a long billiard cue I could touch each of them on the back of the neck! The row between us and them was filled with, I think, security people of both India and Russia, but it was quite eye-opening to me, coming from this part of the world, at the height of the Cold War, to see these situations in which people moved. I can't remember exactly what was said but I do know that Pandit Nehru was very friendly towards them; indeed, that was one of the problems at the time, that fundamentally Krishna Menon and Pandit Nehru had a leaning towards the Left wing and the Russia of that day.

Krishna Menon was, incidentally, that Indian politician whom the boy I taught in Devon had attacked on the aeroplane with a knife, probably because he heard his parents make some derogatory remark about him. Menon was a very unexpected character and at one stage hid from Pandit Nehru, the Prime Minister of India, the fact that the Chinese had actually attacked Indian territory way up in the north.

Because of the inter-connectedness of the British Council, Moral Re-Armament and the families of the boys I was teaching in Aitchison College, that was to say more or less the leadership of the whole country, I often found myself in the midst of quite complicated discussions on religion, politics, economics and social affairs. I discovered to my relief that a great help to me in all this was my origin in Southern Ireland and also the fact that I was a Protestant. To many other people, this seemed to give me some kind of status as a moderate outsider. From the anti-colonial point of view, I was regarded with favour because the Irish had stood up to the English in the sense of the Empire. From the religious point of view I was regarded as less rabid than the Roman Catholics, who seemed to want to get everything directed from Rome. From the British establishment point of view, the fact that I was a Protestant and went every Sunday to the Cathedral, and to that extent flew the honourable flag, I was most fortunate to be quids in with most sides of the debate.

Of course, my own experience of discussions in Ireland – which had been immensely complicated between the various parties in Southern and Northern Ireland, and the different kinds of religion, from Plymouth Brethren right through to Methodist or High Church – made me quite at ease learning the different types of Islamic, Hindu, Parsee beliefs and all the shades of political belief that I came across in the sub-continent.

There were also two other factors. One was that I came from Tipperary, which would often cause people to throw up their hands and say, "It's a long way..." as if to say, you can't expect the people from Tipperary to be very sensible. The other more unexpected aspect to all this came about because my name is Lloyd Mullen. In fact, fully it is Lloyd George Mullen. Sometimes, when I was introduced to people as Lloyd Mullen of the British Council, the hearer would imagine that he had heard 'Lord' Mullen, the British

Consul. This would give rise to a discussion about how British I was – presumably I was from Northern Ireland, though I was from Southern Ireland, and how did I have a Welsh name (which I had to explain as there is an explanation)? Then the assumption was that because I was from Southern Ireland I was a Roman Catholic, and when I explained that I was a Protestant, the person would often give up in confused disbelief that such an animal should be let loose on the planet!

My first tour of three years, from 1959 to 1962, gave me a chance to settle in well because one whole year was spent acclimatising and learning the ropes, the second year was spent developing what I had already learned and getting on with the job much better, and the third year meant that I felt comfortable and was able to have the confidence to innovate various things I wanted to do. That was very satisfactory because it gave me a fair chance to understand the characteristics of the boys I was teaching.

One thing I had not realised until I thought about it was that the boys and adults in Pakistan were very independent; they had very firm, clear ideas and were not at all easy to push around by anybody. In fact, they were quite used to pushing others around and very used to standing still when people tried to push them around! The reason for this, I discovered, was that there never had been any Pakistan in the British Empire. The Pakistanis themselves had never been a subject race; they had been rulers with the Muslim Moghuls in undivided India, then they had been, as Muslims, part of the India that was undoubtedly ruled by the British. However, when the British left, they formed their own nation and were determined to do things their own way; against the wishes and efforts one might almost say, of all the world.

Pakistan is really made up of four large provinces: Punjab, Sind, Baluchistan and the North-West-Frontier, with several different tribes inside each. These four provinces were always independent of and from each other and of and from any central government that attempted to set itself up in Karachi or Islamabad later. And, of course, the people of the North-West-Frontier, the Pathans – sometimes nowadays called Pushtoons or Pukhtoons – have never in all history paid taxes to any man. In fact, they made people pay taxes to pass through… even Alexander the Great had to negotiate his way through the Pass!

It is also a fact that when the Pakistan government wanted to bring electricity into the tribal areas to some schools, clinics and hospitals, the tribesmen would not allow them to do so unless they gave the tribes-people free electricity for their own illegal arms factory at Darra! The government had to agree. And all the time I was there, weapons were being made – good copies of Lee-Enfield rifles and similar – in this tribal area at Darra. They sometimes exploded in peoples' faces, but generally they were sound weapons and used against the forces of law and order.

The rule in the tribal area was that if you killed a person on the road it was murder, but if you killed them off the road it would be dealt with by the local tribes under their individual Khans or rulers. This meant that all the men in the tribal areas carried guns with them all the time, and it was not unusual to see quite small boys being trained to shoot. They became very good shots; in fact, one of the standard pictures of the North-West-Frontier shows a Pathan tribesman high on a mountaintop sniping down at anyone passing below. If you examine the picture, you will find that his face is Greek in origin, the idea being to portray that that part of their heritage comes from the Greeks left behind by Alexander the Great. There are also some Jewish tribes who didn't go back to Israel but went up into that part of the world. And there is the original tribal family belt itself; a very powerful and individual race of people altogether… it's not surprising that they were squash champions of the world for a very long time!

An interesting aside on the relationship between the men of the North-West-Frontier and the rest of India and the British was given to me by Roger Hicks, who had stayed in the Ashram with Mahatma Gandhi some of the time that he was campaigning for the British to quit India. Roger was a friend of the British establishment and sometimes carried secret messages between the two, but he told me that one afternoon he said to Gandhi, "Bapu-ji, if we British do quit India won't those Pathans from the North-West-Frontier come down here and slit your Hindu throats?" Gandhi's reply was, "Yes, of course they will, but what business is that of yours? You British have used that excuse to stay here for the last hundred years and would like to use it to stay here for the next hundred!"

This is very relevant because another of his remarks that Roger told me concerned the time when Gandhi returned from near Calcutta to Delhi at the height of the hand-over of power in 1947. He discovered that the other Indian politicians had agreed with Mountbatten and Jinnah to divide the sub-continent into two separate nations. Now Gandhi had fought against this and had warned the rest of the Indian politicians never to do it; to both Muslim and Hindu he said, "Don't do it!" However, Roger told me that when Gandhi discovered they *had* done it, he almost lost his temper. Indeed, Roger said it was funny at one stage to see the little man jumping up and down with rage! Gandhi had said, "Look, we Muslims and Hindus killed each other before the British ever came to India; we went on killing each other all the time the British were in India and we should certainly have continued to kill each other after the British left India, but one day it would have ended and it would have ended in one country. Now see what you've done – you've set it up in two nations, with national armies, national flags, national anthems, national pride, national aims, national everything! You've dished it!"

There is a wider dimension here, which is really very sad. Roger, Gandhi, a missionary called Charlie Andrews (a famous bishop of the time), and the leader of the Pathans, Badshah Khan (also a believer in non-violence), were all great friends. In fact, Badshah Khan was called the Frontier Gandhi and one of the first Pathans to make sure that women in the family got educated. However, what none of them seemed to have noticed was that at that time other forces in the world were emerging. One was the future of oil; oil was going to play a big part in the whole world. Another was the growth of the other Muslim nations, especially in the Middle East. So that when the independence of India was being considered and then, at a second level, the possible division of India's independence into a Muslim nation – Pakistan, and a Hindu nation – India, the wider dimension was missed. The result was that the division *did* take place and took place with dreadful brutality.

Now it ought not to have, for one of the governors of the North-West-Frontier Province had been Olaf Caroe, a very thoughtful man whose book on the Pathans is still standard. He, as a young Indian Civil Service Officer, had been posted to Aden in the Gulf and while there he noticed that oil was going to be the future. In fact, he coined the saying 'Oil is the name of the game'. So the great players who knew Olaf Caroe and were in touch with him, couldn't plead that they were ignorant of these other forces in the world. It is a shame that the focus was on the difference between Hindu and Muslim which, of course, the outsider, the British, had been able to make use of to stay as long as they could (and did) in the sub-continent.

There had been warnings of the dreadful things that might happen if the sub-continent was indeed divided. Wavell, when he was Viceroy, had told Attlee, the British Prime Minister of the day, that if he had five years or more he might be able to divide the continent peacefully by dividing the Army, Civil Service, postal communications, railways, the whole structure and infra-structure, but he added that, "...otherwise there will be such slaughter in the Punjab and Bengal that history may never forgive us."

Wavell was probably right. The slaughter resulting from Partition haunts us to this day. A colleague in Aitchison College had been on Wavell's staff at the time. Bizarrely, he had the task of proof-reading Wavell's most peaceable anthology, 'Other Men's Flowers', which has calmed angry souls ever since.

It seems almost grotesque now, all these years later, to be talking of the friendship between the Gandhi family in India and the Pathan family on the Frontier; Wavell's book of flowers, the great anthology; oil in the Gulf and Olaf Caroe's remark about it being the name of the game. I can only say that having had the privilege of knowing members of both families and knowing Roger and being close to the man who proof-read Wavell's collection of poetry, I am able to understand how the great tides of history can simply flow round and over the best-intentioned men.

One of the most pleasant afternoons I spent in my first year in Pakistan was in the garden of the home of Badshah Khan's eldest son, Ghani, at a place called Charsadda, near Peshawar. Ghani was married to a beautiful Parsee lady and between them they had raised, of all things, the most wonderful English rose garden in that part of the world. You could have lifted the whole thing and put it down in, shall we say, Dorset or Yorkshire and it would have seemed absolutely right; and this was a man who had gone into the Club in Peshawar and, with his sword, slashed through the portrait of the new ruler of Pakistan, Ayub Khan, because he felt that when the British gave independence to the sub-continent they should not only have divided it but should also have given a new state, called Pakhtoonistan, to the Pathans in between Afghanistan to the north and Pakistan to the south.

The military dictator, Ayub Khan, understandably kept Ghani under house arrest in a very beautiful hill station, far away from places where he could give trouble. That was reasonable because it was always likely that he would raise some kind of rebellion against the central government.

Ayub Khan was in fact a very straightforward and honourable man in many ways and not at all suited to be a military dictator, as is shown by the following episode.

A friend of mine, an old soldier who had come back to Pakistan, had trained Ayub Khan as a young soldier in the British Army and always called him Ayuba. I was with them one day – not in the room but in Murree in the mountains – when Ayub invited the old man to morning coffee, which they had together. The old soldier told us afterwards a tale which was quite interesting. He said to Ayub, "You know, Ayuba, I am very disappointed in you as a soldier." He said, the President blushed and replied, "Sir, why, what have I done?" and he said, "Ayuba, when I was in London, in my house in Wimbledon, and you and the Indians were fighting, I knew exactly what the Indians had between Delhi and you. You could have taken Delhi and then have been in a position to say you'd give them back Delhi if they'd give you Kashmir." Ayuba said, "Oh but Sir, that wouldn't have been fair – they were fighting the Chinese on the other front."

And I said to Ayuba, "Fair! You've been talking about wanting Kashmir and nothing else for a long, long time and yet when you could have taken it you didn't because it wouldn't have been fair – oh, I don't think you're a soldier really!"

This brings up the key point that for both the two organisations I have mentioned – the British Council and Moral Re-Armament – there is the problem that military establishments do not really like them because they tend to go for what is fair, not what is going to help one particular side to win a war. I have known British, Pakistani and Indian soldiers held in check from having much to do with Moral Re-Armament because of that. However, there's another interesting angle on the Kashmir situation.

I was present when two Indians – who knew all about it and had a lot to say and had some influence on the future of it – were talking about Kashmir. Because I had just crossed the border and come from Pakistan, they wanted to hear how Pakistan was getting on and they talked to me about it. Then they discussed what is always called 'the Kashmir issue' in my presence. One said to the other, "Yaar man! Kashmir is theirs – we should give it to Pakistan." The other Indian said, "Yes, you're right… we should but we can't." When questioned, he said, "Well, if we give Kashmir to Pakistan, we will have to rely on the Pakistanis to defend us against both Russia and China." I saw the other stop in his tracks and blanch a little and say, "You're right, of course, we can't." And thus you see a good-hearted gesture, which might have saved the world much pain and agony, stopped by realpolitik.

7
REALPOLITIK

That realpolitik of Communist pressure from Russia and China, Capitalist pressure from the United States and the West generally, Islamic pressure from the people of the country inside Pakistan, and the other Muslim nations, especially Saudi Arabia, and the civil liberal-minded pressure from some of the people in some of the cities of Pakistan, formed the clash in which we all lived in Pakistan in those days and, indeed, in which Pakistanis have lived since the country was founded. Running through all this in varying degrees amongst the different groups was a fear and hatred of Hindus because there was a belief that India's ultimate aim was to re-take Pakistan as part of its own country again.

Indeed, one might say that a prime reason for the foundation of Pakistan was that the people who founded it simply did not want to substitute a Hindu Raj for a British Raj because, through the sheer numbers of the population, the Hindus would have dominated the entire sub-continent after the British left. And yet, amongst the elite of both countries there was a very powerful linkage. Two simple stories illustrate this.

One was in Aitchison College when I saw the Major in charge of the college's Officer Training Corps (O.T.C.), sitting in our staff room reading a newspaper with tears trickling from his eyes. When I asked if he was all right, he looked up and said, "Yes, I'm just reading the names of my former colleagues here who have been killed in the Indian Army fighting against the Chinese." That gave me something to think about.

The other was the fact that in the war between India and Pakistan, an Indian Air Force pilot was shot down over Lahore. He was the son of General Carriappa, the soldier in charge of the Indian Army. He bailed out and landed with his parachute, but broke his ankle. It is a fact that Field Marshal Ayub Khan (President of Pakistan) actually contacted Carriappa, his old colleague; he told him not to worry, his son would be looked after well, they would do what they could for his ankle and that when the conflict was over he would be returned safely. Of course such things did not percolate out to the whole country for the simple reason that there would have been accusations of treachery, treason and so on but, nevertheless, they do demonstrate the inter-twinedness of these two nations.

Daily life went on in the midst of all this and we foreigners were quite well looked after. I can remember once having a bodyguard who produced a beautiful piece of English which I still cherish. When I asked him whether the ordinary police in their uniforms, who he could easily recognise, would know he was a plain clothes policeman looking after me, he said, "Ah, no Sir. They don't know who are we... but we know we are who."

Of course, the expatriates amongst whom we moved also produced their own moments of hilarity. I well remember a British Council Officer – who loved to travel by train and had an ambition to go up the railway, right up the Khyber Pass to Afghanistan – arriving in Lahore, which had in its very famous station a set of cubicles where you could go in and have a wash, shave and dress and so on before getting on your train to the next place, which he did.

While he was under the shower, with his clothes hanging on a hook near the top of the partition between his and the next cubicle, he noticed a hand coming over and fingers trying to get down into the pocket of his trousers in which his wallet was sitting. Instead of quietly stepping out of the shower and grabbing the hand, he shouted, and of course the frightened hand gripped everything and disappeared over the partition wall, along with trousers, shirt, the lot! There was this British Council Officer, left under the shower, his clothes gone; so what does he do? He gets his towel, wraps it around himself, leaps out of the cubicle and runs after this other fellow, shouting "Chor! Chor!" ("Thief! Thief!"). However, the fellow had run out into the beautiful, large concourse in front of Lahore railway station and disappeared into the crowd.

So now we have an Englishman, dripping with water, a towel wrapped round his middle, standing bare-foot in the street! What does he do next? He calls a tonga-wallah, gets into the tonga and says, "Take me to the British High Commission," which the tonga-wallah, well used to the odd behaviour of foreigners, does.

About twenty-five minutes later, he arrived at the British High Commission and went to the nearest house, which happened to be the private residence of the First Secretary, and knocked on the door. It was about eleven o'clock in the morning and the door was opened by the First Secretary's wife. She saw this Englishman standing there, still dripping wet, with his towel around him, asking her for money to pay the tonga-wallah!

That same English woman took part in another economic discussion about the same time, but of a much more serious nature. The British High Commissioner called a private, indoor meeting of the British people in Lahore, which took place in this First Secretary's house. His wife was the hostess. We were only about forty people in number. The High Commissioner explained that he had asked us to come together privately to give us some news. To make it quite clear, he stood on a chair in the middle of the drawing room while we all sat or stood around listening to what he had to say, which was that Her Majesty's Government had asked him to be part of a worldwide answer to a problem that Britain was facing with imports from Hong Kong, India and Pakistan of cotton goods. These imports had increased to such an extent and some of the items were so good that they were proving a threat to the British cotton industry in the north, especially in Lancashire. The Conservative-led owners of the mills had for some time been putting pressure on Her Majesty's Government to curtail these imports. The Government had stood up to their demands but now, on the Labour side of the house, the workers who were losing their jobs in these mills, some of which had closed down, simply had to ask the Government to do the same.

Now that pressure was coming on the Government from both sides of the political spectrum, it had decided to place a quota on the numbers of cotton imports from these nations. From Pakistan, the example he gave was that a British housewife in those days could buy three Pakistani-made boy's shirts for twelve shillings whereas she could only buy one British-made shirt for twelve shillings. As the High Commissioner said, "She is not a fool, so naturally she buys the Pakistani ones; therefore the Government is going to have to put a quota on this."

I stood there saying to myself that I had been in Pakistan for some time trying to help a new nation (with which Britain had close contact) to get off the ground, economically, politically and socially. Having helped a little on the economic side, we were now being asked to rein back and put a clamp on their expanding.

One of my former pupils had gone to UMIST (University of Manchester Institute of Science and Technology) and learned how to produce better textiles; he had come back and expanded his factory using these methods to make these better shirts which were going into Britain… which were now about to be curtailed in import!

At this point I thought to myself: the British Government has been paying the better part of my maintenance out here and they have asked me to help develop the country. Now I am being told, almost secretly, to accept that we have to put a limit to the country's development, and this meeting which the High Commissioner has called is to give us some idea of how to put this matter to our Pakistani friends.

My mind went back to, I think possibly the cleverest man I ever met, the son of a Durham miner who had won a scholarship, first to Durham University and then to Oxford. He had seriously considered taking up international Communism as the ideology of his life, but when he was told that he should treat everybody equally, he asked himself the question: 'Why should I? Some people are lazy and downright crooks; others are very good people who would help anyone in distress. Why should I treat them all the same?' He couldn't find any reason, except that at that particular time he had just met some people who told him that they believed all men and women, wherever and whatever their circumstances, were children of God. While he didn't actually believe in God, he did see that if one imagined every boy and girl born was a child of this one God, then of course there was a good reason for treating them all the same; indeed, they all became members of one family, and this he accepted as a guide for his life.

I recall him saying to me, "When I was thinking about Communism and the fact that everyone should be treated equally, I agreed with that and could understand it very well. However, when they said there was no God and therefore I couldn't think of human beings as 'children of the one God', I realised that, at the very base – the plinth of Communism on which it all stood and which seemed to me to be a fair deal for everybody – there actually was a crack in the middle of that plinth and it was bound to collapse."

This event in the First Secretary's house in the compound of the British High Commission in Lahore really helped me greatly because it meant I was able to get on with my work of teaching these particular boys in this school without worrying about any other philosophic fundamentals of why I was doing it – they were just boys and I was there to help them.

To give an example, I can remember when I had to teach them 'Hamlet'. Now one of the problems of teaching Hamlet to even senior boys is the question of whether or not Hamlet is sane or mad. I had an inspiration one morning and before beginning to teach them I said, "Please clear your desks. Put away all your books and don't think about anything for a moment and then we'll begin." They looked at me a bit oddly and thought, 'What's happening here; has this chap lost his senses or is he going to do a magic trick – what's going to happen?'

Now remember, these were Muslim boys whose marriages in the main had been arranged already, even while they were there (they were aged between about eighteen to twenty). One or two of them might have been married already for all I knew, back in the village. However, there they were, looking just like boys anywhere in a public school across the world. I said to them, "I want you to imagine, you boarders, that you go home at the end of this term, and you day boys (there were a few), that you go home at lunch time, and when you get into the house you discover that your uncle has killed your father and married your mother." The shock was so much that one boy almost vomited; he leant forward and put his hands up to his mouth. "Then," I said, "while you are in this state of uncertainty, you dream or you imagine that your father's ghost appears to tell you to bring revenge on your uncle and kill him." This was no problem for them at all as this is what they would have done in normal life. "However," I said, "while you are thinking about this, you look out of the window and see, by accident, the girl with whom your marriage has been arranged, walking across the courtyard. You think to yourself, 'Oh, my God, how can I think of anything at this time – murder, revenge, marriage'."

From that moment on I can honestly say we had no problem at all in thinking about whether Hamlet was or was not mad. He was certainly confused and everyone understood why, but whether he was mad or sane was left to everyone's discretion and use of the word.

Of course, stories like the one of the British Council Officer who ended up asking for money to pay the tonga-wallah, were recounted all over the world in the various Council Offices. I think one of the better ones I heard concerned our British Council office in Egypt where a very brilliant British Council Officer – a scholar and expert on all his subjects, though not a very practical man – invited his father, who was in his eighties, to come and spend some time with him in Egypt. The old man came, but his son hadn't been very sensible and had asked him to come at the hottest time of the year. It therefore wasn't a surprise to anybody that the old boy died while he was staying in his son's house! His son was at his office at the time, so the head bearer or steward telephoned him to say his father had died and he must come home and deal with the matter. The son is reported to have said that he hadn't finished The Times crossword yet and that he would come home, but would the steward immediately get in touch with the people who took away bodies to mortuaries and morgues because of the heat and that he would deal with the matter then.

He came home at lunch time and discovered that they were coming to take away his father's body at about half-past-two in the afternoon. This was the middle of his normal siesta time, so he gave strict instructions to the steward that when the people came they were not to wake him up. The steward said he would see to that. However, unfortunately, they did wake him up when he found himself being carried down the stairs by the people from the morgue – they thought a corpse had come to life and screamed, dropped him and ran away!

Of course, the story may be apocryphal, but it certainly went the rounds of all our offices when I was in Lahore.

Another odd story, not apocryphal, concerned a member of our staff who came to London on a scholarship. While he was there he wanted to buy some things to take back to the lady to whom he was engaged – they were going to be married in good Muslim fashion when he arrived home. He had never seen the lady, but he had received instructions through his family from her family to bring back some nice Fair Isle sweaters, so he went to Selfridges and asked to see some. He wanted to buy half a dozen, but when he was asked what size he wanted, he said, "They are for my fiancée, but I don't know what size she is – I've never seen her." Now you can imagine the assistant in Selfridges, in the 1960s, moving discreetly down the counter to the head of her department and bringing her back to deal with this strange foreign gentleman who had never seen the lady he was about to marry! Anyway, he bought the stuff and took it back, and it appears to have done its job – I've no idea how, but it seems it was a happy ending!

Pakistan was certainly a wonderful place for an expatriate to be posted in those days because we were able to go anywhere without the slightest bother. I remember with great affection the Kissekhani Bazaar in Peshawar – this was where most of the stuff came down through the Khyber Pass from central Asia, or went up through India and Pakistan into central Asia. Fancy goods of every kind from every nation under Heaven were to be found. Also the characters who owned shops there, and whose families had owned them for generations, were really a delight in themselves – a whole different world. Of course, this has now vanished from the face of the earth, but I am happy to tell you that I still have a few artefacts in my house which I bought there in 1960/1961 from 'Poor old honest Joe', as one was called, and all sorts of other people in that famous Kissekhani Bazaar.

Talking of buying things, I actually bought the material for my wedding suit in Landi Khotal, right up in the Khyber Pass on the border of Afghanistan. I think the material came from China – I'm still not sure to this day – but it was very good material and excellently looked after by the tailor who made my suit. That was something I never expected in all my life to do – to buy my wedding suit material on the borders of Afghanistan!

Of course, it wasn't all plain sailing. One of the outings on which I took a party of boys was from Lahore up into the tribal area to Parachinar. Parachinar means 'four Chinar trees'. One of the boys in my house invited a party of us to his place. We accepted the invitation and took the college bus there. When we arrived at the village, all the boys were put up in the owner's compound.

On the first evening I was asked whether I would like to go with the men of the family to a meeting with another family from across the border in Afghanistan. I went along – three men on one side meeting three men on another side – and we climbed up some steps into a kind of room, under which there were animals at ground level and a sort of thatch over us. There we sat, cross-legged on the floor while the discussions went on, which was in a language that I couldn't understand (a variety of Pashtu). All this time one of our party kept his large revolver in front of him on a big red handkerchief with white spots, and he kept taking the rounds of ammunition out of the revolver, cleaning and shining them and putting them back in.

When I was able to discover what exactly was going on, it turned out that the people across the border had kidnapped a boy from this particular group's tribe. The people on the Pakistan side were stopping those on the Afghanistan side from smuggling a special type of wood out of Afghanistan into Pakistan where they got a much better price for it, and the deal was to be, if it could be, that they would give back the boy if we would allow them to smuggle their goods through our property into Pakistan. I am not quite sure how the discussion ended, but when much later I learned that the hills just over the border where we were, were called Tora Bora and became famous when Bin Laden hid among them in the next century, I wonder what did happen! However, I can say that on the way back to Lahore with my party of boys, I spotted a lovely place to have a picnic. There was a beautiful view looking down over the river, so we stopped just off the road and got our picnic ready while the bearer went down to the river with two big jugs to get some water.

I was sitting idly on a mound of earth just a little behind our bus, while the boys wandered about chatting and taking photographs. Suddenly two shots rang out and I saw the sand go up in two little jets behind my bearer! I didn't know from which side the bullets had come, but they certainly told us to get out of there immediately, which we did.

About a quarter of a mile down the road we met, coming up the other way, the District Commissioner's jeep, headed by one jeep in front and one behind with men sitting on either side with guns at the ready. It was then that we realised that we had quite unwittingly stopped our bus in the centre of an ambush which had been set for the District Commissioner, rather spoiling the local tribesmen's chances. I don't know to this day what their idea was but I'm glad that all of us got out of it alive!

The human cost of the division of the sub-continent into Pakistan and India was shown to me very dramatically one day when the Vice-Principal of Aitchison College telephoned to ask me whether I could use my car to drive him and some of his family immediately to the border with India, at Wagha. I said of course I would – it was about fourteen miles from Lahore to the border. He already had two other cars and as we were getting ready, he explained that he had received a phone call telling him that his own sister (he used the expression 'full sister' – same father, same mother) would be on the other side of the border in a few hours' with her family – they had gone back to their home place in Kashmir and now they were coming down to the border at Wagha. If he could get there by a certain time, they could meet for the first time since the Partition some seventeen years earlier.

So off we set and when we arrived all the family got out of the cars and walked in a small group towards the border where there were soldiers from both the Pakistan and Indian armies on duty on either side. They spoke to the officer in charge on this side, who spoke to the officer in charge on the other side. I stood back and kept well away from it. There was a great deal of discussion about what might happen and at first it seemed that they weren't going to be allowed to meet. However, after the officer on the Pakistan side was convinced that nobody was going to try and chase each other across the border and that this was a genuine family meeting, he spoke again to the Indian officer who, to his great credit, agreed.

It was a pathetic sight to see this huddle of about twenty people from either side of the border being herded behind a small sentry box to talk to each other, hopefully out of sight of other people, and embrace each other and cry and laugh. It was something I shall never forget... seeing brother and sister, children, cousins, boys and girls, kith and kin – talking with each other and then being separated again, very gently. You could see that these senior officers of the army on both sides were worried about their own skins for allowing this to happen, but they went in very gently and parted them. It was very, very sad. However, I was glad to be able to play a small part in that little reunion of a family that I knew so well because the Vice-Principal had been the greatest help to me – he was always called 'Hockey Wallah' because he was so good at the game.

One aspect of life in Pakistan at that time worried me considerably and that was the attitude of the American administration to the country. It was a simple fact that whilst all the Americans one met were very pleasant, generous and good spirited people, the actual policy of the United States administration towards the country was unremittingly U.S. interested. This is understandable, but when you have a nation the size and power of America as it was in the 1960s, and a weak nation as Pakistan then was – hardly a nation at all, more a collection of states or provinces put together under the name of a country – then the difference was very great. The way in which the American policy pushed Pakistan's genuine policies out of the way, quite mercilessly, led slowly to an anti-American attitude which placed the rest of us expatriates in a difficult and delicate position. Our interest was to help the people of Pakistan, but it was not possible to do this without keeping the Americans on side since they had the policy-making money.

This was a great difficulty for everybody, including I think the Americans themselves because all the American expatriates I met were never able to understand why it was that the local people didn't like them, especially when they were doing so much for them. Indeed, one of the sad things was that the Americans had a great longing to be liked whereas the British didn't – they did just what they felt was right and that was the end of the matter. However, the Americans wanted to be liked and it was impossible. Their policies were such that the nations on the receiving end, and Pakistan was very much on the receiving end, as it still is, couldn't possibly like them.

The matter was further complicated by the presence of very genuine American missionaries, Christians, who were not part of this industrial/military complex but were doing all they could to educate the Pakistanis, to give them better hospitals and to genuinely be a part of their betterment and welfare. However, the uncle of my wife-to-be who was across the border – a senior policeman in India – on more than one occasion had to arrest so-called American missionaries high up in the Himalayas. They were ostensibly missionaries but really, as he discovered painfully because he was a Christian, they were in fact spying for America against what the Chinese and Russians were doing on the other side of the mountains in the cold war of those years.

For the average citizen at home here in Britain or in Pakistan, in India or even in Afghanistan, these matters were so confusing as to be hardly worth thinking about since one more or less said we can't do anything about it anyway, we've got to let this happen and hope that it works out well in the end. Of course, hoping that things work out well in the end never works, and it hasn't worked yet, as we see today.

However, all these political considerations were no reason for not enjoying the tremendous hospitality of the Pakistan families whom we met. They were so generous in their time, their parties, and their help in everything they did to look after (and they did look after) the safety of us expatriates wherever we went in the country. I could recount many instances of times we were saved from all sorts of dangers, like floods and mountain falls, where the local people were so kind in coming to help us and get us out of jams we got ourselves into through not knowing the terrain or not knowing where we were going or how long it would take us to get there – they were wonderful, very generous and pleasant people.

With friends at Taj Mahal – 1960

8
Memories Recalled

In those years in the scented evening air of the Punjab or the high mighty mountains, the quietness between them and the Himalayas, I thought occasionally of experiences that I had had before ever leaving Britain. Three in particular used to come to mind and possibly, in some way, shaped my thinking.

The first experience was a sad one. My best friend in school had been a boy from Cork. We'd played in many games together; I'd been invited to his home; we went fishing in his boat off the coast of Southern Ireland and caught pollock and mackerel, and when we left school I went off to teach and he went to agricultural college. He was a keen farmer but, alas, in his very first term he caught viral pneumonia and died. It was such a shock for everybody. Both our mothers were widows and the whole thing left me unsure for a moment what to think about life.

The second experience was the several weeks that I had spent in my summer holidays as an office boy in a stockbroker's business in Dublin. The owner of the business had given me this opportunity to see whether I might like to take up that life later on. It was a very kind offer from a friend. He gave me a lot of experience in the business and trusted me with things that perhaps he shouldn't have trusted such an inexperienced person with – but fortunately they came out all right! I learned, though, that no matter how much money I might ever make or no matter how much interest I might ever take in the economics of this world, and of Ireland in particular at that time, that kind of life was never going to be for me. I couldn't see myself going day by day to a desk and operating in that way; it just didn't seem a serious option.

The third experience was the many, many weeks that I spent tutoring the son of our most well-to-do Irish horse owner. We lived in style: a butler and two footmen always in the dining room; a different silver trophy on the table at lunch time and, if approved, kept there for dinner; two packs of hounds in the kennels; twenty-two hunters in the stables throughout the season; a head chauffeur who drove only the Bentley, and there was a private petrol pump in the yard. The woods on the estate were laid out in the formation of Wellington's regiments at Waterloo. The avenue was a mile long from house to gate, and its edges were clipped clean the whole way. No ivy was permitted on any tree in the entire estate. The house had three hundred and sixty five windows. There was absolute punctuality for every meal. The whole set-up was very well organised in the 1950s and I discovered that the cost of maintaining that style of life and house at that time was £6,000 per month. So, no surprise that every evening dinner comprised a full seven courses with the correct wines served with each course!

The boy I had to tutor was a very pleasant eleven-year-old who wasn't doing well at school – not, I think, because he was unintelligent, more because he was rather repressed by the unhappy family relationships. I remember one instance at the table when he mentioned another lady, quite accidentally and incidentally. His mother slapped the table with her hand and said, "Never mention that woman's name in this house!" The cutlery bounced up and down on the table, solid though it was, and the boy said meekly, "Sorry, Mummy." His father, at the other end of the table, didn't even raise his head; he just carried on looking at his plate. And there I was, sitting in the midst of it! Nobody bothered with me – why should they and why should I bother with their family matters, but it did have an effect on the boy I was tutoring.

Fortunately, he did ultimately pass his examination and got into Eton. His father had told me that they'd always automatically gone to Eton and now the present 'new head' as he called him, wouldn't take his boy unless he first passed the exam. He even went on to say, "I think he's a Red... he won't take my boy."

I used to wander about the estate in the afternoons when I had nothing else to do, and came across a delightful experience which I can hardly believe to this day, but it was so obviously performed that I have no doubt that I am telling it accurately.

I was walking through a very large, open, low-lying field with reeds; it was beginning to go to swamp and I discovered that on one side there was a very damp patch of about two or three acres – the field itself was probably about ten or twelve acres. As I circled my way around the swampy patch back towards the house, I must have disturbed a duck which fluttered away flapping its wings tremendously. It flew off way in front of me, veering to the right and landed on the other side of the field. Then I noticed – and am so glad I did – that from the very point where that duck had taken off, six little ducklings were beginning to wobble and wander their way out of where obviously their mother had been caring for them. They looked very frightened, but then they cleverly formed into a single file and turned away in a big curve to my left, slowly of course, and disappeared underneath some reeds. The mother duck was some considerable distance away to the right and these little ducklings huddled somewhere behind reeds over to my left. I stood still and waited, and then saw the mother duck very cautiously continue her journey right around the field way down behind me. Slowly she came up, occasionally going to earth then rising again, and kept going until she came to where she was re-united with her brood. It was a wonderful sight to see, and even as I recount it now I feel something happy about the universe in the way things happen.

Also interesting were the visitors to the house. Naturally, when the owner was so wealthy and had such a position in the racing and hunting world in Ireland, all sorts of people came – they had their various tasks or were just guests. I recall an amusing incident with the fellow who more or less looked after the business interests of this vast estate from his office in Dublin. He used to come down every Friday and go about the different farms on the estate, ending up at the Home Farm, which was nearest the house. He would then come and have dinner with us in the evening. He was sensible enough to arrive early because I think he rather liked his master's whiskey!

After dinner we would retire to the drawing room and talk about all kinds of amusing topics. It was a general agreement that one didn't talk business – one just had fun in the evening after dinner. One evening this very tall man was stretched out leaning against the back of a sofa. (I ought to mention that all the anti-macassar coverings of the various sofas and chairs in many parts of the house showed hunting or racing scenes.) The butler, Albert, appeared in the doorway, making his presence known by giving a discreet cough. His master looked up and said, "Yes, Albert, what is it?" and Albert said in that wonderful voice of any well-trained butler, "Excuse me, Sir, but the Arend-Roland Comet is outside… I thought I should tell you, Sir." The visitor leant back in the sofa and put his hand right back over his head towards Albert and said, "Oh, Albert, can't you bring it in here!"

Another guest had been A.D.C. to Mountbatten in Delhi at the time of the hand-over of power in 1947, but he had earlier served in the British Army in Egypt. He was also a good polo player. When Anthony Eden and Nasser had trouble over the Suez Canal and the Egyptian leader blocked the canal, I remember our host saying to this guest, "Archie, that's your fault – you knocked Nasser off his pony playing polo and while he was on the ground, called him "…all sorts of a *wog." Now look what he's done, closed the canal – you're responsible for the whole thing!" (* Author's aside – a term definitely not to be uttered today.)

A most delightful visitor to the house at that time was the English wife of one of our Irish backwoodsman peers. She told of how, when her family came back from India (where she and her three sisters had been girls in their teens) and settled in their house in the south of England, they brought with them a mongoose which had somehow or other managed to stay alive and, as she put it, was of great use in their rambling mansion because it got rid of the rats, being able to go down into the places where the rats lived.

She told how this mongoose became such a family pet that when their butler laid out the table for lunch or dinner, they put an extra plate beside her mother's chair on the floor so that the mongoose would come out of its hole in the wall, find its way around the legs of the chairs in the dining room and pick up its food from the plate on the floor and go off to devour it.

She was the eldest of the four girls and the great day came when, from the family's point of view, she was bringing her first boyfriend home for dinner. Naturally, they were all going to be on their best behaviour, so, after a family discussion, they decided it would probably be better not to put down the plate for the mongoose. Everything was laid out as usual, and the butler served the first course – let's say it was a cutlet each. There was no cutlet and no plate on the floor because the butler had been primed… but the mongoose hadn't been primed! It came out, sniffed around and couldn't find its plate, so jumped up onto the table and took the young man's cutlet before disappearing without him noticing. However, all four girls had noticed and were hardly able to contain themselves. The butler, not to be defeated by the mongoose, simply came around again to the visiting young man who looked up in surprise because he knew he had been served already. On looking down at his plate, he saw it was empty, so without saying anything he just took another cutlet and put it on his plate. Now at this, the entire table, the girls especially, erupted with laughter – they could not contain themselves. The place absolutely collapsed and, as this delightful lady put it, "After that, John more or less had to marry me."

Strangely, the graciousness with which she told her story I found almost replicated by our British Council representative in Peshawar at that time. He was an Englishman, a viscount by birth, who had played rugby for England and had resigned his post as a public school master in order to go on a rugby tour with the team. He told me a story which reflects the way World War II and the Cold War affected people's lives.

In Peshawar, near the Frontier where he was the representative, there was a very fine hotel called Deans Hotel, which had been there throughout the Raj. It was a very good, small hotel run by Pakistanis, but almost always had a foreign manager or manageress. The manageress this time was a German lady. The British Council representative told me how he was having a party and went to the hotel because he wanted to invite her. His words to me were, "When I invited her she said she was so sorry she couldn't come – she would love to but couldn't possibly get off duty that particular day and would I excuse her." He added, "There was something so gracious in the way she said this that I thought this girl has some background more than appears here." So he made enquiries, got to know her a little and discovered, not surprisingly, that she was one of the Junkers' family – the Prussians who made so much of the material for the German army and air force. After the war, she met an American soldier who eventually married her and took her to Spain, where they lived for a while. He was posted with his unit to Pakistan, but suddenly went back to America, leaving her behind – he just left her behind in Pakistan! Eventually she managed to get the job as manageress of this hotel on the Frontier.

My friend could hardly believe it. It was just the simple way that she excused herself from attending the party that made him realise there was something more to this girl than first appeared. He was instrumental in getting a number of influential people together and they provided her with some money and sent her off to America – not to join the man who had abandoned her, but at least to a life that was better than the one she would ever have been able to have in Peshawar.

Back at the house where I was tutoring the boy for Eton, there was an interruption to dinner one evening when the butler whispered something in his master's ear. The master sat up and said, "Oh my goodness, I had forgotten. Please ask him to stay in the drawing room and give him a drink." When Albert had gone out to attend to this unknown guest, we were told that he was a very well-known local Irish farmer over whose land the Hunt (of which our host was the Master of Foxhounds) would ride each season. They had to come to a good agreement with him about how, when and where to hunt and what to do if the hunt did any damage to the land. This is a common arrangement in Ireland and everybody does it and joins in.

The conversation in the dining room continued with one of the guests saying, "Because he's a Roman Catholic and you're a Protestant, you had better get over that difficulty by telling him some good story in favour of Roman Catholics!" So it was agreed that mein host would tell the guest how Roman Catholic priests in the South of France had developed a wonderful drink called Green Chartreuse.

We then went into the drawing room and saw this enormous man, about 6' 4" tall and twenty stones, standing looking a little lost but obviously a friend of our host, whom he called 'Your Honour'. 'Your Honour' then began to tell him this story of the priests and the drink, how first of all the taste was developed and then (he didn't use the word 'bouquet') the smell, then the colour and how it took centuries to develop but turned out to be a wonderful drink. It is fair to say that the farmer looked a little bewildered as to why all this was going on, but he accepted the offer of trying the drink. So off goes Albert and returns with a tray of liqueur glasses. I still remember the farmer looking at these tiny things; he could barely get his large hand around the glass, but finally succeeded and we all held up our glasses and he said, "Your health, your Honour," and swallowed the whole lot in one go. Everyone else hesitated and for a few seconds nothing happened; then this obviously hit our guest's stomach and his face started to redden from his neck up. When the redness reached his forehead he said, "God, your Honour, it was surely Roman Catholics made that drink... but a bloody Protestant made that glass!"

Alcohol was, of course, off limits in those days in Pakistan, even though it was fairly well known that what came out of certain teapots into certain teacups in different parts of the country was not actually well-brewed tea!

Perhaps, with so many guns around and many differences between so many groups of religionists and tribal men, it was a good thing alcohol was off bounds.

The law which applied in the Frontier area, as opposed to the rest of Pakistan, was once explained to me very dramatically by my Principal at Aitchison College – the one whose father had been the leader of the great Pathans and he was a great Pathan himself. He enjoyed telling me how his landlady, when he was up at Oxford, used to say to him sometimes when news came through of what the Pathans were doing, "Oh Ali, I hope you're nowhere near those dreadful Pythons." He was able to assure her that he was not near those 'dreadful Pythons' without telling her that he was actually one of the leading ones himself.

As a dramatic explanation of the law, he told me of a fellow Irishman, called Nicholson, who had become a legend amongst the tribesmen of the Frontier for the way in which he brought order to the entire countryside for miles around, including riding into a village where the headman had refused to obey him, so he decapitated the man on the spot with his sword. We don't actually do that nowadays in Ireland but it did bring order to a place even wilder than my own Irish country.

The way the story goes is that there was one of the usual quarrels between an uncle and a nephew over the entitlement to land ownership when the nephew's father died. This was a very common problem. The Jirga, that is the local Council of Elders, met and tried to sort it out but couldn't – the contestants would not agree. Then they held a proper full-scale meeting of all the Khans of the village, senior Khans sitting in the centre, but that still didn't work. So they brought in the junior Khans who sat around the edges, and we now had about twenty people trying to sort out this problem while the witnesses came in front of them and gave their evidence. Still they could come to no agreement, so the senior Khans decided to ask the local District Commissioner – this man called Nicholson – to come and help them in their judgments. It was their place and their law, but the British law would be accepted if it was imposed.

Nicholson duly arrived and they sat him down at a very small, low table with all the senior Khans either side of him and the junior Khans extending out to about twenty men away. The various complainants, contestants and accused sat in the middle. The entire village had assembled.

As the case proceeded there was an old man with very red henna'd hair sitting in the front row who kept interrupting. They asked him to stop and he would for a while, but would then start again. No one seemed to be able to stop him from talking. Finally, they asked Nicholson if he would ask this dear old man to stop interrupting and let them get on with the case. Nicholson, sitting at the table, lifted his revolver – a very large one in those days remember – opened it and took out some rounds and showed them to the man. He said, "Old man, what is this?" The old man said, "A revolver, Sir." Nicholson then said, "What am I doing now?" He put in the rounds, closed it and put it down on the table. "You have loaded the revolver, Sir," to which Nicholson said, "Right! If you speak again I will pick up this revolver and shoot you dead, do you understand?" The old man said he understood very well that he would be shot. So they went on with the case. Of course, it wasn't a full minute before the old man interrupted again, whereupon Nicholson picked up the revolver, leant forward, took aim and shot the old man dead.

When he told me this story, my Principal at Aitchison College added, "Very high-handed you might say, but it brought order to the Frontier." And so it did. Nicholson was the only Irishman within two hundred miles, and this was how he ruled.

There were other Irishmen contemporary with Nicholson – one was Lawrence who was in charge of Lucknow, then the capital. Another was Roberts, who was a soldier in Delhi. These three coincided with what came to be called the Indian War of Independence, or the Mutiny. A further Irishman called Daly, less well known, was further south in Punjab.

When the Mutiny broke out Lawrence held the fort in Lucknow for so long that, even though the British were reduced to killing and eating rats, they did manage to hold out. At the same time Roberts took part in holding what was called The Ridge in Delhi so that the mutineers couldn't get across into the city. Nicholson raised an army on the Frontier and on the way down towards Delhi; he led it in, while Daly raised a levée down in Punjab and led it up to Delhi. The result was that these four Irishmen played such a key part in putting down the rebellion that Roberts won a V.C. Lawrence has had several books written about him, and Nicholson still has a statue standing to his memory. He was praised by all sides of the conflict in North West Pakistan. Sadly, Daly was more or less forgotten.

One of the problems in modern times is that the people of Northern Ireland, from where these men came, were unable to accept the idea that Northern Ireland should be severed from the mainland of Britain. They used to say, "Those people down in London would never have had an Empire if it hadn't been for our forebears."

One of the more mischievous jokes that I have enjoyed perpetrating from time to time is to say to mixed groups of British and foreign, that we Irish pulled off one of the greatest confidence tricks of all history in that we ran this immense Empire all over the world... and we let the British think it was theirs!

The truth is of course that Ireland, both North and South, benefitted enormously from the sacrifices made by people who built and maintained the British Empire because we were always able to shelter behind its defence in the various World Wars and always to gain from the numerous jobs it created as it spread out across the world. So I was always very careful to choose my audience when I put forward that remark, even as a joke.

Peshawar, the city at the foot of the Khyber Pass, has figured in history ever since its first mention by Herodotus in about 450 B.C. and it still figures today. The following two stories in particular are worth recounting:

One was when the British/Indian Royal Air Force, gearing up for war with Hitler, wanted to build an air strip that would take in larger aeroplanes than the strip they already had. Their hopes were dashed because right in the middle of the only really good site available for the new air strip was the grave, the tomb, of a well-known saint which could not be moved without offending people from miles around. So a stratagem was used which consisted of an Englishman – not an Indian (and there were plenty of Indians in the air force at that time) – masquerading as a Pathan holy man and going out each evening to pray at the tomb.

He was seen doing this by villagers, who occasionally joined him, and he went on doing this for some weeks. He then began to look very sad and unhappy, and when asked why by the local people, he said he had the feeling that the saint would much prefer to have been buried on the top of the hill nearby rather than down below in this flat, low-level plain. He said he wasn't sure and asked them to give him more time – which they did. He continued to go there and pray, but things got worse and he looked tremendously sad. Finally the villagers asked him whether it would be an idea if they moved the saint's grave. At this he showed suitable horror, but they said, "If the saint is unhappy, why can't we move him?" The masquerading British officer said he would pray some more, which he did, and after a few weeks told them he had come the conclusion that the saint would not mind if his grave and tomb were moved to the top of the nearby hill. The villagers all wanted to gain some kudos by making this move and joined in heartily. The result of this was a very fine air strip for allied aeroplanes from that point on.

From that time to the present there are two unusual things just beside Peshawar: this very fine air strip (now even larger), and tank-traps in the Khyber Pass. The latter because it was imagined that Hitler might try to come all the way across Asia and down through the Pass, resulting in this extraordinary defence of one of the key areas of the world. And, of course, it was from an underground hangar that Gary Powers flew his U-2 flights over Russia until the famous day when he was brought down.

The other story is from the officers' mess of the Pakistan Air Force in Peshawar. One night in the mess, one of the officers said, "Our Squash Marker who plays here with us is so good that I think we should enter him into the World Championship in London. He would very much like this opportunity so why don't we all throw in a few chips to send him there and see how he does?" There was no problem with planes – they came and went all the time as far as they were concerned – and they would easily find friends in London to put him up, so it was all duly arranged and off he went to London.

However, just before taking part in the championship there was a temporary hiatus because, in the club in Peshawar he always played in bare feet and long trousers. In London they had to discuss what the British public would think about someone coming into the World Squash Championship dressed this way. The chap was given a little practice wearing shorts, which is not actually satisfactory for Muslims – they don't like it much. He also tried tennis shoes and found these slipped all over the place, but he did play finally and, of course, he won. He was quite beyond the reach of all the others.

This was the start of a dynasty of Pakistan world squash champions because his son and nephews all became champions in their turn for several years; in fact, one of them was greatly and most generously praised by an Englishman who became world champion at one stage after they had finished. A friend said to this Englishman, "I think you ought go and talk to Zafrullah because even though he's old now and not playing so well I think he could still teach you one or two things." So the Englishman rang and spoke with Zafrullah and they agreed to meet at a squash court in North London.

Telling the story afterwards, this very generous Englishman said, "I was appalled when I got there. I met this rather old looking man, wearing long trousers and with a good tummy hanging over them, fiddling with an old squash racquet. He just said good morning and was quiet but friendly, so I said, 'Let's just play a game and perhaps you will notice some things I can do better.' So we played and it turned out that, even at his age, this Pakistani player was infinitely better." He went on with the story saying, "When he thought I was going to cry, he gave me one point before the end of the game!"

There has always been this wonderful rapport between British and Pakistani squash players.

I met one Englishman who, on his way back from Malaysia to Britain, broke his journey in Pakistan and travelled up to Peshawar just to see this famous squash court from which so many brilliant players emerged. He told me that when he arrived he could hear some rather slow play going on inside and wondered what it was. Seeing the door at the back of the court slightly ajar, he peeped in and saw two of the new generation of squash players, aged about twelve, standing on their heads with one hand on the floor and the other holding a racquet. They were hitting the ball up to each other against the wall while they remained standing on their heads. He told me that once he had seen that he fully understood how it was that the Pakistani squash players never lost their sense of orientation, no matter how many times they had to swing around on the court.

I was personally fortunate to have a very close knowledge of these men and their doings from my bearer, who at one stage came from the same village as them. He would occasionally ask me if he could be excused the following evening because his brothers – he always called them his brothers – were playing squash and he wanted to go and see them. Of course, I always said 'Yes'.

That man also told me how, in their village, they had a very strict rule about boys and girls not fraternising, not meeting each other privately at all. He went on to explain how in the village circle, between all the houses, there was an open space with two poles – one at each end, seven or eight feet high. If a boy and girl were found talking to each other illicitly, she was put up against one pole and he against the other and her father shot him and his father shot her!

Dreadful as this appears to us nowadays, it went on all the time in the Frontier and was one reason why it was often said that a woman could walk from one end of the Frontier to the other without being molested. This was simply because anyone who attempted to do so knew he would be shot dead.

9
Marriage And More

It was in the last three years of my time in Pakistan that the most exciting of all things that happened to me took place. The young lady whom I had seen acting on the stage of the Government College on my very first evening out after arriving in Lahore, had returned from London; I didn't know this until I was invited to a party at the British Council to welcome her back.

This meeting was unfortunate from my point of view because, sitting across the table from each other, she told me how she had enjoyed Manchester very much and I said, "Wasn't it very wet, because I thought the rain in Spain fell mainly in Manchester?" Now this attempt at being clever on my part produced a most dramatic reaction. The lady went into high gear to rattle off the names of at least ten different seaside resorts in Britain which had higher rainfall than Manchester and how, in certain months of the year, there was hardly any rain in Manchester at all. Never was I greeted with such a tirade of statistics to prove the excellence of Manchester's climate! So I had to withdraw in disorder!

We did meet afterwards, very briefly, in the party but then went our mutual ways. However, I met her again en-passant at church and, gradually, because she was with other people, got to know her friends who began to invite me to parties where she was present. A large number of the people at these parties would be Christians and I discovered that her father had been the Principal of one of the leading colleges in Pakistan. He was now retiring back to his science subjects and was head of the science department of a college in Lahore. She didn't live with him, but on her own in what were called 'Government Officers' flats', because she was a fully-fledged member of the Civil Service. Her name was Promilla Thomas, and she was an English lecturer in one of the leading colleges. As such, she had her own accommodation provided for her.

Gradually we got to know each other; a little tentatively and carefully because the sight of unmarried couples, even foreigners, going about in Pakistan in those days was regarded as a little forward – a slight affront to local custom, nothing more. Anyway, we did find opportunities to meet and on one or two occasions I found myself arriving back at the college too late to get in before the gate closed. I had to climb over and go and get the chowkidar (the night-watchman), to open the gate and let my car through. So you can imagine that in these circumstances it became fairly well-known that I was going out with somebody outside the college!

It wasn't too long before I was able to meet her family. Her father was a very erudite and accomplished man and her step-mother was a doctor. He had been India's tennis champion and his cousins had played Davis Cup tennis for India, so they were well used to the international and the local scene.

After being invited to the house and getting to know the family, there eventually came the time when I had to pluck up courage and ask the father for his daughter's hand in marriage. This I did and was a little nonplussed by the reply, which was direct, strong and straightforward. He said, "I hope you know what you're doing." Any man who thinks he knows what he's doing when he asks someone to marry him is a little foolish, but I pretended I knew. Anyway, it was definitely what I wanted.

In due course the wedding was arranged in Lahore. It was rather hot because we were going to get married at the end of the school year so we could go up to the mountains for our honeymoon in the cool. Sadly, my family were not going to come out, and I certainly wasn't going to ask them to come to Pakistan in that heat as they could have died.

I remember a dinner which Promilla's family gave for us some days before the wedding. As we were sitting down to the meal her father took me by the arm and said, "Son, have a good meal… it might be the last decent one you'll get!" Naturally, we all laughed –

he had this sort of mischievous gleam in his eye most of the time. He was a wonderful teacher and greatly respected throughout the country.

His wife also had a sense of humour. She had married into the family, and her daughter-in-law was already there as she had married Promilla's brother. In the middle of dinner, she said, "How do you find you get on with these Thomases?" So this was the kind of atmosphere in which we met and in which our courtship flourished.

A happy wedding day arrived and we went to the church, all delightful, exactly as it should be until, alas, the bishop who was marrying us, began to feel faint and staggered backwards towards the (fortunately) low altar. He sat down on it, then lay down in a faint. The Best Man rushed forward to help, as did a local friend, and they lifted him up and carried him out through the side door... and we were left. The clergyman who was second in command, took over very well and went on with the service. We were actually married by this time, but the service had to proceed in the proper way.

Suddenly, I began to feel very faint and felt myself falling forward and my new wife pulling me back. That's all I remember. It seems that I, too, fainted and was lifted outside by my wife's sister, who was a bridesmaid, and someone else. This meant that my wife was left alone with the congregation while her new husband and the bishop were stretched out in the cool outside (it was 114°F that day) trying to be brought back to life. Thankfully, we were, but not before my unfortunate wife who, on her way out to see what had happened, collapsed (and I don't blame her) in a faint on the steps near the end of the choir! Luckily, her friend, the American Consul's wife in the choir, saw what had happened and came across to help her outside. So there was as much activity in this nice little green area under trees outside the vestry door as there was back in the church! We were all brought round fairly quickly.

I then had to sign the register. A very old Christian Registrar (who was missing many teeth) held the register book over my head while I lay on the grass and tried to sign it with a biro, working upside down. He said, "Today I celebrate my ninetieth birthday; I was thirty-five years in service and I have just completed thirty-five years on pension." It was as if he had defeated an entire system!

With this in my mind we were raised up and taken back into church. Eventually we proceeded down the main aisle with everyone grinning and laughing, and all our Muslim friends – and there were many in the church – wondering at the amazing way in which Christian weddings were carried on! I am pleased to say that the rest of the proceedings were as normal as could be in the circumstances.

Our Wedding photo… eventually!

The news of this unusual wedding spread so far that very much later my wife was asked to give an account of it on British radio, 'Woman's Hour', which she did. Also it was used as part of the briefing that the Pentagon gave to people who came to Pakistan about the dangers of hot climates.

More immediately, my wife and I went up to the mountains for our honeymoon, in a beautiful place called Nathia Ghali. So many things happened there that it would take a whole book to relate. One was the surprise fact that an old boy of the school I attended in Ireland was there on holiday. He was about twenty-five years my senior and retiring as a director of Unilever and having his last holiday up there. I saw him one morning sitting under a tree talking in the local language to some children. He was in the correct attire for the British Raj on holiday: blue shorts, blue knee-length socks and blue short-sleeved, open neck shirt. I recognised him because he had figured in our Old Boys' magazines. By some extraordinary chance I had on my old school tie when I went across to him and said, "Good morning; you must be..." But before I could go any further with his name, he hastily looked up, put his hand to his throat, hid the open neck and said, "I say, sorry old boy... I didn't think we'd need them up here!" I later found out that what he was really interested in that day was whether his son might have won a race in the Public School Sports in London, held at the White City.

My wife and I enjoyed the most perfect climate one can possibly imagine. As she once said to me, "The only sound I hear is the wind in the trees and the slight movement of the pine needles under my feet." It was a most romantic place for a honeymoon which we can never forget.

All sorts of things happened. For example, because we were sleeping in a strange place, when my wife woke up in the morning she turned over imagining she was still in her own bed, and fell out onto the floor with a great thump, which woke me and I didn't know where I was either. Thankfully, she wasn't hurt. We had many tales to recount about the unusual things that happened. Fortunately they all ended very happily and we were able to get back down to the plains.

On the way down we stopped in a place called Abbottabad, took part in a British Council seminar on the teaching of English and met many of our friends there before returning to Aitchison College. Here we lived in a new house – well, an old house, but a new one for me because I had shifted out of my bachelor quarters into this nice house.

Our first home

Many wonderful things happened thereafter, one of the most amusing coming from our dear old sweeper who used to sweep the house very carefully and assiduously every day. When I wasn't there one day, he asked my wife a question. He knew my name was Mullen and he always called me 'Mullen-Sahib', but he heard my wife using a different word when she addressed me. She used the word 'sweetheart'. So, with great deference, he said to my wife, with whom he was friendly, "Memsahib-ji, is your Sahib's name Mullen-sahib or is it Sweetheart-sahib?"

I was to play a part in arranging meetings between two of our French friends who were the leaders in the European Jute Industry, and some of the Pakistani leaders of the Jute Industry in East Pakistan. Their aim was to stabilise this industry worldwide because they had discovered that a large number of quite poor peasant growers and workers in the jute industry in East Pakistan would often be out of work when there was a glut in the jute market. This was also applicable in some of the factories back in Europe. Then there would come a time when there was a shortage of jute and everyone would rush back into action – factories would re-open, workers would have jobs again for a while, even at better pay depending on the circumstances – and that 'up-and-down' cycle went on.

My French friends wanted to try to build up a 'buffer stock', so that when there was plenty of jute available some was put aside to be drawn on when there was a shortage, thereby keeping the market running smoothly. This way the factories in Europe and East Pakistan would keep going and everyone would be sure of their future and not worried whether there would be a job for them next month or not. However, I am sorry to say that it didn't work out; an agreement was not reached, so the sad affair of the uncertainty of employment continued.

Another much more amusing and unexpected encounter was with the famous and celebrated historian, A.J. Toynbee, who happened to be sitting in the next seat to me on a flight from Peshawar to Lahore. When we were flying over the great River Indus and he saw that I was using my binoculars to look out of the window, he more or less grabbed them from me and said, "Please let me borrow these – I want to see the place where Alexander got stuck with all his soldiers and couldn't get across." He went up and down the aisle looking out of every conceivable window – and because he was such a celebrity everyone deferred to him, as did I – then he returned to his seat and gave me back my binoculars.

He told me how he had been up in Afghanistan inspecting the various roads built by the Americans in the south of the country and the Russians in the north of the country, and where they had met. I couldn't help reflecting at the time on my absolute childish, boyish delight at meeting this famous historian and also at the cleverness of the Afghans in getting one great power, Russia, to build their roads in the north and another great one, America, to build them in the south when they were in the middle of a tremendous Cold War! Indeed, it bore out what my first Principal at Aitchison had said when he told me he believed that the Afghans were by far the best diplomats in the world!

It was quite difficult knowing what was happening in the junior school, where most of the teachers were ladies, because one didn't mix very much with the ladies in Pakistan generally, nor in the school. However, fortune favoured us as there was an older Irish lady on the staff who had known the work of Moral Re-Armament in Ulster before she ever went to Pakistan, so she was able to share with me quite a lot of useful insights. This included the way the children were taught, the way the teachers were trained and treated and the whole way in which the boarder boys especially were brought up before they came to us in the senior school. I have to say they were very fortunate children because, at that stage, they were getting one of the best educations in the world. There is absolutely no doubt in my mind that those people who questioned whether we, in the British Council, should be giving our help to the richest and most well-favoured people in the country rather than to the poorest, had a genuine question but the answer was very simple.

The future of the poor in the country depended on the behaviour of the rich in the country. The rich spoke English and had access to how the modern world worked whereas the poor did not. There was no way that we could even communicate satisfactorily with the poor, who were illiterate and had no facilities whatever, so this was a 'had-to-do' situation – we simply had to go through the rich to reach the poor. Unfortunately, that meant going through politicians who were many times less than wholly helpful to the poor.

An interesting event took place on one of my holidays about this time when I was up in the separate state called Dir. While I was there I had to spend a night in a remote village where there was no rest-house or hotel, so I slept in a room that one of the local people let me use. It had no door or window and I was able to look straight out at the sky.

As I lay down to rest I saw a bright silver star in the sky which seemed to be moving very slowly, so I got up and went outside. It was now very dark and up in those high mountains in the Hindu Kush the sky was absolutely clear. There were other stars in the distance, but this one seemed a little nearer than most and was definitely moving across the sky with a tiny tail of silver behind it. As I watched, an old man emerged from another house. We couldn't speak each other's language but I tapped him on the shoulder and looked up at the sky and he knew enough English to say, "Ji, Sahib, Silver Bullet." Of course, once he said this it dawned on me that this was one of the Russian satellites put up in the sky about that time and it came around and around. The local tribesmen interpreted it in terms of guns and shooting. The name was a good one because it did look just like a silver bullet in the sky.

I had never wanted to be a housemaster but was prevailed upon by the Principal to take on one house in which the boys were mainly Pathans from the North-West-Frontier. This house had a particularly famous room; it was the one in which the Nawab of Pataudi had slept when he was at school and later on he went to university in England and became an international cricketer and played for England. He was always called 'Noob'.

When I was there, his two nephews were in the house and they actually slept in this room. Their father was Pakistan's ambassador to Malaysia and he came to realise that the young sons of the Malaysian princes couldn't ride horses or play hockey very well – there were at that time thirteen princedoms and they took it in turn to be king for one year before passing on the kingship to another prince. He arranged for as many as he possibly could, seven ultimately, to leave Malaysia and come to Aitchison College and learn these skills and generally rough it with others. I had four of them in my house and they fitted in very well, eventually going out riding with many of the boys in the early mornings (five-thirty a.m.).

One of the big events in Lahore, in fact in Pakistan, every year was the Horse Show in February and I well remember Her Majesty the Queen coming as a guest at the Horse Show and watching the boys riding, doing their tent-pegging and also seeing the tribesmen riding on camels. It was all very exciting and quite suited to the 'aristocratic expectations' of the Malaysian princes, who were very pleasant people.

The one game that they did find a little odd was cricket and none of them was ever really able to manage batting, bowling or even fielding. It somehow didn't seem to fit in with their family characteristics, which was a shame.

When they were in my house, the captain of the Indian cricket team (and a member of the Pataudi family), in terms of strict Islamic and traditional aristocratic policies, rather spoilt things by marrying a leading actress in Bollywood!

It is interesting now to look back and see how all this was regarded with a kind of dumb silence, almost as though the noble game of Test Cricket and the rather doubtful world of film star celebrity didn't quite mix, especially when some of the people involved were royalty.

The strange place that cricket has in relationships with India, Pakistan, Britain and other Commonwealth countries is reflected in a very simple personal matter. When I was teaching in Northern Ireland for a short while, Peter Everington, a young Englishman, was my assistant cricket master and became a very close friend. He was very keen on cricket and later went off to Britain and became a member of the MCC (and supported Middlesex forever), and I went off to Pakistan.

Although we kept in touch – and he and I are now godfathers to each other's children – over the years we didn't have very much to do with each other. However, recently, one amazing afternoon in Bangalore, Ireland beat England at cricket in a one-day match! It is quite unheard of, for England to be beaten by, of all people, Ireland, and Peter wrote me a poem on my next birthday to celebrate this strange cricketing event:

They say that English battles won
Were first won on the fields of Eton
But of course we were never taught that much
Of the fields where we were beaten.

But now to lands of East and West
Sky Sports blares out the score
Of how the Irish slew the English
On the field of Bangalore.

You grieving English at Oval and Lords,
Raise up a grim memorial.
But ask the source of Irish skills
Who gave them their tutorial?

On the field of Down in ancient days
Lived a cricket master, Mullen.
In him is the cause of Irish joys
And English faces sullen.

And he took his bag of cricket lore
To a school in Pakistan.
That's how the world knows the sixes and swing
Of Khan and Khan and Khan.

So raise your glasses, one and all,
To the man who opened the door
For the lads of Tipperary
On the field of Bangalore.

I hasten to point out that this poem grossly exaggerates any effect I may have had on cricket in any part of the world. The only connection I can possibly see is that I did have a small part to play in two of Pakistan's most famous cricketers, Majid Khan and Imran Khan. With Majid Khan I am able to say that I did prevent him from bowling a certain kind of no-ball, which he did by throwing. When I no-balled him he said, "But Sir, no one else has no-balled me for that." I replied, "No, Majid, but I think you threw it." The very next Saturday he went to Karachi to play for Pakistan against Australia and 'threw' out their two very good batsmen, Lowry and Burke. The Australian Board of Control protested, and with no television replays in those days to examine the action of the bowlers, the Pakistan Board of Cricket reluctantly agreed that he would not bowl in the rest of the series, which he didn't, concentrating on his batting, which he did very well.

With regard to his younger cousin, Imran Khan, who became much more famous later on, all I can say is that one afternoon when he was a small boy, probably somewhere between about ten or twelve years old, I was asked by my friend, Mr Naseer, to take cricket practice. He was in the net, running down and banging the ball with a cross-bat over square leg's head, mid-wicket's head. I said to him, "Imran, I think that's very good but… one day a good bowler is going to get you out because you haven't got a straight bat. Unless you keep a straight bat to defend against the good balls, you will be got out… remember that the bowler can bowl a good ball just as well as you can play a good shot."

I showed him one way how to do it and the dangers, and he did it. Then, as with all the other boys, I threw him some straight balls from about fifteen yards, which he played, then I threw him some bad balls, which he hit sideways. Finally, I threw him a good ball, straight but a little faster, and of course it got through and broke his wicket because he hadn't played a straight bat. He stood there, looking at me and at the broken wicket. I don't know what he said to himself, but I think it may have played a tiny part in the history of cricket! His subsequent captaining of Pakistan to World Cup victory in cricket, his playboy reputation in Britain, his marriage to Jemima Goldsmith and their subsequent divorce, and his entry into politics, to say nothing of him having set up a very fine cancer hospital in memory of his mother who died of cancer – and where people are treated today without the staff knowing who are rich and who are poor, who are paying fees and who aren't – reflect in some way the whole history of the problems that Pakistan has faced ever since it came into being in 1947.

That history was bedevilled by the unfortunate antagonism which continued to exist between Hindu India and Muslim Pakistan. It was particularly difficult for the boys in the college where I was teaching, since so many of their families had half been left behind in India and half come to Pakistan – some of them had gone to India and not come back at all. There were problems over property, inheritance, etc, but there was also a tremendous goodwill in some people to mend those relations and to bring the two countries to live together in harmony.

This was exemplified by the insistence that the erstwhile Hindu and Sikh temples in our college should be very well looked after.

The Mandir, the Hindu temple, was turned into an excellent library, kept immaculately clean and beautifully decorated so that whenever a visitor did come, and they did occasionally – a Hindu from India, one of the old Maharajahs visiting his old school or his family's old school – they would be thrilled to see how well their temple was being looked after. Likewise the Sikhs and their Gurdwara, because the Sikhs and Muslims of North India had, at that time, a terrible conflict when the Partition of the sub-continent took place. They, too, were delighted that their Gurdwara was being so well looked after. There is no question that this made a very good contribution to the possible reconciliation of Pakistan and India.

My last years in Pakistan were made much easier for me by my wife. After we were married she was able to tell me so many things about the way in which the sub-continent worked, because her family had been right across it in many guises over the years – as sportsmen, as diplomats, as teachers and professors in universities, mixing and working with local people of all religions and with foreigners. They understood a lot about the interaction of all these different communities, which, of course, I did not.

Also, she had in her own right become Pakistan's more or less 'official reception lady' for foreign dignitaries. She was given the task of showing them around, whether it was Agatha Christie, with whom she developed a lifelong friendship, the Shah-n-Shah of Iran's new wife, or Princess Beatrix of the Netherlands. She also assisted in Bhowani Junction, where she met international film stars – some of whom she thought were wonderful and others of whom she didn't have such a high opinion – but she enjoyed that, too. So I was able to learn a great deal at a time really when I needed to because life was changing. We were now almost twenty years on from the independence of Pakistan as a nation and the old orders were beginning to move away but new orders hadn't yet come in. I remember a Communist-leaning newspaper being shut down because it didn't fit in with either democracy or Islam, and there was also the problem at that time that Islam and democracy didn't always fit together! So this was a time when my wife's wisdom was a great help on many occasions.

For the sake of a word, one trivial episode lives with me. The Trade Commissioner in East Pakistan and I were friends. When I was staying with him on one occasion, I was sitting in the back of his car while he was driving and we were talking about what was to happen in the evening. He mentioned that we were just then going to have tea with '*so-and-so*' and in the evening we were going to have dinner with '*so-and-so* else'. There was another passenger in the car who then said, "But, haven't you got a cocktail party at seven o'clock, in between?" With that he took both hands off the steering wheel and said, "Gadzooks! So we have." Now I had never heard the word 'Gadzooks' in my whole life, although I had seen it, I think, in the earliest editions of The Beano and The Dandy and in one or two other comics, but to hear it actually happen in real life is something that I treasure to this day. I had not heard it said before and haven't since, and it's one thing that I will never forget.

My wife was also able to introduce a new and unusual activity into the life of the house and this was to teach the piano to the younger son of the Nawab of Bahawalpur, who wanted to learn how to play. I've forgotten where we had the piano – I suppose it must have been in our house from her family because I hadn't had one before we married. Anyway, she taught him and he became quite good at playing in the elementary way that one can in a short time. That was one way in which life was civilised through my being married.

Another was an amusing way. It was when we later came near to leaving Pakistan. One day in the street my wife said to me, "I have a pension from my job in the Government, or some sort of accumulated fund or other." I said, "You can forget it now because you won't get it in the short time we have left here." We knew that Pensions and Provident Funds and suchlike took an inordinate length of time to come to fruition in places like Pakistan, India and all those erstwhile countries of the Empire. However, we went to the Pensions Office and they suggested we came back the following Monday and speak with the officer in charge, who might be able to help.

Although there were only a very few days before we were to leave the country, we went back on the Monday and were shown into a fine room. It was very nicely decorated, with a long table covered in green baize down one side, three rather splendid chairs in front of it and one chair behind. It seemed to me a very good entry to one's Provident Fund or Pension!

We sat down and waited and about ten minutes later a young man came into the room and went immediately behind a large screen. Over this he said, "Good afternoon… excuse me, I'll be just a few moments finishing this and will then be with you." Eventually he came and sat down behind the table and looked up and said, "Well now… Promilla! Promilla! What are you doing here?" (My wife's name is Promilla, spelt as you see it here but pronounced rather like Pamela). Now this young man and she had acted together in plays in the university and hadn't seen each other since. They talked to each other for a little while and then rather hastily and with a slight blush she indicated me and said, "This is my husband; I've just got married." So we said, "how do you do," and chatted a little, and then they went on talking about the Provident Fund.

He said, "Oh but Promilla, this amount of money is beyond my capacity to sign for; besides, there are all sorts of complications. You went away to England for three years and when you came back you should have had three years of increments, but that has not been put in here, so you are due not only your Provident Fund but it has to be calculated on a higher number of increments than are shown here. I can't possibly do that this afternoon. If you don't mind coming back tomorrow, I should have completed it by then and may even have been able to get my senior officer to sign it because he has the authority to do so."

We went back the next afternoon and, to my utter astonishment, walked out of the place with so much money that we had to buy carpets and other things in order to get the 'money' back to England when we did leave Pakistan, because there were all kinds of currency restrictions and heaven knows what else in vogue at the time. It was far easier to put a nice carpet and some other goods into one's heavy baggage and send it home, rather than to try to fill in all the necessary forms for currency exchange.

This is probably the place to explain a great sadness in my wife's life. She was a very good actress and was offered a scholarship by The Old Vic to come to London and go to RADA and have a full dramatic training, with all her expenses paid. Alas, when she put it to her father he wouldn't have any of it because, in those days, actors and actresses and suchlike were not really regarded as 'quite the thing'. So I was the beneficiary of it... but I am often conscious of how much of a life my wife has missed by not being able to take up that scholarship, because there was no question that she was, and is, a very good actress, and with a very good singing voice, too, in those days. In fact, the reason she took up learning German and became fluent in it was that she was so thrilled with German music.

About this time the British Council were pointing out to me that I had now been nine years out of Britain and it would probably be advisable for me to go back to the university and pick up on all that had been happening in the world of language teaching and linguistics while I had been in Lahore. I was a little torn because the post I had in Pakistan seemed to me to be quite a relevant one; however, I could see also that my future would definitely become more and more out of touch with the rest of the mainstream world if I stayed there, so I decided to come back.

The most amazing experience of my life where money was concerned took place in Pakistan. I was saying my prayers one morning when a clear thought shot through my mind: "Send your friend £25." I hadn't seen him for years, but wrote the cheque and posted it.

Six months later I received the reply:

Dear Lloyd,
Thank you so much for the money. It followed me round various addresses and caught up with me in New York when I had no money at all and my father had just died back home.
I was actually on my knees praying for money when your letter was pushed under the door of the room where I was staying…

Mourne Grange Cricket Team

10
Back To Britain

The British Council offered me a scholarship to Manchester University to spend a year in the School of Language Teaching and Linguistics, coming up to date on how to teach the English language to foreigners. Of course, this didn't mean that I would definitely have a post anywhere after that year was over and, since I had just got married, I had to take the whole situation on trust and bring my wife with me to Manchester.

A most fortunate circumstance was that Promilla had been in Manchester for three years at the very same Department of the University where I was going, so she knew it both professionally and socially; she also knew the city and England. I had been out of Britain for nine years so was totally out of touch. For example, when I left Britain buses and trains weren't heated and when I got back I remember being amazed that a bus was heated around my feet – very simple things like that. Anyway, it was certainly a comfort to know that I was going to go to a city with which my wife was happy, very happy, as was witnessed by the attack she made on me when I said something derogatory about "The rain in Spain falls mainly in Manchester" – which was the opening for how we met again after her return from England. So we bade farewell to Lahore and Pakistan and travelled back to England.

My wife's affection for Manchester is most easily shown by a song which she wrote herself, and the music, and sang on Radio Manchester one happy afternoon when she was interviewed about her time in England as a British Council scholar and now returning as the wife of a British Council Officer posted to Manchester University. This is the song she wrote:

Grey streets of Manchester lie wet in the rain,
Grey streets of Manchester lie cold in the rain,
Warehouses rising high,
No sunset in the sky,
And dirty grey trickles outside the window pane.

Warm hearts of Manchester beat warm through the rain,
Laughter and loving shine bright through the rain;
Welcome is in the air,
Friendship is everywhere,
And music is playing behind that window pane.

Because of the long summer vacation between the end of the school year in Aitchison College and the beginning of the academic year in Manchester, it was possible to go home by ship rather than fly. However, there was one sadness that we had to go through before we left. Promilla had to go into hospital for a small operation because of a pregnancy which had gone wrong (in its very early stages, fortunately). The operation was carried out successfully by one of her old friends and colleagues – a very skilled surgeon – and she recovered quickly. She actually boarded the boat in Karachi only three days after the operation, and in between had travelled down overnight by 'Tez Gam' (the train) from Lahore to Karachi. Fortunately, our heavy luggage was being dealt with separately so we didn't have the burden of that.

The shipping line was the Italian Lloyd Triestino, which we had to take because there were none of the old traditional lines travelling, like the Oriental Pacific. So we boarded 'The Asia' on 1st July and quickly found that our fellow travellers were a most pleasant group of people.

Rather like ourselves, many were going home for a long leave, or going home to Britain or to Europe after a spell working abroad, so that we had much in common to talk about, plus enjoying the leisure of an ocean voyage. We went first to Bombay, the main pick-up point for passengers between Italy and India.

It was a very nice time of the year to be travelling, as the weather was pleasant, but I was not a good sailor and spent quite a number of days trying to get my sea legs. My wife had a good joke with me, as she said, 'playing Hide and Sick' in the cabin, where I tried to keep things down or, when I did get on deck, stood near the rail for fear of disaster. But fortunately, it soon settled down and we got into a very pleasant routine on the ship.

The people to whom we related most easily and immediately were tea-planters going back home on leave or at the end of their tour. This was probably because Promilla's brother was a tea planter and had been so for many years in the north of East Pakistan, so the jargon was easy for us to understand and the situations of life, such as being parted from one's children for a long time or being subject to monsoons, or to trade fluctuations in different parts of the world.

There was excellent entertainment in the evenings, with plenty of swimming and deck games during the day; all the usual fun on board ship.

We left Bombay on 5th July and reached Mombasa on the 11th, having crossed The Indian Ocean, and I was looking forward to less choppy waters for the rest of the way. However, an incident occurred which didn't affect the sea but did affect the people on board very much.

Our ship was supposed to call in at Beira, the port in Mozambique – Mozambique being a Portuguese possession at that time. An international incident flared up when Pandit Nehru took Goa by force. Goa was a Portuguese possession in India, and relations were broken off between the two nations. The Indian Government informed the Italian Government that if their shipping line, the Lloyd Triestino, which we were on, called in at Portuguese possessions, say Beira, then they would withdraw all their coaling facilities from them in Bombay. This would have left the Italian shipping line without any destination, thereby more or less putting it out of business!

The few people on board who were due to get off at Beira were thwarted in the extreme. One of them was from the de Beer family from South Africa, the diamond magnates; he was going to meet his wife who was already in Beira and they had planned great holidays in the African Game Parks and beauty spots. I saw this unfortunate passenger jumping up and down in front of the Captain, who was Italian but spoke good English. I even overheard him saying, "Can't you get a helicopter to come out and take us in?" The captain was so upset and bewildered by this behaviour that he finally took refuge in pretending that he didn't speak enough English to understand all that was being said and put an end to the discussion that way. The ship did not put in at Beira and the disappointment of the passengers who had booked for Beira was very great.

This is probably the point at which to remind ourselves that the reason why we were coming home by ship right around the whole of Africa, rather than coming through the Red Sea and Suez Canal, was simply because Nasser had blocked the Suez Canal. It had remained blocked so international incidents at both ends of the continent made life awkward for Africa's diamond magnate.

We left Mombasa on 11th July and reached Cape Town on the 18th. We just spent one day in Cape Town, arrived early morning and left in the evening, and there again Promilla and I ran into another international incident.

We had the day to spare so left the ship and tried to get a taxi. For the first time in my life I saw something I had only heard about. On the top of the taxi was a big sign in two languages which said 'WHITES ONLY'. Now, my wife is Indian, born Indian and became Pakistani at Partition and has remained so ever since. I remember looking at this taxi and the notice on it with a sense of shock. The thought that went through my mind was that these people are mad... they really do do this! However, the taxi driver in Cape Town had strict instructions to be very accommodating for matters of this sort and hadn't the slightest hesitation in taking both of us in his taxi to this very beautiful city of Cape Town and showing us many places. We saw this very great open air mural to the Voortrekkers who went from the coast inland and more or less created South Africa, of course leading finally to their Dutch wars with our British later-comers.

A German engineer on board, who shared a lunch table with us, told us an absolutely horrific story which concerned him but had a happy ending. He was an oil engineer and was sent by his firm to work in Venezuela. While there, his little child, aged about seven, was kidnapped and couldn't be found. He and his wife had to go back to Germany without their child, absolutely traumatised.

The company made him a promise that he would never have to go to Venezuela again. However, about five years later a very serious problem arose out there and because he was the only engineer in the firm who could handle the matter, he was asked to go back. Very reluctantly he agreed and did go back.

One evening when standing in a queue at a cinema to go in to see a film, he saw a beggar boy, aged about twelve or so, come along begging for money and he recognised, he thought, his own son, five years older! He left the queue, grabbed the child, ran straight back home, hid the boy and next morning took him to the German Embassy. The end of the story is that he *was* the son and they did all get back somehow to Germany, a reunited family, with the child probably the most bewildered of all.

This same engineer got on very well with Promilla because, in addition to speaking German, Promilla had a hobby of card tricks which he shared. Therefore, they were able to talk to each other and show each other card tricks and they decided to swop some. This is how conjurers work, I suppose! One day I witnessed the complexities of them practising and I thought to myself, "These conjurers really know how to do a thing or two."

We were now on the ocean for nine days; a long trip from Cape Town up to Dakar in Senegal. Here the women were beautifully dressed in wonderfully bright, flamboyant clothes, with head-dresses almost as tall as their bodies – they looked like people about to go for a parade or a fancy dress ball, but this was their normal attire.

They also had a very odd economy because de Gaulle in France at that time, was trying to operate a kind of war against some of the erstwhile French Colonies and Britain through them. The price of everything, priced in French Francs, was so high that one of our fellow travellers had a meal in the hotel for which he wasn't able to pay. The rate of exchange was so bad that what would, say, normally be about one pound sterling for a cup of coffee had become twelve pounds, so by the time he had had dinner for six people he was hundreds of pounds out. He more or less staggered back to the ship in amazement.

Next stop was Las Palmas which was delightful. The climate, the spectacular vegetation – flowers, plants, trees – and the sense of old world charm that surrounds that island was wonderful and we were quite thrilled with our day-and-a-half there because it was like a holiday in itself. When one has been on board ship for a very long time, to get off in such a beautiful place carries a special charm all of its own and I remember it even now.

Soon we would be going through more familiar territory – the Straits of Gibraltar and on to Barcelona, our next stop. We then had two days down to Brindisi on the southern tip of Italy, and another day up to Venice where we could have left the ship but, because it was easy to do so, we stayed for another day and went on to Trieste and then came back again to Venice before catching trains to Switzerland.

Here we were met by a Moral Re-Armament acquaintance, Burford Weekes, who picked us up at Lausanne and drove us up to Caux, near Montreux, where the International Conference was being held.

Caux Conference Centre

As we drove up this mountain track I remember Burford Weekes realising, halfway up, that my new wife (because he didn't know her, he only knew me) was actually the daughter of someone he had been at university with in Edinburgh. Suddenly, he took his hands off the wheel and said, "My goodness! Are you Winnie the Pooh's daughter? I don't believe it." Well, we did make it safely and at the top my wife explained that she wasn't exactly Winnie the Pooh's daughter; she was in fact her step-daughter as her father had married again – his second marriage. She was really named Winifred, but in university she was always called Winnie the Pooh.

The onward journey to Manchester was without incident and we stayed with friends of Promilla from her previous time there. This made life easier, settling into a country where neither of us had lived for several years.

The next item on the list was to go to Ireland to see my family and get to know everybody there again. My sisters and mother met us at the airport in Dublin and there was great rejoicing amongst the women because they hadn't seen each other before, even though we had been married this length of time. My mother had been very careful not to come out in the hot weather. We set off in a taxi with me sitting beside the driver and the four ladies behind, all talking, talking, talking!

I asked the taxi driver how things were in Dublin these days and he said, "Very quiet, not much tourist trade, nothing happening… well, there is one thing – you know Mountjoy Jail up here?" I told him that I did know it because all our leading Irish heroes and politicians spent some time in that jail under the British rule. He went on, "Well, the prisoners all went on strike about a fortnight ago and yesterday the warders came out in sympathy with them." Once he said that I knew I really was back in Ireland! A wonderful place to be, where things happen rather differently from anywhere else in the world!

Another surprising thing happened a few days later – at least it was surprising to me, though it may not have been to my wife or my family. I was sitting quietly in the drawing room reading the newspaper and knew that upstairs my mother and my wife were exchanging all kinds of interesting thoughts about, I suppose, each other and life and especially clothes – they were always very interested in clothes. After some time I heard the door behind me open and my mother walked in, passed me on the sofa and said, almost as an aside, "I hope you treat that girl nicely; you know, she's far too good for you!" I suppose I had to accept my mother's judgment since she'd known me for many years. She had only known my wife for several minutes, but that was her opinion – that my wife was far too good for me!

We had great fun because we went on a tour of all the old places, down to the house where I was born and grew up, and we saw Nellie, who had been our nanny's daughter. We stayed with a boy I'd been with at school and his wife, and we went to see the headmaster of the school I had been in, The Reverend Fleming. He was now Rector of a parish down in Cork, having given up teaching. Then we went all round the famous beauty spots of Killarney, Blarney Castle, Glengariff, and stayed with another boy I had been in school with, who was now a clergyman. We then drove back along the coastline, taking in pretty well all the beauty spots and meeting old friends in Waterford, where I had been at school again. We saw the famous Waterford glass factory, met the member of the Board of Governors who had introduced us to international rugby in his day, and saw a famous cousin of mine, a really beautiful girl called Gwen who married a really wild boy called Miley who had been in the school just as I arrived. Then we came back and met my cousins in Kildare at their farm where I had spent so many happy days as a child. We also saw another old girl of the school, and so on back to Dublin, where we watched 'The Playboy of The Western World' in The Abbey Theatre, a very suitable way to leave the country and come back to Manchester. Here we stayed with Promilla's friends again and looked for a flat into which we could move.

Because we were technically 'students', at least I was, it was not immediately easy to get a flat – and good flats were rented to other people if possible, not to students! However, we got news of an ideal flat and telephoned. Promilla put her hand over the phone and said to me, "I think I had better tell her I'm a Pakistani." So she spoke to the lady and said she had just come over with her husband and that she's from Pakistan. The voice at the other end said, "That's fine, that's quite all right." Promilla continued, "My husband is from Ireland." A great "Ooooh!" came down the phone from the other end. However, in spite of my coming from Ireland we were permitted to enter this flat and stayed there for two very happy years.

The flat was ideally situated for the university, taking only a few minutes to get there by bus or car. The actual building in which we had our lectures and seminars was on the south side of Manchester, which was fortunate for us. There were thirty-two students on the course with a staff of about seven or eight. Between us, we had worked in nineteen different countries and represented nine different nationalities. Of course, we were mainly British, but the amount of experience we were all able to share with each other was considerable. The oldest was probably forty-something, and the youngest about twenty-five, which gave a mature, light-heartedness to the entire operation. Whilst very desirable and helpful in terms of our careers, the course was also a bit of a holiday from taking one's own classes... it was a real joy to be able to let someone else try to teach you.

The basic outline of the course was a fairly detailed study of Phonetics, the sounds which come out of our mouths, how they are made and how to teach them to other people who are used to producing different sounds. That was a very useful side of the course, the phonetics. Linguistics was also very interesting, but difficult for those with an old-fashioned approach. We also studied Practical Classroom Teaching. This depends very much on the classroom, who's in it and on the personality of the teacher, but there are certain basic factors which have to be taken into account. The tutors had all been teachers in their time, and so dealt with these matters very coherently, sensibly and very sensitively.

It was a good course overall and for me personally a great joy because Promilla had taken that same course about six years earlier and knew the staff very well. She was on first name terms with the wives and husbands and we were in a constant round of parties and, of course, in Manchester we had access to a very high standard of plays and operas, etc.

We were getting ready to go and see Margot Fonteyn in Swan Lake one evening when we heard that the leading male dancer had broken his ankle and so Rudolph Nureyev had been flown in from Germany for just two performances. The result was that we saw Nureyev and Fonteyn in Swan Lake, which probably is about as high as you can fly in the world of ballet. This was symptomatic of our happy luck all that year.

The British Council at that time was trying to arrange for its officers to be seconded to various Departments in British Universities so that they could keep up to date with their own subjects and also with what was happening in Britain at a time of great change, and be able to represent that in their work abroad. I was the lucky beneficiary of the very first attempt as the Council asked Manchester University whether they could second me to the same Department where I had been working as a student and taken the particular diploma course that they had on offer.

The University of Manchester and this Department were happy enough to have me back as a kind of transitory member of the staff who could fill in extra work for them and also do some research which they didn't have time to do.

One very interesting piece of research was to do with the difficulties that good foreign speakers of English find when they are in the British lecture room. Lecturers have very different styles and one Spaniard who spoke excellent English told me how he was thrown by the casual nature of a particular lecturer who came into the lecture room carrying a rucksack, umbrella and various other bits and pieces. His shirt was open-necked and he was wearing jeans, and he said, "You remember that last Tuesday we were dealing with such-and-such. Well, I was hoping that we could get on today with that but we can't and, anyway, I had such a good weekend fishing that my mind is more or less still down at the river. However, let's get started," and he would go on. By this time, the poor unfortunate Spaniard had written down something about 'fish' and other things and got thrown – he really didn't latch on to the social niceties of what was going on.

Another thing was that certain words which we use normally in a whole host of different ways, are, to foreigners, quite difficult. When I asked the same Spaniard, who was a highly intelligent man, to give an example, he said, "Take the word '*however*'. Sometimes you are saying, 'this is the case, this is the case and this is the case, *however*...', and then you turn backwards on what you've been saying. Then there is another occasion when you seem to say, 'These are the facts, and *however* you look at it, they are going to remain the facts'; in which case the *however* is taking you on in the same direction you were already going. When we hear the word *however*, we don't really know for a while whether we are agreeing with what has gone before or whether we are disagreeing with it and simply going on!"

This type of issue was very useful and made interesting reading, which we were able to circulate to various departments in the University and which undoubtedly helped the lecturers in their handling of foreign students and, we hope, vice-versa.

Another most amusing case that I came across was where a Greek speaking lady had a particular dialect so that whenever she came across an English word with a 'd' in it she was inclined to add a little 'n', a nasal sound, in front of the 'd', making 'n-d'. One evening she rushed in and said, "I'm so sorry I'm late... I want to undress in Piccadilly." My colleague and I looked at each other and thought, 'what on earth?' However, because we knew about languages, we paused and worked out that the lady had actually said, "I'm so sorry I'm late... I went to an address in Piccadilly." Going to an address in Piccadilly is quite different to wanting to undress in Piccadilly!

Another delight was being within easy reach of the Lake District, the Peak District and Scotland – Promilla had cousins in Edinburgh. Of course, we could also go down to London, although that was quite rare.

We were hoping to have a child while we were in England, and indeed did, but things didn't happen as planned. When Promilla discovered that she was pregnant there was a suggestion that it might be a case of placenta praevia. This is where the placenta is underneath the baby and there is a danger that the weight of the baby may break through it. Sadly, when Promilla was seen by the specialist she came out afterwards crying, and saying, "Oh Lloyd, he didn't examine me properly. He just gave me a rough going over and said, 'You're all right, everything's going to be fine'." I suppose I should have complained, but I felt that he must know his job and we just hoped for the best.

Well, in fact, the worst happened; the placenta did break and, honestly, I thought that Promilla was going to bleed to death in front of my eyes. However, she kept her head better than I did and told me to go into the bathroom and get all the towels I could find and then ring the ambulance, which I did. Mercifully, the ambulance came very quickly and whisked Promilla off to hospital, with me following behind in the car. Luckily the hospital was just down the road – Manchester Royal Infirmary – and I caught up with them just as Promilla was being taken to a ward on a trolley. I overheard one of the nurses saying, "My goodness, what a woman. She might be dying and look at her, she's sitting up, telling jokes and trying to make us laugh... amazing!" Of course, this was Promilla all over. She had learnt early on in life that the thing you do when everything is disastrous is to try and keep other people happy. In fact, she really wished that life could be one long party. Perhaps I did, too... but I wasn't quite as enthusiastic about it.

Promilla spent months in hospital, lying flat on her back. To keep busy, she did all sorts of things... even teaching herself more card tricks! Then the great day finally came when there was to be a delivery. That was a terrible day really, when I look back.

The delivery took place at mid-day by Caesarean Section. To the amazement of everyone in the theatre, when the sheet was pulled back to do the operation, there was a biro mark on Promilla's tummy, reading, 'cut along dotted line'. Now you can imagine the horror from the point of view of hygiene, but she had been left long enough lying on a trolley somewhere or other to do this!

Quite wonderfully, a baby girl arrived, and she was passed fit and sent up to the ward. As was usual at this time, I was not present at the birth, but was waiting elsewhere in the hospital. I was given the good news, but then things started to turn into a nightmare. It transpired that when our daughter arrived at the ward, a nurse raised concerns about her health. Although the baby had been passed fit, this little Nigerian nurse said, "No, I don't like this child's breathing; she must be examined again." So she was put in a crèche at the end of the ward and all the nurses were told that she was not to be fed until she had been fully examined. This little nurse then rang Pendlebury Hospital – the children's hospital – nine miles out of Manchester, at Salford, and spoke to the specialist paediatrician. He knew this nurse as a bit of a fusspot and actually said to her that he didn't want to come all the way over and find it was a wild goose-chase. However, she insisted that it was very serious and needed him to come. Thankfully, he did.

The specialist examined our daughter and found that the nurse was absolutely right. Our baby had a condition known as 'tracheaeosophageal-fistula'. This meant that instead of having separate wind and food pipes, she had just one pipe which had to be divided into two. If she was given even a drop of water or milk, she would suffocate and drown! A major operation was required. The consultant explained it to me as trying to separate a thin piece of white thread into two even thinner pieces of thread. It had to happen immediately. I even remember saying to the doctor, "Don't I have to sign something?" He replied, "Yes, so you do – we've got to get on with this," so I signed. That little incident showed me how serious the whole matter was. The operation was to be performed in Pendlebury Hospital, nine miles away.

As if this was not worrying enough, the nightmare worsened when I received a message about Promilla, saying that she still hadn't stopped bleeding after giving birth. I was told, "If we can't stop it, she will die." Having tried everything else, they said they were going to try the old-fashioned method of packing the womb with bandage material. The doctor said, "It doesn't always work... but sometimes it does!"

I remember going outside and standing in a corridor, seeing in my imagination my daughter, miles away now, and my wife in a ward into which I had just seen a doctor running with his white coat flying...

which is something that doctors aren't supposed to do. A hospital chaplain came along and more or less took me in hand. We went to the canteen and talked over a cup of tea. It turned out that, as a young man with a young wife, he had been in the outback in Australia when his wife suffered the same condition as Promilla. Tragically, she died before his eyes because he couldn't get any medical help to save her. When I heard this I realised what a long and wide thing life is and I give thanks for that padré, even though I have now long forgotten his name.

It looked as if Promilla was going to be OK, so the hospital sent me home. When I went back to the hospital at midnight, the news was at least half good. They had stopped the bleeding, but had had to give Promilla a complete blood transfusion, which made her look somewhat bloated in the face, hands and arms, etc. However, of far greater concern to me was that she still had not returned to consciousness. They were worried whether she would ever come out of this state and even asked me to shout at her and hit her in an attempt to elicit some kind of response – can you believe it! Now it's almost impossible to shout at your wife in a case like that, but I did, and I even gently slapped her wrist. Miraculously, the little finger of her right hand gave a twitch – just a little twitch. I told the nurse and this meant they were able to do something.

When a new Sister came on duty, I could see that she was the kind of person I could easily relate to. She was obviously the daughter of an Irish country farmer, probably from Munster where I come from, and very brusque, very tough and used to dealing with all situations. I recognised immediately the kind of Roman Catholic girl who surrounded me when I was growing up. We talked about the problem of my wife... suppose she gets better and comes round – do I tell her about the condition our daughter is in, nine miles away? If I do, and it affects her badly, she might die of shock on the spot! Equally, it might spur her to fight even harder to get better, but we didn't know at that point. The Irish nurse looked across Promilla and, staring me straight in the eye, said, "Are you going to tell her?" I hadn't made up my mind until that question hit me straight, and I found that before I could really think, I had said, "Yes, I am." Her reply was, "Yes, you've got to." Fortunately, Promilla did come round and I did tell her and she fought very hard to see her child, hoping she would come through the operation.

That operation on our daughter took place. The chief surgeon was a Jew, called Cohen; the number two was a Muslim, called Ahmad – amazingly the brother of a lady Promilla knew back in Pakistan – and the third was a Christian, called Fingleton, from Australia. I remember saying to my irreligious friends at the time, "Boy, if there's anything in this religious business I'm on to a winner here – I've got three of them working hard for me!"

The operation was successful but, of course, they wouldn't be able to tell us whether the child would survive, having been so long under the anaesthetic, or whether she would be normal if indeed she did survive. We had to go home but we visited the hospital every second day and rang them at eight o'clock every morning. For weeks the answer was always the same, "Your child has had another night, she's all right but you must understand that she's in a very critical condition."

This went on and on until the great day came when we were sent for to take her home. I still remember the Sister, who had been in charge all the time, saying to Promilla, "I'm telling you this, Mrs Mullen, some people have spent an awful lot of time 'on their benders' for this one, because there were whole days when none of us could see how she could possibly make it and here she is, going home today." That was a tremendous experience for all of us and even as I tell it now, forty years later, my voice breaks because of the incredible emotion involved – the incredible victory it seemed to me, of the National Health Service, of the fortune of being in Manchester when it happened, one of the only two places in the United Kingdom where the operation could have taken place.

We brought her home and, amazingly, she began to thrive at once and we never had any problems thereafter; even those two desperate problems that we had feared, there never was a sign of them. One was that her food pipe would not be wide enough to permit her normal food to go down – it always has done. The other was that, because blood had been denied to her brain for so long under the operation she might be somewhat retarded – that didn't happen either. Finally we were told that only five per cent of babies survive the operation… and Cherry, our daughter, was one of the five per cent.

She is called Cherry, incidentally, because originally Promilla was going to have twins. One of those was lost, and we had decided that if one was a boy we would call him Chester because he was a Man-child born in Man-chester and then, looking for a name similar if it was a girl, we said she could be called Cherry. When we told this to a lady knitting some baby clothes with very bright red wool, she said, "Oh yes, look at this lovely cherry colour… it will be just right." So somehow or other the name Cherry was fixed on for a girl.

Meanwhile the British Council were planning to post me from Manchester to Nigeria, Abraka in the Delta, because there was a new training college starting up there and I was to go and run it. It was totally unwise from the health point of view to move out of Manchester with our baby at that time and the British Council knew this, but they couldn't necessarily make the adjustment. I would have to go alone, which would cause problems for my wife back in Britain.

As it happened, the Biafran War broke out in Nigeria at that time and the area around where the new college was to be opened was overrun by different soldiers. I well remember the British Council officer who was trying to explain to me where exactly it was, being unable to find it on the map; in fact, I was lucky to find it myself. So it was touch-and-go for quite a time whether I would go or not, but the British High Commission in Nigeria intervened and said it was unwise and unsafe for any British people to be posted to the Delta at that point, especially in Abraka, and that we should all wait for a while before we assisted this new Teacher-Training college. They also pointed out that there was no use yet because it couldn't get going because of the war. So I was told to wait and was then given a posting in the English Language Teaching Institute in Portland Place, London, just opposite the B.B.C.

I had been advised that in order to make sure my pension rights were transferred correctly, having taught in England and overseas, I should teach for one term in a school in England.

This was arranged for me in a little primary school in Moss-side in Manchester. It was the last term of this school, which had been condemned, and I have never forgotten some of the events that happened there. The first thing that struck me – so different from all the other schools I had ever taught in – was the sheer poverty of the children. One child used to arrive late in school simply because he had only one set of clothes and his mother had to wash and dry them each day and sometimes this couldn't happen. The other thing was that the headmistress, who had been there for a long time, had seen girls come in, leave the school at fourteen or sixteen and bring their own offspring back into the school a few years later. She was on to the third generation of children in this cycle of near poverty in Manchester.

The children were delightful. I remember once seeing a fight go on underneath a desk between one of the blackest little girls you have ever seen in your life and a white boy, absolutely albino – it was like a caricature of race relations! They were aged about seven or eight and were pulling each other's hair. So I said, "Come on you two, out you come." They came out and stood up in front of me, shivering. I said to the girl, "What's your name?" She hesitated and finally blurted out, "Marilyn Monroe." I had enough sense not to react and turned to the little boy and asked his name; his little voice said, "Gregory Peck, Sir." I have to tell you that I managed not to laugh, but this was the kind of society they came from. There was another boy in that class who had eleven names... one of each member of the Manchester United Football team!

I recollect asking the headmistress and an inspector who passed through one day, whether this cycle could not be broken somehow – this cycle of poverty of the child leaving school at fourteen or sixteen and coming back with their own child. They said the social pressure on the families around there – to leave school, get married, have a child – was so great that no matter how hard you tried, for the majority of those children you could never break that cycle.

On the issue of colour, we had another very amusing incident. Enoch Powell made a famous speech about 'rivers of blood'. He excited the nation so greatly about this that some local people in

Manchester noticed that my wife hadn't appeared in the shops near where we lived for some days, with the little baby who they had seen in the pram, and wanted to know how she was getting on. When my wife didn't turn up they assumed that it was because she had been upset by Enoch Powell's remarks. Nothing could have been further from the truth but they came in a sort of delegation to the flat. Promilla told them that she had heard about it but it hadn't worried her; in fact, she hadn't even bothered to think about what he had said. They said, "We've missed you and want you to come again as you're such fun – you've brought so much colour into our lives." Nowadays, when we have something amusing happening at home sometimes, we say, "Oh but you've brought so much colour into our lives!"

Another amusing event that happened to us there was that we had always invited people to come and stay with us at Christmas. On one occasion my sister was staying with us from Dublin. Promilla had also asked a cousin to come and stay, as there was room for two. However, it turned out later that the cousin brought along her sister, who she always had with her for Christmas, and the sister brought her dog, a big one which she couldn't leave behind. Also, a great friend of mine, the geography master who had been with me in Pakistan, turned up because I had said whenever you're around come and spend Christmas with us, which he did! Fortunately he had brought his sleeping bag with him. Now, by good luck, the flat next door to us in Manchester was being vacated over Christmas by two nurses whom we knew a little, so we were able to park some of our guests in the flat next door and take the rest in our place, including the dog, and we had the Christmas of our lives.

On Guy Fawkes night the Head of our Department gave a traditional party and invited all of the students and we used to have a marvellous bonfire. One of the students was from Japan and was, unusually, a Roman Catholic. He was thrilled to join in and one of the interesting things was relating the sense of humour of Japanese to the sense of humour of us in Britain. This particular night he burst out laughing when, at one stage, I went across and grabbed him and said, "Now, this is where we throw the Roman Catholics in the fire." Towards the end of the evening when the fire had died down a lot and was about two feet high with just embers glowing over a wide space, I whispered to him, "If we go across in a moment when this fire is a little cooler, and lift it up, underneath you will find printed there: *Made in Japan!*" He hooted with laughter and was able to see the kind of fun we always had about things made in Japan.

Moving down to London to my next posting was not so difficult because Promilla's cousin was a solicitor just south of London and helped us greatly in buying a house where we could live within reach of the city. Even when we were delayed getting into the house because one of those 'breaks in the chain' held us up for a few months, he was able to arrange for us to stay in the flat of one of his clients until the house became empty and we were able to move in. That was such a help and started us off in our new posting on the right foot.

11
Some Anecdotes

At this point I would like to break off from the straightforward chronology of this narrative and inject a few incidents, bits and pieces, which I remember very clearly as having an effect on me, both at the time and in my memory later on. The first two concern my old nanny and neighbours in Holycross in Tipperary.

Whenever, as a tiny child, I felt that some people had been unkind or unfair to me or had hurt me in some way, I would go running to Nanny and tell her all about it and she would very often say, "Don't' mind those people, they don't know any better." She used this phrase, "They don't know any better," and would sometimes add, "I'm sure, they wouldn't do it if they did know better. The only thing you can do for those people is to pray for them." She got me to take the line that these people really needed to be helped to become more civilised human beings. However, I realise now, looking back, that what she actually did for me was a tremendous gift because she implanted in me some sense of forgiving people before they actually hurt or harmed me so that when they did do it my first reaction tended to be, "Ah, well, they don't know any better!"

The second involved my old friend the postman's son who, when I went back to Tipperary as an adult years after my father's death, talked to me about the very night my father had died and said how good he had been to all the different members of the communities around there, Roman Catholics, Protestants, rich, poor, sick, and so on. He used a sentence which I thought was terribly kind: "Ah, sure, your parents were role models for people for miles around this place in those days."

The next four incidents occurred whilst I was at Bishop Foy School, the first during the holidays:

One day I was walking down the street in Dublin, just outside Trinity College, when my overcoat caught in the overcoat of a lady coming from the opposite direction and both of us were flung against each other. We both stepped back and I said, "So, sorry…" but as we stepped back we were pulled together again – bump, bump! We looked at each other and realised that a button on my overcoat had gone through a buttonhole of her coat (because both our coats were open and blowing in the wind) and we were brought together in this extraordinary fashion. I still regret that we never got each other's names, telephone numbers or anything because it was the most amazing sudden coming-together with a girl that I have ever had in my life!

Then there was the matter which concerned the master who was teaching us the Irish language. He had gone to Spain for part of the Civil War and had just come back and he used to spend much more time trying to get us interested in the Civil War in Spain than he did actually teaching us Irish. To be honest, to this day I still haven't sorted out some of the things that he told us – I expect he was telling us the truth but it was a very odd situation.

The next was my disappointment at the behaviour of the New Zealand Rugby players when they came to England after the war; they played so improperly that to this day I am unable to relate happily to them when they play, which proves, I'm afraid, that you never get a second chance to make a first impression!

Another was the strange feeling we had when we looked at small steamer ships that came into the River Suir in Waterford during the war, with holes in their sides from having been hit by a shell. It gave one an empty feeling about the war – that something was happening out there on the sea that you couldn't really quite relate to, yet it seemed so calm and quiet with this ship just moored by the quayside with a big hole in its side.

The next incident that I remember very clearly concerned the first master in the school I went to in my job in Northern Ireland. He was a very quiet man and in his childhood had been in Hungary, Romania, Bulgaria and such countries, because I think his mother was an actress or an opera singer there. All these many years later, he used to go off during the summer holidays, in the height of the Cold War, slip behind the Iron Curtain somehow or other and manage to smuggle out some of his relations and get them away to Australia mainly and, I believe, Canada. None of us ever knew the full details and we didn't enquire because in those days such a thing was best not talked about at all, no matter how much you knew about it – and we knew very little except that he did do it, with great bravery.

Also, while I was in that school an amusing event occurred in the theatre one night when the actor who was playing in a pantomime proved to be too fat to go through the hole in the stage – because he was a bad character and was going to hell! There was this tremendous explosion and flash of light and the actor was supposed to disappear… but when the smoke cleared, there he was, in the middle of the stage, stuck halfway down the hole by his fat tummy. A voice from the back of the theatre shouted, "Holy Moses, Hell is full!"

Perhaps the most amusing piece of writing I came across was by Bernard Levin. He wished he, "…could get it into the head of Mr Anthony Wedgwood Benn (whose head, by the way, may be described as the thick end of the wedge) that nationalisation was not the answer." When I repeated this remark, which I thought was rather funny, to an Australian friend of mine, he immediately said, "It's wonderful that you can do that sort of thing in England. Even in Australia, if you were to make a remark like that you would be held to task and it wouldn't be acknowledged as a joke at all."

Which leads me to another Australian friend of mine who often had to make after-dinner speeches and used to preface his remarks with, "Thank you, ladies and gentlemen, for asking me to be with you this evening. I have had a very good dinner and have enjoyed myself immensely and I hope you have, too. I know you are already aware that I come from Australia, the continent down-under, so you are bound to have various opinions about my ancestry. The only thing I would like to make quite clear is that my ancestors were hand-picked by the very best judges in England."

That Australian had worked full-time for Moral Re-Armament, as had Peter Howard. Peter told us how his friend, Lord Hailsham, who, when a Minister of Government, went to Russia to meet his counterpart. In the Russian Minister's office he noticed there was nothing on his desk except a Bible. Now Hailsham was well-known as a Christian and quite a good Christian apologist, too, but he wasn't going to jump at the bait immediately so he stayed quiet until just before the meeting was over. He then said to this Russian, "I notice you have a Bible on your desk… that's interesting." The Russian brought his fist down on the Bible with a tremendous thump and said, "Yes, I have, and in here there are two revolutionaries, Jesus Christ and Saint Paul, and if Christians had lived the way those two had lived, the dark side of our revolution would never have been necessary."

A strange view of life was given to me by a grandson of Mahatma Ghandi who, in an address to quite serious people in Britain, said, "I know that many of you will think that my grandfather was a funny little man in a bed sheet and indeed he was, and did many things that one could laugh at, just as he did many things that one could applaud; however, I would just like to make one comment – my grandfather got up at four o'clock every morning for forty years of his life and never once took a holiday, struggling to give my people values which the British brought to India and without which he knew our independence would not be worth the paper it was written on."

Much more haunting was a remark I heard made by General Montgomery on television when he was recounting the Battle of Alamein. He told how his tank commanders had come to him in the middle of the night and told him they were losing tanks at the rate of nine a minute and there were seven men inside each tank – could they withdraw, re-group and go in again? Monty's next remark was, "I had known this was going to happen and I had my answer ready. I said, No, you stay in there and when the sun comes up we'll see the Germans going off in one direction, the Italians in another and then we'll pause and decide which to mop up first."

An incident occurred while I was moving from Manchester to London. I was sitting in the British Council English Language Teaching library when a person approached me from behind and said, "Excuse me, you're Mullen aren't you?" I looked round and said, "Yes, I am." He was one of the senior officers in our English Teaching Division at that time and he said, "Do you think you can go to India for us on Friday?" Now this was Tuesday! I said, "I beg your pardon?" and he said, "We have to run a seminar in a place called Dharwar and whoever was going has just let us down so we have to fill it quickly and you are about the only person we know who can do it and is free at the present time; how about it?" I said, "Well, I have a wife and a new-born child and am halfway between Manchester and London, moving house, but I'll look into it." It so happened that it was possible for me to go, not on Friday but on Saturday, and finally I got to Dharwar, which is out in the centre of the north of Mysore State. It was a new University, Karnataka University, and I was running a course in English language, especially speaking, for lecturers in Mofussil colleges. ('Mofussil' means rural or country colleges.) The lecturers, staff and students in these colleges were not at all au fait with English but were struggling to carry on in it or the local language. I had a marvellous time there and they treated me very well.

After dinner most senior professors used to go for a long, slow stroll around the beautiful grounds of this new university and they invited me to go with them. I was considerably younger than them but I went along and listened to their conversation and joined in here and there. These men discussed matters in a way that at first I couldn't quite latch on to and then it dawned on me. They would never resort to physical violence to sort out a problem or a question – they would rather walk away from it or yield to their opponent than have it solved by violence. Somehow they made it clear that if you resort to violence you have left your humanity behind and have gone back to the animal stage. This interested me because, coming from Ireland and Europe with all our wars, the attitude was, in real terms, amazing, although of course in theory it is quite easy to understand; but theory is very different from practice in these matters, as we Europeans know.

It was on my way back from Dharwar that I had the most interesting experience of all. When I reached Belgaum and was waiting for the aeroplane to come up from Bangalore and take us on to Bombay, a very tall, Anglo-Indian official of Indian Airlines came up behind me and whispered in my ear, "Excuse me, Sir. I'm not supposed to tell you this, but actually the plane you are waiting for will not arrive because it lost its windscreen wipers in the monsoon on the way down to Bangalore and it can't take off again to come back here until it gets some more. They've had to send them down from Bombay so I'm afraid you're not going to be able to fly tonight; however, it's not been made public yet."

I immediately went back to my taxi driver, having fortunately remembered the golden rule – never let your taxi driver leave until you are satisfied everything is in hand for the next stage. He was eminently sensible and said, "There must be other people on this flight who are in the same pickle as you and want to get down to Bombay. What I suggest is that you all get together and arrange for a taxi to drive you there. I can't because I haven't got a licence which takes me across state boundaries but I'll organise one for you if I can."

Taking his advice, I found four others and my taxi driver took us to the Indian Airlines office in Belgaum and introduced us to the top man of the taxi rank. This man was obviously 'Mr Taxi, Belgaum' because he had the whole thing fixed. All we had to do was go to the Indian Airlines desk, give in our tickets and they gave us back exactly the amount of money that he was going to charge us for the journey down to Bombay.

This great man, 'Mr Taxi', walked out into the middle of the concourse, called a chap over and said, "Bring your taxi here," which he did. "Tell those people to get out," and the poor unfortunate people already in it got out. He then said, "Now take these five people to Bombay." "Yes Sir," was the reply. So we were almost pushed into the taxi and then he said to the driver, "Are you alright, have you enough petrol?" The reply was, "Sir, I have no stepney." Stepney is the word used locally for spare wheel. So he walked across to another taxi and said, "Here, you, give this man your Stepney," (all the cars in those days were based on the old Austin or Morris) and he took out his spare wheel and handed it over! By now our luggage had been put in and we were ready to go.

I sat in the back beside a rather nice, small, very well-dressed Sikh gentleman, covered in bangles and bracelets, coming back from a party after his honeymoon. On the other side of him sat an enormous Sikh, a huge man. In front sat a couple of indeterminate origin and the driver, and off we set.

Part of the problem was the monsoon, which had wiped away the windscreen wipers that were the cause of all this trouble; it had also washed away a lot of the road. There was mud everywhere and we were driving and sliding along the side of the mountain, hoping to get there, until suddenly, this enormous Sikh at the back broke the silence and said, "Look, this bloody fool can't drive. I'm going to drive and when we get to such-and-such a place we will stop and I will give you all dinner and then he can drive us the rest of the way down to Bombay." And that is precisely what happened. The driver meekly got out, came round and sat in the back and the big fellow got into the driving seat and drove expertly. I discovered afterwards that he ran a huge trucking firm, having started at the very bottom of the transport business.

When we arrived where the dinner was to be given, we stopped and had a very good dinner and this man paid for it. As we were standing up, I began to put my hand in my pocket to get out some money but the smaller Sikh touched me immediately and said, "No, no, don't – he would be terribly insulted. Don't do it. Accept your dinner."

After that we carried on and got down to Bombay safely and with better results than we would have had on a plane because this taxi driver drove each one of us to the particular address we wanted.

He dropped me off at the hotel where I had booked because I was going to fly on from Bombay to Karachi and then go on to Lahore and see my wife's parents. There was only one flight a week between India and Pakistan in those days, so bad were the relations between Bombay and Karachi. I rang various friends I had in Bombay and they all had the same story. "Lloyd, we're awfully sorry, we can't come and help you because we are flooded here. My car, even though it's in the garage, is half up to the axles in water."

As I was making these phone calls from the hotel, I noticed that there was an American girl, crying, in the middle of the foyer and so I went across to see if I could help. She had missed her plane and couldn't get back in time, there was no hope. Just as I was getting up from bending down to speak to her, a taxi drove into the forecourt of the hotel and the driver got out and dashed in to shelter. I ran out and shouted, "Driver-ji! Airport ke-pas jana jaldi." (To the airport at top speed, please!) He replied, "Sahib, ap Mussulman ho?" (Are you a Muslim?) I said, "No, I'm not… I'm a Christian." To which he said, "Lekin, ap Urdu-bolne-wala ho!" (But you are an Urdu speaker!) "All right, come on."

I got into the taxi with him and we drove off to the airport. In the spilling rain his brakes didn't work at all, but he dealt with this difficulty by selecting whichever lane on the highway had the least traffic – it didn't matter if it was going or coming – and finally we got to the airport in time. I caught my plane, got to Karachi and all was well.

An unusual meeting had taken place on my way back home to Dublin on one of my leaves. When journeying from Pakistan to England I went via Kenya and Uganda. In Kenya, some very kind friends took me to Lake Naivasha with some others to see the wonderful pink flamingos, which are world famous. When we got there we found that the lake had dried up to such an extent that the water was way out in the middle where the birds were, but there was dry sand for about two hundred yards between the normal edge of the lake and the water, and I could actually see some small trees that were usually under water but were now showing. Someone had to stay with the Land Rover because it was unsafe to leave it off the soft sand where we couldn't drive it as it would have sunk in, so I elected to stay.

I hadn't been there long when I noticed approaching, probably two hundred yards away, an absolutely classic group of very tall Masai warriors with their long spears, walking with great, slow dignity along the path between me and the other members of the party who had gone to the water to see the flamingos.

These Masai warriors were clad in their traditional dress, with the big shield, in the same auburn-red colour that one sees in so many tourist brochures. At first I was a little alarmed. I thought, 'five to one… and they've all got spears and I've only got a Land Rover and they might want it'. I went round and stood between the Land Rover and the path they were following and as I watched, with slight apprehension, I remembered what someone had told me: that the Masai were so proud they really didn't take any notice of other tribes, foreigners, or anybody at all. Indeed, when they came nearer and I realised they would pass about ten yards in front of me, I hoped this might be the case. And it was. They didn't even look sideways at me; they walked slowly and stately by with absolutely no turn of the head in my direction, their spears upright, and passed by as if I didn't exist. And how glad I was because it was a meeting that I had not expected and wouldn't have been able to deal with had anything happened!

Another amusing incident I remember from that visit to Kenya was told by a very old settler whose family had been in Kenya for three or four generations. This man had come to England in earlier times and had brought back a phonograph and some records. Since it was a new thing in that day he showed it to everybody, including the workers on his farm. He had been there so long that he spoke their language, and the sub-dialects, and was very friendly with them. They all gathered round while he played some records and they listened and even attempted to dance to the music, but it didn't quite fit their African style. However, after some time he overheard one of the older Africans, a dear old member of the tribe and an old, old friend of his who had been there for a long time, say to one of his friends, "What a very little thing it takes to amuse a white man!"

During that short visit to Kenya, I was taken by some friends to a farm up on Mount Elgon close to the border with Uganda. While I was there they took me right up to look down into Uganda and pointed out various places and beauty spots. Uganda is a very beautiful country. We saw a village and when I asked the name of it they said, "Cheperaria." Now it was the nearest name I had ever heard to 'Tipperary', my own county in Ireland, so I asked them again and they said, "Yes, Cheperaria." I asked how to spell it and they told me, but said the last letter 'a' is hardly pronounced in speech so that while you read it as Cheperari**a**, it comes out of the mouth as Cheperari, which is very close to Tipperary. I am glad that the other very beautiful green country that has a 'Tipperary' is Uganda – Uganda and Ireland both beautifully green countries.

My mind here goes back to a part of the world which isn't at all green. That is the journey down the mountainside from Kashmir into the plains of India. I made it in very unusual circumstances when a friend, a Scottish lady, Diana Hay-Thorburn, asked me to drive her car down to the plains because she was afraid it would get stolen by some of the soldiers fighting across Kashmir.

After agreeing to do so, I then discovered that she wanted me to take an eighty-year-old friend who was staying with her on her houseboat, a twenty two-year-old girl companion of hers who had come out from England to stay with her and have six months' experience of the sub-continent, and also a large dog which belonged to the old lady. Would I take them down and drop them off in the plains? Firstly, this Morris Traveller had been used for so long on rough country up there that it had almost no shock absorbers left, so it went bang, bang, bang. Secondly, because the Indians were fighting a war against the Chinese, they had requisitioned the road for themselves and there were only certain times of the day when you could go up or down because they were sending up enormous two-hundred-truck convoys carrying equipment – when you met a convoy you simply had to get to the side of the cliff and wait there until the last truck went by.

I think it took two days and three nights to get down, but we eventually made it and got to a place where there was a 'Rest House' as it's called, but it's the only Rest House in the whole sub-continent that I ever came across that had no food, no water, no lamps, nothing, but it was open. So we were able to get in, drag our charpoys into the open air (because it would be too impossibly hot to sleep inside), and set up mosquito nets, which fortunately we had, and aim to have some sleep. Unfortunately, the great dog was a guardian to his own mistress and would not let me go anywhere near her charpoy to help tie up her mosquito net, etc., so the young girl had to do all the running. Finally we ended up with the old lady out in the front, the young girl in on the veranda and, luckily I had another companion with me – he and I slept out in the open.

We managed to deliver everybody safely to their destination, leave the car where it was intended, and go on from Pathankot to the border, where I was able to get across fairly easily through the fortunate accident of meeting someone else whom I knew and he gave me a lift back to Lahore.

One of the most remarkable things about my entire stay in the sub-continent was that I was constantly coming upon people I knew at just the right moment – these coincidences made life much easier than it would otherwise have been.

Probably the most remote and, at that time, little-visited area of the world that we came across was Kafristan, high up, way beyond Chitral which is the northern-most of the separate kingdoms beyond Pakistan going right up to Afghanistan and China.

Kafristan is inhabited by a group of people called the Kalash. No one knows how they got there, what religion they are and why their means of buying and selling is done through cowrie shells, although they are about two thousand miles from the sea in any direction. They have a long tradition of independence. We didn't see the men because they were far away in the hills, herding or looking after distant farms. We saw some of the women who, probably because they had about three or four visits per year from outsiders, had developed a tiny tourist industry of doing some dances in the only clothes they had, a long, brown, friar-like gown (they looked like followers of St. Francis!). They wore very bright caps and had a most pleasing attitude.

Getting to them had been no easy business. We had had to leave our Land Rover miles away and climb over a very high mountain. We had been warned that we should take a lot of water with us. We didn't take that warning seriously enough and discovered that, by the time we reached the Kalash area, we were parched. We found our way down to them finally, and managed to come across what I can only describe as a muddy water hole. We were in such a condition that we just threw ourselves down on the ground and put our faces into it to get what water we could. We couldn't use our hands because we just got handfuls of mud and muck. With our mouths we could sift something out. All thought of what diseases we were imbibing into our systems faded in the need to get some liquid.

After finding a Kalash village and seeing the women dance, we spent the night in a cowshed and next morning discovered that the way out was not to go back up over the mountain, but to go down to the stream nearby and then into a cave in which there was a pathway about two feet wide, close to the side. This pathway became submerged in the water, and we hardly dared to walk on for fear that the next step might plunge us into water beyond our depth – the path was about three feet below the water. However, we were able to walk along, cautiously, clinging to the wall of the cave, until we came out at the other end and were able to climb around some bluffs and get back to our Land Rover, feeling both relief and wonder.

Three other places are worth mentioning, because I was fortunate enough to visit them, albeit briefly. They all contained trees and this is interesting because throughout Pakistan, wherever you go, there are not very many trees to be seen.

The first was up high in a mountain called Tirich Mir, not far from where we were in those valleys I have just talked about, the Kalash valleys. One day we drove along in our Land Rover and went through a pine forest; the trees well separated from each other but giving a very pleasant effect on the light snow beneath them and the view of the high mountain in the distance. Suddenly we came to a landslide and I remember John saying, "Oh, not jeepable!" So we left the Land Rover and walked across a path which the local people had actually worn in the snow with their bare feet. We walked perhaps a mile through this pine forest and came out and stopped in our tracks because there, only about one hundred yards away, seemed to be the base of this great mountain, Tirich Mir. We were at 9,000 feet and it is 22,000 feet high, so if you work that out, you get to about 13,000 feet of absolutely clear snow, just snow going straight up into the sky. We stood there in awe, leaning our heads right back to get a view to the top. My companion said, in the silence surrounding us, "If this was in Europe there would be cars parked for miles," and the only car we had was about a mile away in the forest.

Another forest was entirely of juniper trees. Some say it is the largest juniper forest in the world with some of the trees being about six thousand years old. This was at a place called Ziarat, near Quetta in Baluchistan and, being up on a plateau, it was a favourite summer resort of the founder of Pakistan, Mohammed Ali Jinnah, who had lung problems and therefore trouble with his breathing. These juniper trees have a strange, very appealing colour in their leaves and they create a wonderful atmosphere.

The third set of trees was, in a way, entirely artificial. Not too far from Lahore, in the plains, it was very large and entirely irrigated by small streams which had water taken from the River Ravi. We were again told it was the largest irrigated forest in the whole world, and I could well believe it because wherever you went you had to stop and walk over a little bridge which had an irrigation channel underneath bringing water to the trees. You could actually see the roots of many of the trees reaching into the water. At least it was cool here and a change from the generally hot weather one experienced in Lahore, although whenever we visited that forest we almost always went in the cool season, sometime between October and February.

12
Work In London

I will now return to the straightforward chronology of this tale and say what London felt like after I had been in Manchester and the rest of the world.

I'd never worked in London before and can only say that when I moved down there I realised that 'Respect' with a capital 'R', was out and 'Vulgarity' with a capital 'V', was in. But one was expected not to say so, even though everybody knew it and took advantage of it. The animal had gained the ascendency in men; women had no option but to fit in otherwise they were regarded as old maids before their time. This subtle bullying may not have been the case, but it is how it appeared to me.

Worse still, the British Council and Moral Re-Armament were both wilting under the pressure to sexualise and commercialise. 'Absolute' standards were out, 'relative' standards were in, so each individual could then decide how 'relative' to be. This, of course, had one good side in that it did at least allow individuals to be just that – individuals. But it was based on a false economy; a boom period for western capitalism with lip-service paid to developing the rest of the world. Those of us who were actually in the developing business could feel it.

So much for the background atmosphere to life in London in the early 1970s. Even clergymen had become confused by the tide of animal materialism sweeping over the then, so called, 'free western world'. Many were not offering a genuine alternative life-style. It was a shame and still is.

My own preference in all this had been, from childhood, to stick to what Jesus had said and done in the New Testament. Fortunately they are very short pieces compared with the whole Bible and they are easy to read. The hour I took each morning taking them in gave me a base from which to listen to all that was going on around me and to either join in or lead in the conversation.

Our work in the English Language Teaching Institute, to which I had been posted, was very simple and straightforward, however complicated it might appear to the outsider. Our business was simply to develop better ways of teaching English to foreigners, all foreigners, in their own countries, in Britain, and from all countries and all classes.

Pretty well anyone could come along and register, and they did, both as individuals, and in groups from embassies, businesses and other countries, and there was a wide variety of people to teach. We had three or four different levels, and the classes went on all through the day and evening. We had our language labs and study rooms where we could develop materials and try them out and see whether they worked. On the whole they did.

However, international events, as always, played a part in disrupting what we might call the smooth tenor of this apparently academic-only and educational-only institution.

The first was that Nixon in the United States, and the Chinese were making secret negotiations to bring China back into the world-fold. This was being done by Yahya, the President of Pakistan; he was the intermediary. But the way it affected us was that the Chinese discovered that in their cultural revolution they had killed off practically everyone who spoke English because that was a sign they were Patrician or upper class or whatever, not of the Proletariat – nobody in the Proletariat spoke English. So they were now, at this key moment in their history, short of diplomat interpreters who could manage English.

Britain had no relations officially with China at that time, so the result was that half a dozen would-be Chinese diplomat-interpreters were somehow or other smuggled into England and lived just up the road from us in Portland Place, at the Chinese Embassy, and would sneak out of the door at about one-minute-to-nine in the morning, scuttle down the street and into our building and spend the whole day learning English. They were all dressed exactly the same, they all had exactly the same hairstyles and all looked almost the same and more or less had the same height. I am told one or two of them were ladies, but was never able to tell which, no matter how hard I tried.

However, they worked very, very hard; in fact, one person worked so hard all day long in the language lab that he or she actually caused the machine to melt – some of the insulation in the tape machine melted. Which reminds me, we had the most excellent technician who could do almost anything – put anything right in those days – but even this was beyond him!

Another way in which the international regimes of the world intervened was that Russia, at that time, had the rest of the world, and London in particular, absolutely chock-full of spies – spies doing this, spies doing that, spies doing everything! When Sir Alec Douglas-Hume became Prime Minister, in his quiet, gentlemanly, border-of-Scotland way, he sent home one hundred and fifty-two of them one night. They just had to leave. Next day I discovered I had lost half of two of my classes, they weren't there any more – the Russians were gone! I can only say I had not known they were spies, although I had known from meeting them at parties, that they were not allowed to drink alcohol *during* a party. This meant, of course, that they drank a lot of alcohol *before*, so that whenever we arrived at a party, we found them in a high state of excitement and happiness and telling us what good teachers we were and how much they loved being in England, etc. Perhaps one ought to have suspected they were spies by the way they behaved!

That led to another strange international incident for me personally:

I had attached to me (that was the expression at the time) a Cuban lady who was very good at speaking English and was, in fact, a teacher of physical education and gymnastics back in Cuba and was an avowed Communist. She was very clever and hard-working and was to be taught to become a trainer of teachers of English back in Cuba, and maybe in other parts of the Communist world. The way in which we worked together was that I prepared a schedule for her, which she attended, but otherwise she did whatever I did; for instance, if I made a tape, she made a tape; if I tested a tape she would do so, too; if I was teaching four or five people, she would come along and watch and then try to teach four or five people and so on. Anyway, she disappeared – along with the Russians – and did so in such a way that her desk, which was at the other end of my office, still had in it some of her private things. Her coat, with some pencils still in the pocket, hung on the back of the door, and she never came back to collect them. I made some enquiries but found the addresses and telephone numbers that we had just did not connect; she was nowhere to be found. I was pleased in a way not to have to take any formal action, just let it go, but it was sad that she had gone away without our even being able to say goodbye to each other.

Imagine my amazement when about six weeks later I went into a Lyon's Corner House in Oxford Street, and there she was, sitting down in one of those cubicles that Lyon's used to have there. I opened my mouth with a big smile to say, "Hello, how are you," and she put her fingers up to her lips as if to tell me not to speak. So I sat down opposite her (she was by herself fortunately), and she had no hesitation in telling me the whole story. Apparently when the Russian spies were kicked out they all had great batches of papers, possessions of this and that, and tapes, etc., which they had to get rid of pretty hastily from their own private flats as well as from their offices, and a large number of these things had been dumped on her. Because she was good at English and knew some Russian, she was in the business of sorting them out and even doing some translation. She and I had a good laugh about the whole matter.

The type of training that we gave brought in an Australian girl. She was about twenty-two and had just left university, and she came for some training in language and was very good. She brought me one tremendous gift, which was to tell me of the famous (well he became famous afterwards) Australian writer, Patrick White. I had not heard of him at all until she mentioned him and then I began to read his books which were, indeed, brilliant. So I was not surprised when, years later, my wife and I were with her mother high up in the mountains in North India, sitting on the veranda looking across at a panorama of twelve peaks all over 20,000 feet high, when we heard on the six o'clock news that evening: 'This year's Nobel Prize for literature goes to Patrick White of Australia, that writer from the continent down under who has uncovered for his readers great continents which they never knew lay under their own minds.' That citation absolutely summed him up for me.

He had the ability to pass on to the reader a full picture of, shall we say, three different people having lunch together then, after a siesta, all waking up with the confused thoughts of their immediate events, past history and future hopes going through their minds, and the inter-relatedness of these three people to each other in the past, present and future. He was able to keep all this so clear that you knew on which wavelength you were as a reader and could understand and relate to each person's hopes and fears as they developed. An absolutely brilliant achievement. I sometimes feel he has never been given the credit he deserves, even though he received the Nobel Prize.

One very sad aspect of the teaching that we had to do in the Institute was the fact that so many wives of those we taught couldn't speak any English. You found yourself at a party able to talk to the man you were teaching and maybe to one or two of his children who may have been running about, but there would be his wife, quite often able to speak other languages but not English, and just standing about, occasionally talking to another lady who happened to speak the same language as she did but otherwise more or less silent. This circle of silence which surrounded these ladies was a powerful stimulus to us to try to get as many of them in to be taught as possible, but that wasn't easy because they either had other social arrangements to attend or were far away and couldn't get to the building easily. But it did alert me to the way in which women are excluded from so much of the normal things of life where men don't even have to think – they just arrive and everything is served up on a plate!

A pleasant thing gradually made itself apparent to me when I was commuting in and out from Sutton, where we lived. There was a great calmness and easy pleasantness associated with our work, which certainly was not associated with all the other commuting people I saw around me. This calmness I think resulted from several things.

One was the nature of the work itself, the actual teaching of a class of probably not more than twelve or thirteen people, and the actual production of material for these classes, whether it was written or to be spoken.

Then there were the people involved. It didn't take me very long to realise that the actual people who decide to work for the British Council are a pretty calm lot compared with others. There may be many reasons for this – one is that they are not fearfully ambitious to get to the top and make thousands of pounds, another is that they are very happy to have the chance to expand in what they are interested in doing, which is, in the particular case I'm talking about, language – the teaching and the learning of language – and that, of course, necessarily means calm.

Another point, of course, is that they are essentially interested in other people. In a classroom it is not a matter of the teacher teaching, it is the matter of the pupil learning, so that if a teacher is to be successful he almost has to be, by definition, more interested in his audience.

This is probably the place to say that in general I found I was very fortunate to have decided to work with the British Council, simply because my colleagues throughout were such pleasant people, they really were, and part of the reason undoubtedly was they had decided to take up a line of action that would help others rather more than it helped themselves. Now I don't want to suggest that we were perfect. No, I remember the following two statements which show both sides of this:

The first side was one of our most senior officers saying the British Council was probably the last great organ of state where a human being could get paid for following his hobby. The other side was the opening remarks of an introductory course for new recruits when the leading man in the recruitment area of the British Council said, "Gentlemen and ladies; I cannot emphasise too strongly that the British Council does not exist to provide careers for you. It exists to establish and keep good relations between Britain and the rest of the world, especially in all our cultural fields; that is our main business and it will put a considerable strain on you, so let's begin on that basis."

Another statement I remember being put forward by the finance boss, when he once said, "Of course, the problem with most institutes is that once you have paid everybody their salaries there is no money left to do anything else!" Hoots of laughter. But all these statements proved there was an attitude of reality in the Council.

Very similar, too, I found the attitude of my friends in Moral Re-Armament. Many of them were well-known and worked for no salary at all. How they lived, God only knows. But their main aim was always, for want of another expression, the other guy, the other country, how to help the other fellow and once that was achieved the other fellow was very happy to help you, and all sorts of relations built up over the world as a result.

So I found that a great deal of my life was surrounded by people who were not only pleasant to each other but pleasant to everybody else, whereas I was constantly hearing from my commuter friends when I spoke with them on the train or at the station, that there was 'this row in the office' and 'that row somewhere else' – quite dreadful. I just counted myself very fortunate; no credit to me, it just happened that way.

Another unusual and unexpected coincidence happened at this time. My wife and I were still living in Sutton, just south of London, and we drove around the place to see an area of the world that we didn't know at all, and came across the village of Ewell. It seemed to be one of the more appealing places in which we could settle and live maybe in the future and we decided that if we ever wanted to buy a house around the area, different from the one we were in already, we would try to find one in Ewell.

This brought us into contact with various estate agents and in talking to one of them and saying we were in the British Council, he mentioned that a friend of his also worked for the British Council in Peru and he gave us his name. Would you believe it, that chap had been with me on my course in Manchester and we knew each other very well. Not only that, but his father had at one time been the Vicar of St. Mary's Church in Ewell. So there was a kind of 'coming-home' effect – long before we ever did come home. He told us a lot about Ewell, having been brought up there as a boy.

This meant that my wife and I, having been at home in Manchester because of her history there, now had the feeling of being at home in Ewell, even before we ever went to live there!

Due to our daughter, Cherry's, very difficult start in life – and because the specialist had told both Promilla and me that we should not attempt to have another child because almost certainly Promilla would die if we did – we decided that Promilla would just attend to our child during her early years and that's what she did… she literally looked after her almost every moment of the day. It sounds like coddling, but actually it worked in the long run because we were told that even a very simple thing such as any sign of a sniffle, cough or cold, had to be dealt with at once for if it were allowed to develop and get down into Cherry's lungs or chest that might be the end of her. The result of this was that Promilla always kept anything that might be needed to stop a cough or cold.

One day when Cherry was about three or four years old and had a friend playing with her in our house, the other little girl coughed and Cherry said, "Oh no! Don't cough; my mother will chase you all round the house with a spoon!"

Anyway, the 'chasing around the house with a spoon' worked and, fortunately, Cherry survived the early years, including surviving, mercifully, what Promilla saw with horror from the window. Cherry went out into the back garden, saw a luscious wriggling worm, picked it up and swallowed it! So Promilla seized the child and went straight down to our doctor in the surgery nearby; he was one of those doctors who, in those days, you could more or less go in and see straight away. He wasn't at all upset and said, "Bad for the worm but not at all bad for the child. She'll be all right. It might even come out in one piece, but it doesn't matter if it doesn't."

On one occasion Cherry got a touch of mumps, and when the doctor came – he wasn't her usual doctor, he was standing in for him – he examined Cherry and asked if she had been vaccinated.

Fortunately we said she had and he said, "Thank God for that, otherwise she was a goner," just like that! We lived a little bit on the edge that Cherry might pop off if we didn't take good care of her, but Promilla really did spend all of her time looking after the child and the result we see today – a married lady with two healthy children.

My life in many ways was quite different because in my classes I was meeting people from parts of the world I didn't know. I can think immediately of people from Mexico, Venezuela, Hungary, Bulgaria and from different countries in the south of Africa, and it was fascinating to me to see how, in the same class, all these human beings speaking the same language, English, would be so different from each other. It seems obvious when I say it like this but actually, when you see it in the classroom, it is a very lively matter.

I developed a question which I used to ask the people at the beginning of the class which helped. It was this: "You've all paid your fees and we'll be meeting twice a week for the next three or four months and we'll do the best we can to improve our English together." I always made the joke that I was an Irishman and hoped my English would be a little bit better at the end of the course, too. I would then say, "Now, be honest about this, make up your mind and tell me what you think: Who here really wants to be mistaken for an Englishman or Englishwoman when they speak?" Usually out of sixteen there would be silence and maybe one head would nod, a few others would shake vigorously and I would then be able to say, "I can see your reaction, but if you have a problem between your head and your heart, that is to say if you want to be a very good speaker of English but don't want to be sympathetic to the cultural-values of the English people, then you will have more of a problem than your fellow students who are happy to learn." They always accepted this as truthful and they also accepted it as a matter of money; they had paid their fees and if they weren't going to back-up their money with their full enthusiasm then that was their decision.

The other thing was that many of them wanted to function in a particular area, medicine, engineering, etc., and we were able to devise classes for them and let them go off into that particular group when the time arose.

One other interesting type of teaching that we had was at the very top level – these were people who more or less spoke English perfectly but wanted to make sure that their idiom and reaction was almost as English as you could make it. They would be a very disparate group, usually the last class in the evening, and I found many funny and unusual things happened. For instance, on one occasion while we were in the middle of class there was a car crash outside in Portland Place and almost everyone got up from their desks, dashed across to the windows and looked out. They saw two cars that had banged into each other – nothing happening; then slowly the drivers' doors of each car opened and out got two men, one from each car. They stood still for a moment; one went back to his car to get out some documents and the other fiddled about in his pocket and got out a notebook, and then they approached each other slowly. They stood together and obviously asked each other questions and gave answers and wrote down things and then helped to disengage the two bumpers that had got entangled. Then, would you believe it, they shook hands and got back into their respective cars, one reversed and they both drove off. Now, the foreigners in the classroom couldn't believe it. Was this really how English people behaved? One lady said, "My goodness, if that had happened where I come from in Caracas, there would have been fifty people around, all fighting within a minute!"

Actually, that has something to say about language and how it fits in. Language is only an expression really of the culture of a place or the culture of a family or the culture of a country.

That same lady was an architect; her husband was also an architect in Rome and they used to commute at weekends – he would come one weekend and she would go to him the next weekend and so on. They were well-established people, aged about forty.

One of the members of our class was a doctor from Hungary, a heart specialist. He arrived late one evening and rushed into the classroom apologising. He said that as he came along the road he saw on a billboard a notice that the Swiss ambassador to Venezuela had been abducted, so he stopped to buy the paper. Before he could get any further, this lady from Venezuela said, "Good, I hope they kill him!" We were all appalled and asked her why; she was apparently at that time very opposed to her government and if any country, such as Switzerland, was so foolish as to recognise her government by sending them an ambassador and that ambassador was subsequently abducted, then serve him right and serve the country right and she hoped they would learn a lesson. Well that, too, wasn't exactly the British way of doing things and everybody learnt a little more – certainly I did.

One of the great advantages of the four years that we spent between Manchester and London before going abroad again was that we were able to pick up with my family in Ireland – mother, sisters, cousins and other relations – and my mother was able to see her only grandchild, Cherry. Promilla was also able to get to know many more of my family and I was able to get to know some of hers in Scotland and around London. This has helped greatly because as time has passed we do at least know who we mean when we use a name, like Cousin June, or Ethel and so on, whereas up to then we really hadn't known who we were talking about when we were occasionally listening to news of other relations or even our own relations. So that made quite a difference in building up the family.

It also acted as a forewarning of the kind of England that we might one day return to and it is certainly a fact that we didn't really want to return to London more than to anywhere else, even though we have done so now. If we had had a choice in the matter, we would have gone to our favourite place, Kirkby Lonsdale near the Lake District. In fact, we have stayed down here mainly due to health and family reasons and not country, because both Promilla and I are fundamentally country people; we can't completely enjoy living in the somewhat cooped up area of London.

13
SOUTH INDIA

One of the built-in excitements of working for the British Council was that I never knew what my next posting might be. Of course I had some say in the matter if I wanted to but, basically, one was selected for a particular post because it happened to fit the way other people were posted and what the demands from the rest of the world were at any one given moment. So I was, at first, very surprised to learn that my next posting would be to Bangalore in South India, to an organisation called the Regional Institute of English. This body had been assisted by the British Council for some years and existed to train the Teacher-Trainers of English in the four southern-most states of India – Tamil Nadu, Mysore, Kerala and Andhra Pradesh.

Things can easily become confused here because each of these states had a different capital and they also had different languages. I am going to put them down just for the sake of the family who come after.

Tamil Nadu's capital was Madras and its language was Tamil; Mysore's capital was Bangalore and its language was Kannada; Kerala's capital was Trivandrum and its language was Malayalam; Andhra Pradesh's capital was Hyderabad and its language was Telugu.

English was spoken pretty widely throughout all these four states by the educated élite but the point of the operation we had to carry out was that these four southern states wanted to assert their individuality against the capital of Delhi, up in the north, by developing their knowledge of English. They did not want to have to speak Hindi and take examinations in Hindi and be judged by their performance for civil service positions; they wanted to stick to

English and their own language because this is what had been left behind by the Imperial power in 1947.

As you can imagine, there were some tensions connected with this and there was a Central Institute of English in Hyderabad where many more aspects of this problem were worked out.

My particular business was to be the Director of Studies in the Regional Institute in Bangalore where I had many different assistants, basically four from each of the states. They would deal particularly with the students who came from those states and we would all manage together, we hoped, to improve both their English and their ability to teach it.

Promilla and I were very fortunate in being able to rent out our house in Sutton while we were away and, indeed, we have been fortunate on every occasion when we have done this, either in Sutton or Ewell, in contrast to many of my colleagues. The tenants looked after our homes very well and we had absolutely no problem at all.

We had equally good fortune in arriving at Bangalore to be met by the British Council driver. He had been a driver in the Indian Air Force, where he had taught the drivers of the most senior officers before he retired and came to work for the Council. He was an absolutely splendid man.

On our way from the airport to the house where we were going to live, we asked him about various things and I've never forgotten his reply to Promilla when she asked him, "Massudi, these theatres you've pointed out to us, are they busy, do they put on plays?" He very straightly said, "Oh yes indeed, madam, and there might occasionally be one which you could enjoy." And there were indeed occasions which we were able to enjoy.

This Muslim man gave one-tenth of his salary every month to support an orphanage for girls in Bangalore. He was altogether a most honourable man.

Having been there for some time he was able to assist me greatly settling into the job because he could get me to any place almost immediately without any bother. He also knew virtually everyone and was a good judge of when to tell me to be a little cautious about arrangements and when it was okay to go straight ahead, because he knew the story of Bangalore for the last twenty years.

This was very useful because we had to adjust to South India. The people of South India are very different from the people of North India and the people of each of the four states in which we were now working, were very different from each other. As Massudi, our driver, was a Muslim, my wife was able to relate to him very well because of her experience in Pakistan; he also knew of some of her relations who had been in India and in the Indian Army. This was extremely helpful because it created a safe platform from which to operate in occasionally tricky situations.

We had to begin from scratch with servants and in the matter of food and cooking, and there we came into the difference again between North and South India. Domestic settling-down was more difficult than academic and administrative settling-down. We had inherited an enormous house, the original property of a prince, and our drawing room was more than twenty-two yards long, that is longer than a cricket pitch! When we arrived, my predecessor's heavy sea baggage was hiding behind a pillar at one end of this room!

As Director of Studies, I was out-posted from the British Council into an Indian Institution and this meant that I did not have responsibility for the British Council Library in Bangalore, which was very efficiently run by a local librarian.

My boss from the British Council point of view was the Regional Representative in Madras. Fortunately an Irishman, he was the son of a bishop whom my mother knew well and a very learned man. He was very keen on acting so he and my wife got on very well because they had plenty to talk about whenever we met. He was also a brilliant man and a very good administrator. He told me he had learned his administration from his father, who believed that administration consisted of nothing more than keeping the details straight and 'keeping-on, keeping-on'.

His first 'keeping-on, keeping-on' instruction to me was to get out of the house we were living in as soon as I possibly could and find another because, legally, the British Council had no proper agreement concerning its lease. The reason for this was that the owner, the prince, had in his older years gone off to Benaras and had become a Holy Man there and left matters in the hands of his Bangalore solicitor. This solicitor was particularly obtuse and it was never clear to whom exactly we were paying the rent, though we paid it, and what the conditions were about who should maintain the building or anything. Mind you, it was all very well done and we didn't have expenses but, nonetheless, it was a highly unsatisfactory situation. So I immediately set about looking for a new house.

We were very fortunate in that the British Council's solicitor's wife worked for an estate agent in Bangalore. She told me of a beautiful house that was coming on the market for renting and we went along to see it. It was absolutely splendid, on Mahatma Gandhi Road, with beautiful gardens, an avenue one hundred yards long and a large turning circle in front of the house, with plenty of space around it. The floors throughout were Italian marble – very cool in Bangalore, which has a wonderfully comfortable climate anyhow – and also the interior design of the house was such that the servants could arrive in any room along their own stairs and passageways. The entire scheme was excellent. From the outside it looked like a small Scottish

Our Bangalore home

castle and, in the grounds, which unfortunately were badly looked after, there were fine trees.

The moment I saw it I knew that this was out of the question because the rent would be far higher than the British Council would permit me to pay. However, we met the owner, who turned out to be a very kind man, a very big business man indeed, and he knew where he came from. His father had begun selling oil by carrying oil cans from one house to another when he was young and from that moved up to a donkey cart, a bicycle, then a small van. His son carried on the business and by the time we met him he was 'Mr Oil South India'. He was a very humble man in addition to being very wealthy, and he was quite open and told me that he was willing to let us have the house if we could tell him how much we could pay. I told him what the maximum was and he immediately said, "Well then we'd better let you have it for one rupee less," which he did! Of course, I understood the reason; it was simply this:

If such a beautiful mansion was occupied by a member of the Civil Service, the Army or any leading Indian, the owner would never be able to get them out, such would be the legalities of it, whereas he knew that we in the British Council, having said we would go on such a day, would go on that day, and indeed we did.

The benefit to us as a family was enormous because it was the most beautiful place in which to live. It was very convenient, very calm and cool and with plenty of space for our growing daughter to run around in.

My wife maintains that the real reason he decided to give us the house was that our little daughter crept up behind him at one stage and put her hand into his and said, "Grandpa!" and this softened his heart so much that he gave us the house. Now this is a very feminine way of looking at the situation, and probably it's right, but I have to tell the whole story.

The house had three garages set out in different parts of the grounds and inside one of these the owner showed me his son's 1929 bull-nosed Austin, in beautiful condition. It was so polished and clean that they kept a sort of tent-affair over it in the garage which could be raised by a pulley when you wanted to take it out.

This car led to another discovery about Bangalore – the discovery took part in two stages. The first stage was that one of our previous British Council colleagues in the Regional Institute of English had decided to retire and stay on in India. He lived out of town, in the middle of the sticks really, and he had, would you believe it, a 1929 bull-nosed Austin. His driver would drive him to the airport in Bangalore and then take it back to his house in the country. Meanwhile he boarded a plane, went to Bombay, changed, flew to Heathrow and was met by his brother who took him to the car park where he got into his other 1929 bull-nosed Austin! Now those who can better that story must be very few and far between.

The second stage was that Bangalore had a tremendous number of vintage motorcars, all in almost pristine condition and owned by all sorts of people. Because Bangalore is about two hundred and fifty miles from the sea in any direction and is on a slight elevation, but not too high, it seems to be the ideal place in which to keep the metal and gadget parts of motorcars in working condition with the least trouble. Just as there is a 'Brighton Run' in England every year, so in Bangalore there used to be this wonderful 'Bangalore Run' of vintage cars when all sorts of amazing motors came out of their hiding places and took part in a splendid procession.

Promilla immediately set to work on the garden and in a very short time had, with the aid of a good, hard-working gardener, managed to clear out a huge amount of undergrowth and debris and get it all taken away; she soon had these beautiful trees set off by very neat, tidy beds surrounding their base. One of the trees was found to have a tiny shrine at its base, which the servants were convinced was a special Hindu place. Promilla encouraged them – she had sufficient knowledge of India to know that this was the thing to do – and they cleaned it, put new whitewash on it and brought flowers there every day and were very serious about it. Later on in our time there, I got seriously ill with some disease – no one knew exactly what it was, not even the doctor, although he kept coming every day as I was delirious and sick. We had a beloved – and I have to use the word 'beloved' – sweepress, Munneamma, who was a beautiful lady of about sixty years of age and always arrived to work with flowers in her hair and always swept the place immaculately. When she knew that I was ill, she went to this shrine every day and spent about five or ten minutes praying that I would get better. When I did recover she was able to say that it was because she had gone every day and prayed… we were inclined to think it was because the doctor had come every day and spent ten minutes at my bedside doing something with medicine! Who is to know the truth? Maybe they were both working together. Anyway, I am very grateful to them both for their consideration and here I am to tell the tale!

About twenty-five yards out from the side of the house down in the grove of trees, was an enormous tamarind tree, very tall indeed, and hanging from it a child's swing. It was by far the longest rope swing I have ever seen in my life. Cherry, of course, loved to get on to this and be pushed and I remember thinking to myself, as she got higher and higher, 'Good heavens, one day if she lets go she'll fly out over the wall into the next compound.' It was a great experience for her and she loved it and we loved watching her on it – it was thrilling.

One day it was almost too thrilling because while she was sitting on the swing by herself (her nanny was inside in the house looking out but not closely enough), a tribe of enormous monkeys arrived. They swing through the trees in India – you never know when they'll come and you never know when they'll go, but you certainly know when they arrive, probably about seventy to eighty, or maybe one hundred of them.

Suddenly, the entire garden was full of monkeys; they were up in the trees, down on the ground and running around. Promilla looked out from the side door to see Cherry, sitting on her swing, right in the middle of these monkeys. Cherry was about the size of a small monkey compared with the biggest ones in the tribe and any one of them could easily have grabbed her and gone off with her; a horrifying moment. Promilla merely said, "Cherry! sit still," and walked out slowly through the monkeys, who get half frightened, but they don't just run straight away. You have to have great courage to walk through them and Promilla walked slowly over to Cherry. Mercifully, when they did break ranks and run away, they didn't take Cherry because Promilla had arrived in time to put her arm around her, lift her from the swing and take her back into the house safely. But it's probably as close a time as we ever came to losing Cherry and not at all a way we would ever have expected to lose her!

Another consequence of Bangalore being so far from the sea was that it was used by India for atomic development because it was the furthest possible land-base from either the Americans or Russians at that time of the Cold War. Because of this the city of Bangalore has slowly grown to be the Silicon Valley of India.

The very opposite of this Silicon Valley idea is remembered by our family as 'a mouthful of mud'. It came about that we were going to some party with Cherry and her nanny one afternoon. I was sitting in the back of the car, behind the driver, when a car coming from the other direction went through some sort of puddle in the road. Out of nowhere splashed a large amount of muddy water through the driver's side window, missing his head but hitting mine and it went straight down my throat! Now you would imagine that one's family would give one some sympathy – not at all! It was then, and remains now, a source of high hilarity!

Another piece of amusement occurred when our Chairman of the British Council, Lord Ballantrae called on us. As he got out of his car, he smiled as if to say, 'Now look, I'll put you at your ease and then you can put me at mine'. He said, "Good morning, Mullen, have you had a good morning?" I replied, "Well, no Sir, not quite so good because our dog has just had pups all over the house." He stopped and looked at me and said, "Great God, I'll write to The Field about that. I've never heard of a dog having pups." His wife, who was Joyce Grenfell's sister and looked just like her, came round the back of the car with an expression which said, 'Oh, my husband's always like that – don't worry about him, he's not at all as bad as he seems.' With that we went in and had a very good lunch; fortunately Promilla is wonderful as a hostess.

We chatted about many things and it chanced that he was an expert on the history of Bangalore and of India. He had been a Chindit himself, and he knew about Churchill having been in Bangalore as a young subaltern in the army and raising his polo team and beating the best British Army teams in North India. However, what he didn't know was that we had in our office in Madras a British Council officer called Churchill who was, in fact, a grand-nephew of the great man.

In our chat he asked me how the place was and I pointed out that our servants' quarters were quite good but that, "Once upon a time they had actually been the stables for the polo ponies." I could see his eyes glazing over as if he was going to hear for the ninety-ninth time in his life about Churchill playing polo, but what I actually said was, "Those stables housed the ponies of the great grand-uncle of one of our British Council staff in Madras." Whereupon he looked at me, burst out laughing and said, "Oh you bugger, you had me there!"

He was a wonderful chairman to have; he spoke up for us in the House of Lords and was very, very particular about his behaviour. His grandfather, father and he had all been Governors-General of New Zealand; he always read the first lesson at church services, and he always wrote his thank-you letters either in the car or plane immediately after he had left a place where he had been given a meal or some sort of hospitality. He had been a lecturer in French at Sandhurst, where, the story goes (because he was six feet six inches tall and always wore a monocle) that one day he came into his class and found sitting in front of him a dozen Officer Cadets all with monocles in their eyes. He didn't say a word, merely went to the blackboard, rubbed out whatever was written on it, turned round and faced the class, took his monocle out of his eye, flicked it up in the air like a coin and caught it in his eye socket as it came down, and then went on with the lesson as much as to say, "Now, gentlemen, do that!"

My wife's prowess as a producer of plays became fairly well-known and one day she found herself approached by the students of the university who had learned, off by heart, the various parts of a play without actually rehearsing and putting them together with cues and the like. Now the title of this play is enough to stop you in your tracks before you even begin – it goes like this: "Oh Dad, poor Dad, Mama's locked you in the closet and I'm feeling so sad." Yes, that's the title! So they asked Promilla if she would produce the play for them. What a time she had trying to organise all these people who knew their parts but had no idea when to say them; she managed to sort it out and did quite a good job with them in the long run, with some good reviews.

We decided to send our daughter to a Roman Catholic Convent where the headmistress was an absolutely brilliant Indian Nun. I sat quietly to one side while she and Promilla discussed education, India, young children, our particular child and what might be done if and when she came to the school. To me it was a revelation of two highly intelligent people talking with utter clarity about complicated issues. As we walked down the driveway, Promilla said, half into the air, half to me, "You know, Lloyd, there aren't many better things in the world than a bright, hard Indian mind." And she was right, there aren't. Absolutely brilliant.

Cherry loved that place and one of the things that happened later, without us knowing it, was that her photograph was sent in for some Miss South India beauty competition and she was chosen to be one of the finalists. We were all summoned to a hall in Bangalore for the prize distribution day and Cherry was the winner of her particular age group. The way the judges had judged the children was to have them up on the stage, wandering about amongst them with toys and games and they watched the children while they played. Cherry's name was announced as the winner, so Promilla took her along to the side of the stage and pushed her up the steps and told her to remember to say 'thank you'. Then the person who was presenting the prizes bent down and congratulated her and said, "Very well done… Now Cherry, you can have whatever you would like in the whole world – what would you like?" And turning to the audience and putting her fingers around her breasts, said, "I want big milks like my Mummy"! I don't think we will ever forget the shout of laughter that hit the roof; really it was the only time in my life that I thought the roof might come off! Mercifully, Promilla was still standing down off the stage and was more or less hiding behind a side curtain until the amazement had calmed down and order was restored.

It was at this stage that I learned something about our daughter that I hadn't fully appreciated. She was very clear-headed and determined. One day I returned home at half-past-five from an engagement that had gone wrong and I had told Cherry that I would be back at five o'clock. I attempted to explain what had happened and that I was sorry I hadn't arrived on time. She merely looked at me, very hard and very straight and – aged four or five – stamped her foot definitely and deliberately and said, "Oh well, if you won't do, you mustn't say." I've remembered that many times since when I've been tempted to say, "Yes, I'll do that," and then I remember that it's just possible I mightn't be able to and am a bit careful then – 'If you won't do, you mustn't say'.

Another 'saying' that brings some happiness was when my boss in South India, from Madras, came up to give me my 'annual interview'. We sat down in our garden (Promilla had chosen a beautiful view and some lovely outlooks for him) and he said, "My goodness, Lloyd, people all over the world pay about £250 a day just to have a place like this to look at and here you are living in it and we pay you to do so! Gosh, this is wonderful," and it was wonderful. Then he began the serious business of the annual interview by saying, "Well, Lloyd, you and I need hardly go through this frightful ritual because both of us are Irish Protestants and neither of us can sin happily." We roared with laughter – thus spoke the voice of the puritanical Irish bishop's son, who didn't want to be puritanical in the least, nor I.

Another thing he said, which of course one isn't permitted to say nowadays because it brings other people into the annual interview and may be regarded as politically incorrect, was, "You know, Lloyd, Promilla is your best asset," meaning, of course, that she was able to hold the show very well together when I couldn't. She and I have had many jokes about it since because I've taken the line that an asset is a little ass!

On arrival in Bangalore one of the rituals we had to go through was to join the Bangalore Club. This was much more fastidious than many clubs in the world, partly because some very important – or so-called important thinking empire builders had been members, including one Winston Churchill in his young days. When you joined the Club you had to go to a meeting in the evening, have drinks and shake hands with every member of the committee. One of the committee members had been deputed to tell the story of how Winston Churchill had been drummed out of the Club because he hadn't paid his dues. Now this was a way of politely telling you that you had better pay up or you'd be drummed out of the Club, too.

I enjoyed our time at the Club; it had a very good swimming pool, all sorts of amenities and one did meet lots of interesting people passing through. Indeed, membership turned out to be very useful when the Indian Government wanted to close down all the British Council libraries in India simply because a Russian building had fallen down in Trivandrum – the Russian Cultural Institute hadn't told the Indian Government anything about it, they'd just built it without anyone knowing. The result was that Mrs Gandhi got so angry to discover that all sorts of things were happening in India that she didn't know about that she said, "Every single foreign Institution must be either under our Government directly or under its own Government directly – none of these in-between things." Now the British Council is a bit 'in-between' so… we were going to be closed down.

Promilla was playing bingo, would you believe, in the Club with a gentleman whom she didn't know very well but she played with him every time she went there. He was very nice and courteous and always asked her how I was. One day she said I seemed to be worried about something, so he asked what it was. She replied that she didn't know but it was something to do with the library. Anyway, he said, "Send him to me," and gave her his card. She gave it to me later and said, "This man would like to see you; he might be able to help you." I looked at the card and saw that he was Chief Secretary, Mysore State. Now the high and mighty spend months trying to get an appointment with this man, but my wife played bingo with him and I got one immediately! I went along and he said, "Well, Lloyd, what's the trouble?" I told him, and he said, "Goodness, are you serious?" I replied, "Yes, I am." He then said, "I haven't been told a thing about this – I didn't know about it," so I told him the whole story. He picked up the telephone, spoke in two different languages, neither of which I understood, put the phone down and said, "I hope we've stopped it."

The very next day the Indian Express carried a major article on the front page saying how Indian students were going to be deprived of their best source of information when the British Council libraries all over the country were going to be closed down and that it was something that must be stopped immediately; no sensible government could dream of doing such a thing. And it was stopped.

Promilla loves dogs and we had a small spaniel in Bangalore called Penny who developed an ability to run around the top of the wall surrounding our entire compound; it must have been about a quarter of a mile. She would bounce along. Occasionally there would be a branch of a tree growing in the way but she would jump over it and carry on running round and round and loved doing this. One day, unfortunately, she fell off and hurt her shoulder but, luckily, when I

Family with Promilla holding Penny

picked her up I could actually feel in her shoulder where the sinew had become a bit twisted and I took the risk and gave it a little twitch – and it worked, she was okay. She was a lovely dog and we had great fun with Penny.

Cherry was growing up and learning how to do things; for example she came back from her school one day, sat on the bottom step of the stairs and said, "Mummy, I think Geoffrey likes me." "Oh," said Mummy, "how do you know that?" She said, "Well, whenever we are playing he pulls my hair." Thus was an early realisation of romance.

But a more practical realisation of her young way of looking at life was when she discovered that our way of trying to hide things from her so she wouldn't understand that we were talking about her, was to call her 'the younger generation'. I've never forgotten the afternoon I came back home from work with an invitation to a party. I told Promilla about it, handed it to her and we talked about whether we could go or not, when a little voice said, from under the desk where she was playing, "Is the younger generation invited?" That put a stop to our gallop!

When I now flick over the pages of my diaries from those days, especially in Bangalore, I get the impression that I was almost never out of aeroplanes, flying out of the four capitals of the four southern states of India, but of course that's not true.

The most scary of all the flights was from London to Bangalore because the first section was to Bombay. When I checked in at Heathrow and said, as a last minute thought, to the lady at the counter, "By the way, what route are we following?" she drew herself up as if to explain the self-evident truth to a child and said, "Sir, this is our main New York/London/Moscow/Delhi/Bombay flight," giving me the impression I was very lucky to be on it. Actually, I was very unlucky to be on it because in those days we had clear indications that as British people we should not fly through Moscow unless it was absolutely necessary. In this case it was not necessary, there were plenty of other routes to follow had I known or had I thought; but I hadn't thought and it was too late so I had to go on the flight. The first thing I noticed was that pretty well everybody got off at London and it was almost starting again with a new set of passengers. There were only three of us – yes three – sitting in that enormous plane on its way to Moscow.

So that was the first vaguely eerie indication of something to come which certainly did come when we got to Moscow and landed. There we were told to sit in our seats until checked in. Along came a police officer or an army officer, I don't know which, but in uniform, and while I sat in my seat, he asked me for my passport and took it away, having written in his notebook the seat and aisle in which I was sitting. After a while someone came and told me I could leave the plane, which I did, taking my briefcase with me. At the exit door I found that instead of just steps down to the ground there was a tunnel made of canvas which had been brought right up to the plane and which went all the way down somewhere, I presumed to the airport. The steps were inside but I couldn't see out and no one could see in. The other two passengers and I went down this tunnel – a mysterious place it was – and came out into the airport where there were various desks. We were more or less led by the hand and told to check in here and there, and then to go up to the restaurant, which I did.

As I was going in I was stopped and told I must leave my briefcase outside and not take it into the restaurant with me. That was a bit tricky – fortunately there was nothing in the briefcase of any interest but I did manage to put it down against the wall in such a place that when I got into the restaurant and sat in a particular seat I could look across my table and see my briefcase was still there, but I sat more or less ready to make a dash for it in case anybody else picked it up.

After a very long, lonely, eerie, quiet time, the meal was over. I can't remember what I ate but it was very plain. The whole atmosphere was dull, dead, and frightening. Then along came the policeman and tells us that we can go. We were more or less followed out of the restaurant, where I picked up my briefcase, went down the steps, out through a door and back up the steps through the long tunnel of canvas and into the plane, where I was instructed, quite firmly, to sit down in the seat which I had earlier vacated. Since there were now a few more passengers in the plane, about six more, I had no difficulty in getting to my seat. Now I'm sitting down, I have my briefcase but I have no passport, so what to do? I made a sign to the air hostess; she knew what I was going to ask her and waved her hand saying, "Passport coming, Sir," and sure enough the passport did come. I looked inside and saw it had been stamped, that was all, nothing interesting.

After a short while the plane took off and we did indeed get to Delhi and finally to Bombay, but even as I recall the event after all these years, I'm saying to myself, 'My goodness, that was a time in the history of the world when people just disappeared in places like Moscow, businessmen especially, and weren't heard of again', so I was jolly glad to be heard of again as I got out at Bombay, where I had to change locally and get the next plane on to Bangalore with a great feeling of relief.

There was another reason for having a feeling of relief when I reached Bangalore, which was that I had no trouble changing flights in Bombay. In those days the seat you had booked on a plane within India itself was not always sure to be there when you arrived at the airport. The reason for this was that India was increasing its numbers of ministers and senior civil servants and so on, but not increasing its number of planes and flights so if someone dubbed 'VIP' arrived at an airport, it was quite likely that another deemed to be less important would be bumped off the plane and the other person would get the flight. That had not happened to me and it was always a relief when it didn't.

However, when my twin sister, Ruby, flew out to join us for a holiday in Bangalore, we went to the airport to meet her; the plane arrived but she didn't get off it. She just wasn't there! It would be too tedious now to explain how we found out, but what had happened was that in Bombay airport, when she went to her flight she discovered that she had indeed been bumped off it for someone else to be put on! She didn't know what to do but, fortunately, as she was going through immigration, an Irish nun whom she had sat next to on the flight from London to Bombay, was beside her and Ruby told her what had happened. The nun said, "I can well understand this; I tell you what, you come and stay with us in the convent and we'll try and sort this out."

My sister certainly had a good knowledge of Irish nuns and trusted them completely so agreed to go with her, at the same time saving herself the trouble of trying to find a hotel in a strange country. While she was staying with these nuns, they got in touch with their former pupils, girls or maybe even boys that they had taught years ago and who were now working for Indian Airlines or had positions of responsibility, maybe the parents of children these nuns were now teaching, and between the nuns and their friends they managed to get my sister on the flight down to Bangalore the next day, where we met her.

You can imagine that in between I had my wife jumping up and down beside me saying all sorts of things, from, 'ring the Prime Minister here and ring the Prime Minister of England and get them both to sort out these matters'!

One journey that I made, not by plane but by car, was to Ootacamund in the Nilgiri Hills. It is a place that is generally called Ooty and is remembered by most of the older generation as being famous for the billiard table in the club on which a young subaltern, called Neville Chamberlain, developed the game of snooker while all his companions were away for the weekend hunting jackals – and hunting in proper pinks, too, with more or less British fox hounds. When they came back he had developed this game of billiards. When I spent the night in Ooty I stayed at the club. I looked at this table, moved the balls around on it, trying to imagine him taking billiard balls, putting little marks on them in different colours and developing the game now called snooker, in which each ball is completely coloured.

Another connection with an Irish nun concerns the Maharajah of Mysore's palace, in Mysore. This lady was tutoring the Maharajah's son and we got to know her. She very kindly said that on a certain day this palace was going to be handed over to the new Indian government that was taking away the princely kingdoms and that she would be able to show us over the palace if we could get to it the day before handover, which we did.

She showed us over this wonderful place, which had a Durbar space on which they could have one hundred elephants on parade, and where they had a Distinguished Strangers' gallery that could hold a thousand people, and also where they had in the corner the Maharajahs' golden throne, which, as I looked at it, I thought could be stolen by any clever people with a helicopter if they were able to drop down, hook it up and take it away – which they didn't as far as I know!

But we did come across one very amusing comment on the human race when we got into the great Throne Room, which was absolutely splendid. It was built with British metal supports, huge pillars which had been brought out from England by ship, unloaded at Madras and brought up by train – goodness knows how – all the way to Mysore and put into this palace. It was an incredible experience to see this and even see the names of the factories where they were made printed on the bottom. But there we were, in this great Maharajah's Throne Room, with beautifully etched glass on every side, huge chandeliers, all very magnificent, and we heard some noise next door. On asking what was happening, we were told that a film company was making a film connected with some story in Indian history. We were allowed to peep in and there, in a much smaller and rather tawdry room beside the great Throne room, a Mock-Maharajah's throne room had been set up and Indian actors were being filmed as Maharajahs and Maharanis and Courtiers of all sorts. I couldn't help feeling how odd it was that human beings were, in one room getting rid of the real thing in the name of political progress I suppose, and in the very room next door trying to make it all up again, in a very tawdry fashion.

Just at the foot of the golden throne we were shown a small stud. It was explained to us how, at the great Festival of Diwali (the Festival of Lights in the Hindu religion), the Maharajah of Mysore had traditionally been the very first one to be allowed to light a fire or show a light on that day; every other fire or light of any kind throughout the entire state of Mysore (several million people) had to be put out and there was total blackness over the land. When the great moment came for this Feast of Diwali, the Maharajah would be standing there, in front of his throne, waiting for his courtiers to tell him it was the right moment. He would put his heel on this stud and press it and, of course, with electricity, lights came on all over the place and immediately lights went on spreading right across the whole state of Mysore – a wonderful scene to imagine from the air, if you were in an aeroplane looking down on all this blackness, to see all the lights spread out.

While we were in Bangalore, my wife's brother, his wife and two daughters were in East Pakistan, now called Bangladesh because it had broken away in the war from Pakistan – the countries, instead of being West Pakistan and East Pakistan, were Pakistan and Bangladesh.

My wife's brother was a tea planter and finding it extremely difficult to get anything in or out of the country. Anyway, he was very fortunate in that an old-fashioned habit of British tea planters came up: 'Home Leave'. This home leave was applied to Indians and Pakistanis, members of the firm, so they were due for home leave in Britain as they had inherited their British predecessors' places. Now he had two visas for himself and his wife to travel to Britain.

He had written to us in Bangalore asking whether we would have his younger daughter to stay with us while they were away. She would have a good holiday with us and our daughter who was about her age, so we wrote back and said, "Yes, please do send her." His other daughter he had sent to boarding school up north just over the border in India, and she had a visa to travel to and from her school.

So all the arrangements were made for us to receive his younger daughter and we were waiting to hear which flight she would be on when, quite unexpectedly, we received a telegram from England saying the entire family, parents and children, were now in England and we would shortly hear details of their journeys. My wife's brother had decided to leave Bangladesh for good and go to Britain. He was able to do this with his wife on their Home Leave visas and was able to bring his older daughter on her visa. The letter we had sent to him saying, 'please send your daughter to us in Bangalore', he had used to get her a visa which she used to go to England!

Another feature of our flying to and from Ireland and England to India and Pakistan was the way in which we could look down and literally see the ground beneath, growing less and less brown and more and more green as we came from east to west. By the time we reached Ireland it was as green as green can be and this was always the beginning of a kind of holiday feeling which ended up many times in the west of Ireland, in Killarney, Donegal and also of course, in the Lake District in England. These were the places of peace for which we always set out when we got home.

One of the things I discovered when I got near my own home place of Tipperary, was that I began to feel quite light as if a heavy rucksack of effort was slipping off my back and the strain of the world out there was going, going until it was gone.

One of the old friends we met was Kingsmill Pennefeather, the elder brother of Lionel who had introduced us to the Oxford Group years and years before. He was by this time a great light in the breeding industry in Ireland, both with regard to cattle and sheep and had kept his common sense very well into old age. When he died, the obituary in the Irish Times was a whole page and ended with the famous sentence, "...and as if to demonstrate that he had retained his faculties to the last, on the night before his death he scored a grand slam doubled re-doubled at bridge when missing one ace." Those people who know about bridge will gasp at such a performance by a ninety-one-year-old.

Another person I met on one of these holidays home in Ireland was known by the nickname 'Rations'. He had been in charge of food at one of the VPSC camps to which I had gone and he and I had become very friendly. A very sad thing happened from my point of view which I never quite got over. I heard that he was down in Tullamore and I wanted to go down to see him, but when I looked up my finances I had exactly £1, no more, and the return bus fare was 17s.6d., I thought, 'that leaves me with half a crown and if anything goes wrong I'm in trouble'. So to my great shame and sorrow I didn't go to see him and you can imagine how distraught I felt when not long after I heard he had had a nervous breakdown. I really was very confused and felt that if I had gone maybe some things we might have said to each other could have prevented it. The other thing I said to myself was, 'imagine being so conceited as to think you could possibly prevent a person from having a nervous breakdown'. All these things went through my mind. I am very happy to tell you that he completely recovered and the next time I saw him, several years later, he was a very happily married Methodist clergyman.

Methodism in the centre of Ireland and in Dublin at that time was very strong. My own father had conducted Methodist evening prayers in a hall in Dublin which was frequented by all the youth of the city after their regular Sunday services. There was also a school in Dublin, called Wesley College, and from it came some very great rugby players. An interesting sidelight on that school was that almost all the Jewish people sent their children there. There were not so many Jews in Ireland in those days – and there may not be many now – but certainly Wesley College was very well known for its Methodist and Jewish connections and I have had many happy times connected with it through my friend, 'Rations'.

I seemed to have clergymen as friends – for some reason people whom I had known in my youth became clergymen. One of them was a Baptist minister and he was ruthless and brutal in his assertions of the realities of life. I hope he was wrong, but I do remember him saying to me, "Lloyd, don't be naïve, people behave in strange ways; when I go to take over a new parish I assume such things as: ...the lady who plays the organ is having an affair with the gentleman who takes the collection, and the person who reads the lesson is likewise having an affair with the first church warden." I didn't believe him, but was at least willing to think he thought that!

A much more pleasant story concerns not someone I really knew but Bishop George West of Rangoon. This saintly man, who had no voice – he could only whisper, but he could whisper very loudly and be heard all over the place – had spent years in Borneo in Dyak villages converting as many Dyaks as he could to Christianity. Suddenly, he found himself, in mid-life, called into Rangoon (in Burma in those days) to be Assistant to the Bishop of Rangoon and not long after (I don't think he was responsible!) the Bishop of Rangoon died and this good old man became Bishop of Rangoon.

In addition to having no voice, he had plenty of hair – it grew not only out of his head but out of his eyebrows, out of his ears, out of his chest up over his clerical collar, out of his cheeks, and the backs of his hands – he was covered in hair. He was like a great bear; indeed he was… about eighteen stone and perhaps six feet two tall. He was a kindly man, much loved by all who knew him – so loved in fact that when he retired he was given a present by his friends of a journey round the world so that instead of coming back from Rangoon the usual way, over the erstwhile British Empire to London, he was taken the other way around, right across the Pacific and across America, across the Atlantic and part of Europe, too, before actually coming into Britain.

On the way back, he was staying with one of his friends in Los Angeles and one night remembered that he had to put a letter in the post box which was near the gate. He walked out, padded out really, in the pleasant evening air, with his dressing gown on, just down a few steps into the street to the post box and then walked back. He was very short-sighted so did everything more or less by sense, but when he got back to his bedroom and opened the door he realised it was the wrong room because this one was air-conditioned, so he backed out and went to go to the next door. As he went towards it a young lady opened it. She was dressed ready for bed and when she saw this enormous, hairy man standing there she gave a screech and said, "Who are you?" He replied, in a deep whisper, "I'm the Bishop of Rangoon." Well, that story has gone round the world and has the great merit of being true.

Much less pleasing was a story that I picked up between England and one foreign country which will remain nameless, because it concerns men who were working in England making a reasonable amount of money, who, when they went back to their country were seized by thugs, dacoits, tied to chairs and made to reveal their bank details, account numbers, sums and so on and if they didn't they had their knees chopped off – a dreadful thing. I have to say that this was connected to the political leadership of the country in which it happened, so that amongst all the stories one picked up in this peripatetic life that we lived, some were wonderful and some were quite dreadful.

Perhaps the crudest, most unsavoury story we came across concerned a Cabinet meeting of a particular nation where one of the cabinet ministers referred to the Prime Minister by his nick-name. The Prime Minister slapped him down immediately with the words, "Look, just because I sleep with your wife it doesn't give you the right to call me by my nick-name in Cabinet." All the other members in Cabinet stayed silent. So you can imagine what the whole country was like if the Cabinet was like that.

During one short interlude in Britain I was asked to take part in an exercise whereby senior French civil servants from the Fonction Publique in Paris would come across to Whitehall and senior British civil servants would go across to Paris, the idea being that they would improve their English and French respectively and also get to know how the civil services of each country worked a little more than they did already.

Because I had to deal with the person who arranged all this on the French side, I learned a lesson because I kept saying that we would be able to do this and that and then we would see how it had gone and move on to the next step, but my French counterpart wouldn't have that at all. "No," she said, "...we must do that, finish; start again, do that, finish." I said, "Suppose it doesn't really work and we discover as we go along?" To this she replied, "No, it will work, we won't begin to do it unless it works." As the plans progressed it turned out that neither set of civil servants spoke the other's language as well as they thought and things were a little slowed down. I found that working with my French colleague was really quite difficult but it taught me the difference between various people's attitudes to work and plans and progress.

A quite different event in Lahore with a Swedish friend taught me another lesson. He had a very expensive camera, I think it was called a Hasselblad. It wouldn't function properly so he sent it to the manufacturers in Sweden for repair. However, they sent it back saying it would be more expensive to try and mend it than to buy a new one as something was bent inside and they were sorry but the insurance would only cover part of the cost. As it would be very expensive for him, I suggested he take it to who we call the 'camera man' down in the bazaar, which he did. The old camera man, who spoke only a little English but was illiterate otherwise, took it and looked at it and said, "Oh, big new camera, big problem, big problem – you come back in week." So we left the camera with him and came back in a week.

Imagine my Swedish friend's horror when he saw a white bed sheet spread out on the ground in this man's yard with all the separate bits of the Hasselblad camera set out on it. This man picked out one piece from the middle and showed him how it was bent and he said, "This funny new metal, funny new metal, Sahib, not good metal." The story has a happy ending: one week later we returned and he had assembled the whole camera, in full working order… for twenty-five rupees!

At that stage in my life I always felt a very relaxed Celtic communication with the universe when I was at home in Ireland. A very easy belief in divine things and a very happy acceptance of Christian worship in whatever tradition. That became different when I went to England, and especially when I went to London where so many of my fellows did not actually believe. They had quite different ways of life from what I was used to, and when I was with them I turned more to my commitment to try to find God's will for the world for the sake of all the people in it rather than this kind of gentle Celtic acceptance of the universe. In the cities where I worked there was no Celtic aura at all.

When I was in and out of Pakistan and India I was very happy with the sincerity of the worshippers all around me in their various ways. There were Buddhists, Hindus, Muslims, Parsees and Jews, and people who were plainly spiritual but would never actually tell you what faith they professed. There were also non-believing Communists who were quite sincere in their efforts to make the world a better place for the poor.

All of these were people with whom I could work quite seamlessly on the basis of the standards of Moral Re-Armament, about which many of them had heard and with which they could all agree although many found the standards too difficult. We all knew there was a great battle going on between good and evil because the state of the world's economy in the middle of the Cold War made it plain that some of us were profiting and the rest of the world wasn't able to join in. This was an imbalance that we all felt had to be put right. Whether we worshipped God in our different ways or didn't believe in God at all, there was this uniting factor of trying to put things right. We all agreed that if we didn't try to put things right ourselves we didn't have any right to blame the politicians, journalists or revolutionaries for the state of affairs.

The most effective operators turned up in the most unexpected ways. I remember that in Kerala, a very rich landowner gave away all his property and lived very poorly in a little hut. He set up a trade union for the poor people and he acted as the secretary for it, because his upbringing and connections enabled him to do so. He spent his whole life doing that genuinely for the poor, so I was not surprised to discover that the state of Kerala was the first to elect a Communist government. Nor was I too amazed when the central government in India closed it down and wouldn't allow a Communist government in Kerala.

All this varied experience convinced me that there was a force for 'good' working in the world, even as there was a force for 'evil', and that these forces moved against each other. Each one of us in our daily life has to decide which side to help. There is no standing on the side-line; whatever we are doing is either going to help things in the world get better or cause things to get worse.

In this situation I was very happy to work with the British Council because it was working in such a way that it took no notice at all of people's politics, religion or class; it just went on trying to find ways of helping Asians and Africans to negotiate the world which Europeans had created and which had spread to America, Canada and Australia. Though it seems strange now when the world is mixed with all races everywhere, back in those days Asians and Africans on the whole were only trying to make their way into what was then called 'the West' or the modern world. The notable exception to this, of course, was the Japanese who had entered the modern world in their own way, far over on the east side of the world from us.

There were practical difficulties on the ground. One of those that I encountered in South India was a gulf between the university pundits who believed in English literature as the be-all and end-all, while there were many in the education institutes who saw the English language as the way forward in all disciplines. I was very happy that at the end of my time in the Regional Institute of English in Bangalore, the tenth anniversary celebrations were actually centred on a conference which was aimed at bridging the gap between these two sides of the picture and I give here a small part of the report as it was written by the professor who was sent from abroad to watch it and to make his comments on how it went.

Report On A Visit
October 1973

To The Regional Institute Of English At Bangalore, South India

My visit to Bangalore was mainly in association with the celebration of the ten years of operation of the Regional Institute of English. In association with that celebration, a seminar on Harmonizing Language and Literature in the Production of Textbooks had been arranged. I attach to this report the Programme that was distributed at the beginning of the seminar.

(HERE THE PROGRAMME AND REPORT)

I enjoyed very much my stay in Bangalore and wish to thank the British Council for the opportunity to make this tour. The various officers of the British Council with whom I had discussions in Bangalore appeared to me to be working extremely well under difficult circumstances. They had, as I have observed in every other part of Asia and Africa that I have visited, the complete confidence and respect of the local community. This is, I think, the most commendable attribute of any group of foreign workers in a developing country. Mr Mullen, for example, works at a very low key in the Regional Institute of English, and yet from the discussions that I have had with members of the staff of the Institute, has their complete respect both professionally and personally. I think this is indicative of the esteem with which the British Council is held in South India.

(signed)

FRANCIS C. JOHNSON

14
Sri Lanka

Just as I had been the last British Council adviser in South India, I was moved on to be the last of a series of Council Officers advising the government of Sri Lanka on its English language teaching programme. It had a special unit in its education department devoted entirely to this.

Here I found, as I had among the staff in Bangalore, men and women infinitely better informed about and technically better equipped to deal with the situations facing us than I was, yet I was accepted and welcomed most graciously. My predecessors had dealt with the separate areas of Teaching Methods, Textbooks, Curriculum, Examinations and Radio. I had to draw all their conclusions together with my colleagues and bring the entire programme to an integrated conclusion. The funding for my work came from a scheme called Aid to Commonwealth English and it was administered by the British Council, so because of the initials, ACE, I became known as an Ace.

Ace in those days meant a racing car driver. Nothing could be farther from the careful way I had to make my way along the good but narrow roads in this island, where wild bear, wild buffalo, elephants and large wild lizards would emerge at any time from the side of the road. Certain routes had very good bus services but passing a bus, no matter in which direction, was an event in itself! The island was beautiful and it was difficult to keep one's eye on the road, so distracting were the lovely views from many sides; going up the mountains or down to the sea, the whole place was full of wonderful things to look at, all sorts of flowers and trees, absolutely glorious.

We made many memorable trips to Galle, Vavuniya, Kandy, Nuwar Eliya, Polonnaruwa, Anuradhapura, all places that have figured since then on the world's standard tourist attraction map and, of course, in those days, too, there was the strange historical interest of, say, The Hill Club in Kandy which was operating in the absolutely traditional colonial style of an old Empire Club. It was dangerously easy to feel permanently on holiday in such a place, especially as the Sri Lankans had a great penchant for holidays. They had more holidays per month or per week than any other country had in the whole year!

Fortunately my friend, Roger Hicks, had advised me to look up an old friend when I arrived at Sri Lanka, which I did. She was a first class motorcar racing driver, horsewoman and photographer, famed for taking photographs of leopards up trees. She certainly helped me to keep my feet on the ground because she was able to help us in our relationships between Sinhalese and Tamils, and explain which beautiful things could be grown but couldn't be exported because of the lack of refrigeration facilities, etc. She was a really up-to-date lady and never let us feel that we were able to just come to her beautiful island for a holiday visit!

Nonetheless, the first date that my counterpart asked me to put in my diary and keep free was a three day cricket match between Royal College and St. Thomas's College. It was called 'The Royal Thomian Match', and every year pretty well all business, even including the government because most of the people in the government were from either of these colleges, came to a halt while they watched the cricket. So it was that I spent those three days watching cricket and meeting the great and good of the land.

On one occasion I witnessed my counterpart with four of his erstwhile contemporaries from school meeting their old Latin Master, falling about laughing at jokes. When I was able to get close enough to listen to them, imagine my amazement to find that they were talking and joking in Latin – yes, Latin – not English, not Sinhalese, not Tamil but Latin! So they were quite an educated group into which I had fallen, and these were men between the ages of fifty and ninety!

Of course they did have Roman, Dutch, Portuguese and British Empires behind them and many Sri Lankans had Portuguese, Dutch or English names. One important social group was called Burghers, because they were descended from particular foreigners who had inter-married with the local people of the island.

Within our own family, a very nice mistake came to light which we still laugh about. I wrote home to my mother after I'd arrived, and because I didn't make my letters very defined, the words 'Sri Lanka' appeared a little unclear. I received a letter back from my dear mother, addressed to me at the correct address but the country was called 'Sky Larka'. We still joke about asking my mother whether she would come and skylark with us in Sri Lanka!

We actually arrived in Sri Lanka only a short time before Christmas and one of the things that we did more or less immediately was to find a church where there would be Christmas services. We found a Scottish Kirk on the main mall in Colombo, called St. Andrew's, as you can imagine for Scotland, and we went along and settled in about three-quarters of the way down on the left of the central aisle, ready for the service. Because there were some decorations for Christmas we allowed our little daughter, Cherry, to stay on the outside near the aisle so she could see what was happening up at the front.

The service began with both the choir and little children trooping in, singing, 'Oh, Come All Ye Faithful' and they went right up to the altar rail. In front of this had been set out about ten small cushions and ten small microphones. Children from the Sunday School who had walked in with the choir, knelt down on some of these cushions ready to speak into the microphones when it was their turn. They had learnt a poem which told the Christmas story in couplets; each child would say two rhyming lines and the next child would pick up the story and they would go on – from the angels, the shepherds and the star, to the end... the birth of Jesus in the manger. To our horror we realised that Cherry had disappeared and when we looked up to the front we found she had knelt down with the other little children, all about the same size, on one of these cushions just opposite a microphone. My wife said we must get her back, but I said to leave it as no harm could come, just a child in church – the Sunday School mistress would look after her.

They began these couplets, nice rhyming lines about the star and the wise men, and we expected that when it came to Cherry, the child on her left would say his lines and the child on her right would say her lines and the story would go on. Not so! Cherry knew two lines of poetry and she was determined to say them. So what happened was that quite suddenly in the middle of this calm, beautiful Christmas story, a clear, distinct voice was heard to say, "Two little sausages frying in a pan, one went pop and the other went bang!" Then the next child went on with the Christmas story. You can imagine the heads that shot up in the congregation to look at this intervention and went down again, and then the shoulders shaking and quivering with mirth and giggles. But what could we do!

Sure enough she was returned to us, but not immediately. She was looked after with the other children and at the end of the service we all went out, down some steps under a very large porch where we were asked to wait for our children. So there we stood and thought no one would know which child belonged to us. Again we were foiled because when Cherry came out of the door in the middle of all the other children, she said in a loud voice, "Mummy, how did you like my poem?"

The British Council has various ways of getting newcomers to be well-known in the community to which they are posted. They hadn't practised this one, but nothing could have been more successful because from then on we were known as 'Two little sausages frying in a pan parents', and that's what we were.

Colombo is a comparatively small city and our house, which was more or less in the centre of it, was only a short distance from my office which, strangely, was in the racecourse building. The racecourse was not being used when we were there and the building had been developed by various parts of the Civil Service. The Education Department had a few offices there and I was given one of them. This had some advantages, the greatest being that I was alone and far from other people without interruption when it was necessary to create new material or read reports when they came in.

It had the disadvantage, of course, that when I wanted to find out something from a colleague (because we didn't have very useful telephones to be honest), it meant driving down to the Ministry of Education or one of them coming to see me. So it wasn't an ideally efficient method of working but it was satisfactory.

And satisfactory, too, for another reason. We discovered the Sri Lankans were very pleasant, easy-going people. The most obvious manifestation of this was the way they smiled at you in the street. There was none of the downcast eyes or averted looks that one had met in various communities in India or Pakistan or Bangladesh. These people were cheerful, smiling, laughing, always ready for a joke, and indeed they had a great sense of humour. They were also very musical and Promilla had a great time singing in various musical groups.

The disadvantage, if there was one, was the climate. In the city of Colombo the temperature very rarely went below 80°/85°F and the humidity very rarely went below eighty per cent. It really was a very difficult climate from the point of view of clothing. The neck of your collar was dirty by eleven o'clock and you had to be ready to change your shirts a couple of times a day. This was acceptable to those who lived there all the time, but to those of us who were used to a different kind of life it was an irritation. My wife suffered much more from it than I did because she had to spend almost all her time in Colombo city, whereas I was able to tour all over the island – go up to the hills and mountains, go down to the seashore and so on and it was a much more pleasant life that I had.

One blessing that we had in Colombo and Sri Lanka generally was a really good ayah called Agnes, who looked after Cherry most carefully. She came from a convent where they had trained her very well in both housework and education generally and she was excellent. However, she was so excellent that after she became a good friend of my wife and was talking to her one day when I was away, she ventured to mention the other families for whom she had worked and who had given her very good recommendations to us (we didn't know them personally but we knew who they were and who they had been). So there was Agnes, explaining to Promilla how it was very interesting for her now to be living in a house where, in her words, "When the master goes away on tour another master doesn't come into the house, or when the madam goes away on tour another madam doesn't come into the house." Little did she realise that she was giving away the paramour secrets of all those people who had recommended her to us!

Another side shoot from her very good care of Cherry was that Cherry began to speak and think very well and act logically. One afternoon, at about two o'clock, her voice sailed down from upstairs in a rather lordly fashion, saying, "Mummy, is Daddy going to run me to my violin lesson or shall I ask nanny to ring for a taxi?" The tones of voice were such that we decided from then on that a good deal of walking to and from violin lessons was probably the best way to attune our daughter to the modern world!

We made one mistake while we were there and that was attempting to develop a good garden with a nice new flowerbed, train a new dog called Merry, and teach our daughter to ride a bicycle, all at the same time. The immediate result was disastrous. All three of them ended up in the same new flowerbed with much damage to everyone!

Meanwhile I was having the time of my life, going all over this beautiful island to very remote places where there were seminars held for teachers to be trained in better methods of teaching English and better methods of speaking English themselves. This was possible because my counterpart, Lennie, had been a school inspector to begin with and was a very, very conscientious one. He visited remote schools and knew exactly how far the teachers had to walk to get to work, or what bus or train they could take, because the primary school teachers in Sri Lanka were almost all married women who got up at five o'clock in the morning, saw their husband off to work after breakfast, got their children off to school and then walked, often miles, to the school where they taught or to the bus stop to get to the school. They then made the return journey at about five or six o'clock and went through the whole rigmarole of feeding their husband and children again. They were really a most outstanding group of women.

Another thing that surprised us – it shouldn't have but it did – was how good they were at singing and acting. The reason for this became apparent as we got to know them. First of all they naturally have good voices and a sense of rhythm. The second point was this: Throughout the British Empire (the whole Colonial period) they had very much resented being regarded not as Ceylonese, which they were in their island then called Ceylon, but rather as 'little Indians'; little Indians who didn't give as much trouble as the big Indians gave on the mainland. This caused them to react in a very telling manner. They decided that anything the conquering group who came into their island could do, they would do better, so consequently they learnt how to sing beautifully in English, German, French and Italian. We remember going to concerts where, to our astonishment, the singing was not only of high standard but it was in the language of whatever nation the song came from.

Also the singing in St. Andrew's Church was of a very high standard indeed with one of the singers quite the best baritone we had come across. We discovered he had been the chief star at the Sydney Opera House one Christmas, but he had only done it because he needed to make money for his nephews who had been left orphans when his brother was killed. He did not go abroad again, though many companies tried to persuade him to go and sing for them. He set the standard for singing and acting for the entire island.

Promilla sang in a choir where the choir mistress produced the most wonderful phrase to tell the tenors that they weren't singing very well. She stopped the proceedings and shouted, "Oh you tenors, you are worse than awful… and that is an under-exaggeration!"

A wonderful piece of Pavlovian conditioning became apparent when Cherry made great friends with our little dog Merry. At twelve o'clock Merry would sit on the front step of the veranda waiting for the British High Commission vehicle which would bring Cherry back from school. Cherry would get out and they would have a great hug. This happened Monday to Friday, but on Saturday and Sunday, come twelve o'clock Merry would go and sit on the front step waiting for Cherry even though she was upstairs calling to her or walking around her. No, Merry would sit waiting for the vehicle.

Cherry was also beginning to learn what it is to be a lady. On one occasion, a guest in our house – she was a great friend of ours – came a little early for a party. She had on a beautiful, low-cut, red dress which inspired Cherry to say in a very polite and nice way, "Excuse me, but your milks are showing."

I have mentioned how bears, elephants, lizards and leopards represented danger in the island of Ceylon. There were others, too; many types of snake, which were quite venomous, and also the tarantula spider. I came to know about this when Lennie and I had to spend the night in a remote school and slept on wooden beds in a school room. Above Lennie's bed there was a gap in the ceiling. When I came back from the bathroom I saw him waving his towel towards this gap and enquired what he was doing. He said, "If there's a tarantula there I want it to fall down now and not when I'm in bed!"

Another unexpected event on that same tour occurred when we were guests of some people who gave us a very good dinner. I was asked if I would like pickle that was five, ten or fifty years old. Yes, *fifty* years old. So of course, I said I would have some pickle that was fifty years old. It was almost like chocolate or paste, but it was wonderful, absolutely wonderful.

Most people think of tea gardens, tea plantations, tea planters, tea factories, when they think of Ceylon because it has been very famous for its tea for a long time, with the best flavoured tea growing on the high slopes and the more solid, steady 'body tea' as they call it, growing down lower. The local people don't use the word 'plantation' so much as 'garden' – they call them 'tea gardens'. Just below these tea gardens are rubber plantations and below those, and down to the sea shore, you get the coconut tree plantations.

If you drive – and it only takes about an hour and a half from the coast to the top of the hills – you go first through the many coconut trees, where you see people up tapping them; then you go through the rubber plantations, and sometimes you see in the midst of them huge fields of pineapples grown by the dozen; and then you get up into the tea country.

They say that the best tea gardens would have their tea plants growing so closely together that you could roll a bottle down, and it would roll smoothly over the tops of the plants to the bottom of the plantation. That seems to me to be a little bit hopeful – I've never tried it but it does look possible.

In the midst of the populous areas of all these plantations there aren't many wild animals to worry about but in the parts of the island where there are not so many people living, there's the danger of these animals that I've already mentioned. Down on the coast there's another danger that is not really appreciated and many people who visit Sri Lanka as tourists fall foul of it.

Sri Lanka, in the Northern Hemisphere, is surrounded by sea and there is nothing between it and the South Pole. The water between it and the South Pole sends up very deep, strong, silent currents, which sweep around the island and carry off quite a number of hapless bathers each year, even though there are warnings on the beaches: "PLEASE DO NOT SWIM OFF THESE BEACHES." What often happened was that there would be a lovely lagoon behind a coral reef or a small island and a good strong swimmer on the mainland would try and swim out to that reef or island. He would put on his goggles and look down at the wonderful tropical fish that are to be seen all the way across but, without realising it, when he is about half or three-quarters of the way there, he is beginning to be swept quietly to one side or the other and, strong swimmer though he may be, he is just slowly, deeply taken away, around the other end of the island, out through the opening of the lagoon into the sea and he ends up somewhere between that little reef or island and the South Pole! It is very sad but it happens every year.

In Colombo City there is a very long street, down one side of which is nothing but a long, long warehouse with, written on the wall the full length of the street, 'BROOKE BOND'. Across the road opposite, there is another long warehouse with, written on its wall, 'LIPTON TEA COMPANY LIMITED' and these two announcements more or less define the whole business of Sri Lanka. Most of the occupations of foreigners who come to Sri Lanka are connected with the tea industry; the making of tea chests, for instance, is very big business. Then, of course, the shipping business all the way from Australia to Britain used to stop at Colombo and put down empties or pick up tea chests full of tea. When unloaded, the people at the other end had plenty of space to put cargo back into the ships and have it taken to Sri Lanka, so actually the cost of some transport by ship in that part of the world was occasionally quite cheap because they were going back without anything in the hold, which had been full of tea chests.

The climate was so sticky and hot that most outdoor sports were not taken seriously and a great deal of time was spent on singing and acting, if possible inside air-conditioned buildings.

While we were there we had many amusing experiences connected with the stage. Most of the programmes would be put on in the Lionel Wendt Theatre which, when we were there was a modern, arty-crafty type of building painted entirely black on the inside so you had to light it up with whatever you were going to do in sense of colour.

Promilla was in constant demand to produce plays, one of which was 'The Happiest Days of Your Life' and she was able to manage the unusual conditions. I remember we were asked to look after the actor, John Hurt, for the evening and take him to dinner. When he heard from Promilla that her father had refused to let her take up a scholarship which she had been offered at RADA, his jaw actually dropped open. Luckily his cigarette stuck to his bottom lip, but I still see him looking shocked. There was a story behind it because he personally had had a bit of a struggle to get onto the stage originally when his parents had more or less set him up for a very good job offstage.

An unexpected proof of how keen the whole nation was on music came when I was asked to present the prizes at a Piano Teachers Association which had had competitions amongst themselves. I had been expecting twenty or even sixty piano teachers; there were over two hundred! They were being given awards for different successes throughout the year.

This did help to explain how it was that if you went for a walk in the evening you were never out of reach of some piano playing or violin or musical instrument which was being practised by a child under tuition from a teacher. They were very keen and, of course, they were very good singers.

The most ridiculous manifestation of this focus on music came in the airport one night when I was seeing some people off who had been on the island on a musical tour. Over the loud speaker came this announcement: "Will Mr A Cello please report to Gate *so and so* because the plane is shortly going to take off." And this was repeated. Of course, what had happened was that for safety reasons a seat had been booked for the 'cello belonging to one of the members of the musical quartet and the person had checked it in as a 'cello. It was good fun to hear a 'Mr A Cello' being asked to board the plane.

The American lady conductor of a concert told us a wonderful story of a time when she and her husband were in Cairo, attached to the American Embassy there. They were trying to 'match-make' two young friends and they took them to dinner at Shepheard's Hotel with the idea that these two young people get to know each other better. Alas, zip fasteners had just replaced buttons in the flies of men's trousers and they didn't always work as well as they should. Unfortunately, the young man's fly had slipped open; it wasn't disastrous, just a little bit of white shirt to be seen. However, when he asked the girl to dance, she kept making excuses that she didn't know the tune, couldn't do the dance, or she was just going to start her meal – any kind of excuse to get out of dancing with him because she didn't want to be seen on the dance floor at Shepheard's with a man whose fly was open! Anyway, she managed to get word round to the lady conductor (who told us this tale). The conductor whispered it to her husband and he managed to tell the young man, who, under cover of those beautiful white linen tablecloths that Shepheard's Hotel always had, managed to make good this situation. He again asked the young girl to dance and she said, "Yes," so he stood up with her to go to the dance floor and, in so doing, took the tablecloth, glasses, everything, right across the floor! The band didn't actually stop playing – in fact it hurried on playing even more quickly – but it has been a wonderful English language exercise to ask people for an adjective to describe the look on: (a) the girl's face; (b) the man's face; (c) the band leader's face; (d) the head waiter's face; and all the other guests, how did they look? A dreadful moment... but very amusing for those not involved.

The amusement afforded by our forays into the world of music and drama seemed to be endless. We were asked on one occasion to look after some actors who were part of a large number of British actors putting on a show in town. They insisted on having one day off and that was a Sunday, so they all met on Saturday night in various houses and had different people put them up and look after them. We had about six or seven people. One of our guests was Mrs Bandaranaike's helicopter pilot. (Mrs Bandaranaike was the Prime Minister's wife.) We all had a very good evening before everyone going off or going to bed.

There was nothing for them to do the next morning except to go down to the beach, in buses which collected them from outside the Galle Face Hotel. I drove the people who had been staying with us down to the hotel and they got on the bus ready to be taken to the beach about thirty miles down the coast, a beautiful bay. One of the men, however, was missing and wasn't to be found. Everybody was complaining that they were going to be late so finally they went off without him, saying, "He's always a nuisance, leave him, let him be." Now what had actually happened was that he had made a deal the night before, in our house, with the helicopter pilot.

After all the others had gone off down to the beach, the pilot would take him to where the helicopter was, fly him down to the beach and land amongst them, and this is what they did! You can imagine the astonishment of all these people on the beach, sunning themselves, going in and out of the water and talking about how this chap deserved to be left behind because he was always late... when suddenly a helicopter appears in the sky, comes down nearby – of course blowing sand in every direction – and as it lands, out jumps their friend in his swimming trunks, waving his towel and shouting, "You rotters, you went off and left me and I had to go and get a helicopter to catch you up." Well, no comment is necessary on this sort of behaviour.

In the midst of all this hilarity I was very fortunate to have an excellent British Council Representative, known as 'Chinese Fred' because he spoke Chinese. Also Lennie Goonewardene and his team in the Language Unit in the Ministry of Education who were responsible for English, were absolutely first class. So these two groups of people, both of whom had a say in how I was to work, worked together – so well that my life was really very easy. I'm not saying that the technical problems of radio work (we didn't have any film work in those days) and the problems of making sure the textbooks and curriculum and examinations all kept in line with each other were easy – they weren't – but I had such an easy background to my work that I was able to do it fairly comfortably and without much bother because of the sheer good manners with which everyone behaved.

My wife and Chinese Fred's wife became very good friends and used to do things together. One day in a bookshop in Colombo they came across a book called 'The Rajah from Tipperary'. They bought it on the spot and brought it back to me. It turned out that the Rajah from Tipperary was a chap called Thomas who had gone from Ireland to England, got on a ship to India, and become the gunner of a Maharajah's state. The Maharajah was killed and he married the Maharani, or she married him in order to keep her position, and he did very well. It was discovered that this Thomas was actually a distant ancestor of my wife whose name was Promilla Thomas, so I often feel amused at the way in which the tentacles of the British Council reach back into history as well as all over the world.

An added bonus was that our daughter, who was growing up, had a wonderful opportunity to learn how to swim in the swimming pool at the club in Colombo; very safe, very pleasant, always good weather and always people to play with and swim with and she blossomed marvellously. Also in the afternoons there was an art class, run by an old lady who had a great gift of bringing out the talent in young people and we have to this day in our house the head of a horse which Cherry moulded when she was about six or seven – and it really is a remarkable piece of work for a child to have done in just an afternoon.

Certain other things are memorable for the truly unexpected way in which they came about. One afternoon I was sitting in my drawing room looking out across the veranda down the avenue towards the gate into the quiet suburban street outside, when a well-dressed man walked up the street, crossed the road in through our gate up the avenue and disappeared to the right where the main hall door was. I waited to hear the bell ring or hear some talk, but nothing happened. The next moment this man appeared through the doorway of the drawing room, came across to the sofa on which I was sitting, and said, "Excuse me, I hope you will forgive me butting in like this. I'm the brother of *so-and-so* (and he mentioned a minister of government) and there are a few things I thought you people should know." I didn't even ask him to sit down at that point but said, "Oh yes, it sounds interesting, what is it?" He replied, "The Russians are unloading weapons about thirty miles off the coast and these are being brought in to the south of Sri Lanka." He gave me the name of some points and continued, "…they are being picked up there by various people in different cars…."

At this point he handed me slips of paper with the registration numbers of the vehicles written on them "…and they are being taken into the jungle to be supplied to rebels who are preparing for an insurrection." I said, "That's quite interesting, please sit down," which he did and improved his story. He said he thought we should be aware of this. I thanked him and said that as he probably knew, the British Council didn't get involved in this sort of thing and had he told our embassy? He said he hadn't but would just leave it with me now. With that he got up and went away.

Now I didn't quite know what to do because one of the things we in the British Council are always very careful *not* to do is to get involved in any way with this sort of thing, for no matter how lightly you get involved you can't 'dis-involve' – you can't get out of it again because you've done something in the rigmarole of events.

I was very fortunate in that the following Sunday, after the church service at St. Andrew's, in the rectory over coffee I met the Naval Attaché of the British High Commission and I thought, 'this is my chance'. I told him what had happened and gave him the pieces of paper on which the car registration numbers were written and I said, "That's it! I'm not having any more to do with this." He said he quite understood, to leave it with him and I was not to worry.

I didn't worry or think about it again until about a month or six weeks later when again I met him over coffee after church on a Sunday morning. I said, "By the way, were those numbers any use – did anything happen?" He replied, "Yes, thank you very much, they were all absolutely correct and I've much more to tell… but it's not for you." I replied, "Certainly not, you keep it to yourself!" It seems the story was true and someone was rumbled in some way or another.

Another unusual event connected with that church took place after I had agreed to become an Elder of the Kirk. Three of us were inducted as Elders one Sunday morning. We stood in front of the altar and the clergyman said a few words, wrote something in a book and prayed, and thus we became Elders. On my right was the Head

The Induction of Elders

of the Voice of America and beyond him was the Ambassador of South Korea. I couldn't help thinking to myself, 'Is there anything other than Christianity that could possibly bring together three such disparate fellows, in a Scottish Kirk, in Sri Lanka! The outreach into various parts of the world was so great that I almost burst out laughing; I didn't I assure you, I took it most seriously but there is an element of fun in all this.

A great deal of our time was spent touring the island to visit different schools to see how they were getting on and hold small seminars of perhaps only twenty or thirty people from the local area, especially teacher-trainers if it was possible to get them together. This gave me an opportunity to see the beauty of the country – it really is a beautiful island.

Other outstanding things we saw were the old cities of Anaradhapura and Polonnaruwa. These were discovered about one-hundred-and-fifty years ago, when a young Englishman went into the outback at the instigation of a very large-minded boss, just to see what he could find. What he found was a wild bear, disappearing down into a hole in the ground, reappearing and going away. At great risk the Englishman descended into this hole, with a torch, to see what was there and, to his astonishment, he found that this wasn't just a hole. It was fully brick-lined; it had a floor of bricks, walls of bricks and even a roof of bricks – what on earth was going on?

So he got out and returned to headquarters, asked some engineers to come back with him and they discovered that this was the remnant of a whole city that had once been there. It had actually been wiped out by malaria, completely, and the jungle had just grown over it; just grown back and covered it, and there it was, waiting to be discovered. It had been well uncovered by the time we saw it; as had the other hidden city, Polonnaruwa – very similar.

We also saw some very strange and unusual cave paintings in a place called Sigiriya. To get to those one had to climb up into a cleft in the rock and view them from close up.

These old cities and the cave paintings are very well known in the tourist trade but to us, who just came across them on our way to and from our daily work, they were decidedly increased bonuses.

Another interesting event was the climbing of Adam's Peak, a high, cone-shaped mountain which happens to be in the way of the rising sun in the East in such a way that the sun casts the shadow of Adam's Peak right across the whole island. You can actually stand on the top and see the shadow of this tall, cone-shaped mountain right across the island and see it getting smaller and smaller as the sun rises higher and higher.

There was a myth attached to this. If you walked up Adam's Peak you would not feel tired. This is because it was sacred to Buddhists, Christians, Hindus, Muslims and almost all the religions.

I was asked to take part in this, which I did, and, having climbed from, say, six o'clock in the evening until midnight, waited up there until the sun began to come up at about four o'clock, watch the shadow, and then walk down again, it is actually a fact that I did not feel tired and my legs did not feel worn out. Whether this was psychological I don't know, but I do recall it as a fact which I did not expect to find true.

One Saturday evening the Secretary to the British High Commissioner rang us in a great hurry and asked if we could possibly go round to her place to make up a party for dinner because her brother, who was a Major in the British Army, was on his way home from Hong Kong to Aldershot, England, and was staying overnight in Colombo and was able to leave the ship to come and have dinner with his sister.

In the middle of the party we discovered the Major had spent some of his service in Borneo. Promilla's sister had been posted to Borneo and had told us a story we could hardly believe.... about a German husband and British wife. Both were trick cyclists, who after the war went to do some research into the head-hunters of the Iban. This was a good lark in itself, researching into the psychology of the head-hunters! Anyway, after some time they set up a clinic in the jungle and it was given the address 'Seventh Mile Mental Hospital', because it was seven miles from the nearest main post office in one of the villages there.

They stayed there and had their mail delivered to that address and after about sixteen months they took some leave and returned to

Europe, first to Germany to see the husband's people and then to England, to Colchester where the wife's family lived. In Colchester the wife was driving her car quite slowly down the street, when she went round a corner and came upon the back of a circus. The elephant bringing up the rear pushed back his foot and stove in the front of her car! So she wrote to the insurance company explaining that 'while she was shopping in Colchester one morning an elephant had kicked in the front of her car'. As it happened they were intending to get a new car anyway, which they subsequently did.

On a later occasion, they went to visit a stately home which had peacocks. While they were looking around the house and having tea, their nice, new, shiny car was surrounded by some of these peacocks, who had seen the other peacocks in the reflection and pecked at them. The couple returned to their car to find a windscreen wiper missing and lacerations all over this lovely new vehicle. So again the wife wrote to the insurance company to explain that 'while she and her husband were having tea one Sunday afternoon, their car had been surrounded by peacocks and absolutely destroyed in its appearance'.

The insurance company wrote back saying they had just about come to terms with the elephant and would she be so good as to give them a little more time to think about the peacocks. In the meantime, since they understood she was returning abroad to where she worked, would she be so kind as to let them have her forwarding address – which of course she did as: 'Seventh Mile Mental Hospital, Borneo'. It is not recorded exactly how the insurance company replied to that address but everything was sorted out in the long run.

The Major immediately said, "I knew that couple; in fact, one of my first jobs after the war was to keep an eye on them because we thought that he might be a Nazi on the run using his English wife as a cover in erstwhile British Colonial properties. I actually went to that place, Seventh Mile Mental Hospital, to check they were all right, and they were. The most amazing thing about them was that they were each over six feet three inches tall, so they weren't likely to be able to hide if they were spies!" Anyway, that was the story and I was very surprised to hear it could be verified.

Another most thought-provoking event took place one evening when I was returning from an expedition in the north of the island, near Jaffna. I was going more or less due west for a while, as the sun was setting, and I suddenly found I was being asked to stop by people at the side of the road. The reason was that a little further on, only about a hundred yards, there were two Hindu Temples, one on either side of the road. On this particular day there was some special kind of procession about to proceed across the road. It was interesting to watch and I saw them going slowly across the road, between me and the setting sun. I was able to see the outline very clearly and remember distinctly how they reminded me of the Holy Communion processions that I have seen so many times in high churches in British churches or British cathedrals. The outline could easily have been people carrying the chalice and all the garments, from one part of the cathedral to another, and here it was, from one Hindu temple to another. I couldn't help feeling that there seems to be a 'sameness' in all our religions.

One thing that surprised me greatly was the arrival of a new British Council representative when Chinese Fred moved on, and I had the job of taking him round and introducing him to various people. One evening we were invited to a party. I had expected it to be a small party of perhaps twenty people, but when we arrived there were about sixty or more people there, in a big room. I said without thinking, "Oh goodness me, with such a big crowd, there's bound to be some relation of Promilla's here." Now I said that because Promilla's family had spread all over India and Sri Lanka and it was very unusual to go to a big gathering of university people and so on, without meeting someone who had a connection with her. The new representative was rather surprised by this and said, "Lloyd, are you sure, do you really mean that? Don't you speak a little too quickly?" I said, "No, there's bound to be someone." So he walked to a group of six men standing there and I heard him say, "Excuse me, my name is *so-and-so* and I'm the new British Council representative. I wonder if any of you gentlemen know a Mrs Mullen – she would have been Miss Promilla Thomas." One of them said, "Promilla! Where is she? I haven't seen her for years; I grew up with her!" It turned out that this man was some distant cousin whose parents had died and he had been brought up in the same house as Promilla. So I had to introduce him hastily to Promilla and they fell to talking about old times while I went on with the new representative.

I must say this new rep remembered the incident many years later when we were on home postings in London. I was waiting to cross Trafalgar Square to go to the main office just under Admiralty Arch, when I was plucked by the sleeve from behind and there he was. He said, "Lloyd, do you think that in this crowd of people here there might be a relation of Promilla?" I did burst out laughing.

Cherry consults the Buddha in Sri Lanka
(Two heads are better than one!)

15
Back To Pakistan

My next posting was to Karachi in Pakistan, as the Regional Representative for the Provinces of Sind and Baluchistan and the Language Teaching Advisor for the whole country. It was a very interesting posting but it began with a firm request from headquarters to, "...sort out the premises problem." It had come about that the British Council in Karachi, which had been the capital of Pakistan before it moved to Islamabad, had offices in a very large, old, central building. This was ideally placed in the city, but perhaps too old and too large for our present purposes and also not properly leased. In fact, when I left London to take up the post, our lease on the property had run out and we were, so to speak, squatting in it.

So I arrived in Karachi with this 'albatross' round my neck of having to do nothing to begin with except sort out the premises problem. Naturally, my very first day I asked the secretary to bring me the file. It was quite clear that we, the British Council, had given a firm undertaking that we would leave the premises on such-and-such a day but we had not done so. Our legal advice was that there was no need to do so and we could stay as long as we liked while trying to find new premises. Now this was not going to be easy because we didn't have all that much money to spend on the rent and also the world was just beginning to develop about this time and there was competition for property. However, I wasn't inclined to do anything too quickly until I had found out exactly what the situation in the country was, and indeed in the city.

Luckily I met a missionary family who were old friends of Promilla's, and became new friends of mine, who were in the business of architecture, contracting and building. They were missionaries but they built churches, they looked after churches, they built houses and looked after missionaries generally. They were very helpful people so I had a chat with them about the situation.

On the staff in the British Council were two or three local members who had been there a long time and who knew all the city scandal and all the city's inner workings. They were able to tell me a lot of things about who was who and what was what and who had influence and who hadn't. However, none of this was getting me very far and, at the most unfortunate moment possible, a crisis arose!

A very senior and wealthy businessman, and also very pleasant I discovered in the long run, wanted to take over our premises as part of a very complicated deal between three or four major companies, based in Switzerland, Pakistan, Australia and London. This complicated deal involved property and shares, as well as the shifting of business headquarters. It was all going ahead until the British Council stopped it in its tracks because nobody had ever thought that the British Council would not agree to keep to its word and get out of these premises on the day that it said it would.

So I had been approached by junior managers of this great businessman's empire, senior managers, members of the board, all sorts of people, and I had said I certainly wanted to get out as soon as possible but couldn't because we had nowhere to go. I had to explain that the British Council's work had to go on and that the legal position as I understood it was that we could stay in the premises, but, from the point of view of good relations, it was undesirable and that I was trying to do my best to get out.

So what happened? Well, one day I was in the middle of what is called a 'Cash check', a spot cash check. Once a month I went to my accountant's desk and said, "Stop. Please show me where your cheque stubs are, show me where your petty cash is, show me where your invoices are." I checked the whole situation, right there on the spot, including putting cash out on the desk. It was quite a demeaning thing to do to one's accountant, I felt, but mercifully I found it always tallied and we were always very happy about it. But what should happen? I was right in the middle of it when I had a rather frightened secretary (an excellent girl) come down and say,

"Mr *so-and-so* is upstairs. He has come personally to see you about the premises." I'm afraid I said, "Tell him he'll have to wait; I'll be up in a few moments. Explain as best you can that I'm in the middle of a spot cash check."

I hastened through it and when I went up I found him standing outside my office. He had refused my secretary's invitation to go in and sit down and had refused her offer of coffee; so I said, "Good morning. How are you? Come in, we'll have some coffee," so we went in and sat down.

He came straight to the point and said, "Why won't you get out?" I replied, "There are two reasons: I've nowhere to go, and also it looks to me as if Mr Bhutto is going to be hanged and if the British Council leaves the country at this point, when a former prime minister is about to be hanged, people will say, 'Ah! The Brits have given up on Pakistan,' and all sorts of things will follow, so I can't poss…" He stopped me in my tracks and said, "You're absolutely right, you're quite right; I've never thought of that. So, what do we do?" I said, "What we do is try to find premises that I can afford. I have an ideal one but it's well beyond my reach and I can't ask our London office to put up so much money; after all it's the British taxpayers' money and they have to get value for it. I haven't even asked what the rent is but I know it will be probably two or three times what we could afford to pay." When I told him where it was he agreed that it would be ideal – he knew the house and its owner – in fact even better than our present premises and offices. "How much money are you able to pay?" he enquired. I replied, "I can't tell you that but it's pretty well known around town because my predecessor has been trying to get premises for a long time." We went on talking and he told me about his recent tours and so on and then he left.

At three o'clock that afternoon, in the middle of my siesta, I was awakened by a telephone call. You've imagined it, yes? This telephone call told me that the premises, the beautiful house which I wished to rent for the British Council, was on the market and immediately available, at exactly the sum of money the British Council had ready to pay! I paused for a moment and then said, "All right, deal done. I'll come… where are the papers and we'll sign."

And so we got into the finest property in Karachi – beautiful grounds and building. The library was able to fit right across the ground floor while the first floor gave us all the office space we needed, and more. It was a triumph of good fortune for me and there we stayed all the time I was in Karachi.

The library in our new building in Karachi

My friend, the missionary architect, came and inspected it and told me that it was ideal. But there was still one snag: it had to be passed by our senior legal adviser in London. He had to see the terms of reference and it had to be within budget. As luck would have it, he was travelling back from the Far East and put down briefly in Karachi because he had to change planes.

My missionary architect friend had prepared a document stating that the building was in excellent condition, well worth about three or four times the rent that we were being asked to pay for it and he recommended that we should take it since we would never get another such opportunity. So we did and I signed; I signed to pay British tax payers' money, about five or six times beyond my competence. I shouldn't under any circumstances have agreed to commit the British Council to pay so much money, but I had the authority that at least the senior lawyer in our legal section was passing by when I did it and I had this document from the architect. And we got it.

I need only remark that about four months later a short, rather terse note went about generally that 'Officers were reminded that there was no circumstance during which they could commit the British Council to money beyond their competence'. At least it brought a smile to my face!

Another event which brought a smile to my face was through the senior office manager, a Mr Qureishi, who had been there a very long time and was regarded as a quiet, serious, dull but very efficient man. He was anything but dull and when this happened I roared with laughter… I received a note, which everyone had to sign finally. It read:

> *Will all those officers whose grandmother is going to die on the last day of their annual leave, please let me know now so I can draw up the 'Leave roster' with certainty that we will always have cover for our work. For ease of reference, a list of the names of those officers whose grandmothers have died on the last day of their leave in previous years is attached.*
>
> (And the list was attached).

I still laugh when I think of that note going round the office and people deprived of their only way of lengthening their leave illegally!

Another thing I smile at is how Promilla decorated the first landing of our home. We had quite a nice house in Karachi out in the suburbs. It had two storeys and the staircase was modern, wide and with a big landing after about ten steps. The wall which faced you as you went up to the landing was plain white and Promilla felt that it was too dull and uninteresting, almost like a prison or hospital and not like a home. She didn't like it at all and didn't know what to do about it. One day I returned from the office to find that, with the help of others but mainly by herself, she had painted on this white wall a green field with a blue sky above it and some white clouds in the sky. In the foreground of this field, right on the edge of the landing, was a white fence – a nice, neat, tidy white fence – about waist high and in the distance there were some sheep, sleeping. It was a very pleasant scene… well done by Promilla.

It was always part of the bargain that if Promilla was so good as to follow me all over the world, to this place and that, once we got there she was allowed to decorate the house the way she wanted it.

We had many people to stay on and off and some would drink a little more alcohol than others – I'm happy to say we never had any trouble with alcohol at all but this was the nearest we came to, shall we say, a misunderstanding. One night a guest who had been drinking a little extra after dinner said he felt tired and would go up to bed because he had work the next day. So we showed him the staircase and bade him goodnight. He knew upstairs and how to get to his bedroom. He walked up the first flight of ten steps but didn't turn right to go up the next flight out of our sight; instead he went up to this white fence which Promilla had painted on the wall and attempted to put his two hands on it and throw his leg over it in an attempt to get into the field. I am able to tell you that he recovered without our help. He felt his head, feet and hands touching the solid wall and he turned round with a little "Hmm, hmm," and said "Well, goodnight," and went on up the stairs. I still think Promilla regards it as one of her more minor triumphs!

My work was intensely interesting because Baluchistan and Sind are both fascinating provinces – Karachi a most problematic city, and the English language teaching situation throughout the country was very varied.

The province of Baluchistan covers a vast area of Pakistan, but the number of people living in it is quite small compared with the other provinces. It was actually when I was teaching in Lahore years before that the Sardar, or leader, of one of the tribes of Baluchistan, the Jamali tribe, though he was only a boy of about eighteen, explained to me what he believed to be the difference between the peoples who made up Pakistan and also the different ways in which the colonial rulers had attempted to deal with them.

He said that what the Baluch liked most of all about anybody was the concept of respect; this was very important. The Baluch respected one another and respected outsiders (until they discovered that the outsiders maybe did not respect them). This mutual respect had manifested itself in British times in that an army officer, when he moved into a certain area with his troops, would go ahead himself and meet the leader of the local area, give him a small gift and receive a small gift in return. They would even have a meal together, and he would say he wanted to bring two or three hundred soldiers through his area and on to the next. The Baluch leader would say, 'Yes, that could be done but could it wait until tomorrow or the next day'.

In this manner the British learned a lot about the local Baluch people but the Baluch people also learned a lot about the British. They had time to see what weapons the soldiers were carrying; they had time to see what sort of plans they appeared to have in mind; they had time to count them and make sure that exactly what the British commander had said was indeed true. In this way Baluchistan and the English got on very well, which was good because it was the southern end of the North-West-Frontier Province and also the western edge of Pakistan, as it became, but it was undivided India originally, and went out to Iran in the desert.

In fact there was a place called Zahidan on the border, right out in the desert where any army officer who misbehaved himself in British times was exiled. That tradition was carried on by the Pakistan army – when one of their officers misbehaved they simply posted him to Zahidan out in the desert between Iran and Pakistan.

This Baluch concept of respect was very important in that it made for a peaceful way of resolving disputes and avoided unnecessary bloodshed. It also led to a growth of trust between the soldiers and their officers which resulted in the fairly unusual occurrence after the Independence of India and Pakistan, that across the Straits of Hormuz in the kingdom called Oman, the army of the Sultan of Oman was actually an army of Baluch soldiers with British officers who used Urdu as the common language. Indeed, the old boy from my old school who had gone ahead of me into the Indian Army and up onto the North-West-Frontier, was for some time after he retired, in charge of the Sultan of Oman's horses and cavalry and because he was a fully trained vet he was in a position of great respect. Again, this business of respect even extended to the animals – the horses, the camels and the mules.

Here, as an aside, I tell the story of one of my bearers in Pakistan who had been a muleteer in the undivided Indian army. It came about when we visited some Moral Re-Armament people up on the Frontier. They were a very old Pathan family whom we didn't know, but they received us very warmly. They had amongst them an elderly lady who had never married – this is very unusual amongst the Pathan families – and this lady ran what I can only describe as a 'stable of down-and-outs' and she always tried to do her best for them. When she heard that I was looking for a new bearer she immediately disappeared into the recesses of their house and emerged with a cringing individual in near rags who stood in front of me. She said he would be a very good bearer. So I said, in Urdu: "Apka nam kya hai?" which is, "What is your name?"

To my surprise he answered in very good English, "Sir, my name is Munawar Din."

"And what job did you have?"

"British Army, Sir" came the reply.

"Really. Did you fight in the war?"

"Yes, Sahib, I fought in the war."

"Where did you fight in the war?"

"Iran, Iraq, Scotland..."

Before he could go on, I said, "Excuse me, Scotland?"

"Ji, Sahib, Scotland."

"Are you sure you were in Scotland?"

"Oh yes, I was."

"Could you tell me the names of any towns that you remember in Scotland?" Straight out of his mouth came the word, "Glasgy."

"Glasgy?"

"Yes, Sahib, big city, Glasgy."

Now that he had pronounced it as 'Glasgy' I knew he was not telling lies so I asked him what he had been doing in Scotland. To my amazement he was able to explain that the great leader, Winston

Churchill, had an idea of attacking the Germans down through Norway and that to do this he wanted to land in the mountains of Norway, which had been occupied by the Germans. He wanted to land mules and soldiers who would be able to exist in the mountains and gradually drive the Germans down and out, and to get these mules, Churchill had arranged for Indian muleteers and mules to be brought all that way.

Well, I listened to the story in more amazement than I had of this lady producing this man in the first place – but that's not the end of the story. The end of the story is, of course, that I appointed him and that he became a very good bearer indeed, bang on time, precise in all his movements, quite different from the wretched, bedraggled creature whom she had more or less dragged into the drawing room in their house.

This mention of the drawing room reminds me to emphasise another point about the Pathans and the Baluch. They did not make much difference between the people in the house and the servants. Indeed, in the evening in the cool, very often both the family and the servants would sit out on the same charpoys and talk together. This of course meant there was a great 'esprit de corps' to be found in sub-groups of these tribes.

This concept of respect among the Baluch and of dealing with them in a respectful manner was to play an unexpectedly large part in my own life some years later on but enough of that for the moment – we will come to it.

The other tribe, the Sindhis, down south on the Indian side of Pakistan, were great traders. They were very good at buying and selling and lived quite a simple life out in a very difficult and quite dangerous desert. There were far more Hindus in Pakistan in the Province of Sind than in any other part of the country because they had been able to live with their Muslim neighbours in a very reasonable manner so that when the continent was divided and the holocaust occurred between the Muslims and Hindus it did not hit Sind in the dreadful manner it hit the rest of the continent. They were, however, always regarded as peripheral to the main events in Pakistan. The Sindhis stayed within their Province of Sind; a few of them did come out to do trading but that was all. They were not a major influence in the whole country, as were the Punjabis.

The Punjabis were the most numerous, the best at farming, the best educated. They had Lahore in the centre as their capital. They were very traditional – indeed, some families had been on the same piece of land from long before Jesus Christ came on the Earth and they were settled there forever. Some of them carried with them the names of places that they had come from, like 'Mazari' – the Mazaris would have come from Mazar-i-Sharif – and so on. But basically they were a very settled, quite rich farming community who had also played a big part in the building of cities, roads and railways right through from south to north and, of course, the River Indus, whose water had watered them, and other rivers, too.

The Punjab means 'Panj-Av', five rivers. We have the word 'av' in our English language, as in 'Avon', the river Avon. These rivers were used to irrigate the Punjab – the province which supplied grain for the whole of India. It became the breadbasket of India for a time.

The city of Karachi where I lived and had my office, was a kind of melting pot of all these different tribes; and also another group of people, and a very important group. They were those Muslims who had fled from India at the time of Partition and settled in Pakistan in the port city of Karachi, which was then quite a small port. They brought with them all the skills of having worked in the Civil Service, of having run their own large businesses in India, and of having an international outlook because they were doing business with all parts of the world when they were forced to leave India and settle in Pakistan. They were refugees really from the holocaust and they settled mainly in the city. This meant two things.

It meant: (1) They had no ownership of land in the new country to which they had come, and (2) They had almost an entire ownership of the Civil Service skills and industrial skills needed to build up the new country.

They were called 'Muhajirs', which really means 'refugees', and they brought with them a new kind of connection into the India which they had left behind because not all the family came. They had left brothers and sisters, cousins, aunts and uncles; they had left whole businesses, vast properties, lands all over the place; they had left a knowledge of their neighbours – who had been neighbours in India but were now no longer neighbours as they had been left behind – and this unbalanced the new nation of Pakistan.

When I settled into Karachi I discovered that the attitudes of all these various people, especially the Muhajirs, were quite different from one another. The Muhajir attitude was cosmopolitan; the attitudes of the other peoples were mainly limited to within the sub-continent, almost tribal, especially the attitude of the North-West-Frontier people, who felt they belonged to the north of the country and up into Afghanistan. They felt they were very different from the rest of the people in Pakistan, and indeed they were.

There was also another and dwindling group of people left behind, one might say, by the Independence of India. They were the Anglo-Indians, mainly Roman Catholic but some Protestant, and the Christian Indians who are now Christian Pakistanis. The reason that they are well worth mentioning is that they occupied a very large number of the secretarial posts in the different businesses, in the running of airports, etc., because they had more or less fitted into the British way of doing things right up to the time of Independence.

A good example of these people would be the band who played every Saturday night in Faletti's Hotel in Karachi and where my wife would dance to the music. They were Goans, who came from Goa originally, Roman Catholics, of Portuguese origin and Indian origin, and produced the latest, most up-to-date music for the expatriates and the élite people of Karachi to dance to. This again was a dwindling group because large numbers of the new Muslim community were not able to fit into the way in which the Europeans had lived and, indeed, some of them disapproved of that way of life.

It is easy to see how challenging it was for the British Council to try to find a proper approach to this new situation and decisions about where to concentrate effort, how to train people and how not to involve people in things that wouldn't be of any use to them, because this new country was full of new people, all of whom wanted to try everything. Well, we couldn't do everything but I was fortunate in two things.

I had been in the country before, admittedly several years before, and so knew how the families worked because I had taught the boys and seen them grow up. I knew something of the inner workings of the families of Pakistan and in Aitchison College we had had families from all over the country. That is point one.

Point two was that, by sheer good luck, just after I arrived in the country it became the turn of Pakistan within the British Council arrangements to have what was called a 'Policy Review'. A Policy Review meant that the most senior officer possible came out from headquarters to make an in-depth attempt at finding out all he could about the past, present and future of the British Council in the country. In my particular case it was a Deputy Director-General who came out and he had a reputation of being extremely efficient and also extremely abrasive. He used this abrasive method to get to the root of things, both within the British Council itself and also with those people with whom the British Council dealt in the country.

He was indeed abrasive and indeed quite frightened some of the members of staff whom he met in Karachi. Fortunately, my predecessors had been very efficient officers who had set up arrangements very well indeed and trained the staff extremely well, and these staff had been in their positions for some years so that they were well qualified to deal in a quiet, calm, efficient way, with the rather rough questions that he from time to time threw at them.

However, this was as nothing compared with a near miracle that changed the whole tone of everything when he asked to meet a very famous Pakistani newspaper man who had retired as editor of a leading English newspaper. The editor – I knew him a little – had agreed to a meeting on condition that everything that was said was off-the-record and would not be reported for many years to come.

So I arranged this meeting – actually on the veranda of the upper storey of this beautiful new building which I was able to get in Karachi. The setting was lovely, looking down over the garden, quite private, a nice place to have coffee in the morning; and there these two men sat. Now they were men at the top of their careers – and each knew very well what the other wanted and what they themselves wanted. The discussion began with the usual polite, "Good morning, how do you do, how are you?" but very quickly jumped into the Deputy Director-General saying, "What earthly use is the British Council to you? Of course, I know that nations have to have diplomatic relationships, especially if there is any kind of military involvement, but why do you need the British Council here at all? After all, couldn't we just get on with ambassadors? You don't need this large library – you could arrange all these things yourself, couldn't you?"

Now the former editor, looking him straight in the eye and putting his thumbs behind the lapels of his coat and down his jacket as much as to say, 'Hold on, we must talk sense here', very calmly said, "You will forgive me for saying that Britain is no longer as powerful as she used to be and we in Pakistan already regret that we can see Pakistan will now never become as powerful as we had hoped. Nonetheless, it remains a fact that Britain is central to the Western World and Christendom and Pakistan is central to the Eastern World and Islam." He actually raised his hands together and as his fingers intertwined, he said, "It is essential that these two cultures should be harmoniously intertwined."

This set my senior officer back a bit and, after a moment's pause, he said, "Oh, all right, yes, yes, I can see that, but how… how?" Then, very slowly and deliberately, the editor pointed with his finger down through the floor of where we were sitting and said, "Down here you have a library and in that library I can read the history of the development of all your institutions in Britain and throughout the British Empire and I can also read, in translation, the history of the institutions of all the other nations of the world. Now Pakistan is a new nation and we could go in whatever direction we like – for example, we could go with the Americans, provided we were prepared to pay their price; neither the Russians nor Chinese have at this moment so much to offer that we would go with them, but there are other nations that have lots to offer. However, it is not easy to deal with them because of the language problem, so we in Pakistan have decided that we will do things the British way and that means that we need not only your library, we need people to teach us how to use that library to the full. We need to be able to use it in such a way that we can send some of our best people to Britain to your universities so that they can come back here; we need to be able to send our army officers to Sandhurst. There are so many things we need to be able to do – even how to build new trains, motorcars, aeroplanes when the time comes, almost everything – and we could, by doing things the British way, find it much easier than by doing them any other way. And, of course, we hope to bring about this rapprochement between East and West, Christendom and Islam."

An added bonus to our lives in Karachi was that, in addition to having very good office staff, we had an excellent set of servants in the house at home, left behind by our predecessors. Not only were they excellent in their work but one of them came from that very same part of The United Provinces of India from which Promilla came and they were able to speak to each other in a kind of local language which carried all sorts of nuances of understanding that otherwise wouldn't have been possible. In fact, it turned out that our head-bearer, Nayyaz, had begun life as a helping-hand little boy in a garage where Promilla's Uncle Stanley, who was the D.I.G. Police in that area, used to get his motorcars serviced, so Promilla received extra respect as the niece of the head of police in the area from which Nayyaz came.

Also it turned out that our mali (gardener) came from more or less the same place – he was older – and when Promilla's father came to stay they discovered that they had known each other years and years ago, long before India was divided into India and Pakistan. They talked to each other so much that Nayyaz actually said to Promilla, "Memsahib-ji, you should have seen them talking, talking, talking – neither of them listening!"

Nayyaz was very efficient, as exemplified by the occasion when Promilla had gone to Lahore to be with her family and I was on my own in Karachi. A group of unexpected guests suddenly arrived on their way from England to Australia and I had to put them up for one or two nights. One man had his wife and child with him and the other two were separate. Fortunately, we had enough bedrooms but I was a bit alarmed in the office, and when I rang Nayyaz to make sure some arrangements could be made while I organised for a driver to bring them in from the airport, he recognised that I was a little worried. I can still hear his voice over the phone, saying, "Sahib, do not worry, all will be well. Only one thing I ask you if I may, please. We have no tonic water. Please ask driver, Zahoor, to stop at the shop on the way home and bring one crate of tonic water."

In fact, when I did get back to the house to be ready to receive them, I discovered that not only had Nayyaz set up three separate bedrooms, but in the one where the child was to be with his parents, he had even found a few toys from some cupboard or other and set them out for the child. He had put magazines besides the beds for the others and also flowers in the rooms. So I recognised at once that I did not have any worries on that front.

Another great help at this time was Promilla's friendship with a local American lady who was the choir mistress of the Karachi choir in which Prom sang. This American lady, Jane Subjally, had married a former Indian prince who had come to Pakistan and set up a shipping line and more or less given up all his pretentions to royalty and maharajadom, but he was very well into the entire scene and able to give us very good pointers on what to do and what not to do.

One of the things he remembered from his days in the British Army, when he had fought with them in Burma, was that when they were coming down the Burma road, with the Japanese trailing after them very fast indeed, he suddenly realised that one of the British army trucks which should have been carrying people to safety, had stopped and the driver was out at the side of the road saying his prayers. Now our friend, whom we called Shuja, was fortunately a Muslim and a senior officer in the army so was not over-stepping any religious line when he walked over to this man and said, "What are you doing?" This man replied, "Sahib, I'm saying my prayers, five times a day… it's time." Shuja said, "Look here, you will be saying your prayers in Heaven in a few minutes if you don't get up and get out of here quick. Now go on." So the soldier got up. That soldier was later to become General Zia, President of Pakistan, and he was President of Pakistan when we arrived there just at this point and had Mr Bhutto in jail. So we were able to learn a great deal about General Zia.

One interesting thing about him was that whenever he came to Karachi, General Zia always called deferentially on Shuja, to thank him again, and again, and again, for saving his life from the Japanese.

To complete the family, so to speak, we had a very good school to which Cherry, our daughter, was able to go. It was an international school and the head mistress was a very strong English lady who really knew how to teach and how to bring children up. She gave Cherry a great start because she had this ability to fix on a child personally and make sure that the entire school and entire staff took into account what that child's needs were. Of course, she was able to do that because she had a limited number of children and a very good background to each of them, but still she took immense care and we were forever grateful for the start she gave Cherry, because Cherry was shortly going to have to go off to boarding school.

The other 'person' to complete the family was the dog. We had left our little dog, Merry, behind in Sri Lanka when we went home, so now we had arranged for her to be sent to Karachi. The Assistant Office Manager, who was the real know-how man, came to me and said, "Sir, when the person is ready to send you the dog, tell him to send you the exact flight on which it is coming and then let me know and after that we will do exactly what is needed."

Sure enough, we got the exact date that the dog would be arriving and the manager said, "Now, what you have to do is to go down to the airport with the driver, park the car, then go to the office and simply say you have come to collect your dog. Don't give them any other details at all; they may ask for papers and if they do just say you haven't got them."

So I did that. I got out of the car and went to the office and said, "Excuse me, I've come to collect my dog." The person at the desk looked up and said, "Your dog, yes, all right. What you have to do is go out there and go in the second turning on the right, go straight up, through Arrivals, then on through Customs, then pass the Police Checkpoint and then out onto the tarmac." So, I asked, "Will they let me?" He replied, "Oh yes, just tell them you've come to collect your dog." So I went along, was stopped at every point by people in all sorts of uniforms and I merely said, "I've come to collect my dog."

They replied, "Oh yes, on you go," and they passed me onto the next person. I must have said it about six times. I got out onto the tarmac and I had been told to go and see Mr Tarmac. Now Mr Tarmac was the boss of the entire airport staff out on the tarmac. I did see him – fortunately he was a big fellow. I went across and said, "I've come to collect my dog." "Ah," he replied, "Yes, you've got to go down there, quite a long way off, to that office. Walk right through all the offices – it's rather a glum place, Sir, I'm afraid – but go to the end and there you will find someone who will tell you." I went down there; it took a long time. People did ask me what I was doing, so I told them I had come to collect my dog.

I turned into what was almost like an aircraft hangar with all sorts of dusty little offices on one side and the other, walked right through them all and at the end was an office. A man was sitting there, so I said, "Excuse me, can you help? I've come to collect my dog." "Your dog, yes, wait a moment." He called someone and said, "Help this man to find his dog, will you." The other man said to me, "Come on, come out here and we'll have a look." He took me down to where there were three or four small kennels which are used to transport dogs by air. Sure enough, Merry, our dog, was in the third one. I said, "That one." "Right-oh, we'll put her on this trolley; you know the way you came? You just push the trolley back... if you don't mind doing it yourself. I can send a man with you if you like." I said it was all right, I would do it.

Merry was very sleepy because she had been tranquilised, and I pushed her out onto the tarmac and everyone was now very interested, "Ah, that's your dog… what a nice little dog. Now you've got to go in there – she's got to go in with the arriving luggage."

Now here was a moment of alarm. The kennel had to be lifted up and put on to the carousel which carried the luggage. I was asked by the chap in charge to get up on the carousel and go through the hatch with the kennel to make sure it didn't fall off.

So, people waiting for their baggage on the other side were treated to the spectacle of a man, in all white clothes, hanging on to a portable kennel with a dog looking out sleepily from it. When we got down to the end, they then saw this man jumping off and – with the aid of a bystander – lifting the kennel down and putting it on the ground. I went across and got a trolley, lifted the kennel onto it and pushed it down towards the exit, where of course I was stopped. "I've just been collecting my dog," I said. "Your dog, of course… on you go, on you go." I went out, where the driver of our car, Zahoor, was waiting. He took the kennel from me, pushed it in the back of the car and said to me, "Get in, Sir, quickly." I got in and we drove straight off out of the airport and back to our house where we unloaded the dog. Promilla was there to welcome her and I went back to the office.

When I got there I saw our 'office fixer' and said, "Thank you very much. That was very quick and easy; I didn't have to do anything. They just sent me through arrivals, sent me through customs and through the police checkpoint, and the same thing on the way back." He said, "Yes, Sir; you see, they thought you had travelled on the plane with the dog – that's why they let you go through so quickly like that. In about four months' time you'll get a request for various documents concerning the dog, but by then we'll be able to ignore them. Is the dog all right?" I said, "Yes, as far as I know, very well, thank you."

This happy and most fortunate settling in to my new posting in Karachi was finally topped off by something I couldn't possibly have managed to arrange. A new Assistant Representative, Brian Clarke, came out to join me. He was quite the best Council Officer I met the whole time I was there; he was absolutely wonderful and so easy to get on with – so marvellous at understanding the needs of the rest of the staff and able to pick out what was important and get on with it efficiently… budgets and that sort of thing.

Our household was completed by our night watchman, or chowkidar, called Yar Khan. Yar Khan was a Pathan from a village to which he could never return because he had killed a man there and if he went back he would be killed in his turn, so he stayed all the time down with us in Karachi. He became a great friend of Merry, the dog, and Merry became his great friend. He used to say to us, "Merry is my chowkidar; Merry looks after me." Indeed, he actually trained her to sit beside him on the edge of the veranda. He would give one signal, a sort of guttural sound from his throat, and Merry would go off and do one circle of the entire house – round the front, down the side, along the back, up the other side and back to where he was and sit down. She would do that right-handed. Then he would give another signal, very similar to the first, and she would do the same thing but in the other direction. Then he would give a third signal, slightly different again which the average person wouldn't notice, and Merry would rush to the gate and put her head out through the iron bars at the bottom where she could see out into the street and maybe bark, maybe not, and then come back and sit beside him. Those three signs were his way of dealing with Merry and Merry's way of dealing with him; she looked after him very well. So we had double safety all the time – either from our own chowkidar or from our dog.

An important point to make here is that because he was a Pathan he was one of the many, many Pathans in Karachi, and especially in our area, who were acting as night watchmen to the people who employed them. Pathans were really loyal to their employers and to their friends who were working for other people. The result was that they had a very firm control over the whole area where we all lived and this was important because if any strange person came into the area, they knew immediately that he was not a local – he might be a thief or might not, but they passed the word on from one to the other and kept a very careful eye that way.

This was very important because it was a well-heeled area of the town and we had some minor sheiks from the Gulf coming and staying in rather fine houses for a short period while they went off into the desert to look for buzzards, kites or hawks of some kind. Of course, you can imagine the kind of people who were sometimes attracted to be near these sheiks, who were quite capable of handing out a thousand rupees as a tip for some small piece of work done well.

Sad to say, Yar Khan took ill while we were there and died. It was very impressive to see how, because he had paid one rupee per month into a Pathan insurance scheme, the day after he died three very respectable Pathans arrived with a minibus and a coffin. They took his body with great dignity, put it in the minibus and drove to the airport where his body was flown to Quetta. There it was taken by another minibus to the place where he was buried, back into his own village... where he could go in death but could never have gone in life.

That simple insurance scheme and the way it was all carried out with such dignity says something about the nature of the Pathan life, which is so often misrepresented in the world.

It is of interest here to record also that this excellent Assistant Representative was from a family in a place called Graiguenoe, about a mile and a half beyond Holycross where we lived on the other side, so we had these two Tipperary connections in Karachi. Indeed, the family of this Representative had actually put in the communion rail in our little Holycross Church where I was brought up and spent the first seven years of my life coming and going. There was a plaque on it just to say it had been erected by this family in memory of one of their uncles, I believe, who had been killed in the Boer War. So there was a strange kind of linkage which followed me round the world from Tipperary, wherever I went.

It is rather sad to record that at this time when General Zia was President of Pakistan and when Mr Bhutto was hanged, later on General Zia himself was shot down out of the air in some strange, unaccounted for aeroplane accident, with the American ambassador on board, I think.

There were so many stories of blood and thunder surrounding General Zia, including one – which I'm sure is apocryphal – about his early career as a Captain. He was sent to Jordan by the Pakistan Government because no officer senior to him would go. The job was at the request of the rulers of Jordan to get rid of malcontents from Palestine who had come into Jordan. Captain Zia, as he was then, agreed to go and he got rid of them by the simple expedient of saying, "I am going to divide you into two groups, tell you to go, and if you don't go I'll come and shoot you." The story is that he did divide them into two groups and when they didn't go he went along and began to shoot one or two – not himself personally but his unit – and they very quickly fled out of Jordan. Now, whether this story is true or apocryphal (and I hope it's apocryphal), it did have an effect in the Pakistan that I met at this time. Mr Bhutto was being hanged, for a crime which the general opinion was – in Karachi anyway, as far as they would tell it to a foreigner – that he was guilty. However, the lawyers had not been able to establish that guilt properly in court so the whole matter was left in a little cloudiness and that's where it remains until this day.

One of the more extraordinary achievements of my Assistant Representative at that time was to go up to the north of the country where a Jeep containing four British geologists had gone over the edge and deep down into a ravine, killing none of them but leaving all four in a desperate and difficult condition. It seemed that nobody was willing to take responsibility for them. I remember him coming to me and saying, "Lloyd, what on earth are we to do? They are British geologists, genuinely trying to do some work – they are not spies or anything – and nobody is willing to take any responsibility for them up in Islamabad. Shouldn't we do something?" So I said, "Brian, tell me, what about the insurance on these people?" "Well," he said, "I can check it out but it should be all right." So I finally said, "O.K. Brian, off you go. Do what you can and try to avoid landing the British Council in the financial doldrums if you possibly can." And he went off.

Suffice it to say, within a fortnight he had managed to get those four people out of the ravine, into Pakistan Army airplanes, down into Pakistan hospitals, and onto British Airways flights to London, where each one was met at Heathrow by his own GP and family and taken to hospital and looked after and they are all well to this day. They certainly would not have been alive had it not been for the simple clear-headed determination and ability of my Assistant Representative in Karachi.

So you can imagine what a life I had – excellent support at home, excellent support at the office, all across the way. You have to have support because you are, after all, the Regional Representative (that was my title) and people judge you by what happens.

Perhaps the way to make a link with the Baluch and Oman is to say that the only loss we suffered was a superb secretary, who got a much better job in Oman and went off there to earn far more money than we in the British Council could pay her at that time.

I remember one of the more difficult things to swallow was a very senior person in Pakistan coming in asking to make arrangements about his daughter going to university in Britain. This was easy enough to arrange and was all attended to, but while he was with me he told me that there was a certain young lady in the P.I.A. (Pakistan International Airlines) who, every time she came back to Karachi from flights abroad, would go right up the whole length of the country by any means whatever, usually by aeroplane, as far as the Swat Valley (which later became famous), and then would return to the coast, to Karachi, and go off into the great wide world again on her next flight where she was a stewardess. Now he was certain that the only possible reason for those journeys up to Swat and back again was to pick up consignments of drugs and sell them in London or America or wherever and there was no way that it was possible to stop that. He was quite helpless. He explained how and why and all the legalities, but that sort of life was going on under our noses and there was nothing we could do about it.

While I was in Karachi, the representative for the whole of Pakistan, who was based in Islamabad, went home on leave and I was asked to go and stay in Islamabad for some weeks and run the show. That was revealing in that I came to understand that Islamabad was a sort of ghost city! There was hardly anybody in it at all, except ambassadors and their staff and international organisations and their staff, a few very senior Pakistani ministers and their staff, and that was it. There was a little night life in the hotels but nothing that you could really relate to very happily. It was an empty and unwise life because the view which these international representatives got of the country was of a neat, tidy city which had grown up in the past twenty years. I myself remembered well driving through the area long before even a single piece of road was laid out for the city to be built. We used to drive up to the mountains through that area and there was nothing there at all and now you had a nice, neat, tidy, modern city but it wasn't alive. It wasn't natural at all.

The reason why it had come into being was that Field Marshal Ayub Khan, the first Military Dictator, found that his army officers and his civilian leadership were totally enmeshed by the business interests down in Karachi where people were constantly flying in and out from India, from the Gulf and from all over the world, with huge sums of money available to give to any Pakistani who would arrange things for them in their own country. Remember, Pakistan had not been in existence long enough to command the allegiance and patriotic love of people who had come to Karachi City from all over the world; so if they were offered thousands, even, in some cases, millions of dollars, naturally they took the money and did whatever the foreigner needed, so Pakistan never really got a chance to settle down, even after Islamabad was created and the entire diplomatic enclave moved there.

One thing the British Council had in Islamabad which really was useful was a first class Parsee accountant. He could tell you down to the last penny exactly what the situation was on any budget sub-head you wanted to ask him about and he could do this because he was very fierce with anybody on the staff who wanted to release more money than he felt should be released. While this made him very popular with the people in London, it didn't make him at all popular with people on the spot who often wanted to get things done in a hurry and needed a little more money than was immediately available.

There were various other things about the office in Islamabad that I was never able to relate to because of the lack of human interaction with the general public. The general public hardly materialised while I was there; whereas down in Karachi the general public was in danger of flooding your whole operation – so many things to do, so many things to ask about – but it was a 'real life' relationship with the country.

Because of that real life relationship we were very glad that we had a beach hut out on the edge of the sea, about five or six miles out of town. It was nothing very special and anyone else would have thought it a little squalid for a seaside place. For example, four or five miles away to the right was a ship-breaking yard, and to the left you could see a large part of Karachi town reaching out along a peninsula. However, in the middle you had a very nice piece of sand and water in which to bathe and swim. Indeed, Promilla, trusting that her natural skin wouldn't burn, stayed out in the sun so long that she got sunburnt and we had the unusual event of me actually rubbing camomile lotion onto her shoulders to try and ease the burning feeling. She also made a collection of stones – she loved to collect stones – from the beach which she brought home and we still have a few in our back garden here in England.

Another thing that kept Promilla busy at this time was a production of 'Blithe Spirit' which she put on for the British expatriates there; she got them all acting in it (some of them were very good indeed) and she produced this slightly shortened version of 'Blithe Spirit'. She had acted in this before and so knew it pretty well. It was great fun and the whole community loved it and joined in because it was not the sort of thing that was commonly done in Karachi in those days and unfortunately hasn't been done since either.

Of course, in the midst of all this peace and quiet and happy work for the British Council, the Russians invaded Afghanistan. One of the first things that happened was that all the unnecessary Americans in Afghanistan left the country and came flooding down into Pakistan to get aeroplanes and whatever they could to get back to America.

We were asked by our High Commission if we would look after two or three of these Americans, and we did. A very nice couple stayed with us, an elderly couple about seventy years old maybe, who were advising on some electro-engineering businesses. When they arrived at our house, the husband stopped dead in his tracks and said to his wife, "Look, will you look!" and he was looking at Promilla. He was a tall man and he put his finger – taking advantage of age I suppose – right down on the top of Promilla's head and turned her around, 360 degrees, and said to his wife, "Just look, everything – the face, the hair, the shape, the voice – every bit of it is Jemima."

Now, Jemima was the girl in Kabul who had looked after the American commissariat. She was an Armenian and apparently, in these Americans' minds, Promilla was an absolute twin of this girl. In fact, they found it hard to believe that Promilla wasn't Jemima herself come to life in front of them in Karachi. So this gave rise to another interesting thing which came much later on in our lives, actually it was when we got to Uganda:-

One night we were invited to the Russian ambassador's annual reception and when we arrived, his wife, with whom Promilla was a good friend, took her down the line of staff to shake hands with the various members. When they got to a man in white uniform, the naval attaché – even though Uganda was landlocked – they stood looking at each other and the ambassador's wife said, "My goodness! Look at them. Twins!" Despite the fact that one was masculine and the other feminine, they looked exactly alike and, would you believe it, he was Armenian. So, the rest of that particular evening was spent by Promilla and this man going round the guests pretending to be twin brother and sister and then admitting who they were and so on.

But... back to Karachi.

The situation was quite serious because the Americans were starting to help the Afghans stand up to the Russians which gave an opportunity to all sorts of people with different agendas, from just plain nationalist feelings to outright jihadist tendencies to every other imaginable political attitude, to get weapons and fight in Afghanistan. This was a difficult place in which to fight because there are all sorts of mountains you can hide behind and come down on top of your enemies, especially if other people were foolish enough to give them weapons, which of course the outside world was doing at that point – the Russians from one side, the Americans from the other. But there was a lot of death in between, sadly.

Anyway, this American couple stayed with us a few days and then went back to America and that was the end of our 'Armenian episode', as we called it.

It is important to say that in Promilla's ancestry, in her actual family background, there was an Armenian influence through the Armenians who fled from the Turks, in about 1912 I think it was. Some of them came across into India and married into Indian families; one of which was the Thomas family in North India, because they were Christians as were the Armenians.

A much more amusing though rather convoluted international mix-up which Promilla got involved in was one night at a dinner at the American Embassy in Karachi. She was asked to sit at a particular table with the wife of the Chinese ambassador. Now this Chinese ambassador's wife spoke very good Urdu, not English but Urdu, and because Promilla spoke Urdu, she translated for this lady. Later, as we were going out of the party the American ambassador took me by the elbow and said, "My wife tells me that your wife speaks excellent Chinese." I really didn't have the heart to attempt to explain that this was not exactly the truth!

Of course, it was a great joy for me to be able to meet, both by chance and by arrangement, many of the boys whom I had taught in Aitchison College years before and who were now grown men in their jobs. As I toured round the place, especially in Sind and Baluchistan, I would meet men who would suddenly say, "Oh, Sir," and then I would have to adjust and remember that he was such and such a boy and looked either as he had done as a boy or now looked quite different as a man. This made for a kind of continuity of regard for Pakistan as a country and these boys as individuals. However, it was apparent to me – sadly apparent to me – that they did regard themselves as individuals and members of their tribes but hardly as Pakistanis.

The concept of what it was to be a Pakistani was very difficult to establish because it had no real root in the ground; it was a kind of political arrangement that came about at the end of the British Empire and it never really settled into a proper, correct and unambiguous identity.

I was fortunate enough to be able to visit the two great cities of the Indus Civilisation; the cities of Mohenjodaro and Harappa. These two cities were right out in the desert and it was only sensible to visit them in the cool season – what we would call our winter – because the heat of the desert in the summer would be too much to bear. When one got there it was very exciting to see buildings which were five thousand years old – they had been two or three thousand years old when Jesus Christ came on the world. Also they had links, strange and unique links I think, to that part of the world in Mesopotamia from where the Jews had originally set out for Palestine. This was established by the fact that they had some bitumen which was carried from Mesopotamia down to these two cities, which were at one time on the River Indus – that's why it's called the Indus Civilisation. Bricks made in this valley were bituminised, so that five thousand years on they were still able to stand up to water flowing over them.

Indeed, water was brought into the house at upper storey level so that at the lower level you could push a tile back and water would flow down for you to have a shower. Then it would flow out through bricks, again bituminised, underneath your wall into the street. In the street there was a long, covered drain, again covered by bituminous bricks, which went on to the end of the city and carried the water right out and away.

Now this still amazes people because the artisans who made these cities also produced intricate and small artefacts which couldn't have been made by an uncultured people. The suggestion is that the River Indus changed course and literally shifted away across the desert, maybe because of some slight earthquake, and left these two cities without water, without any means of sustenance. The people who lived there (and left behind quite an interesting script which has never been deciphered) died or moved elsewhere and became absorbed into the civilisations round about, as in Punjab and Sindh, and we've lost these peoples of these two cities.

However, we still have pieces of their pottery – a large number of pieces – and when we parked our Land Rover at the entrance, there were two potters still making pots in exactly the same design as those made some five thousand years ago. You could walk a few yards away, pick up the shards of those old pots, push them together and get the same kind of pot as was being made in front of your eyes by a man sitting at his wheel.

I think the thing that impressed me most about the cities was the fact that in those drains, which went down the length of the street – and they were straight streets for long distances – every twenty-five yards there was a manhole with a proper cover. The workers responsible for keeping the water flowing, could lift the manhole cover and remove any dirt or garbage that was blocking the water flow. This city maintenance suggested a very high level of civilisation. My driver remarked to me as we walked about the cities and saw all these things, that it was a better place to live than his own village where he came from and many of the present day towns in Pakistan and India. He was able to recognise from the local level exactly what happens when civilisations flourish and civilisations die.

One way in which I saw a civilisation developing concerned the bearer whom I had appointed up on the North-West-Frontier. After Munawar Din had been with me some years, he wanted to leave because he knew that I was going to leave Pakistan shortly and he would have to get another job. He had heard that there were factories opening in the city where they were going to make metal nails and had asked for apprentices to learn how to do this job. So he asked me whether he could have one night off every week in order to go and work in this factory and then after some time, one whole day off. Naturally I agreed, and I am very happy to tell you that just about a fortnight before Promilla and I had to say goodbye to Pakistan altogether, that young man found a very good job for himself in one of the factories in the city.

One of the places where one could eat out very comfortably in Karachi at that time was The Yacht Club; they still had the old rules of dress and behaviour which lasted into the modern era. An unfortunate Dane who had come out to do business turned up with his Pakistani friends to go to dinner one evening, but was stopped from going into the dining room by the head waiter, who very politely said, "Excuse me, Sir, but in this dining room gentlemen are required to wear suits." The Dane and his Pakistani friends pointed out that he wasn't wearing the conventional type of suit, but a very ultra-modern style where all the different parts – the trousers, jacket, tie and shoes – were all toned in slightly different colours of brown. However, the headwaiter stood his ground with the famous remark, "Sir, no Sir – this dining room, same coat, same trousers, same coat, same trousers dining room, Sir," and the unfortunate man had to go away. He did of course come back about twenty minutes later in a suit and they all had dinner together. But it remains an interesting point that the waiter was able to stand up to club members who tried to slip, as he thought, something past him.

Another story which came out in that Club one night was from a friend of ours who had arrived in the country about four months earlier. He told us that he was sharing a big house with another family until they could get another house and then the families would live separately. He and this new man had discovered that they had their own birthdays on the same day, their wives birthdays on the same day, they had been married on the same date and one or two other amazing coincidences. When we got back home my wife told this to our head bearer, Nayyaz (who came, as I told you, from the same part of India that she came from and they spoke the same dialect) and when he heard this story he said, "That won't happen again for three thousand years!"

Laying a wreath on Armistice Day

16
Home Again

There now occurred something which certainly won't happen for another three thousand years! I was given five months home leave! Such a long period of home leave from overseas service was quite unheard of and probably against all the rules of the Kings of England, the British Council and any other organisation you can mention. It came about in this way:

In the British Council, London-appointed officers who served overseas had it made quite clear to them that their home leave was an entitlement, but it was not a right and it would have to be foregone if necessary. It could only be taken according to the 'exigencies of the service'. Now in my particular case this meant that the space between my last two postings – Bangalore and Colombo – had been so small that it had only been possible for me to be given short amounts of leave, so that my full entitlement was now very large… five months! However, this was more than could reasonably be given to anybody. I never really discovered why it was given to me but I suspect it was because the British Council had one good point going for it. Most of its senior management were officers who had come up from the bottom, been right through the system themselves, and knew all the difficulties and advantages. They knew when somebody was skiving and when somebody was working properly, and they decided that I was to be allowed to do this because of my past history. There is no other reason for it.

So the result was that our leave began in London on 12th April 1980 and ended on 12th September. Within those five months we saw our daughter into her first term of boarding school, through her first long holiday and back into school for the start of her second term. We also saw the sale of our existing house and the purchase of our new house in Ewell (where we still live).

We had the confidence that our home in Karachi was being looked after by a well-settled and responsible group of servants who would look after the officer standing in for me while I was away, and also look after our own particular interests. Nayyaz had a long history with our family and there are one or two small stories about him that are worth telling.

One concerns the famous battle at Kohima. He had been some sort of mess bearer in the army up at Kohima. However, he got lost in the confusion of the fighting and didn't know where to go. He was wandering about one day trying to find some of his unit when a British Army truck went by and an officer saw him and shouted, "Nayyaz! Come, jump up." So Nayyaz jumped up and got in with this officer. He asked, "Sahib, where are the others?" The Sahib simply replied, "They are all dead, Nayyaz." Just like that. And when Nayyaz told me that story he just stood still for a moment and then turned away and went off.

A more amusing story about Nayyaz is when my wife picked up the telephone in our house in Karachi and got a crossed line between a man and woman who were obviously making an illicit tryst to meet somewhere. It ended up with one saying to the other, in a language which she didn't fully understand, "I'll meet you at the corner of such-and-such a place." The other voice replied, "Well how are you going to get there?" The first person said, "I'll wear my burkha." Promilla called Nayyaz to the phone and said, "Listen here, Nayyaz, what's happening?" So he listened for a while and then put the phone down and said, "Madam, the burkha is the cover for everything!"

His sense of responsibility came out in another unusual way one night at a party when one of our guests was perhaps drinking a little too much. Nayyaz sidled up behind me and said into my ear, "Sir, such-and-such a sahib I think drink too much; may I put water in his whisky?" So I said, "Yes, do, Nayyaz, put water in his whisky."

This was the level of service and servants that we had. They were near to being family and were very loyal to the British Council because they had worked with the Council before I arrived and would work with the Council after I left.

Another interesting, faithful servant of the Council was very useful in the library. He had worked as a peon – that is really as a general cleaner and tidier-upper of things – for a long time but he had, over the years, managed to acquire one great skill. It was simply this: whenever a book went missing and the librarians, their records, all their shelves and correct places did not uncover it, they would send for him. He would listen to their story, think, and very often would go straight to some shelf and take out the book! That is literally true and they did rely on him at the last gasp because if he couldn't find it then the entire system was incapable of operating to find it!

Another odd and very helpful thing that happened when I moved in to the new Karachi office concerned putting in a new telephone. We experienced great delay, but one member of staff came to me privately and said, "Sir, my sister is married to the man who is in charge of giving you the right to have this new telephone. He is well known as one of the richest men in Karachi because of all the money he collects from people who want to get their telephones put in quickly. All this delay is only in the hope that you will give him some money to do this, but don't, Sir, because once you do that he will keep at you forever, so just wait." The result was that we did wait and operated the British Council office without telephones, but we did have telex of a kind in those days, and whilst I was under considerable pressure from people to get the telephones in 'at any cost', I *wasn't* prepared to do so because of what this faithful member of staff had told us.

A very satisfactory event took place while I was there in that the British Council librarian in Karachi, who had been serving faithfully and efficiently for a very long time, was awarded an M.B.E. This was a great joy for him personally and also to all the staff who had worked with him because they felt the recognition given to him was some sort of recognition for the entire operation in Karachi, bearing in mind that Karachi had been the capital of Pakistan when all this started and remained the centre of the British Council operations in the country.

And yet it is strange for me to remember now that throughout all these very interesting and exciting times in my life, one of the memories that kept coming back to me, as the most precious almost, or the most calming, was in Sri Lanka when we had gone to a very remote part of the southern coast to visit some schools. In the evening we were taken to the southern-most point of a peninsula just to see the way the moon set on this particular piece of sea. We were actually in a grove of cashew nut trees and, standing in the calm of the tropical evening, looking out across the water – really at the South Pole which was in the next hemisphere, miles away – the wide, light green calm of the sea and that cashew nut grove and my friends a little distance away talking quietly among themselves, remains with me as one of the most peaceful experiences in my whole life; quite different from the excitements of London, Dublin, Karachi and the great cities of the world. In some way this filled my heart from the bottom up, and my nerves, so that it was possible to deal with all these other cities in a calm way.

A good example of the way in which these cities operated comes from one evening when my wife and I were invited to dinner at the home of the great businessman who ran so many hotels and finally took over the British Council office that was in existence when I arrived in Karachi and played a very instrumental part in our acquiring our new office. My wife knew his wife very well because, though he had kept her in purdah, my wife was able to go in behind the purdah-screen and got to know her, so we were quite at home in her house. We sat down to dinner and my wife said, "I have never seen such a wonderful dinner service before. What is this – these knives and forks – sort of dark gold – is it brass?" And my host said, "Promilla dear, gold, not brass, gold, gold-plate." So everybody sort of gulped and thought 'oh dear!' Well, you can commit a faux pas, but if it ends up with your host being able to say, "Gold, gold," then perhaps you've given them the opportunity of showing they're onto something you're not!

Another very memorable but much more sombre occasion was the Armistice Day celebrations in the Karachi Commonwealth Graves Commission cemetery where British and other allied soldiers were buried. During the service the representatives of various countries and institutions walked forward with their wreaths, the head of the institution carrying the wreath and laying it down. I felt that as I was a Southern Irishman and hadn't actually fought in the war but one of the members of the British Council staff, a senior peon, had fought and had served the Council for a long time, that he should be the one to walk forward with the wreath; I should have to go beside him to lead him because he wasn't quite sure what to do. Anyway we did that and he turned out in a magnificent white uniform, tall turban – he was a tall man anyway, 6' 2" – and he carried the wreath and put it down with great dignity. I stood beside him, a much smaller man. He stepped back, stood still, saluted, turned round and we went back to our place.

I was very surprised and very heartened over the succeeding weeks at the large number of people who told me that they thought it had been a wonderful idea for this man to put down the wreath.

We knew a large number of the other representations in Karachi from the different countries, and their servants. If you had a large reception it was a useful custom to be able to borrow some servants from other delegations – and this was quite common practice.

I do remember an incident, not in Karachi but in Dhaka, when I was having breakfast one morning with my host who was a diplomat. His bearer, who had been serving at the French ambassador's party the night before, was regaling him with all that he had overheard, and I thought to myself, 'My goodness, how careful one needs to be to guard one's tongue when you have servants and bearers around you all the time.'

This relationship between employers and their servants led to some exchanges of language which were very amusing. Once I remember a bearer being unable to say precisely what age his son was. He tried to say he was between five and six, and my mind went back to a little boy in Aitchison College, who, when asked a similar question said, "Half-past-five, Sir!"

Despite Karachi being a very cosmopolitan city, there was less humour there than I had known up in Lahore. I think the reason is that in Lahore most people were Punjabi and they knew each other from pre-Partition days when there were Hindus, Sikhs, Muslims, Parsees, Christians all mingled up together and they had standard jokes about each other, one community playing off the peculiarities of another community and so forth.

One of the more amusing ones concerned two Sikh gentlemen who came back to Lahore to visit some of their Sikh shrines in Pakistan, as it now was. They were going to go north up to Rawalpindi and got into a train in Lahore – but it turned out to be the wrong train actually. They got into the top berth and asked the Pakistani man in the bottom berth where he was going. He told them that he was going south to Karachi on business, whereupon they said, "These clever Pakistanis, they're well advanced. They've got trains with the top berths going north and the bottom berths going south – goodness, how do they manage it?"

Whilst on my extended holiday in Britain, only one really alarming event took place and that was when Cherry fell into a canal somewhere near Sheffield. The water was flowing quite quickly towards a mill wheel about a hundred yards down. We were on the other side of tall, metal railings and couldn't get to her and for one moment of horror, we thought she was 'a goner'. Thankfully, our friend who had been with her managed to grab her, more or less by the collar, and hoicked her up onto the bank. It was very cold and we wrapped her in all the clothes we could find, put her in the car and drove home at top speed, managing to save her from getting pneumonia – having saved her from one death we then saved her from a second.

Of course, one reason maybe why I was able to have five months leave was that the British Council required me to go on courses in management and finance. They counted this as work and not as leave so that diminished, as it were, the ridiculous length of my home leave.

I do remember one course particularly. It was a management course and the people who organised it had some of those 'initiative games'. They divided us into about five or six groups, each of, say, six people. The game our group was asked to play was a sort of Lego. They chucked a pile of bricks into the middle of our group and the idea was to build a particular kind of structure – we had a specific plan, like a small church – in the quickest time possible. We all set about our tasks and ours was going very well indeed as we thought, until just at the very end when we were more or less putting in the last pieces. Unfortunately, a slight push in the wrong direction and the whole structure collapsed. Far from coming first, we came last!

Discussing it afterwards with a Maltese friend I had made, he said in a kind of mournful, thoughtful way, "Ah, yes, haste, too much haste – the seedbed of our Western self-destruction." I've often thought of that remark when I was in a hurry to get things done: "The seedbed of our Western self-destruction!"

Promilla's sister, Tina, was married to Andrew Norris, a British Council officer so she understood the whole situation of our daughter going to a new boarding school. Promilla's sister-in-law was a niece of Ravi Shankar and had grown up in India in a very civilised situation, extremely cultured. So there were these two ladies in England, along with another lady married to a cousin of Promilla's, really from the Argentine, all of whom had children of their own. We knew that Cherry would be in safe hands no matter what hour of day or night her plane touched down at Heathrow or Gatwick on her way to or from boarding school, wherever we were in the world. This was a great comfort. They were all living within thirty or forty miles of the airports and they were extremely helpful to us.

This was another gift that most of our colleagues didn't have. I can remember conversations with many colleagues on the fact of having to get strangers to look after their children, having to find changes to their plans because their leave didn't fit or they couldn't get back into their house because it had been let out and somebody was still there – all sorts of complications which are common to those who live this peripatetic life, but we escaped all that and looking back now I can only say how grateful we are for this.

Also, the fact of Cherry having lived with us in Pakistan, India and Sri Lanka meant that she was able to fit in quite easily with the other girls in her boarding school. This was because they, too, came from all parts of the world and it was a common thing for them to share their experiences with one another.

Happy as things were with us in England, it was impossible not to look back at the countries in which we had worked and see that they were far from happy. There was division between Tamils and Singhalese in Sri Lanka, divisions between various groups in Pakistan, and there were differences between many of the states of India. While all these countries were progressing in what might be called the material way and doing very well and we in the British Council did our best to help them, too, nonetheless, it could not be said that they were progressing in a peaceful way, either with themselves or with their neighbours. This was a constant source of worry because you sometimes felt that you might well be painting your own cabin while the whole ship was sinking!

As a schoolmaster, I was haunted by a verse written by Frances Crofts Cornford about the English poet, Rupert Brooke, when he was setting out from Britain:

A young Apollo, golden-haired
Stands dreaming on the verge of strife,
Magnificently unprepared
For the long littleness of life.

I used to wonder whether the boys that I had taught and for whom I had some responsibility, had been prepared for life and whether they would regard it or come to regard it as a 'long-littleness'. I had been fortunate in that as a tiny child I had somehow picked up the idea that life wasn't just a thing you lived, it was a purpose. You got on to doing something to help other people and there were very specific things that I saw.

I saw the whole war winding up and people trying to save freedom, which they did; and then I saw after the war people trying to re-build Europe and the rest of the world, which finally they managed to do, and it was all our business to help everybody else in that job.

We also saw that there were whole nations coming to freedom that hadn't existed before the war, and these nations, in which the

British Council had helped us to work, were developing. But, all the same, there was a feeling that within these nations, while groups of people had particular purposes there was a lack of over-arching purpose to make the whole world work in a way that would help everybody and this was a constant problem.

For me it was no problem in my heart because I had always known that there was a good purpose for the world which God had in His keeping and that He could and would find ways of revealing to each one of us what we had to do to help that forward if we tried.

The concept which held me in all this was the Christian concept of Love that one was meant to, and was able to, love people of every persuasion whatever – even if they were absolutely anti what you were doing, you could still love them in a way that might help and if it didn't help at least you could make sure it didn't hinder their lives. But all around one sometimes had the negative feeling that the forces of evil were managing to do their work without people realising it and it was very necessary to go back to the belief in one's own heart that God would win eventually, not for His sake but for the sake of the people of the world whom He loved.

A particular instance of this, which was very painful, happened in my own country of Ireland in the late fifties and sixties. Having failed to get the students in Paris, or the trade unions in England to create mayhem, the international anarchic people – in their attempt to demonstrate to the new nations of the world that parliamentary democracy might not be the way ahead – managed finally in Northern Ireland to isolate two figures on either side of the divide. A young girl and an older clergyman became polar figures for different groups of people. I think without ever realising it, each one, in their own sincerity, actually helped to contribute to a huge amount of trouble in the world.

I have to say here that this is the sort of thing you could never prove to be a political truth but for those who come after me I am only saying it's as I saw it and believed it to be at the time.

This lack of love for the other party in any dispute, whether individual or collective, was the most obvious missing factor in the entire attempt made by different governments to move forward to a happier world.

Another saying which somebody quoted to me and which haunted me at this time was:

You are as near to God as you are to the person
from whom you feel most divided.

I have to say I am glad I was on home leave when these thoughts surfaced very strongly in my consciousness and I had some peace and time to consider them, but the more I think about this one the more I find it a tremendous challenge that if I become divided from other human beings or just one other human being, then I am in some way becoming divided from a God who has been extremely good to me.

In an unexpected area of experience this saying was summed up for me by one of our great Irish rugby players who captained the Lions. When asked about professionalism, money and sport etc., he said very firmly, "Look, it matters desperately who is going to win, but it doesn't matter tuppence who has won." Now that attitude to sport seems to me to be a wonderful way of summing up a good attitude to life.

A good attitude to life for me was severely tested one morning when I was trying to cross Berkeley Square and get out of the traffic to get to the other side. I was standing on that nice piece of greenery in the park, moved out onto the footpath to cross the road to where there used to be a Lloyds Bank, and was waiting there, watching the cars going by but I just couldn't break through the traffic, which I thought I would be able to do, because there were so many cars.

I began to notice that so many of these cars were really rather good ones, and the longer I stood there the more I noticed that some of them were Bentleys and Rolls-Royces and cars that I didn't have or even think of buying or owning. The more I saw of these going round and round preventing me from crossing the road, the more I found myself beginning to wonder why I shouldn't try and get some of these things and go about life in an entirely different way from that I was currently doing. It is genuinely true that I could actually feel the tentacles of materialism creeping up around my lungs and heart and mind and brain, and I did for a few seconds understand the grip that the desire, as it were, to be rich and powerful apparently in one's own eyes, can take hold of people. I had always thought up to that point that they were ordinary people just showing off a little, but, no, I began to realise in my own heart that this could be a terrible reality that could spoil your life completely!

That branch of Lloyds Bank on the other side of the street, which I did finally manage to reach, played another and rather amusing part in our lives. Once, when we were abroad, the manager of the bank wrote to my wife to say she had a current account at the bank but no deposit account and if she put her money on deposit it would gain some interest, whereas it wasn't at the moment. My wife loves a good joke – she was writing books at that time, hoping to have them published, short stories mainly – so she wrote back saying:

Dear Manager,

Thank you very much for your kind letter but do not worry, the milliooooooons are about to roll in. Meanwhile, I depend for my necessary and unnecessary expenses on my husband's account.

Back came a letter:

Dear Madam,
Though you are far away and out of sight,
We wish you success with all you write,
We have today credited to your new account
Forty two pounds, two shillings and sixpence,
...the exact amount.

Signed:
The Manager,
Lloyds Bank,
Berkeley Square, London.

That was a civilised era in which we were living!

Of course these five months gave us the opportunity to build up relations with the family – my own family in Ireland and Promilla's family in England – and we were also able to settle into the community where we began to live in Ewell. We were fortunate in that Promilla's cousin was a solicitor and did most of his work from Ewell and had been instrumental in organising the legal side of our house selling and buying. He was also able to introduce us to various churches around the area but we really didn't decide on any one in particular because we were going back to Karachi.

However, we did decide on the house at Ewell because from its location within five minutes we could get into any library, doctor's surgery, dentist, wherever you wanted to go. Another good reason for buying it was that we knew I would ultimately have a home-posting and there was a railway station right behind this house with only half-an-hour's journey to Waterloo or Victoria; it was also only half-an-hour from Gatwick and Heathrow.

Fortunately, we both had the idea that when you buy a house you really buy a place, a position in the world. The property that we bought was not exactly the style and kind of house that we would have liked to buy for ourselves but it was a most practical one in that while we were abroad we had no problem in letting it out. The great thing was that the various tenants looked after it. At one stage we even had four teachers living together in the house and, bravo for teachers, they looked after it very well.

All this meant that when we returned to Karachi after our leave we were very relieved in our minds to know that our daughter, our house and our relations were all well integrated together and would look after each other while we were away. It's a remarkable thing to have such good fortune as relations and friends who can look after both the medical and legal sides of one's child's life and you leave it entirely in their hands. We had met the house master at the school where Cherry was going to stay and we were very happy with him – he and his wife were exceptionally pleasant people and very sensible.

So back in Karachi we started again. Life was very similar; nothing much had changed whilst I was away and the main thing now was to make sure before I left the place that all the things we wanted to do were done. I think to a degree they were, although I must say I found my farewell tours rather sad because I was leaving a place to which I knew I wouldn't return to live in again and which had been a part of my life since 1959. During the time that I had been in Pakistan, from 1959 to 1982, the whole world had changed so much that one hoped that what one had done had contributed to something but one could never be sure.

Anyway, I paid a visit to Quetta and it was on the flight there that all sorts of interesting things happened. First, when we got to the airport in Karachi the plane couldn't take off because there was bad weather – you must remember in those days the planes were quite small – but we did finally take off and halfway there a bit of a hiatus occurred.

There was a discussion between the pilot and the airport at Quetta about whether we should go on or come back. We were able to hear a good deal of this because it was one of those planes where there was only a curtain hanging between you and the pilot and his navigator. They decided to go ahead and see if they could land.

The thing to understand here is that Quetta is in a dust-bowl. It's down in a valley, surrounded by mountains, and the distance that the plane has to fly in before it can land is not very long. It has to be accurate and it can't be upset by bad weather.

It looked as though things had gone wrong because I distinctly heard the pilot's voice saying, "Well, Quetta, why did you let me come this far if now I can't land because you know I can't turn round to go back to Karachi, I haven't got enough fuel, so do the best you can for me and tell me what advice you give me now." The advice must have been that they should take the plane down low enough to follow the road and this we did; the plane followed the road into Quetta. However, our sense of direction was rather upset when we saw, quite clearly, the navigator and the pilot turning the map of the road which they were looking at, right side up! We thought we'd been going the wrong way for a while, wasting fuel! Anyway, we hadn't and we eventually landed in Quetta.

I was able to go round all the various colleges and offices and meet the people who had been so kind to me and helpful all the time I had been in Pakistan, thank them and go on my way. The British Council was much appreciated in that part of the world.

It was a very different farewell in the Province of Sind. There was a kind of mourning for Mr Bhutto who had been hanged and who was lying in state in his own home place. I asked the driver to take me there. We had to go right around his house, which was in a very rural spot far away. We drove between buffalos and mudflats and countless people, almost pilgrims, who were coming and going from what was becoming a sort of shrine to the Sindhi leader whom they revered and whom the rest of the world hadn't really, in their view, fully appreciated.

On the way we had seen the great Sukkur Barrage which goes right across the Indus River, exactly one mile wide at that point, and were able to understand briefly the immense engineering work that had gone into the irrigation of that part of the world.

I had now heard that my next posting was to be as Director of the English Language Management Department in London. This was a great joy in that, apart from the fact I would like the work, we would be at home for our daughter's next years in boarding school. It turned out when we did get home that we were there for the remainder of her time in school because she had had two years before we arrived home and then she had five years before leaving – by which time I was ready for another foreign posting. Also, she knew how to live in Britain, which she more or less reckoned we did *not* know, having been so long abroad! She had even at one stage in her journeying, brought Promilla's father, who was old and whose eyesight was not so good, to live in Britain and handed him over safely to his son at the airport.

So when we arrived back in Britain and went to the school to see her and take her out for the weekend, we were quite aware that it was really she who was looking after us and making sure that we would behave in the sensible manner in this new milieu that we hadn't been in for so long. I am sure that from that day on she has felt a little more responsible for us than we have for her!

It was a good thing, too, that we were home because one or two events took place for which our presence was needed. One development was that she was good at art and her art masters, both the junior one and the senior one, felt that she should be developed and got her to do some extra work outside and arranged for her to take her portfolio to various places.

One weekend Cherry was to have an important interview and take her portfolio. The senior art master arranged everything and the junior art master left her portfolio for her in the art room, but when she went to collect it, alas, the art master had gone off with the key and she couldn't get in. This created such a problem and such a disastrous situation, she felt, that she used some 'unparliamentary' language to her house master about the matter. This language was the reason for us to be called to the school and we went to see the housemaster and Cherry.

Our daughter hadn't really fully expected us to come along and take her side because it seems some of the other parents more or less abandoned their children and left them to look after themselves. Anyway, we were there to support her.

Now because I was a school master myself and being in the presence of two other masters – the house master and the art master – we were a sort of club who understood how such a sad thing could happen. We also understood that Cherry had a perfect right to be upset, although she had no right to use unparliamentary language. We sorted it out as best we could and when we were trying to, as it were, present it to the public, the house master was sitting at his desk, I was sitting just beyond on the opposite side and our daughter was standing a little to the right beside his desk. We were negotiating a sort of happy way out of this unfortunate affair when, suddenly, Cherry slapped the desk quite hard with her hand three times and said, "No, no, no. You are only trying to gloss over all this. You are not dealing with this properly. Things are going to be different around here from now on!"

When I view this situation in perspective and think of a thirteen- or fourteen-year-old child, taking her housemaster and her father to task at the same moment about how life ought to be lived, you are faced with reality in a sudden and unavoidable way.

The happy ending to all this was that throughout the rest of her time in boarding school, Cherry was quite carefully looked after by the art masters and the whole art department, and towards the end of her time there she was able to do very well by going out into other places to learn more.

Another fortunate thing was that her mathematics master told her that she wasn't very good and might do badly in the G.C.E. Fortunately, Promilla was able to take her to some teachers out of school who quickly discovered that she wasn't bad at all but just needed to be re-oriented on what she was doing and, thankfully, in her G.C.E. her best results came in mathematics.

Also in that school she took part in various unusual things, such as the school children's edition of the United Nations where they visited The Hague for a debate – in the proper chamber there. Her business was to represent East Germany of all places, in a debate on the desertification of various parts of the world. While this might sound a little odd it certainly helped in widening her understanding of the world and the way things were done.

Another thing in which she took part was a business exercise in which various groups of children had to produce a product, market it, sell it and then show the accounts with how much it had cost, how they had sold it and whether it made a profit in the long run. This exercise was very useful, too. I remember when I asked her what she had learned mainly from it, she said, "Well, you must have a good accountant who can tell you exactly how much money you have at any point when you want to know what to do next." She also made the point that you have to have a product that people actually want to buy. She compared the success of her group with some other groups who produced very good products but very expensive and people didn't want to buy them, at least not at the price that would re-pay the production cost.

One of the more unexpected sights that I saw as a result of these programmes was her standing on the platform at Ewell West Station, just behind our house, with a little briefcase and going off to an appointment with the Ambassador of Sudan to discuss with him desertification. She also managed to get some sort of interview with, not the East Germans who refused to have anything to do with her, but with the Russians. As she said: "They wouldn't listen to me, the East German Embassy; they took no notice of me so I just went round to the Russians and asked them to tell me about it... and they did."

All this time Promilla was having success with her writing, with short stories being published in various magazines, like Woman's Weekly, Bella and The Lady. Also with her poetry; in fact, she wrote one poem which won the Daily Express competition for the best love poem in honour of the four hundredth anniversary of Romeo and Juliet.

So these incidents helped to give our time in Britain all a bit of a lift, and my going up and down to London daily to the office was relieved by these pleasant happenings back at home.

Commuting daily to and from the office was not too much of a burden I discovered. The only unfortunate thing was that I seemed to have lost eleven umbrellas in one year, if the tally was correct, leaving them on the train when I got off. I did once leave my briefcase on the train, and that was a worry, but I managed to get to the last station, I think it was at Dorking, and sure enough the briefcase was still there when the train arrived and I was able to get it back, but these mishaps weren't too prevalent, fortunately.

We were also fortunate that we had excellent help in making the alterations and additions to our new home. One of the alterations was to put a door through to the dining room because, believe it or not, one didn't exist when we took on the house. Another addition was to extend the dining room so it could have a music corner with a piano in it, and also to build a study for Promilla and myself to the end of the house. These were very well done for us by an Irish friend, a builder, who not only gave us the lowest estimate but also gave us such good quality of work that a near neighbour, who had retired as an inspector of building, came across one evening to enquire politely who our builder was because he had been watching him and was surprised that he taken such trouble to put in all the correct foundations and do all the correct and proper things that such a building required.

We also put up a separate conservatory/playroom at the end of the garden so it was possible for Cherry to use it later on for an art studio, and we could use it for a store-house for the bric-a-brac which inevitably collects when you live as a family. Importantly, we could have it as a separate place for children to play if it was wet outside, and they could still be watched from the kitchen window by their mothers or others. These additions made a considerable comfort to our lives and made the house much easier to let when we were abroad.

Another small advantage which accrued from these buildings was that behind the conservatory we were able to keep our garden rubbish and plants that weren't doing well, our bins and anything that we wanted to hide from public view. It was also a place where you could get on with a dirty job without upsetting the main garden, like making compost or planting various cuttings in pots before they were ready to go out in the beds. It turned out to be a very useful area which we hadn't actually thought of before we put up the conservatory.

The house and surroundings turned out to be a good, useful spot in which to live and we more or less made up our minds that we wouldn't move from it until we had retired and tested it out as a permanent place to live.

There was one disadvantage which was that we never really furnished it to the best possible standards simply because we knew it was going to be let out and we had no guarantee that people would treat good quality furniture or good quality anything with the best behaviour but, in fact, they did and we had no problems at all with any of the lettings all the time we were abroad until the time we retired.

We discovered that an excellent idea and place for summer holidays was Lancaster University's Summer School. They ran an excellent series of courses on everything from fell walking to chess, from novel writing to weaving or painting, and we were able to go there together as a family and have different courses for each of us at our own interest and age. I personally used to go off fell walking and probably walked most of the fells in the Lake District. Promilla took creative writing and bridge and Cherry did whatever the children did when she wasn't able to be with us.

These holidays had one great advantage which was that from the moment you arrived you were looked after by the students, who carried your luggage and showed you where to go, and you literally did not have to touch money – unless you went into the bar – for the whole holiday; it was all paid for in advance, all arranged and it was a great relaxation to know that everything was done for you. It was a holiday. Even on the walking holidays I remember there was an easy section and a hard section and the people who took us were real experts in their field. Lancaster University was greatly to be congratulated on how they managed this because it was a wonderful advertisement for them. I don't know if they still do it but if they do I recommend it to anyone who is reading this.

Throughout this period of our lives Promilla also got an opportunity to do some of her first love – acting. She took part in the production of 'Oliver' with which the Ashley Centre Playhouse opened its first production in Epsom. She was Oliver's friend, the housekeeper.

She made enquiries about a writing circle and discovered that there wasn't one in Sutton. However, as a result of Promilla's enquiry and that of another lady, very soon the Sutton Writers' Circle was founded and Promilla was able to take part in it, being a founder member. She went on with her writing and also played bridge.

The other thing that we did was to more or less settle on St. Mary's Church in Ewell; it was the village church not far from us on the London Road and we began to go there regularly. There was a new vicar who had come from Wales, the Reverend Richard Hanford, a very learned man and very good musician and we got on well with him. I remember him saying of his friend, Rowan Williams (who later became much more famous) that he was an absolutely disgusting man who walked down the road and came back to you speaking another language, so brilliant was he!

St Mary's, Ewell

I am happy to tell you that many years later when that vicar finally retired from St. Mary's Church, Rowan Williams came on the last evening and preached the sermon at his farewell.

I suppose I have some fellow feeling as an Irishman that they were both Welsh and all this was carried on in the English language which was the language he used to impart special pastoral and spiritual care to my wife and myself when we were affected by serious health problems. He was the best possible help in time of need.

Even his departure bequeathed us something more lasting for, at a party to welcome his successor, we met a total stranger, Valerie Wood, who has become such a close family friend that, with great sensitivity and patience, she has put together this whole memoir in presentable form so the rest of the family can read it, typing and ordering it from start to finish. What was facing me as an awkward chore, she transformed into an absolute delight.

17
More Work In London

And so I took up my post as Director of the British Council's English Language Management Department in London. My office was just beside Admiralty Arch and I used to walk from Charing Cross Station, across Trafalgar Square, to reach it, during which time certain stories from far away kept surfacing in my mind. One of them concerned a boy called Akbar Ali.

Akbar Ali was a real nuisance in Aitchison College when I had been there in the sixties. I never had any dealings with him before but everyone was always talking about the trouble he caused, so you can imagine how I felt when one day I began the new school year with a very good class that I'd already had for two years and was now going on to its third year before taking school certificate, and I came into the classroom at the beginning of term and there, sitting in the back row by himself, was Akbar Ali. So I said, "Good morning," to the rest of them and then said, "Akbar, I see you're here, how's that?" He replied, "Sir, the headmaster told me to come here because I failed my exam last year and everybody thought I was going to leave the school but my parents sent me back and now I have to try and pass my exams and that's why I'm here." Now I knew instantly that the headmaster had done this without telling me because I would have kicked up a fuss about having a very good class likely to be interrupted by this boy, whom I didn't know in fairness.

Anyway, there he sat at the back, and as the days passed he moved up a little. It wasn't very long before he began to interfere with the lives of the boys on his right and left and small disturbances were beginning to break out with the lack of attention on their part, increasing irritation on my part and increasing irritation on the part of some of the other boys who wanted to get good results.

It came to a head when he did something that upset everyone, so I stopped the class and said, "Everybody, put away your books. Come up here Akbar Ali. Stand there." He did; he came up and stood right in front of my desk. I was standing beside the desk. All the other boys looked a little apprehensive, and I said, "Now, Akbar Ali, you have a choice. You can go straight out through that door," pointing to my left, "and never come back in here again, or you can go straight back to your desk and work and I will guarantee to get you through your examination. Do one or the other but do it now." (The third possibility, that he might have knocked me out because he was a big strong boy, I didn't mention!) He quivered a little, shook, opened his mouth to say something but stopped, then said, "All right, Sir, I'll work." He turned round, went back to his place and sat down.

I said to the other boys, "Get your books out again and we'll go on as if nothing has happened and you won't talk about this to others if you can possibly avoid it. Forget it's happened."

Sure enough, he was as good as his word and he did pass the exam! He left the college and I forgot all about it until the next Christmas when I received a rather bulky envelope. It was a rather unsightly kind of letter, all rough and rugged, and had come from Zahidan. Zahidan was right out in the desert on the edge of Pakistan on the borders with Iran, far away – a place to which in British times officers who misbehaved were posted. It turned out that Akbar Ali's father was posted out there in the Pakistan army and Akbar Ali spent time there with him.

I opened the letter and took out a piece of white cardboard, cut probably from the top of a shoe box and bent into the shape of a card. It had a hole bored at each end with a piece of red ribbon forced through and tied in a rather awkward looking bow. Inside was written:

Happy Christmas
Sorry, Sir, they don't have proper cards out here.
Akbar Ali

Do you know, even as I try to record this all these years later, my voice breaks. That is absolutely true. That's the quality of the kind of boy that I had to teach in Pakistan.

Another story that kept surfacing in my mind concerned a boy called Ali Hassan who had been in my boarding house. Now Ali Hassan became well-known in the college because when he returned from a school trip to the Sukkur Barrage down on the great River Indus, he had hidden under his seat, all the way in the train and later in the college bus, a live, young goat which he had bought in the market near the Sukkur Barrage.

This was not discovered until I found the goat in his bathroom – the boys had rooms with a dressing room and then a bathroom behind. There was this goat, tethered nicely, chewing away on some food he had prepared for it. I asked Ali about it and he told me exactly what happened. I spoke to the master who had been in charge and he said he didn't know a thing about it. Ali and I managed to get rid of the goat, quietly and by agreement, but he was very upset because he loved this goat and was very attached to it.

Slowly, the story of his attachment to animals and this goat emerged. It transpired that Ali Hassan had been sitting in the front of a motorcar with his father driving, when his father, in a fit of temper, turned round and shot dead his wife and her sister in the back of the car because he felt they had been 'gabbling and talking too much as women do', so he said. Understandably, this had an effect on Ali Hassan.

The next part of the story was that he turned up one day at our house (I was married by now), with a beautiful brooch made from peacock feathers of several different colours and carefully entwined together. He'd got the feathers by picking them up at the local zoo, which wasn't too far away. He gave this feather brooch to my wife, to thank me for 'having been nice', as he said, 'about the goat'. Well that's another story – and he came from the same area as that boy with the Christmas card.

Another thing that stuck in my mind about the difference between cultures concerned a boy from central Punjab. He was going home on holiday and I said goodbye to him. He said, "Oh, Sir, I love going home because as soon as I get back into the village I'll take off my blazer, trousers and tie, put on shalwar-kameez and throw my tennis racquet in the corner, then I'll be myself again." 'Be myself again'. Of course, we were taking boys from being themselves into being the sort of stock product of the Public School across the world. It has troubled me occasionally when we imagined we were doing great good for them to remember that maybe we were also alienating them from things they knew and loved and understood.

An area where the difference between our culture and theirs definitely clashed came out in discussion between two friends of mine. One was the son of a Trade Union leader who had founded trade unions in undivided India and had then set up trade unions in West Pakistan; the other was a close friend of the owner of the biggest commercial and engineering manufacturing enterprise in Pakistan. The two of them had met through Moral Re-Armament and had become friends and were able to keep their industry going by always talking about problems and difficulties as they came up.

Now this son of the Trade Unionist came over to England, where he had several jobs and became trained in various skills, then went back to work in the big engineering enterprise owned by his father's friend. He was a foreman of a particular section of the factory. One day he and a nephew of the owner, who was taking over the factory as his father grew older, met in a particular workshop and were talking about the business. They were discussing the way in which various machines worked when they came to a very large machine which required twelve people to work it properly. It emerged that this machine could be operated with only six attendant workers, which gave rise to a discussion which went more or less like this:

"Suppose we laid off six attendant workers... what would be the best way to manage it?" The foreman, whose father was the Trade Unionist, said, "I don't think we can do that easily because suppose the six men running the machine were to get the salaries of the twelve men, workers in other parts of the factory would be upset and demand higher salaries." "Oh," said the nephew of the boss, "I wasn't thinking of doubling their salaries, just that we could save money by operating the machine with fewer people." The other young man said, "That's the trouble with you, you want European standards on Asian salaries!" They remained friends, but this problem of European standards on Asian salaries continues to this day.

Another train of thought which came to me at this time was the other way round, where you have Asians on European salaries, and it came about like this:

When I went to Lahore in 1959, I opened an account in Lloyds Bank because I'd banked with Lloyds here from when I left school. A nice young man opened my account, a very friendly fellow who I discovered later had acted with my wife in plays when they had been at university together, and we became quite friendly. After a year or two I noticed he was no longer in the bank but had opened up a finance business with a friend on The Mall. I didn't quite know what they did there and I had no occasion to use them so I wasn't worried about what was happening but, later, when I was home on leave in England once, I met him in Park Lane, living it up very well indeed. It turned out that he was working in one of the senior positions at the Bank of Credit and Commerce International, which later became known as BCCI and, I am sorry to say, figured in a tremendous scandal and had to be closed down ultimately.

It was very painful for me because one of my English friends who worked for senior institutions over here, pointed the finger at BCCI during its rise and fall, and was a few days later moved from his position to another part of the institution for which he was working and my friend, the Pakistani friend, had encouraged other boys from the college where I taught, to work in this large bank and, indeed, some of them were working there.

Now it's fair to point out that they themselves did not actually benefit greatly personally (by way of salary or increments) from the way in which the bank worked but, unfortunately, that bank cheated lots and lots of investors of all sorts of things. It was never really properly recognised as a bank even – it was only a deposit-taking agency.

However, it had more or less come to the end of its tether when I was starting my work in London and it was a little embarrassing occasionally to meet boys whom I had taught and who were now men, who had worked for BCCI without some of them realising what was going on, whereas of course many of the others did. There was also a rather personal thing in that the city from which the founder of the bank came was Lucknow, which was my wife's city, and somehow or other the obloquy seemed to fall on Lucknow for no other reason except that he came from there.

But that, too, was in my mind as I began working in London in this international set-up because I was the Director of a Department that was really responsible for our English Language works administration all over the world.

As a background to almost all my teaching and education work I had kept the verse in mind, to which I have referred in earlier chapters. It's the one written by Frances Crofts Cornford about the English poet, Rupert Brooke, just before he went off to the war, particularly in the direction of Greece. This was how she saw Rupert Brooke, a very handsome young man with the best possible education behind him and a great poetic talent:

A young Apollo, golden-haired
Stands dreaming on the verge of strife,
Magnificently unprepared
For the long littleness of life.

For those of us fortunate enough to have had a purpose in life of course it doesn't seem too difficult, but for those who don't have a purpose or an aim or something to keep them focused then, of course, life is a 'long littleness' and a very pointless one, too. There is a lot of debate about why we're here and what we're doing and that's all understandable, but I think it is the responsibility of teachers and educationists to make sure that at least their pupils get a chance of developing a purpose. They may use that chance or they may not, but they should be given a chance.

I had come back into this Management Department and inherited a very straightforward style of work, very well done; I didn't have to make any changes, it ran more or less on fairly straight tramlines. It was also my good fortune that the quality of staff I inherited was probably 90% as good as it could have been, especially the two more senior officers who were stalwarts on whose shoulders I was able to stand for the early part of my time there.

Because I didn't really know anything about London or our office in London, except what I had been able to glean from our office overseas and various courses I had been on, I was very careful not to try to give them any idea that because I was the director I felt I could tell them what to do; that would have been disastrous. I did call each one of them in turn and said something like, "Now, look, you're in charge of your own area and you have to do these various things and know much more about them than I do. All I can say is that if you do your work well and it comes out right I will see that you get the credit, that I can promise you. Equally, if you do make a mistake and something goes wrong, please don't worry, I will take the blame. If I'm foolish enough to allow you to make a classic mistake in my department, then that's my responsibility. The only thing I beg of you is that if you *do* make a mistake, come and tell me immediately or as soon as you realise it, and the two of us will try and get out of it."

They all worked very well, though I did notice that at first they were a bit hesitant to believe that I would keep to my word. However, I was very fortunate in that one of the very best of them had the opportunity some time later, when a vacancy came up in another part of our organisation, to go and take it. I was able to recommend him most strongly, with the result that there was some evidence to back up what I had said about making sure they got the credit for what they did.

Indeed, a little later on I overhead two ladies in the department talking to each other – I happened to be the other side of a screen – when one said to the other, "Isn't it nice the way Lloyd tries to get us all off, promoted or whatever; he does as much as he can for us." The other said, "Yes it is, but I'm not sure that he always does the best for himself." This sounds like inverted boasting but I was very glad to hear that, because at least they appreciated that I recognised them which, oddly, was something I discovered wasn't always expected amongst people who worked together. Sometimes people seemed to have the feeling that their colleagues were trying to do them down rather than raise them up.

Another line of patter that I developed had to do with briefing other officers who came into the department in the early part of their career, not to do any work but to listen to what we had to say. While this bit of patter was really outside my domain – it wasn't to do with English teaching alone, it was to do with the whole generality of their service – I felt it important to say it because divorce was becoming a bit of a problem in the British Council. I remember over-hearing that it was second only in numbers to our Members of Parliament, so I thought in fairness to new recruits I should at least say something. And this was the patter that I developed:

"Unless you are one of the most fascinating foreigners in the country to which you are posted, you will not be doing your job as a British Council officer. Equally, if you do not meet the most fascinating people in the country to which you are posted, you will not be doing your duty as a British Council officer. When fascinating people meet fascinating people, fascinating things happen, and one of the things I think it is good to decide right now, while you are sitting on that chair there, is that nothing too fascinating is going to happen to you which might result in domestic troubles."

One lady, a new recruit, suddenly gave a little jump in her chair, put her hand to her mouth and said, "Goodness, I've just got engaged!" At least she had understood the point and by her reaction maybe gave a sign that she hadn't quite thought the whole matter through.

I discovered from the very start that there was an uneasy relationship with the literature department – just as uneasy as I had known in the South of India – where there were some people who felt, quite rightly, that literature was totally different from language teaching. On the other hand, administratively it didn't necessarily have to be shut off in a separate department because for business reasons its expenses could be combined with the expenses of the language department. However, this is not the sort of argument that goes down well with real artists. By real artists I mean people who really are literary people, who write poetry themselves, write short stories, and meet and talk with others who do that. That relationship was always a bit uneasy, but I tried to let it slip past as much as I possibly could without interfering in areas that I didn't fully appreciate because, of course, in the literary world there are all kinds of relationships that you can't possibly know about from the outside.

A most happy perquisite fell my way as a result of the connection with literature because each year there was a major conference held in Cambridge University. I had to go up to the University to check that it was actually happening so I would be able to authorise payment of the bill when the time came. I naturally chose the day when George Steiner was there giving his lecture. He was the major critic of the time – a wonderful literary expert.

On my way there I had a most amusing time with a great lady who sailed in front of me in the queue at the station where I was waiting to buy a ticket. She said, "Would you mind awfully if I went in front of you? I've got to get to Cambridge today and really feel I may miss this train." I said, "Not at all, madam; if the people behind me in the queue don't mind, you buy your ticket." I happened to overhear which train she arranged to get a ticket for so when I had bought my ticket I went over to her and said, "I hope you bought the right ticket but, just to say, I'm going on a train which leaves later than yours but arrives before you." She replied, "Really, do the railways do that sort of thing?" "I'm afraid they do, madam, but if you'd care, I'm sure you can come on the same train as me and we'll get there sooner." She said, "Really?" I added, "Perhaps you'd like to have a cup of tea before..." She said, "Do you know, I've had such a dreadful day, I'd have a cup of tea with anybody!" Thus we began. Another thing I recall her saying was, "My husband's a judge; he has a very good salary and I can do more or less what I like!"

She sat opposite me on the train and we were sharing a four-placed table with a married, older couple, who it turned out had had a very happy experience with the British Council in Nigeria. When they discovered I was from the British Council and was going to a seminar held by them, the most tremendous 'mutual admiration society' broke out and I'm afraid other travellers in the train were treated to a quartet of something which they must have regarded as a little self-opinionated.

We arrived at the station and I was met by the local representative in Cambridge, a very nice Scottish lady, about 4'10" in height. I had told my tall 'friend', the wife of the judge, that if possible I would give her a lift because she didn't seem to have any arrangements made, so I said to the person who picked me up, "Would it be possible for our friend..." and then realised I didn't know her name. The Scottish lady gave me a look as if to say, "Oh! it's like that is it!" Anyway, we all got into the British Council car. The Scottish lady drove with her hands above her head, looking out through the steering wheel at the road ahead. The tall lady sat beside her like an Afghan hound sitting beside a Jack Russell. I got in the back and we set off for the University.

Now it was getting late and, very pointedly, the British Council rep said to me, "I've made arrangements for your evening meal because the kitchens are closed at this time but they'll save one for you; I'll pick it up when we get there." I have to say that while this was directed at the tall lady as if to say, "You'll have to starve, you won't get any food," when we did arrive my Scottish friend and colleague went around behind the scenes and made sure that the tall lady did get a good meal and we all had a happy time.

I learned afterwards something that made me adjust my opinion of the tall lady. She had two daughters who were totally deaf from birth. She was attending a Conference on Audiology in the same college as our British Council seminar.

Another very revealing association which I had with the Literature Section of the English Department during my time in London was a review of the Council which was carried out later and in the report that came back, we, as an organisation, were praised very highly for the close contact that we had with all the different people and the different arts of the countries to which we were posted and where we were working. But there was one important caveat which went like this. The author said that 'while I found wherever I went that the British Council officer who looked after me could introduce me to all the leading lights in the arts of the country, be it sculpture, painting, music, literature, anything you like, the fact of the matter was that because the British Council officers themselves were not in the top flight of poets, novelists, painters and musicians, there was a genuine gap between the organisation and the local arts people. It was not quite enough to bring out the best artists, poets and writers from England to meet them; the Council needed to re-think how it could go back to one of its original principles which was that, on the whole, people who were very good at a particular art or shone in a particular way would be posted to a country and there would be other administrators who would look after them.'

Of course this is a long running debate and it is very expensive to do both at the same time. However, I mention it here because it was mentioned in an actual observation which the British Council itself asked for at that time.

A telling observation by George Steiner was that he was very disappointed children and adults no longer learnt as much poetry by heart as they used to. He seemed to suggest that this was because modern education has confused learning by heart with learning by rote. By rote, of course, meant just by sound without thought, and he did actually emphasise the need for us all, however experienced, to consider what we meant when we said we had learnt something by heart. He felt the expression 'by heart' meant that the poem, piece of prose, verse from the bible or whatever it was you had taken in to yourself, was now a part of you – it was in your heart – and that this was far different from learning by rote. By rote you cast it in and out of your mind as you want it; by heart it was a part of you no matter what circumstance in life cropped up, and he felt this was very important.

I remember now, by a strange coincidence, that when I was signing off the authority to pay the bill for this seminar, there fell on my desk also a very much smaller bill for a seminar that had been held on the South Coast. The British Council was paying for it, but there was no detail attached, so I wrote a note on it asking: 'Who attended this seminar? How many people turned up and was it any good? etc.' You can imagine how I felt when I had the reply that nobody had attended the seminar and they didn't even know whether it had taken place! They assumed it had because it had been arranged and the bill had come in. So I'm afraid I sent it back and said they would have to check up on it because I wasn't going to pay for something that we didn't really know about!

All of which reminded me of another incident way back in the 'sixties in Pakistan when the Principal of the college had asked me whether I would very kindly go along to a hotel in Lahore where the Nawab of Bahawalpur was staying, and ask whether he might please pay his bill. He apparently hadn't paid his bill to the school for some time, which was typical Maharajah and Nawab practice right throughout the whole history of India. It was also very difficult for other, shall we say, local people to go along and ask Maharajahs to pay their bill, and even though the Principal could have gone himself or could easily have sent an office messenger to ask for the bill to be paid, especially when they had asked for it in writing many times and it had been ignored, it was felt that, as a foreigner, if I showed my face it might exercise a little more pull, particularly as the two boys were in my house. Well I did go along and we had a nice chat and I presented the bill. I don't know how he paid it, but he did say that he would and I think that, having given his assurance to me as the boys' housemaster and as a person from another country, he would have felt honour-bound to actually pay it, although this was not the kind of thing that normally Maharajahs and Nawabs did.

Another interesting piece of tittle-tattle about monarchs and money concerns the receipt I saw in the museum at the end of The Mall in Lahore, the Secretariat Museum, which was signed by Queen Victoria having received one million pounds sterling from an Indian Maharajah for the State of Kashmir. Of course, this did not work out very well since the good Queen sold an entire state of Muslims to a Hindu Rajah, and while it was perhaps reasonable at the time since she felt that we needed a lot of money to pay for the cost of the Sikh wars which had just ended, nonetheless it persists to this day in a very, very expensive aftermath.

Here a link with another queen. Amongst my 'commuting friends' from the station behind my house up to Waterloo each day I met a few people with whom I formed, I wouldn't say friendships but at least acquaintanceships, because I discovered that other commuters were very cautious when talking to each other and perhaps my Irish accent and cheerfulness and wanting to talk upset them a little! Anyway… one lady dropped a large number of papers all over the floor between us in the train so I helped her to pick them up. As I did so I found that one of them was referring to a poetry competition and I immediately said, "My wife is a poetess and she loves writing poetry and she loves competitions. Do you think I could possibly have a copy of this from you?" "Yes, of course." So it led us into a little conversation, albeit a very cautious conversation on her part.

We met I suppose once every two months for the next year or so and it turned out that she was actually busy producing a book by poets who went along to the Tate Gallery and viewed various pictures and then wrote poems about them. From time to time I heard a little of the difficulty of this and how it was progressing. I more or less forgot about it until one evening I was waiting on the platform at Waterloo for the train, at about half-past five or so, when suddenly my arm was clutched. It was this lady who had run up to me and said, "The Queen has asked for my book!" "How marvellous, that's wonderful," I replied. Then it came out what the book was and I got a copy of it, and am very pleased to tell you that because my daughter is an artist and is married to an artist, it was well worth a discussion point in our house and has remained so to this day. However, the delight of this highly professional curator because the Monarch had asked for a copy of her book, did reveal to me something of the British spirit.

Other equally memorable, though more amusing, things happened. One was an unfortunate 'flu epidemic which more or less decimated the typists, secretaries and assistants in the office so that my boss had no secretary – those were the days of secretaries – and he had to get one brought in from an agency outside; this lady originally came from Australia. She came in the morning and worked for him. He was doing some work on the Middle East and one of his letters was to The Yemen. When she produced it for checking, she had written Yemen as "Ye Men," so he pointed this out to her and it was corrected. In the afternoon he dictated a letter to Oman. This came back as, "Oh Man." So he pointed this out to her, a little testily – maybe a little unkindly – whereupon this wonderful Australian lady said to him, "Say, where do you get all these men from?" This became a kind of joke throughout the office for a long time. Whenever there was a big crowd in the office people would say, "Say, where do you get all these men from?"

A more thought-provoking incident occurred in our home life at this time. One of the joys of being back in Britain for some years was that we were able to have as guests in our house members of family and friends whom we hadn't seen or hadn't been able to entertain for a long, long time, if ever. One was the wonderful assistant I had had in Karachi, a young man who had been in charge of the VSO programme in Papua New Guinea. He stayed one night with us and slept in the guest room. Very shortly afterwards we had a big gathering of family in the London area for a wedding and the lady who came to stay with us was the wife of one of the brothers who couldn't come. She slept alone in the very same room where the previous guest (who had the connection with Papua New Guinea) had slept. This lady was reputed through the family to be psychic, to have all sorts of different views about life, death, ghosts, spirits, etc. When she came down to breakfast the next morning I naturally asked her how she had slept and she said she slept very well, but added, "One very interesting thing you know, although I slept well I had very vivid dreams last night about a place I've never been to – it was about head hunters in Papua New Guinea. I specifically saw the decorations on their face and body, and the headgear and clothes they wear – of course I knew this from pictures in books – but definitely it was a very strong, lively atmosphere both within my head and it seemed to be surrounding me, too."

I have to say that I immediately thought of my friend who had come back from Papua New Guinea, with his head full of all the knowledge of the different tribes, because he had gone almost everywhere looking after a dozen or so VSO's in remote parts, and I fell to wondering whether there is a kind of electricity that goes on inside our heads and stays in places where we've been. It is recognised that certain places produce a certain atmosphere and it is acceptable that many churches and chapels produce a particular kind of atmosphere, but this specific set of feelings connected with the head-space above a particular pillow-space did make me think a lot more seriously about this. I tend to look upon it all as a sort of coincidence, and that more or less gets rid of it as a problem, but I'm not convinced that it has been got rid of really from my own mind.

A home posting I quickly discovered did not produce all those unexpected interesting incidents that one was constantly meeting overseas, but I did have one which really took me so by surprise that I remember it vividly to this day.

I was leaving the office on 22nd December for Christmas leave that was going to go on until 3rd January. On my way out I was stopped by a total stranger coming into the office, who said, "Excuse me, but you're Mullen aren't you?" "Yes," I replied, "Who are you?" He told me he was *so-and-so* from one of the offices down in Whitehall, and said, "You manage this department that looks after English Language teaching and so on throughout the world. Is that right?" I agreed that it was and he said, "Could you possibly spend some money for us before April Budget-end?" "Probably, but how much?" I asked. He then mentioned such a large sum that I had to stop him and say, "Wait a moment, that much money would spoil anybody's Christmas leave, but it might indeed set the same person up for the whole New Year. If you are willing to come back here on 4th January at nine o'clock in the morning, maybe we can sit down and see what we can do. Is that all right with you?" He paused a moment and then said, "Yes, I'll come; do you think you can do it?" I replied, "I'm fairly certain I can, but I still have to look into the details before I commit myself." "All right, I'll see you then," he said, "Have a good Christmas." "Have a good Christmas yourself," I said and off he went.

I did have a good Christmas and hoped he had, and he certainly did turn up on 4th January at nine o'clock. I'd come in the day before and had arranged with a member of my staff who was very keen to get a lot of projects going in his area, to take the details out of his top drawer and have them arranged in decent order on his desk. When 'our new friend from Whitehall' arrived, I asked my colleague to bring along his various projects, which he did. Everybody was very happy!

I asked how this money suddenly became available and it turned out that for political reasons one of our areas of government management had withdrawn from an agreement with other people but, of course, when you withdraw from an agreement you may still have plenty of money budgeted as if you'd gone ahead with it and that's indeed what had happened. This man's particular department didn't want to lose the entitlement to that money, so they were able to pass it over to us and say they had spent it.

My colleague was able to get twelve projects dear to his heart solidly off the ground before the financial year ended and passed on into the coming year with that money. It was a tremendous boost for him and for us too because we felt that Providence was on our side. It did provide very good English language Teacher-Training for people in a large area of the undeveloped world.

About this time a new horizon opened up in that we were asked to do some work in China. We hadn't been doing any work in China at all and this was an absolutely new beginning. Everybody was very interested and I remember being called with my Controller to the Director-General and Assistant Director-General to discuss how this may happen. Eventually the discussion came around to money and I was asked a question that I hadn't really been able to work out so had to answer on the spur of the moment. The question was: "How do you think we can budget for this operation because we simply do not know all that may or may not happen when we start and we haven't really sufficient control because once we begin we don't want to withdraw; on the other hand, we don't want to begin at too low a level. So what do you think?" Faces turned towards me – silence. So I said, "Well, when I go on holiday I budget for the fares, hotels, happinesses and frivolities, and everything that I think it's going to cost for my family and myself, and when I get what looks like being a genuine figure, I then double it, because that's what the holiday is actually going to cost!" After a second there was a howl of laughter because I think everyone recognised the truth and they said, "Gosh! Yes, that's it. Let's budget like that – let's do a realistic costing and then double it." Now, of course, it was done much more efficiently than that, but at least I had the pleasure of watching people rejoice and going on holiday in China!

I hope members of my family who read this will recognise that this is a memoir of memories and a very personal memoir of memories, not of facts, because I'm writing about how I felt about something at the time rather than checking up on the exact details. It's a very foolish administrator who believes that he understands actually the facts of what happens at any time. But anyway, the point I want to make is almost an apology for not bothering to get the facts right, but at least telling the truth about how I felt. For instance, we came away from that meeting with our Director-General with a very happy feeling that the top brass in our organisation were going to go ahead with something that was very important and we would have to play an important part in it and we would be able to do so. Of course, one of the best things was to make sure that we were able to go into it on a happy, agreed manner from the very beginning.

In fact, I sometimes think when I look back at the work I had to do, it was really rather like singing in a choir. It is a fact that if everybody in a choir is very happy, the sound which comes out is better than what comes out if you merely get the technicalities correct from an unhappy choir. It is difficult to explain why that should be, but it is a fairly well recognised fact in the musical world – something to do with the quality of projection – and it was exactly the same in the work that we did in our English language teaching and English language Teacher-Training. Whenever we were really happy with what we were doing it did work definitely better than in places where there was uncertainty or conflict or anything that prevented going ahead with a smile on the face.

Naturally, one of the most pleasing aspects of this five-year long home posting was that we were able to spend time with our daughter from the age of twelve to seventeen, and as already mentioned, we were able to meet up with all our relations and friends again who we hadn't seen for a long time.

Because we lived in Ewell and our daughter's boarding school was not far away at Addiscombe, beyond Croydon, it was very easy to come and go, and my wife, while I was working, was able to go and see Cherry and take her to various things connected with her mathematics and art or anything which needed attention.

I, too, had an opportunity to pick up friendships with erstwhile colleagues and also with new, younger colleagues. This was interesting because the new younger generation who had grown up inside Britain while I had been abroad for several years, were so very different from those that I had known at their age before I left Britain way back in the sixties. It was very important for me to know more about the country that I was representing when I was abroad because it certainly was a country that had changed and was changing immensely in its attitudes to a whole range of quite important subjects. Tremendous strides were also being made in the whole area of language teaching itself, which was really our primary concern.

Perhaps the biggest difference between what I would call the older generation and the new younger generation was dramatically shown one day in our house in Ewell when my next door neighbour, a lady of about sixty-five years of age, met a cousin of ours of about the same age. When they were introduced to each other in our drawing room, they both stopped in their tracks, looked at each other and almost took a pace backward. In the odd silence with which we surrounded them because we noticed something funny was going on, one said, "Hut 22" and the other, after a moment, said "Yes, you were Hut 8 weren't you?" and there they checked themselves and fell to talking a little over to one side of the room.

It was later that we learnt they had seen each other but had never spoken to each other when they were both engaged in the work at Bletchley Park during the war, where the top brains of Britain more or less worked out the German codes and the ENIGMA machine was famously de-coded, and they worked together for quite a time – not together in the sense of being with one another but in Bletchley Park without the one knowing what the other was doing.

I do know from a book which I later read, that our next-door neighbour had been one of those who went to Bletchley Park at the very beginning as part of a so-called 'Hunting Party' to open up the whole thing and discovered that her job was the highly intellectual one of making sure food was sent up by a kind of pulley to Alan

Turing, who had more or less developed the computer and who was working in a loft at the rear of the barn at the back of Bletchley Park and had to be fed, and she then had to collect the empties when he put them down. That was amusing enough to think about but that certainly was how the war was won.

Probably the most significant point that came home to us was that here we had a next-door neighbour and a cousin who had been engaged in winning the war, won it, and never said a word about it. Indeed, our neighbour was horrified when some time later people were allowed to break their silence and talk a little about what had gone on. She thought this was betraying the past in no small manner whatever!

It was the greatest comfort throughout this whole period that our house was within two minutes walk of the railway station. While I had been uncertain about buying a house in such a position, Promilla was absolutely certain that it would be a good idea to do so because it would save so much trouble and hassle with the car and so on, and she was perfectly right because I would be back home, perhaps upstairs in the bathroom at the back of the house, washing my hands after the day, and I would look out into the station car park and there would see people with whom I had travelled on the train still walking down the long car park to pick up their car to drive home. We definitely gained I would say a whole hour of time for togetherness each day and that, when you work it out over five years, is well worth having.

It also meant the other way around, that if we decided at six o'clock in the evening that we wanted to go into London to see a show, we could just about manage it by getting the train and then taking a taxi and probably be sitting down in the theatre at just about the time the show was starting. That, too, made life easy, because it was the same coming back – we didn't have to get in the car after we got off the train, and drive through the long, dark evening – we just walked round the corner and were home. And, incidentally, it was silent! We were very surprised that we didn't hear the trains in our house, partly because of the nature of how the property was built and partly because the nature of the trains was improving so much about this time.

18
UGANDA

My next posting was as Representative in Uganda and one might have thought that this was a change from the convenience of five years in London in the English Language Management Department to the inconvenience of a nation that was just coming back to some sort of peace after the upheavals of the Idi Amin years, the Obote years and the take-over of power by Yoweri Museveni. It is true to say that the place was really very dangerous for everybody, and also the simple things – like telephones, water supplies, electricity supplies and the condition of the roads – had fallen into gross disrepair over the long period of sad internal strife the country had suffered.

However, I actually welcomed it because from very early days in my life I had felt that Kenya and Uganda – what used to be called East Africa as a unit – was a very attractive place in my mind and also because of schoolboy stories I had read about it.

Before I actually left London I was sent to Dublin on a course dealing especially with the use of Foreign Aid in Subsaharan Africa and, of course, this included Uganda very much. I enjoyed the course tremendously and felt very proud that it was so well done. To be back in my own country and see things being very well done gave me a great deal of pleasure. However, a small event occurred which made me realise that the attitudes of the rest of the world to Ireland were fairly well established. The evidence was this:

On the last night of the course we all went to a great party in one of the nearby pubs; we must have been over one hundred people. There was a great deal of Irish dancing and singing by a family aged from about seventy down to about seven. It was hilarious at times and very moving at times, but always the standard of music, dancing and joke telling was very high. At the height of some hilarity I happened to hear behind me two people speaking in French. I think they were the French Director and the Greek Deputy Director of UNESCO at that time. During the laughter they said, "Yes, this nation is very amusing, but underneath its high hilarity there is a 'tristesse profonde'. The way they said it emphasised the meaning – 'a profound sadness'. In other words they said that Ireland had at its root a deep sadness. I have to confess that I have never felt that deep sadness myself, but I do know what people mean when they talk about it. I don't think it's actually valid, however it alerted me to any attitudes I might find when I got into Subsaharan Africa.

The second most interesting thing before I left was meeting a lady from Uganda, a senior educationist, who came to my desk in the British Council headquarters. She had heard I was posted and came along to say hello. In the midst of the conversation we talked about one particular Teacher-Training college and she told me how to get there and said it wouldn't be too difficult because all I had to do was to drive south from Kampala, just drive straight down, keep to the main road and turn left at the equator! This expression delighted me because in Ireland we used to have jokes about going straight down the road and turning right at the turf to wherever you wanted to go! So I felt strangely at home with this place, both in modern terms and in my childhood outlook before I ever started.

My wife and I were fortunate in that we had each grown up in countries which did not have modern conveniences that the rest of the world had. Her upbringing in India and mine in Southern Ireland meant that we were well used to having to collect wood for fires, water for drinks and cooking. Also, there were no such things as telephones in our early childhood homes – electricity came along later. We were well used to the basic difficulties, if you call them that, or perhaps the better word would be realities, the basic realities of country life.

We quickly discovered that we need not have had any worries at all about the realities of life in Uganda because we found that the people were so pleasant – that was the first thing. The second thing was that the vast majority of the people were Christians – that was a very easy point of understanding. Thirdly, those that we had to deal with at every level spoke really very good English and the matter of communication was not at all difficult. We also noticed that although the people were poor, they did do their very best to dress well. For instance, the ladies used to turn themselves out in the most gorgeous outfits and the men were always clean and tidy. Also they were very sophisticated in their attitudes to other people and had long term plans in their dealings… as, for instance, that lady who called on me at my desk before I ever left England. She and I were more or less friends before we met on her own turf.

I discovered as the days went by that the Ugandan people were extremely well equipped to deal with outsiders. So well equipped that I was there for about six months before I realised they had many, many different ways of – for want of a better expression – getting their own way or getting what they wanted. I found the reason for this was that throughout history they had been there in the centre of Africa, right in the heart of it, with nowhere to go except into Lake Victoria, which is bigger than Wales. They had to fend off all the other tribes of Africa who kept coming at them from every possible direction – north, south, east and west – and they had learned how to negotiate; they were really skilled negotiators, such that the word 'stranger' and concept 'stranger' hardly occurred in their language at all. If a newcomer appeared on the scene they would immediately say, "Ah, come in, have tea. You must be tired from where you've been. Has it been a very long walk for you to get here?" They were quite willing to take not only half an hour but half a day to find out where this new person had come from, what he or she did back there and what he or she wanted to discover here. One of the questions that would be asked, very tactfully, was: "And what was it that the people back where you came from were hoping you would tell them when you went back there?"

The skill at negotiating with the other tribes of Africa they transferred in more modern times to the Arabs and Europeans who came into Africa and they had very good success in dealing with them, particularly in the fact that land ownership in Uganda remained entirely with the Ugandans. Even the British Imperial power preserved that, whereas just over the border in Kenya the land was taken and a great deal of it was owned by white settlers, white farmers, and also by Indian settlers, Indian business people mainly… but not in Uganda.

The Ugandans consequently were totally without any feeling of inequality towards the newcomer. They talked to you on a completely straight level. They didn't feel that you were the interloper boss. They might regard you as an interloper entrepreneur looking out for your own interests and they would know how to deal with you on those terms, too.

But when we consider how dreadful the relationships were between the Africans of the Congo and the foreigners who came in to meet them there, and the Africans of Kenya who met the British in Mau-Mau, we can see what a difference there was. I am not quite sure of the origin of this difference but I think it had something to do with the kind of 'Missionary Enterprise' which set up schools in Uganda, both Catholic and Protestant, and where the missionaries appear to have been 'well-to-do' people in their own countries who had been to leading schools and were now setting up in Uganda what they felt to be a leading school for the people of that country.

Indeed, one of my colleagues in London told me before I left how she had been a schoolgirl at Sherborne School in Dorset where they collected money for a school in Uganda called Gayaza (she gave a penny a week I believe) and this school benefitted from their donations. They thought they were helping a school in the middle of Africa – which they were – but imagine her astonishment when, having left her school, gone to university and then on a tour of the world and, as it were, dropped in to see this school, found that the girls and the Gayaza School were so similar to her own school back in Sherborne that she wondered what on earth she had been thinking all those years ago. Here were people completely on a par with herself!

So successful were both the Protestant and Catholic missionaries in their own areas that the schools they ran produced pupils and adults who were loyal to Catholicism and Protestantism rather than to Uganda! The British Government in Uganda decided it was necessary to try to stop this polarisation. They took various steps to try to do it, but one was very interesting in that, at government expense, they set up a school called Ntari and brought down from Juba in the Sudan a very well-known, successful young schoolmaster from Scotland, called Crichton, who became headmaster of this school and, with his staff, he set it out as an entirely new type of school, one which would not have particular religious affiliations although it might have Christian standards.

I became very friendly with a senior civil servant who said he had been a boy at that school from the very first day it began. He told me that the boys were all assembled in the hall of the school (their parents, from different tribes all over the country, had left them as boarders at this school). The headmaster led his staff on to the platform in this hall (a mixed staff of British and African people; the language they spoke was English) and he stepped forward and said to the room full of about one hundred and twenty boys, all between the ages of ten and fifteen, "Whose school is this?" There was a long silence and he repeated, "Whose school is this? Is it for us on the staff standing here? Is it for your parents who have left you here and gone back home? Is it for the Government who has paid for all the desks and chairs and buildings? Is it for you boys, who we hope will learn something… as we hope our staff will teach you something? Who is it for?" One brave boy said, "Sir, it's for us." "Yes… So whose school is it?" A few boys joined in and said, "It's our school, Sir." Then the headmaster said, "Well, if it's now your school, who should make the rules?" A long silence and one timorous voice finally squeaked, "We should, Sir." "Of course you should," said the headmaster, "Well, please do that. We'll come back in about an hour and you can tell us what rules you have made," and he led the staff off the platform out of sight! This left a hall full of boys from many different tribes, many different parts of the country, many different backgrounds… Protestant, Catholic, animist, all sorts.

We don't know what went on exactly. My friend told me there was a discussion and a very quiet discussion because the boys were very worried rather than very pleased by this development.

The staff came back and said, "Have you made the rules?" They replied, "Yes" – they spoke in little bits – mainly they had made a time-table, but they had produced two very telling rules indeed:

Rule 1: Boys should not be allowed to make remarks about other boys' families.

Now that rule in one moment swept away tribalism, absolutely.

Rule 2: Big boys should not be allowed to break little boys' beds.

That is the way they worded it and there you have, in one sweep, the entry of democracy. Those who had power and muscle were not to be allowed to lord it over those who had not.

"Good!" said Crichton, "then those will be the rules," and from that point they went on and the whole school developed along those lines. For example, from the very start it had an Honour Tuck Shop. There was nobody in charge of the tuck shop; it opened and you took your bar of chocolate and put your money down on the counter and left it there. No one to check. The school had no boundary; there was no such thing as being on the school premises or off; you could go anywhere so long as you were in time for your next game, next class, next assembly, whatever.

In no time at all a totally new attitude to education began and one attitude was that the boys never felt cowed down by authority of any sort, religious or political. And if I tell you that, while I am writing this years after, the President of Uganda and the President of Rwanda were both boys at that school at that time, you can see that this did have some powerful effect on the children.

Alas, the other thing which had a powerful effect on the children of that time was the near poverty of the entire country. Once you left Kampala city and went out into the country in any direction you found that the people were inordinately poor, really very poor indeed; it was a struggle for them to keep their families together, to keep their children fed and clothes on their backs all the time. Of course, this did not mean they didn't try to go to school – they did. One of the problems of going to school in those days was that you had to walk a long distance and you had to pay some money up front. If you hadn't got the money you couldn't go and if you didn't have good food in your tummy you couldn't walk that far. Life was very difficult right across the countryside.

And what a beautiful countryside it was. It was green, it was lush, it was four-thousand feet above sea level, it had its own eco-system based on a huge stretch of water in Lake Victoria and the Mountains of the Moon to the left, the great bank of Ruwenzori as it stood there. It also had its own set of clouds that used to rise up above it and blow in different directions, and according to the directions in which those clouds blew and according to the directions in which the dry air blew down from the Sahara and according to the direction in which the evaporating water of Lake Victoria blew, you had this special climate for the country of Uganda. Bananas grew freely. I planted some dwarf Asters near our house. They were meant to grow to about six inches and in about ten weeks they had grown tall enough for me to park the Land Rover in their shade!

One never needed to use a fan to keep oneself cool and one never needed to use a fire to keep oneself warm. Any wonder that the local people had been able for generations to walk about simply with no clothes on at all and enjoy life. That was their prerogative. I used to wonder sometimes at us foreigners wearing suits and ties inside buildings made of concrete where we needed fans to keep ourselves cool!

This lack of money in the countryside and this high level of educational readiness for development was a great divide with which we had to tussle. I am glad to say that we did tussle with it and I think it would be fair to say that the actual administration of the country improved greatly as a result of the training given by those people who came from outside. We in the British Council were one group – and an important group – but also I feel we had to admit that there was developing throughout the country as more money appeared on the scene, a degree of corruption with which we in the West were not able to deal, and with which we in the West have not yet been able to deal in our own society.

There were two kinds of sadness which this economic situation inevitably led to in the countryside and the cities in Uganda at that time. In the countryside it was often a plain fact that the only way in which a young mother of, say, three children could make enough money to keep those children in food was to sell her body to the men of the local area.

At the same time the well-educated men in the towns were able to get the new jobs which were coming on stream because of the inflow of Aid money from outside and there was inevitably a development of corruption because this money was in the form of cash which had to be spent in different ways. Those who got into positions to decide how it could be spent – whether they were ministers or secretaries or whatever in the Government – were naturally tempted to divert it, if not into their own pockets, at least into the pockets of their own tribes or their own group. And this happened despite the best efforts of the Roman Catholic and Protestant and other religious denominations and also the best effort of the traditions of the society itself, which society actually did not have a tradition of handling money.

I came across one very sad but very telling example of this international corruption one afternoon when the lady representative of a major foreign donor organisation was passing through Uganda. I wanted to see her in Kampala to make arrangements for joining our British Council efforts with her efforts in one or two particular projects. She was in a great hurry and told me over the phone that if I could get to her for about ten minutes in the office where she was, then she might be able to give me some time. So I did. I dropped everything, rushed across, got to the office and when I arrived I said to her, "This Secretary of Government, Mr *so-and-so*, he's a very honest man and I'm very glad that we can deal with him." She immediately burst out, "That man! He is so honest! Do you know he won't even take money for himself let alone for his group. He is the biggest obstacle to our plans for this country!"

Thinking it over afterwards I realised that her own personal chances of promotion within her own organisation rested a little on the success with which she would be able to push forward the plans that that organisation had for various different countries; in her particular case, Uganda. And here I saw how it was very difficult to step out of the coils of corruption that international finance was wrapping around both the developed world and under-developed world.

On another occasion in a quite different context a person said to me, "Look, Lloyd, what you are saying is perfectly right. This project is ill-conceived, ill-advised and will not really benefit the country greatly but I can tell you that four thousand jobs back in the West depend on this project so no matter how much you protest you are not going to get anywhere!" And that was true. And I had to face up to the simple fact that my own salary was being paid out of money, some of which was being misused by the countries to which we were 'donating' it.

I came across a book, called 'Africa's Mountains of the Moon', by Guy Yeoman – a very revolutionary but possibly right answer to this whole problem. He was radical. He suggested that we stop all our Aid programmes, take all the money that those programmes cost, divide that money up into small parcels and give it month by month to any girl in, say, Uganda, who had reached the age of sixteen and who was not pregnant. The monthly payments would cease when she became pregnant and they would begin again after the delivery of the baby and for another nine months. If she became pregnant again then they would cease.

His argument was that: (1) it would give the local women power that they had never had in their whole lives, and (2) it would mean that they had a very strong financial and immediately relevant incentive not to bear children. Whether it would have worked or not we don't know. It was never tried because people said, "Oh, the men will steal the money," "Oh… this and that…" But actually it could have been as good an answer to the whole problem of how to develop a country according to the mōrēs of that country, as any other.

Another way in which this situation diminished women greatly was that the women in the cities where all these men were getting better jobs and better salaries and had more money to spend, discovered that one of their only ways of surviving in the midst of all this materialistic scramble was to sell their bodies for ever higher prices to the men around them. This led to a very sarcastic and cynical expression throughout society – it was called 'Thigh Power' – and it almost came to be an accepted part of the way in which the whole society worked, just as it had long been accepted in the West in the field of starlets gaining places in films, or in the whole mannequin industry. Worst of all was the effect that it had on the next generation of children growing up into adolescence and adulthood, seeing that this was how the society actually operated its surplus funds.

Expatriates were often tempted to confuse this situation with an age-old tradition in the African villages. Basically their thought was that it took a village to raise a child and the village consisted of a certain number of men and a certain number of women, and it was not always clear which men were with which women or for how long and, generally speaking, you could have said that throughout life there was a fair sharing of both men and women on each side. Now this gave rise in European minds, especially Missionary minds, to the thought of promiscuity and almost sin, whereas in the African mind it did mean that concepts like jealousy, concepts like ownership of women, concepts like widowhood, concepts like being orphaned did not exist because each child belonged to the village and each adult in the village felt some sense of ownership for each child. Indeed, in one or two languages there is no singular for a child to talk about 'my father', they tend to talk about 'my fathers', because it is not always clear which of the men in the village would be his or her father. This was perfectly reasonable and it also meant that the whole idea of property being passed down from father to son was not present. What was present was that the property of the village was passed down to the children of the village.

Of course, as time went by everything altered slowly, but the advent of the Muslim Arabs and the European Christians did have a very powerful impact on this whole society. It was the development of this society after the troubles of getting independence from the Imperial powers that we were living within while we were working in Uganda.

Our business was to transfer from Uganda to Britain and from Britain to Uganda certain levels – if possible the highest levels – of expertise in various branches of the sciences and arts and this I think we contrived to do. For example, we were able to increase the number of women who came from Uganda to Britain, and of course we also had the problem of trying to extend that out amongst the tribes because there was no doubt that those tribes which lived closest to Lake Victoria, closest to Kampala and closest to the centre of things, on the whole had better access to education and modern know-how than those who were farther away out on the borders, let's say Congo, Sudan and Kenya.

One industry was developing which was a great joy for us when we were off duty and that was the tourist industry. Uganda is absolutely beautiful; it has a wonderful supply of wild animals in their natural habitat; it has a lovely climate; it is a very small country and it always gives the foreigner the feeling of being, though very strange, very soft and comfortable, but at the same time vaguely threatening.

The **vaguely** threatening element was **actually** threatening when we first arrived and there were still soldiers in uniforms, with guns, and eyes bleary from drugs, wandering about here and there, who held you up, and they more or less hoped you'd give them some money before they would let you go on. But those things quickly passed away.

The worst we ever encountered was when a man put his gun through the window, across Promilla, into me and asked her to hand over her handbag, which she did and he just looked in it – there wasn't anything in it – and gave it back to her and took the gun away; but just for a moment you feel the reality. Our driver gave us a very good piece of advice when I asked him one day why he didn't speak to the person who once stopped him; he said, "Sir, I never talk to those people because if you once start talking to them, then they ask questions and you have to answer them and then there will be trouble." That lesson I learnt and I just didn't say anything and they didn't shoot me and always went away.

The roads throughout the country were murram roads, a sort of red mud, quite good for driving on, and they did take you to where they said they would and the journeys were short enough to be able to spend the night at an hotel which the tourist industry was just beginning to build up and where you could enjoy yourself peaceably and peacefully and where the service was quite good, and then go on to the next stop, especially out to the Game Parks on the edge of the Congo.

That was wonderful because there you really were alone in the centre of the world. You could go to a place where there was no sign of civilization in any direction and just sit there and watch, and slowly the animals would emerge from where they had hidden when you approached. Some were very big animals – enormous elephants; some were quite small – hyenas, warthogs, and in one particular place there was a splendid collection of topis and zebra.

In that particular Game Park I remember we had a hilarious moment when we went down there on a Saturday. Now the previous Friday had been a great day in Kampala because it was the opening of the very first 'Zebra Crossing' in the city. Various dignitaries, police authorities, etc., lined up and school children were there and everybody was taught the importance of this zebra crossing and practised it. Motorists had to come along and stop when they saw a child walking out or an adult holding up their hand and walking across. There were no accidents and it was lots of fun.

The next day we went to this park and as we were driving along, right in the middle of it actually, our driver, Charlie, suddenly stopped the Land Rover, kept the engine running, and said, "Look, Sir, Madam! Look up at about two o'clock; there is a herd of zebra." He had sharp eyes because way in the distance, yes, there was a large herd – normally you don't see more than about six or eight zebra together there but this was maybe twenty or so and we watched in silence, apart from the low running of the engine. In the Game Park you never switch off an engine because if you switch it off and by any bad luck it didn't re-start, then you had trouble.

Now I don't know what it was, it might have been a lion, but something frightened the zebra and they turned, the way they do, as one herd heading in one direction more or less straight down the hill for us! They came thudding down and what a tremendous noise they made as they came; they thundered across the road about twenty yards in front of us, putting up dust in every direction. We stayed where we were and watched them, and they went on about another eighty yards down to our left and then they stopped, skidding to a halt, digging their hooves into the ground, turned back around to look at us... and then a great silence.

In the middle of the silence I said to Charlie, "Charlie, I'm so glad you stopped at the zebra crossing." I shall never forget the hoot of laughter that man gave. His head almost went through the roof of the Land Rover and it took quite a long time for him to stop shaking with laughter before we went on to see the topi who were down in the dip of the river in front of us.

Very large animals, topi, and exactly the colour of taupe, too. A sort of cross between a deer and a cow. They were very quiet and unthreatening but very beautiful to look at. I don't think it was a lion that upset the zebra because in that part of the Game Park I can't imagine there were that many lions otherwise there couldn't have been so many topi, zebra and warthogs.

A lovely story about a warthog happened at Mweya Lodge in erstwhile Queen Elizabeth National Park. In that park they built a very fine dining room and reception and checking-in area, and between the dining room and reception there was a wide open foyer with no doors – big openings on either side about twenty feet across, ten or twelve feet high which allowed the air to blow in up from the lake and kept the place very cool and airy while you were having your meal or checking-in.

Animals were very common; by the time you got there you'd seen them on all sides as you drove to the place in the safety of your Land Rover. But you'd left your vehicle now and had checked-in and gone to have lunch in the restaurant and the next thing you saw was an animal running through the hallway between the reception office and the dining room. That's nothing – just a little fellow... you weren't sure what it was. Then came a warthog, really moving – it ran at top speed in at one side of the building and out of the other. All right, look up, a warthog, not a particularly dangerous thing, and people began to look back at their plates, pick up their knives and forks when suddenly a lion raced through after the warthog. That did make people sit up and look around and make sure they weren't next in line for extinction! I don't know if the lion caught the warthog because they went way out of sight before we could see.

That reminds me that there was a marvellous notice on the inside of the door of our chalet. Our chalet, along with others, was about one hundred and fifty yards from the main building, up a slight incline to give you a good view; you had to walk there and walk back. The notice on the inside of the door (I wish I had taken a photograph) said more or less this:

> *Management regrets very high price of service to room. This because long distance from kitchen and smell of food make danger life of bearer carrying tray from main house to bedroom. Please forgive delay if danger come.*
>
> *Thank you*

Well, danger never came to us but something approaching it did one night when, in our chalet, I woke up and heard a sort of sniffing noise. I got up and looked out of the window – there was a thin gauze curtain covering the glass in the window which you could see through – and there outside about six feet away was a massive hippopotamus cropping the grass. He was enormous and sniffing as he did so. I thought to myself, 'If he just fell or rolled over towards me he would knock down the whole chalet and bury us all alive!' Anyway, he didn't and it must have happened many times when people awoke to find these great animals just beside them.

Another great draw of tourism was the attraction of the source of the Nile. It was only about twenty miles from Kampala on the road to Jinja and there you could actually see where the Nile flowed out of Lake Victoria. It was about a quarter-of-a-mile wide at this point and there were various trees across the way and a rather fine little pool at the nearby edge where the water of the lake ran in, curled round, came out again and went back into the main stream. In this pool fish would get caught for about five or ten minutes before they managed to re-emerge into the main stream again. So always above that pool there hovered anything between four and twelve kingfishers; black and white ones mainly, enormous kingfishers, diving down and catching their prey time after time and no one able to prevent this.

Promilla went down to have a look at close quarters and, unfortunately, slipped into the water. We managed to grab her and haul her back onto dry land again but I'm afraid I've been teasing my wife ever since about the tidal wave that she created right down to the Mediterranean – and if you think of the thousands of miles there are between that point in the middle of Africa and the Mediterranean Sea and all that the Nile has to go through to get there, you can see that the joke must be very irritating for her after all this time!

We visited one of the more interesting places that the Nile goes through, and that was Murchison Falls. Named after the President of the National Geographic Society at the time they were discovered, Murchison Falls is only twenty-two-feet wide and through that narrow gap flows the whole river, which by this time in places has been almost half- or three-quarters-of-a-mile wide, flowing powerfully down to join the Albert Nile. The Victoria Nile comes out of Lake Victoria while from another set of lakes to the west comes Albert Nile; they meet and go on down through Sudan and Egypt to the Mediterranean.

Murchison Falls in British Imperial times had boasted a wonderful hotel where you had to dress for dinner, where you could have proper wine with any of the seven courses, party into the night and then drive back to Kampala or Nairobi the next day.

I found it very hard to believe when driving along the same route that the grass was higher than the Land Rover; there were places where it was just impossible to be certain whether there was a foundation or a marsh in front of you and I had to get out and check with my feet before I drove across it. Then, in the middle of all this wild jungle, I came across a fine metal notice, beautifully set up, still standing, slightly swaying and creaking in the wind. It was very rusty, but clearly stated in large letters: "ELEPHANTS HAVE RIGHT OF WAY." I suppose when I saw that I realised that the people of the time had either a great sense of humour or a great sense of self-preservation – or both!

And those people also had very bright ideas for the future of Uganda. One idea was that it might become a homeland for the Jews. Another idea was that it might become the base for the Institute of Development Studies which was set up after the war to help bring the civil servants of all the countries gaining their freedom through the 'sixties into some good training for civil service action. However, the bright sparks in our security services spotted that it was very likely to become a hot-bed of left-wing ideology and that the leaders of the new-coming nations would be trained to look towards Moscow and Peking rather than to London and Washington. So that idea was scrapped and the Institute of Development Studies was instead set up on the campus of the University at Brighton, where I had the pleasure of attending one or two courses, and excellent they were.

The contrast between the actual physical realities of daily life on the ground and the hopes for the future which we were planning in our work was so great that it would have been easy to say we were living in cloud-cuckoo land, but we weren't, and this was possible because of the excellence of the office staff in the British Council in Kampala. We were housed in the High Commission building – this was forced upon us for security reasons – but the actual quality of our staff was very high indeed and so my personal life was comparatively easy because, while I had one leg in the realities of the day and another leg in the hopes for the future, it was these excellent staff who made it possible to feel that one day it might all come to fruition. And it did. We had considerable back up from our office in London but, nonetheless, if we had not had such good local staff it would have been a very depressing scene indeed, as it was for some other people in other Institutions who I met from time to time.

A feature of our security arrangements were hand-set radios which all of us carried and it meant that we could be in contact with each other and with the security people who were detailed specifically to look after the High Commissioner. These radios were not always easy to operate and occasionally my wife and another lady, whose name was Gladys, found it a little confusing to get things right but they were often able to contact each other and have a chat which might break-down in the middle or go askew but then they would get back on-line. However, none of the conversations on these radios could be kept private – they were overheard by anyone else who happened to be listening in at that time, so the conversations between my wife and this lady came to be known as the "Prom and Gladys Show." And this Prom and Gladys Show relieved many people's tensions from time to time in hoots of laughter.

These radios actually helped to save our lives on one occasion when a fire started in the middle of the night downstairs in our house. We didn't wake up or become aware of the smoke but our dog, Felia, who slept in the corner of a very big bedroom, came across and tried to wake us up – she had never done this before (she was a wonderful dog) – so we got out of bed and even then didn't know what she wanted but decided finally that she just needed to go outside. Then we had the business of opening all the security doors upstairs and downstairs, which took some moments, and went downstairs where she immediately went straight to the door of the sitting room. We did, too, and opened it and out came clouds of smoke, absolute clouds of smoke. The building was so cleverly built that the smoke had been kept in, almost hermetically sealed in by the closed door. However, we were able to get on the radio to the Protection Team who looked after the High Commissioner and to whom we had access in an emergency, and they quickly spread the word around and got onto the fire brigade and after some time, with the help of our Quick-Response team and our servants and those from other peoples' houses, the fire was put out, but it certainly was due to our dog, Felia, and the hand-set radios, that we were able to save the house at that point.

And a very fine house it was, too, surrounded by well-cut and very well-levelled terraced lawns with the correct layout of avenue, plenty of space for parking and turning cars and situated on the road that led to the Commander-in-Chief's house, which meant that we almost always had a good supply of electricity, water and telephone connections.

Our domestic staff were simply sophisticated in the most wonderful way. I have never forgotten when Promilla was showing a

Our Kampala home

would-be gardener around the grounds (he had applied for the job) and they came across Felia's droppings in the middle of one lawn. He turned to Promilla and said, "Madam, do you allow the dog to '*defecate*' in the middle of this lawn?" Promilla answered the question in the negative and carried on showing him around where, in another part of the garden, she pulled some plants out of the ground and said, "I don't like these, we can perhaps get rid of all of them and put in something else." And as she looked at them, around the roots there were tiny bits of plastic falling off and she said to the applicant for the job, "What's this plastic doing here, can you explain that?" He said, "Yes, madam, the people who put these plants in probably didn't realise that the plastic isn't '*biodegradable*' so that's why it's there." I think Promilla gave him the job on the strength of those two words alone!

But there is an even more amusing tale to tell which involved him. We were all sitting out on our terraced lawn as darkness began to fall (it did at about seven o'clock) and were watching the fruit bats – which about this time suddenly rise up in the air from the trees with a great clatter of wings and form into a tremendous darkening of the sky and fly away down to the lake to feast on whatever things came out at that time. This particular night, just after the bats' display, dinner was over and everyone had gone off duty when I was asked by the High Commissioner to do something very early the next morning. I was able to do it but it would have meant asking Robert, our cook, to produce an early breakfast. He wasn't around so I asked the gardener if he would to go to Robert's quarters when he came in from his day off and ask him whether he could do this.

When the time came, the gardener came back to me and stood in front of both Promilla and me and said in very respectful tones, "Excuse me, Sir, the cook presents his compliments to the master but says he feels he is too drunk to appear before him. However I shall make sure that breakfast will be ready." I thanked him and let him go while Promilla and I looked at each other and thought how wonderfully well trained such people had been by those before us.

It is very sad to relate how, only a few years after we had left Uganda, both the cook and the gardener had been swept away by the tidal wave of AIDS which had ravaged Uganda all the time that we were there. The fact that Uganda was the first country in the world to acknowledge how devastating it was and how many people had it and how quickly it was being picked up, didn't make the actual experience of it for those of us who watched people get thinner and thinner and die before our eyes, any easier.

The actual disease itself was called SLIM when we were there because it hadn't come to be called AIDS in any official way throughout the world then. It was called SLIM because people just got thin and died. Large numbers of our friends disappeared from view. Men and women of all ages; men and women of all types of society; men and women from all parts of the country.

In fact, one of the briefings that I felt bound to give to those people who visited Uganda under the aegis of the British Council was, "Please remember that you can jump in and out of bed with any number of people you like but you are certainly going to jump out with AIDS at the end of it all, so try not to do it."

I did have one amusing come-back on that from an elderly couple who, as they went away, their tour over and they had done whatever they had to do, came to thank me. The wife looked at the husband and said, "It was rather fun to think that at our age you had the vision of us jumping in and out of peoples' beds, but anyway, we haven't done it and we're going home healthy!"

The Army was being decimated by AIDS, as were those areas of the country where the Army was posted, and while it was normal to accept that people were dying right, left and centre, it nonetheless was quite alarming to find that at one celebration of an event I went to, of the forty-eight people present only three of us did not have AIDS. We were there to celebrate the fact that there was some improvement in the conditions under which they were looked after, but there was no question in anyone's mind that before very long they would all be dead and this was a difficulty to live with. It is to the credit of Museveni, the President, that he made no attempt to hide the horror of the situation; indeed one might say he tried to use it to get people to re-adjust their habits of living.

Of course there were other ways in which one could die, as we came close to discovering one late evening in the Game Park over in the centre of the continent. We were with our daughter, Cherry, and a friend of hers. We were coming back to Mweya Lodge and the driver, who was experienced in the Park, said, "I think if we drive up onto the old air-strip at the top we might be able to get a very good view of the buffalo and elephant coming to their evening water-holes." So this we did.

It was a lovely, clear, still evening and as we sat in the Land Rover looking out we could see about thirty or forty buffalo in single file, and as many as fifty or sixty elephants slowly plodding their way towards the water-holes. Everything was in silence, no lights around, and I was imagining that this must have been a bit like the world shortly after the animals had been created.

There we were, all quiet, and suddenly Cherry, from the back of the Land Rover, said, "Goodness, look at that huge black cloud." And sure enough, way across the lake, there was the mountain and then this huge black cloud and then at the top a little more of the

Cherry on holiday

mountain. What it was really was the entire massif of Ruwenzori, the whole length of The Mountains of The Moon, standing between us and the setting sun in the west and absolutely clear with the three little tents of white on the top where there are three peaks which are permanently covered with snow, right on the equator. Without thinking, I said, "That's incredible, we'll never see that sight again; everybody out, gently, don't bang any doors, just look at that; that's Ruwenzori, The Mountains of The Moon – wonderful!"

We got out and stood beside the Land Rover. Cherry and her friend walked about twenty-five yards in front to get a better look over a little knoll, which they undoubtedly did get, and there was silence except for some birds chirping away to our left. Occasionally these birds would stop chirping and then start again, and about the fourth time this chirping started I turned to look in their direction as I thought I might see them there… that's when I saw the lion! The lion had his belly close to the ground and was moving forward slowly from cover to cover and I realised that Cherry and her friend were in his sights!

I should never have let anyone out of the Land Rover in that part of the Game Park. Anyway, I hissed Cherry's name and fortunately she caught the hiss and turned round. I beckoned her and they came back very, very slowly while my heart almost stood still with my brain calculating how fast lions can run, how fast girls can run, the angle of this ... oh goodness me, what a dreadful moment. Anyhow, they came back and got into the Land Rover as the lion gave a low, disappointed sort of growl and hid under the foremost bush. That was a great moment to look back on now that everything is well, but at the time it was dreadfully scary indeed. Frightening.

Viewed objectively, Uganda could be seen in those days as a very dangerous place where you might easily die – from wild animal intervention, from AIDS or from human activity, guns being shot off all over the place from time to time. In fact we did have tracer-bullets through our home family compound one evening, quite a lot of them. We never discovered quite who was chasing who with them, which party was against which. Just as we'd had the same thing in Aitchison College in Lahore in the 1965 war (Pakistan against India), and as we had known back in Ireland in the old IRA days, bullets whizzed about. Yet somehow the whole atmosphere was not unsafe.

A very welcome interlude was a visit by Myra Leach. She came back to her own childhood home – a coffee plantation out in the middle of Uganda – and was able to meet families whom she had known growing up and who were now running the coffee plantation, as her father had before her.

The Leach family had played a very leading part in the introduction of Moral Re-Armament into Uganda in those old days and a kind of religious revival known as 'Balokoli' started as a result of their activities. Balokoli was really Accentuated Honesty, which found people returning cattle they had stolen, land they had stolen, even human beings they had stolen. All sorts of unhappy things were sorted out in those old days.

Myra Leach had actually met her husband through their common association in the Oxford Group and they were married in Uganda.

I had been great friends with them when I was teaching in Devon so it was a great joy for me to meet her again and hear how the children had grown up and what they were now doing. The fame of the Leach family – particularly her father-in-law, Bernard – as the leading English potters, had grown; Michael and his brother David were still leading potters at home and very acceptable to the old people of Uganda who remembered them with great affection.

Myra loved wandering around Namirembe Cathedral where I think she had been both Christened and Confirmed before going back to England to live, as she did for ever really. It was refreshing to see how she became a young girl again in the places where she had actually been a young girl and didn't know how to behave other than as a young girl in those wonderful places because Uganda is essentially a young country. It is a 'country' country, beautifully green, full of flowers and full of all kinds of wonderful birds, one of the most natural, unspoilt countries in the world. As indeed Myra was a natural, unspoilt girl even when she was a grandmother! It was quite charming to have her as a guest.

She was absolutely fascinated one evening when we had dinner in a hotel in Kampala. A party of about twenty American ladies (they used to be called the 'Blue Rinse Brigade') came into the dining room. They were in great form, talking to each other, shouting across from table to table while the dinner was being served and suddenly in the middle of it all, one of the ladies said, "Say, is this Kampala? I thought it was Nairobi. I've been sending my cards one stop wrong all the way along our itinerary!" I shall never forget how Myra exploded with laughter – a kind of innocent laughter, that such a thing could occur when it couldn't possibly have happened in her day; tourism didn't exist when she was a young girl in Uganda and here it existed in one of its most ridiculous forms.

There was a very high standard of dramatic work in Kampala especially. Very good plays were written by local Ugandans, produced and put on in the different theatres. They were quite simple theatres but the plays were anything but simple; they were quite complicated and very clever, well done to a very high standard and very well attended. One of the electricians who worked in the British High

Commission was actually a very successful producer and director of such plays.

Amongst the various British Council activities we brought out a production of Macbeth, which was very well done, and I have never forgotten President Museveni, sitting next to me, when he heard the line from Macbeth: "There's not one of them but in his house I keep a servant feed," meaning that he had a spy in all his enemies' houses. Museveni leant forward and slapped his fist into his open palm and said, "Very good advice from four hundred years ago." So I was relieved to think, as the British Council representative, that the President of the country was really paying close attention to the dramatic offering that the Council had brought out to his country.

Promilla, having discovered that the Deputy High Commissioner could do a very good imitation of Elvis Presley, wrote a pantomime for the expatriate community, which was produced in the British High Commission compound. It was a variation of Cinderella and in it she had made use of this 'actor'. Cinderella was produced in the usual way as a pantomime, full of local jokes about the ugly sisters, etcetera, etcetera, but there was a king, and this king wanted to sing all the time but the rest of the actors wouldn't let him; they said, 'Stop him, don't let him sing'. So Promilla worked the plot round to the fact that at the very end Cinderella was going to get married and because the king after all was the prince's father, they would allow him to sing at the last moment. I was astonished when this tremendous bugle fanfare went up and everybody stood to attention and stamped their feet. There was a sudden moment of silence and they announced, "The King." Round the corner came this splendidly, open-chested, chain-dangling, imitation of Elvis Presley with the Deputy High Commissioner singing, 'Be My Teddy Bear', and he sang it so well that ladies in the audience between the ages of forty and sixty were absolutely transfixed – you saw the years drop off them onto the floor round their seats; they clenched their hands together, screwed up their faces, turned away, looked back, couldn't believe that all these years had been shed and here was Elvis back again!

Off stage I once was present at a most interesting conversation between an Indian lady who was working in the country and a senior

Ugandan lady discussing the various different customs of their country, with particular regard to women and the relationship between women and men. Both were surprising to me in this way:

The Ugandan lady was telling the Indian how in her particular tribal group the custom was when a boy and a girl were to be married and the arrangements had been made between the two families, an older aunt (beyond child-bearing age) of the girl's family would spend sufficient time with the fiancé, the young boy, (a) to ensure that he wasn't impotent or had a disease, and (b) to teach him to be gentle (they knew I was listening as I was standing there, so the two ladies weren't at all secretive about this matter). The next morning the sheets, which had to be pristine, were taken by the aunt and inspected to make sure that the girl had indeed been virginal.

Now the Indian lady for her part had an interesting tale to tell of the way in which in her particular group, if a husband and wife had a quarrel and the wife did not want the husband to come near her, she took a pair of shoes belonging to some other man and put them outside the bedroom door and went inside and closed it. So long as those shoes were there the husband could not enter the room – this was the custom because in that local society it was a matriarchal tribal set-up. I must say I thought of my own Ireland and couldn't imagine what our ladies and men would have thought if they'd listened to this in broad daylight as a sensible conversation!

Namirembe Cathedral is on one of the seven hills on which Kampala City is set and it figured largely in our life there. Two events I particularly remember. One was when we were in the middle of an ordinary service and the preacher had gone into the pulpit. A little disturbance at the back began and when we turned round we saw a man wheeling a bicycle up the main aisle while the service was going on. He took the cycle right up to the altar steps where one of the other clergy came down to meet him. They whispered together a while and the other clergyman went to the preacher, who listened, and then the preacher announced, "John has just come to church with his bicycle; he has been praying for a bicycle for the last four years because he needed one badly for his work and now he has one and has come to thank God for it. He wants us all to join him in blessing the bicycle, so perhaps we could all do that together." We all bowed our heads and the preacher said a few words of blessing for John's bicycle, then John turned and led his bicycle down the aisle and out of the door.

A quite different occasion was rather grand when a new bishop was being enthroned. When the enthronement had properly taken place, the bishops all had to leave the scene and go into the vestry and together sign some great book of ecclesiastical importance, so that for a moment the remaining clergyman didn't quite know what to do but seeing the President sitting in the front row alongside his wife and others, he went down and whispered to him. The President demurred but finally agreed to say a few words and I've never forgotten how Museveni began. He went up the steps very deferentially, wearing a double-breasted grey suit, and turned round and almost sheepishly pointed up to Heaven and said, "Well, of course, there are no Presidents in church, but I see I'm expected to say something about this new Bishop," and he went on for a while and sat down again. But I did think that was a sign of some real value in the man.

All this time that we were in Uganda our daughter was fighting in the first Gulf War on the borders of Saudi Arabia and Kuwait, stationed mainly at a place called Al-Jubail. She was a member of the QARANC, the Queen Alexandra Royal Army Nursing Corps, and she told me that there she had the sad business of looking after more Iraqi wounded soldiers than Allied. She said, "Daddy, they weren't properly trained at all; they were just teachers, accountants and so on who had been conscripted very quickly. They didn't know how to fight and they were almost glad to get across to our lines to be well looked after." Anyway, that having been said, she did tell us about how a Scud Missile was, in the night, taken out by a Patriot right over the place where they were staying. She said the explosion was so powerful that she almost felt the entire universe had exploded and then added, "And that was the one thing that actually we had not been trained for – the horrible, dreadful moment of silence after the explosion." She said, "I remember feeling myself in the dark, my arms and my legs, and saying to myself, 'Yes, you're still alive but where are you?'" She didn't know what had happened. And then the stuff began to fall down all around the place and they were able to come back to real life.

But it was a very interesting experience and led to a very interesting joke which she told us over the phone, from Al-Jubail to Kampala would you believe! It went like this:

"Daddy, Daddy."

"Yes, Cherry."

"Daddy, what did the Scud Missile say to the Patriot?"

"Oh, go on, tell me," said I.

"Are you taking me out tonight?"

Young people can always laugh and joke even in the midst of war. Some of my uncles died in the First World War and some of my colleagues died in the Second, yet, thankfully, my daughter did not die in the first Gulf War. I myself, because of the accident of age really, never fought in any war, and I would be a little dishonest if I didn't admit that I feel slightly guilty at having hidden behind so many brave and dead people in the world who have kept freedom alive for the likes of us.

A strange thing happened one night when we went to the airport in Kampala to see Cherry off on a flight back to Nairobi and London. We arrived at the airport and discovered that there was some unexplained hold-up. The plane she was to travel on had to come down from Nairobi, land in Kampala, turn round and go back to Nairobi and then on. The lights in the entire airport began to go on and off; it seemed they might fail entirely or maybe there was some jiggery-pokery afoot. Then I heard a voice quite loudly saying into the telephone to Nairobi, "Well Nairobi, if that plane doesn't come down here quickly and turn round we won't be able to get everybody off, so please make up your mind what to do." Part of the scene here was that the airport in Kampala was actually controlled by North Korean technicians who were always at odds with the South Koreans, who also had diplomatic representation in Uganda. On this particular night it transpired that the South Korean ambassador was returning to Kampala from Nairobi and for some reason which we never discovered, the North Koreans wanted to kidnap him.

We didn't know this until afterwards but the way it worked out was that the ambassador's wife, waiting for him in the lounge, came to my wife, who played bridge with her, and actually fell on her knees and implored my wife to ask me to take her husband in our British Council Land Rover back to Kampala because she felt that if he went in anything else he might be abducted. Promilla told me this and I said, "No, we can't have anything to do with that sort of thing; we don't know how many of us would get killed; we don't know the true story at all; we don't know what's going on – we simply have to keep out of this," and I went outside.

Suddenly everything went dark, absolutely every light in the whole region went out. We were right on the edge of Lake Victoria – you might say we were in the middle of the African countryside because we were some miles out from Kampala and Entebbe, and there we were in this silence and blackness, waiting for a plane. We waited, then the purple lights down the centre of the runway began to flicker on and off and sure enough, through the silence there came the sound of a plane and some lights came on and then the plane did land. We were told we must get our daughter (and the other passengers) onto the plane in ten minutes because it was going to spend ten minutes on the ground, turn round and go back to Nairobi and make the connections there. That we managed to do… just, but when I got back into the main lounge I discovered that, while we managed to get Cherry on the plane – and hoped that her luggage would catch up (which, incidentally, it did later) – the rest of the people were still sorting themselves out.

The first thing was, I met the Deputy Vice-Chancellor of Makerere University, an extremely angry man, and also an extremely angry Minister of Agriculture, both of whom I knew. They felt they had been held up in Nairobi by the Kenyan authorities as part of a policy of deliberate harassment of Ugandan politicians and officials who had to pass through Nairobi on plane journeys from the rest of the world to Kampala. Anyway, they sat down and waited for their luggage, so did the South Korean ambassador who came into the lounge, and the other passengers.

Having rushed out to get Cherry into the plane before it went away I came back to find there was a great deal of unease and anger in the lounge and when an announcement over the Tannoy asked for the South Korean ambassador to go down to the luggage bay to claim his luggage and verify it was actually his, his face went absolutely white – I remember noticing that particularly. There was utter silence and he refused to go.

Just at that moment my driver, Charlie, came into the VIP lounge – a thing he would never have attempted before, but he managed to get in somehow because he knew somebody at the door. He came to me and whispered that there was a motorcar full of men waiting just behind the South Korean ambassador's car.

This more or less decided me and all four of us stood up – my wife and myself and the Deputy Vice-Chancellor and Minister of Agriculture – and, taking the South Korean ambassador and his wife, both of whom were shorter than I was, fortunately, we more or less pushed them along between us. We all went out of the lounge, down a few steps, carrying such bags as they had, and pushed them into the back of the Land Rover, which Charlie had managed to reverse up near the entrance to the lounge, close the door, stack the suitcases along the window side and got the Deputy Vice-Chancellor into the front seat. The Minister of Agriculture's driver had waited all the time and he didn't require a lift, so we closed the doors and set off. But in the worry of the moment we forgot to speak to the South Korean ambassador's own driver in his car, so what he saw was his ambassador and wife being taken into the back of another Land Rover, obviously in his opinion being abducted. So he drove up very sharpish right behind our Land Rover as we drove slowly out of the airport, bearing in mind that a Land Rover can't accelerate very quickly anyhow. We went along very slowly followed by the South Korean ambassador's car and behind that a motorcar containing four strong men – obviously wanting to keep as close to us as they could.

My real worry at that point was that there were road blocks all the way along (dating from the Idi Amin years) between Entebbe Airport and Kampala, probably three or four of them. All motorcars had to stop and a soldier on duty came and looked in and, generally speaking, didn't ask too much and let you go on after a pause. But I have to say that I was really worried when we were held up by one particular soldier who stood in the middle of a road with a torch – remember it was late at night and very dark. With this hand-torch he swept it to and fro across the road until we stopped but, fortunately, Charlie, being very experienced in this sort of situation over the last ten years or so, never actually stopped, he drove very, very slowly, just moving gently along. The soldier looked into the car, actually put his hand along the side as we went by and then waved us on with his torch. I was so grateful that no bullets came from anywhere, which they might easily have, because I had visions of crowning an already undistinguished career with the death of an ambassador and a Deputy Vice-Chancellor in a British Council car at an airport in the middle of Africa!

Anyway, we went on slowly, slowly and after about three-quarters-of-an-hour, such were the roads in those days with potholes everywhere, we did get into Kampala and to the South Korean ambassador's residence. Even there, there was a moment of tension because it was padlocked and guarded by two night watchmen who took quite a long time to verify that indeed this was the ambassador and his wife, but in a strange Land Rover. Where was their Land Rover? Where was their South Korean driver? (They had in fact been held up and separated from us at various road-blocks along the way; also Charlie had taken a safer, different route). They finally agreed they would open the gate… but they wouldn't let us in. What they would do was, if we reversed slightly, they would let the ambassador and his wife and their luggage out of the Land Rover and into the ambassador's residence.

Meanwhile the Deputy Vice-Chancellor of Makerere University was jumping up and down with rage at what the authorities in Kenya had caused to happen, and full of how he was going to tell President Museveni that this sort of thing must not be allowed to be done to officials of his own regime and representatives of other countries. Anyhow, it all worked, although it was even further held up by the ambassador's wife, falling on her knees and clutching Promilla around the knees and thanking her profusely for having saved her husband's life.

After that we were able to drive away back home, meanwhile hoping that somewhere in the air Cherry was reaching Nairobi on her way back to England and that her luggage was catching her up if not already with her.

Enquiring in the office next morning, I discovered there had been an incident the previous week when a North Korean diplomat disappeared in a building in Kampala which housed some of the officers of the South Korean Embassy. Of course, it is impossible ever to get the actual true story that goes on behind the scenes in this sort of event, but I am glad we are all here able to tell the tale.

There have only been one or two other occasions when I was so genuinely afraid that disaster might strike us as we travelled. One was when Promilla and I took a taxi from Delhi up into the mountains in the north of India to see her relations. The taxi was a very poor quality one and broke down in a few places on the way, but we did finally get close to our destination when the driver told us that we had to decide whether to go on a long way round and possibly run out of fuel because there wouldn't be any petrol stations on the way at which to fill up, or whether to take a much shorter route through very dangerous tiger country.

I remember thinking to myself that either way we were going to be losers because if we broke down (and it was very likely that we would) on a remote track in the jungle with tigers prowling about, there wasn't much hope for us. Otherwise, if we went round the long way we'd simply wait longer for them to come! Anyway, we decided to take the short route, which only took about forty minutes, although I can honestly admit that those forty minutes were spent looking out of the window, not admiring the scenery, which was wonderful, but fearing we might see a wild animal at any point.

Another occasion, much more friendly-seeming, was in Uganda in a channel of water called the Kazinga Channel joining two lakes; a very fine channel with a reputation for having crocodiles at one end and hippos at the other but not both at the same end so they didn't fight each other. In this channel, where we often went on a launch trip, it was very exciting because we could see all around us on the banks a most wonderful display of birds and also wild animals of every kind. However, in the channel itself there were hundreds of hippos, yes, hundreds of them – often the water was so thick with huge hippopotami that one felt you could step out of the launch and walk across them to the bank, stepping from one hippos back to the next. There was always the fear that one of these vast animals might just bump into your boat and knock it over. The driver of the launch never seemed to think this was likely at all and we did it many times. But between hippos, tigers and Korean diplomats, I have to say that I *have* been frightened in my life.

Fear of an entirely different kind was underneath the surface of our minds all this time. Cherry was fighting in the Gulf War; things were very uncertain there and even though the Military Attaché in the High Commission in Kampala very kindly kept me up to date with the progress of events as far as he could, we were worried that something might happen to our daughter. In view of this, we agreed that Promilla would leave Kampala a little early and go back home to be there in case any news arrived. We didn't feel we could possibly have bad news reaching some of our relations in England and then them having to tell us – that would have been too much altogether. So Promilla left early and went home and I stayed on for the remainder of my tour, which was, of course, going to be my last few months in employment.

While I was scaling down, so to speak, and making my farewells and getting things ready for my successor, an event occurred which was to change almost everything in the world. That was the attack in October 1990 by the forces led by Paulo Kagame and Fred Rwiygema into Rwanda from Uganda. This attack took place as part of the long running Tutsi/Hutu rivalry for control over Rwanda. The Hutu had, in democratic terms, a huge majority, but the Tutsi had been very much favoured by the Colonial powers and they felt they had a right to far more of the running of the country than Habyarimana, the Hutu leader, was prepared to give them. Museveni, who in strictest terms was in charge of those who made the attack, was not in the country at the time – he was in Washington on a tour of both America and Europe – and when the news came through to him that they wished to go, wished to attack, wished to leave Uganda, he merely said, 'Let them go' ... and they went.

This is no place to recount what has happened since then with all the murdering in Rwanda. Suffice it to say, that attack acted as a trigger for the displacement in Central Africa of more Africans – by death or disablement or refugee status – than occurred in the whole history of the slave trade, and the oddest succession of rulers has taken place. For example, when my wife and I used to drive in Kampala up to Makindye Hill, to a place called the American Club where we were able to play tennis and swim in the pool, we'd pass by some very poor shacks and allotments and plots on the side of the road. At that time, in amongst them lived a man who had been a leader in the Congo and who had sought refuge in Uganda when defeated, and there he was, without even a bicycle! However in the midst of all this he had to be actually lifted from that place and that condition and put into the Congo as a leader. His son, Kabila, is still there to this day.

The three men, Museveni, Kagame and Rwiygema, had all been boys together at Ntari School – that school where the headmaster, Crichton, had introduced a much more far-seeing type of education. By a coincidence, one of my colleagues at Mourne Grange School in Northern Ireland way back in the 1940s and '50s, did for a time become a member of the staff of that school and teach there also.

Fred Rwiygema was shot dead on the first day of the attack from Uganda into Rwanda, leaving only Paulo Kagame, now President of Rwanda, and Yoweri Museveni, President of Uganda.

Many natural glories of Uganda remain forever in my mind – mountains, lakes, beautiful long vistas of green, trees, birds – but two man-made places exist also and I don't think I could ever forget them. One was a co-educational boarding school right in the centre of the country on the edge of a lake. This was run by a Roman Catholic Father and his staff. I happened to visit it on the day of their Annual Regatta. They had several boat races which took place on the lake, and several swimming races in a proper swimming pool beside the lake. I remember being surprised that this was a truly co-educational school in that the boys and the girls were treated exactly the same; for example, in the boat races one House had a team entirely of girls, the other had a team entirely of boys and a few others had mixed teams. I asked about this and said, "Surely it's unfair, the boys will beat the girls quite easily, won't they?" and I was told, "No, not at all. Each team has its best oarsmen, its best rowers in the boat; if the best rowers are girls, they're in, and if the best are boys, they're in."

Boat Race on the Equator

Likewise in the swimming races: there were short races and long races and each House put up its best swimmer; there was no such thing as the best boy or the best girl, it was the best pupil.

This was also reflected in the fact that the head of a House could be a boy or a girl, the deputy could be a boy or a girl, some of the prefects were boys and some were girls, a mixture, entirely equal. This was very unusual. I recall it very clearly because I have heard people say that many of our co-educational schools aren't really co-educational schools, they are, "Boys' schools with girls in." That may be true, I don't know, but I cannot forget this school right in the centre of Africa.

The other place was the Owen Falls Dam, not too far from Kampala where the huge River Nile is blocked off by this immense dam. There are great turbine-holes which allow the water to go through the dam, through its arches, and down into the river and ultimately on to the next country, Sudan, and so to Egypt and to the sea, the Mediterranean. It was always exciting to see this because of the vast amount of water sometimes and the small trickle of water at other times.

This difference between the vast amount and the small trickle led to a constant joke which used to be played on my unfortunate neighbour in Kampala. He was the Egyptian ambassador and his fellow diplomats used to love to say to him, "Can you come to our party on Saturday night... Oh no, of course you can't, bad luck; you've got to go to The Owen Falls dam and count the drops of water to make sure you get enough down into Egypt. Sorry about that!" This old, old joke never failed to amuse. He was very generous about it. Also, his wife was very generous to my wife and gave her some lovely presents from time to time.

My last call in saying farewells was to Mrs Museveni, the President's wife in State house. She and I had known each other for some time, but it was not the correct thing for her husband to have anyone other than an ambassador or High Commissioner to say goodbye, so his wife invited me and we had a long and interesting chat about the past and the future. The last thing she did was to ask me to pray with her. So we did. We said a prayer together in that empty room – there wasn't even a bodyguard in the room as I remember it – and there we shared prayers and said goodbye and I came away.

But that was not quite the end because the next day when I arrived at the airport and was waiting in the lounge to be called to the plane, her personal assistant, a lady I knew, rushed into the lounge and came over and gave me a Ugandan scarf for my wife and a Ugandan tie for me. We still have these to this day and remember Mrs Museveni's kindness when we wear them.

The plane journey itself was enlivened greatly by the fact that it was the pilot's retirement flight and an announcement was made shortly after take-off, "Today is Captain Piet van Riet's retirement flight… Champagne will be served." I signalled to the air hostess who was standing at the front and she came along to me and I said, "Today is my retirement flight also." She replied, "Really, is it exactly yours?" I said, "Yes," and she said, "It's not exactly his – his was on Thursday but he had to put it off until today… I know this because I'm his wife."

So I sat there and the Champagne came around and we drank it, and after a little while she came back to me again and said, "He wants you to go into the cabin." So I stood up and went into the cabin and met him. We shook hands and this man, who appeared to be younger

Fit for retirement

than me, was absolutely like a child with a new toy. He was bubbling with excitement. This was his retirement flight; his entire career had been a great success – positively there were sparkles coming out of his skin. He kept taking me to this side of the plane, to the other side of the plane, pointing down at all sorts of wonders on the ground below, famous old pieces of archaeology, wild animals, rivers, all sorts of things. He was so excited that after a long, long time I said to him, "Thank you very much for this but there's a whole plane load of people back there, worried stiff at two old men drinking Champagne in the cockpit." He burst out laughing and said, "Yes, you'd better go back to your seat." So I went back feeling what a happy retirement flight both of us had had.

Owen Falls Dam on the Nile

19
Retirement

And it was all happiness when I arrived home, too, because not only had Cherry survived the war in the Gulf but also our neighbours and many in the village of Ewell had been so kind as to send her all sorts of comforting things through the Army mechanism in the Gulf, referring to her as 'our girl in the Gulf'. And so, when she did finally come home there was great rejoicing amongst all the neighbours, neighbours whom I have to say have been extraordinarily good to us all the time that we have lived in Ewell.

However, Cherry did have certain hang-overs from the war. One was a dreadful feeling of wanting to scratch herself, under the arms and the back of her neck, because of all the sand which had more or less permanently lived and lodged on their bodies while these soldiers were fighting in the Gulf. Another, of course, was a release of tension that was necessary. This release came in the most blessed way imaginable because our great friend in America, Jane Subjally, who had retired and was living in Seattle in her home place, invited us to go and stay with her. Now our heavy baggage was just on the way from Uganda, so I decided I would stay in Ewell and Promilla and Cherry should go off to America, which they did and they had the most wonderful time on the far West Coast of America, driving down from Seattle to San Francisco, through the Sequoia trees, that wonderful Oregon Coast, and having the time of their lives without me to blight it!

I am happy to say that our heavy baggage arrived in good order with everything intact and nothing missing.

This is probably the place to tell a little story that I used to tell quite deliberately to embarrass Promilla from time to time. It's not true but we used to have a joke about it. It went like this:

When we came back from any foreign posting and our heavy baggage arrived, I used to say, "Everything has arrived safely, absolutely everything except one spoon was missing from a particular set and a waistcoat from one of my best suits." Then the story went on to say how my mother was going to come and stay with us wherever we were at the time, and part of the plan was to get the house nice and clean before my mother arrived so Promilla would be proud of it… and me… and that I should have a bath! We made much fun of getting the place ready and the water hot and me getting off my clothes and discovering there, under my vest, the waistcoat! This story was a dreadful embarrassment to Promilla and she used to beg me not to tell it, because she said somebody would believe it! Well, I hope the reader doesn't believe it, but on the other hand I want to say we had much fun out of it!

Another slightly more serious stratagem we pursued was that wherever we went we stuck to the old adages of my first posting overseas to the Punjab, which was: When you pick up the beaker to have a drink, put in a little water first for the scorpion and throw it out. When you go to put on your shoes, give them a little shake and throw out the scorpion. When you walk into the bathroom, don't do so in your bare feet, open the door first and look in to make sure there isn't a snake on the floor. Equally, with snakes be very careful when you go to draw back a curtain or open a door that there isn't a snake neatly and warmly snuggled up on or inside the curtain or on the window or on the edge of the door; give it a little shake from a distance first and be ready to step back if he does hiss at you.

It only happened once in my whole experience and that was when I returned to Lahore and my faithful servant, Munawar Din, went first of all to open the door and he did discover quite a large snake had curled up nicely in the cool of the room and was there ready to have a go at him when he opened the door! Fortunately he was able to deal with the matter very well.

A few months into my retirement I met Mrs Museveni again at a Moral Re-Armament conference in Switzerland and one of the things she asked me to do was to set up a charity in Britain for the orphans in Uganda who had been left behind by the AIDS epidemic.

I did help her a little with that and others and an organisation called UWESO, Uganda Women's Efforts to Save Orphans took off the ground and it has gone on ever since, slightly changed in its emphasis as the political and medical realities of the situation have altered.

A very simple remark by our daughter, Cherry, when I was discussing with her some of the changes in behaviour amongst ordinary people, helped me to see how things had changed. For example, when we grew up two things were absolutely wrong: one was to boast and the other was to show off. Yet, when we got back to Britain, we found there was a tendency towards what we now call 'celebrity culture' – a kind of way in which people advertise themselves. This was considered absolutely appalling behaviour to us and in discussing this with Cherry she made this point in a very simple sentence, "Ah, no Daddy, you and Mummy couldn't possibly understand the modern world, you are the fag-end of Empire." I repeat that, 'the fag-end of Empire'.

That was her way of summing up a standard way of behaving – good manners really – that appeared to have gone out of the world. She could see it I think because she had been with us on many foreign postings as a child, grown up learning how to entertain at parties and how to be entertained by people, how to travel in aeroplanes across the world and back and she had also been to boarding school, art school, the army, trained as a nurse and fought in a war, so she had an experience of life which we simply didn't have and she summed it up in this way – we, not she, were the fag-end of Empire... although perhaps in the Gulf she was part of the fag-end of Saddam's empire.

I kept a few stock phrases up my sleeve for those who asked me what it felt like to be retired. One was, "Well, it's a matter of substituting switches for servants," and when they went on and asked how that was, I was able to say that it meant if you wanted light you now turned on a switch and didn't have to ask someone to bring an oil lamp or a candle, and if you wanted hot water, likewise you turned on a switch to the kettle or your heating system and hot water came straight out of the tap and you didn't have to ask someone else to go and boil a kettle and make hot water; indeed, almost anything you wanted, you just turned a switch and it came on.

Another thing I used to say was, "I'd always regarded work as a serious impediment to retirement." That they didn't always like but at least they recognised I was trying to have a joke, and when people pressed me a little I used to say, "Well, if I was ever to write an autobiography I could begin with the sentence: 'I had reached the age of sixty and had had a cup of tea brought to me in bed every morning of my life before I realised I was a poor man'." That sentence, though not strictly accurate, was sufficiently accurate and had the merit of asking people to read on to the next page or so to find out how that had come about.

Of course, it had come about as a matter of being an assistant master in a prep school where the staff wanted you to be on time for breakfast or for your next duty. Likewise, working in climates abroad, you were expected to work with the help of people who would see you through the difficulty of the climate.

The biggest difference I suppose between working in Britain and working abroad in the areas of Africa and Asia was that you didn't have any siesta in Britain. In Pakistan, for instance, my first job overseas, you got up at five o'clock, you finished at two o'clock, you had lunch and a siesta until half-past four, maybe five even, and then you worked again until about eight when you had dinner. After dinner you took a brief walk and many of the local Pakistani people wore the same clothes for dinner as they would wear when they went to bed. Then you went to sleep and got up again at five o'clock and the amount of sleep you got at night and in the siesta was sufficient to see you through the rigours of the climate.

Two small items helped put a shape on my life in retirement. The first was that I was asked to edit our Parish magazine. That had to come out once a month on the last Sunday, so that meant there were some deadlines to be kept to. The other was that there was a meeting of a group of Moral Re-Armament people in London every Wednesday morning at half-past-ten and anybody was welcome there. After I had been overseas for so long and was a bit out of touch with the centre of things here in Europe, I went along to that meeting. So these two regularities – of Wednesday mornings and lunch times spent in London, which is not far from where I live in Ewell, and producing the magazine – kept some sort of boundaries in life, which meant that you had to decide what days you went on holiday and what days you didn't.

A Wednesday morning group

The other availability was the time to go and visit old friends, members of the family, especially within Britain itself and Ireland. One of our happiest visits was to Ireland, to County Tipperary again, to see an old friend from school days, who lived in Cashel with his wife and children. He was able to tell me a rather interesting story about the estate nearby from which my first Moral Re-Armament friend had come.

Many years ago one of the servants in their house had left Ireland and one of her children had made good in America, earned a lot of money, come back and as the social scene had changed within Ireland, had bought the estate where her family had been servants. This was a very successful effort and they put the place into good condition with their American money but, alas, found that living in such a place was just too lonely and after some time they more or less abandoned it and came back to live in the town.

I thought this showed something about the way society had altered in my lifetime, especially in Ireland, but also altered in the very home in which I had grown up between the ages of three and eight. Glenree it was called, and it was now lived in by Michael Lowry, the local Member of Parliament; in Ireland we call them TDs. He was a very nice man indeed, very pleasant, and showed my family and me around the whole place. He had improved it and I was very happy to see it in such good condition. He even showed me a little place on the wall of the coach-house, low down, where generations of whitewash had not fully obscured the pencil marks that I had made as a child years ago, so my wife took much pleasure in writing her name in pencil underneath my name from all those years ago.

Old Glenree

Other details intrigued me. One was that the good old grandfather clock which had been there when I played around in the hall as a boy, was still there, although in a slightly different position. Another was that the enormous bath (I think it was made of iron) in which my twin sister and I used to be washed when we were tiny children, was still there and when I showed amazement at this, that such an out-of-date object should be kept in this very modern house, he told me that the builder whom he had asked to take out the bath said, "Oh no, that's a very special kind of bath; you wouldn't be able to buy that for thousands of pounds; it's antique… you keep it." And he kept it. And there I stood, looking down into this veritable well where I remembered that we used to throw sponges at each other because she would be at one end of the bath and I would be at the other, with my mother or one of the maids trying their best to keep us quiet while they gave us a bath before going to bed at night.

Outside, though things were very well kept and maintained, there was a little sadness in that there was no tennis court. He told me he couldn't get people to come and work on the tennis court – people who would always be ready to roll it, mow it, mark it, keep it well surrounded by wire netting to prevent the balls going all over the place – he just couldn't get people to work like that; they all went off to the towns for other jobs where they were paid more money and where the work was not quite so hard. That was one sad thing but socially perfectly understandable.

The other was that a portion of the wall around the big, enclosed garden, where we had so many apple trees and vegetables, had fallen down just a few days before my father died and there it was still, fallen down, it hadn't actually been repaired. There was no real reason to have it repaired because it was still high enough to keep animals out but, nonetheless, my mother had always regarded it as a slight omen when she looked back and I couldn't help but get a peculiar fluttering in my stomach when I saw it.

The great old oak tree which stood in the front of the house and where my sister and I used to climb up and read comics, was still there. I was told it was five hundred years old; I'd always believed it was three hundred years but to learn that it was five hundred years old and that he and the entire countryside around were very proud of this old tree, made me feel very happy.

In the nearby town I saw the school we went to. It was now lived in by a family and was a normal house and it was rather odd to stand

The 500-year-old Oak Tree

in their drawing room and look at the wall where the big map used to hang and where Mrs Walshe told us about the world that we later went out into.

A little farther north, in County Kilkenny, we had a great family gathering in the house of my cousin, Bertie's, daughter and her family, and she assembled as many of the family as she could and we had a wonderful afternoon. Her father-in-law had been a well-known character in that part of the world, a social leader in many ways and a great collector of ancient motorcars.

So it was a glorious home-coming for me personally, but also for our daughter to fit into the past. As Cherry said to me after we had come away, "Now, Daddy, I see where you are coming from."

Another place we went to while we were there was the house at Gaile where we spent a few days at the time my father died, and I was able to show them the very spot on the gravel in front of the house where that white laser beam had come down from outer space at the moment I heard Daddy had died; and it had touched the ground just in front of the wheel of the motorcar Uncle Eddie was driving. And that rounded-off some kind of life experience for me.

Promilla, where the white beam struck

Another related joy of retirement was to be able to go down to Sussex and spend time with the old friend who had been at the same school as I was and had been in the Royal Army Veterinary Corps on the North-West-Frontier Province of India in those days. He wanted to know all about Ireland and the families who lived round about where we had all lived in Tipperary, and also he wanted to know about the situation on the borders with Afghanistan and Kashmir and that area where he had been so long ago. I was amazed at the accuracy with which he remembered the names of the villages, the streams, the various events that had taken place almost a hundred years ago it seems.

I was a dozen years into retirement when the biggest surprise of my life arrived in the form of the letter which I quote below:

Islamabad Policy Research Institute
House # 2, Street # 15, Main Margaila Road, F-7/2,
Islamabad Ph:(92-51) 9213680-2. Fax:(92-51) 9213683
Website: Www.Ipri-Pak.Org,
Email: Administrator@Ipri-Pak.Org

Ref No: VP/Gen/55-2003 June 26, 2003

To: Mr Lloyd Mullen
C/O Defence Attaché
Embassy of Pakistan
London UK

Dear Mr Mullen

On behalf of the Islamabad Policy Research Institute (IPRI), I would like to invite you to visit Pakistan. We would be glad to arrange the visit between mid September to mid October 2003. This period is suggested so that Aitchison College reopens after the summer vacations and before the start of the month of fasting (Ramadhan). Please confirm if this period is suitable from your point of view, otherwise suggest dates during which it will be convenient for you to visit Pakistan.

The tentative programme of your visit will be finalised in consultation with you and Aitchison College, Lahore.

We would appreciate, if you could let us know the places you would like to visit, and nature of activities you would prefer so that these could be incorporated in the programme.

All expenses involved in the travel and lodging would be covered by the IPRI.

With regards,

Sincerely,

(signed)

Dr Imtiaz H. Bokhari
Vice President

To say that I was surprised is not strong enough; I was stunned, absolutely stunned, for two reasons. First, this invitation had come out of the blue without any warning whatever, without any reason given – it just arrived on my desk in Ewell. The second thing was the sheer generosity of it. I was going to be able to choose when and where and how much, irrespective of the cost or the awkwardness to my hosts of the timing. For busy people this is almost unheard of and I wondered what on earth was behind it. Anyway, I went to see the Defence Attaché in the Pakistan High Commission. I knew him a little already and he was extremely helpful and almost more generous than the letter itself.

The result was that I finally took off from Heathrow, travelling First Class, on Sunday, 5th October and arrived in Islamabad on Monday morning early, to be met at the foot of the aircraft steps by a gentleman who took me to give me a cup of tea while he handed my passport to someone else to clear my luggage and told me we would talk together about the programme until we were ready to leave the airport. This reception was so kind and unexpected and so without trouble that when we did finally leave the airport and I was driven to the best hotel in Islamabad, I began to wonder why on earth this treatment was so good because a lot of trouble had been taken to arrange it and it was quite clear to me from the behaviour of the people who met me that they were extremely anxious to make sure everything went well.

Everything did indeed go well and the next few days were spent talking to the staff of The Policy Research Institute about various elements of the success or failure of Pakistan internally and externally and their foreign policy and their internal policy. They took me on a visit to Taxila, which is a very famous archaeological site, very large, dating from pre-Greek times, and showed me everything there. I had been there before but very much in a tourist capacity rather than in a proper archaeological study capacity. They also gave me dinner in the evening and introduced me to the leading lights of their universities and Foreign Policy areas. I found that these men were younger than I was and some of them I could possibly have remembered as boys, although I wasn't too sure, except in one case. Then they gave me a journey up to Peshawar to speak to people in the University Institute of Education and Research.

It was on this journey from Islamabad to Peshawar that I noted the difference from the old days when I had been there before. In the 'sixties I had gone up this road, driven myself in a motorcar, and to various other places, had got out and walked, wearing just a pair of shorts and shirt and maybe carrying a rucksack to bring stuff back, but now this was not the case. I was inside a motorcar and behind and in front of me there were jeeps carrying soldiers with guns at the ready; they went first and they came last and I was in the middle! I noticed this tremendous difference and I thought to myself 'My goodness, all our efforts at education and the development of the world have led to more of a closing down of it rather than an opening up of it for the people of the world'.

However, the drive from Peshawar up through the Khyber Pass right up to Michni Post was very exciting, particularly because halfway up we ran into a hail storm and the hail stones were as big as table tennis balls. Fortunately, because we were in a very powerful car they bounced off the roof and didn't come through, but there we stayed for some time.

I also remember having pointed out to me the narrowest part of the defile where a camel could get through with one bag on one side but not with two bags and where, even to this day, only small jeeps can go through, certainly no large lorry. That was very interesting because up above it, about forty-feet above, there was still a little look-out post that some English General had placed there years ago so that he could fire down on anyone who came through the defile.

To stand up at Michni Post and look down into Afghanistan from the border and then return to the Khyber Rifles Mess for lunch has been the ambition of several politicians and army people throughout the generations and here it was all being given to me for reasons I didn't know. I can only say that the lunch was excellent, beautifully served, and after lunch we all went out onto the balcony and sat down and were treated to a wonderful display of dancing, Waziri, Chitrali and Khattak dancing by the different Regiments to which these men belonged. They came from various parts of the North-West-Frontier and this was a way that the army had of keeping them extremely fit and extremely disciplined for all these dances are wild dances, extremely energetic, some with swords swinging, all sorts of acrobatic leaps in between and they go on for a long time.

The soldiers who performed them, in groups of about forty or fifty, were lathered in sweat by the time they finished and were obviously very glad to get off the lawn and out of their uniforms and back into some sort of comfortable clothing again, but, for those of us who were sitting in comfortable chairs, it was an experience of a lifetime.

On Thursday I flew down to Lahore where I was met and taken to Aitchison College to stay in the Principal's bungalow. The Bursar and his wife gave me dinner in the evening in their special restaurant in a new part of the city that had hardly been evident when I was there, and they were able to tell me how the city of Lahore had grown since the time I knew it. Of course it is true to say that fifty years had passed and there's no doubt it had probably doubled in size. One delight was that the Bursar's wife had been taught by my wife in college and she kept asking me how Miss Thomas was and telling me about the great fun they had when Miss Thomas was teaching, so by the end of the evening I knew a great deal more about Miss Thomas than I had ever imagined possible!

Another joy was to have dinner with one of the best pupils I ever taught in my life who had been extremely successful in his accountancy business but had, most unfortunately, gone totally blind. I was able to pick up from him and his wife their efforts to have blindness treated very well in Pakistan, and all sorts of different Institutes that they had started and different programmes to help those who were afflicted with blindness.

One early morning, sitting on the veranda in front of the Principal's bungalow and looking out over the tennis courts where I had played my first game of tennis in Pakistan way back in 1959 – on the very day that I saw my wife for the first time on the stage that evening – I noticed that there were no birds flying around the way they would have been, especially the hoopoe; I wanted to see the hoopoe – Lahore was always full of hoopoes. When I asked why there were no hoopoes I received the sad news that they no longer came to Lahore for the simple reason that the actual pollution of the atmosphere around the city was so great now that not only did birds not come but sometimes aeroplanes couldn't land because of the fog which was caused by this pollution. I could hardly believe this because the air had been so clear and crystal when I first arrived, and now I saw what a dreadful change had overtaken this beautiful city.

Then came a rather urgent message from Islamabad to say that the Prime Minister, who wanted to see me, had been held up in Washington for another day and would I please, if possible, be sure to remain in Pakistan and not return to Britain until he arrived back. This meant that I had time to go around Aitchison College and see it in its modern dress, so to speak – that was, of course, full of computers, full of the very best equipment in educational terms. However, I did notice one thing and that was that the boys themselves, although extremely well turned-out and extremely well-behaved, had far less international experience and were far less well versed in dealing with foreigners than they had been in my day and I could only put this down to the closing-down of the world which I had noticed on my road trips up and down all the way to the Khyber Pass and back.

The extra time that I had in Lahore enabled me to see the junior school's swimming gala and I noticed how it had advanced only very slightly from what it had looked like half a century before, but the standard of swimming was wonderful because the best boys in the houses took part. It was all very well organised with the ladies of the junior school looking after the very junior boys who seemed to be so disciplined that they just went in straight lines as they got out of the water after their swim straight back to where they should go.

It also meant that I arrived back in Islamabad the next day in a very peaceful state of mind and was looking forward to meeting the Prime Minister in the evening, because he had just got back from America that morning. I think both of us were glad to have had a little rest before we met.

I was taken aback when he came straight into the room where I was – in his own Prime Minister's residence – and said, "I want to thank you very much indeed." So of course, I stood up and said, "Prime Minister, it's wonderful to see you now as Prime Minister.

Congratulations… I hope all goes well." "Oh!" he said, "we'll talk about that in a moment. I just want to thank you for how you spoke up for the Baluch in London." I replied, "Beg pardon." He said, "I want to thank you; you apparently spoke up on our behalf at a meeting in London, did you not?" And then it all came back to me.

Pupil and Prime Minister

There had indeed been a public meeting in London where I'd been present and where some disparaging remarks had been made about the people of Baluchistan – so disparaging that I remember getting to my feet and interrupting and telling the assembled group that I had had the privilege of teaching boys and students in three continents all over the world and though they were mostly all the same, some were better than others and it just happened by sheer chance that one of the best ones I ever taught was a boy from Baluchistan who was now the present Prime Minister of Pakistan.

I had no idea that somewhere in the audience there was somebody who apparently reported this back to the Pakistan High Commission in London and then it went back to Islamabad to the Prime Minister himself and he, of course, remembered me because he had been a boy in my house, and immediately gave an order that I was to be sent for and made a State Guest.

Now, of course, because I was a nobody it couldn't be done just like that, so the Islamabad Policy Research Institute was used as the vehicle to get me out to Pakistan to meet him. And what a meeting it was, wonderful. We talked and talked and talked.

Then he did what the politicians of that area do, after friendship has really been re-established, after everybody is on a very even keel – and he even apologised to me for being late but he said he felt he couldn't actually refuse President Bush when he asked him at the last moment to stay over an extra day in America – he turned to me and said, "Well, have you anything for us?" This was his way of saying, "You've come a long way, you've seen a lot of things since you were here before… do you have any advice?" I had carefully thought what I wanted to say if I got the opportunity, and I said it. He was very taken aback and spoke across me to the Head of Security and said, "Is what he is saying…. (he couldn't get a word for it: right, true, proper)…. proper (he ended up with) – is it the truth?" The head of Security looked equally uncertain but after a while he nodded his head and said, "Yes, I think it is, we can easily check it out anyway." So he said, "All right, it's very difficult you know but, all right, we'll do that."

And then we went on to less serious matters and had a very friendly chat and finally I left, but just before I came away I said, "Prime Minister, congratulations, and I hope that the rest of your term will be wonderful but I do want you to know that everything that passed between us in this room I will make quite public to all my friends, be they Irish, English, America, Japanese, Indian, whatever, except that one thing that we agreed we would keep between us when you asked me." He looked at me and said, "Mr Mullen, there is no need to tell us; we know you and I understand. Moral Re-Armament was very strong in the College when we were there all those years ago. I hope you have a good journey back and do keep in touch with us." So off I went. I got on the plane the next day and came back to London, thinking that was probably the second most exciting thing of our retirement so far.

The first had been, actually, the fact of Promilla's winning the Daily Express competition for a love poem in honour of the four hundredth anniversary of Romeo and Juliet. Out of thousands of entries across the world, she won first prize – and £500 to boot! I shall not forget the scream of delight that I heard in our kitchen when I was in the dining room – her head almost went through the ceiling with delight.

What had happened was, she had seen this competition in a paper one day; I was at my desk, she was at hers, and I said, "Why don't you write something and put it in?" She did. She just sat at her desk and within two hours produced an entry, turned round to me with it in an envelope and said. "Post that for me." I posted it and we forgot all about it. It turned out to be the winning entry. This was it:

The Games of Love

I wish I loved you as I am, myself,
Not as this other being, who can sense
Your entry to a room, yet, nerves intense,
Ignore your presence, disregard your self.

This other self plays games of high pretence;
Aware of your approach across the room,
Coming to share my laughter, I presume,
I walk away with artful innocence.

My proper me, with hyper-sharpened ear
Is swift to answer silent telephones;
In your most formal notes seeks undertones
Of hidden meanings, secret love made clear.

As I am me, I long for love returned,
My other self pretends your love is spurned.

Our daughter, Cherry's marriage to fellow artist, Peter Blundell, has been another highlight of our retirement and the subsequent birth of her daughter and son.

'Lowlights' we might call them, have been the successful quadruple by-pass operation which I had and the successful triple by-pass operation which Promilla had, both in St. Thomas's Hospital in London. We were very well looked after through Epsom Hospital and our local Bourne Hall Medical Centre here. These events have kept the family going and look like keeping it going for some time.

A rare privilege came my way through my friendship with the Luwum family of Uganda. The Archbishop had been killed in Idi Amin's time and it was decided that his statue would be one of the last ones to be put up over the great West Door of Westminster Abbey. Ten niches had been left throughout all history to be filled in as and when the Church of England decided. It was decided that these niches should be dedicated to the Christian Martyrs of the twentieth century and that ten significant figures would be chosen from all parts of the globe for having died in pursuit of their faith.

If you go there today you will see, third from the left, a statue of Archbishop Luwum, and third from the right you will see a statue of Esther John, a young girl from the sub-continent of India and Pakistan. Beside Luwum you will see a statue of St. Elizabeth of Russia. I mention these three because they refer directly to the privilege I had of being in the Abbey on the day when these statues were unveiled.

A Lambeth Conference was in progress and many of the bishops and archbishops from all over the world who were present at it, were in the Abbey, all together on the left-hand side of the aisle. On the right-hand side were the families of the martyrs and each family had been entitled to bring one friend to the Abbey with them. I was invited by the Luwum family.

The reason for mentioning St. Elizabeth of Russia is that her great-nephew, Prince Philip, Duke of Edinburgh, was present as a representative of her family and he had brought, as he was entitled to do, a friend. He had brought his wife, Her Majesty the Queen, who was, in her own capacity, going to take part in the unveiling ceremony. It was strange to see her sitting alone, a little ahead of the front pew of those of us on the right-hand side, but it was also a sign of equality between all the different peoples of the world represented by these sacrifices made by the ten people whose statues were outside.

The girl I mentioned, Esther John, had been well-known to my wife's parents in Lahore because of the tragedy of her life and how she came to be martyred. She had for a while been looked after and sheltered by them in Lahore, so she was almost a part of the family.

One of the feelings that one came away with from that service was that we people in the world are one family and however much we may kill each other, when it comes to final thought we are but one group together and we remember that.

This led me back to a thought I'd come across in George Steiner's work some years before where he had written that he could somehow imagine a great genius like Jane Austen putting down her pen, slipping away to have a sip of tea and a biscuit and thinking to herself that she was reasonably satisfied with what she had just written. Steiner said he found it much more difficult, nearly impossible, to imagine Shakespeare slipping away and sitting down and thinking to himself 'that last bit of King Lear or Hamlet', which he had written, 'was really rather good'! However, then Steiner went on to say that when he looked at and read the 15th, 16th and 17th chapters of the Gospel according to St. John, he found it utterly impossible and he described these chapters and some other part of the Bible as 'Absolute Revelation' – nothing else but Absolute Revelation, no human composition involved.

Another effect which this set of ten statues and the day of their unveiling has had on my life is that whenever now I walk round the front of Westminster Abbey or in Parliament Square, around about that centre of London where so much of the government of Church and State is carried on and the great hall opposite of the Wesleyan Methodist Hall, I am not in any way in awe of the greatness of it all. These ordinary people, Luwum, Esther John, Elizabeth and the others there, have brought it all down to earth and brought it down to earth in a very earthy way, too. The whole thing seems almost normal and natural and it is the great buildings – the Cathedral, the Houses of Parliament – they are the ones that seem almost strange and unreal, sometimes almost unrelated to real life and yet very much related to the best things in life.

Many of these best things have been encapsulated for me in a Daily Reading book which I keep, which was co-edited in his retirement by the British Council Officer who first of all criss-crossed, so to speak, with Moral Re-Armament in my life and who later turned up at Lahore when I was already there.

At that time the British Council offices in Lahore were good offices but were in a horrible place at the end of a rather narrow, mucky street which was very often flooded and occasionally full of cow dung because of the way in which the city worked. I remember saying to him that I felt really the Council ought to get out of that place and get into some better premises just for the public image of the Council. He said to me, "No, it's impossible, it's too expensive, London would never wear it. I'd have a dreadful fight to get them to agree to that and, of course, with the rest of the British Council in Pakistan who take some of the money." So, in thinking about this afterwards, I said to myself, "If I'm not prepared to fight with him to get better premises, I can't expect him to fight with the British Council in London or the people in the City Council in Lahore." So I did; I put up a bit of a fight and said, "No, it's appalling, we can't go on like this, we've put up with it for too long, let's get out."

The short of it is that he did, and he won his fight, and the British Council in Lahore shifted into very fine premises. I hope they're there to this day, if they haven't closed down, but they were very fine premises indeed and not at all difficult to get when it came to the fight.

I think the fact that we won that particular fight helped me a little much later on when I was retiring and coming back to London after several years overseas. I knew that back in London I would meet lots of people who had worked together in Britain and Europe for thirty or forty years when I wasn't around and I would be a bit 'out of it', because some of these families had even married into each other, they had taken part in the same sort of campaigns, they knew a great deal about the way in which the Western world worked, which I didn't, so I really prayed very hard to find out what I ought to try to do when I did get back in retirement, and I had a very clear thought that crystallised in my mind and it came out like this:

Fight so that Jesus Christ is at the heart
of those at the heart of Moral Re-Armament.

Now this gave me a widening of the mind that saved me from one of my great worries. That widening was that I had had the immense privilege over the previous forty or so years of working with Buddhists, Jains, Hindus, Muslims and many different sects and groups of these religions and also people of no religion or even overt Communism, who, when they applied the simple standard of absolute honesty to their own lives and to the actions that their organisations took, had definitely produced a much better life for those around them and indeed a much better life for themselves in most cases. So I wasn't actually afraid of this injunction, I just took it on board and it has given me a pointer of what to do and what to try to do all the time.

One thing I didn't spot when I retired first was that there was a basic difference between working in The Third World and working in Britain. In The Third World you could almost always see some actual material improvement in the lives of the people around you as a result of the application of absolute moral standards to the situation in which they existed, but back in Britain the need was almost the other way round. Materialism had got such a grip of the Western World that the advance of absolute morality would almost certainly have brought about a different way of living, a different kind of attitude which would be at odds with the rampant materialism that was taking over the end of the century and the beginning of the next century.

The way out of this conundrum, I discovered, was to concentrate on the human individual and not worry about anything else, not worry about the circumstances around, just concentrate on the future happiness of the individual with whom I was concerned, because, once I remembered that, then there was a central core of common sense to what I was doing. All around me I could see that politicians, sociologists and economists had very little idea of how to manage the countries of the West in any sort of common sense way.

I remember my mind going back to that day in the 1960s when I saw the Major of the Pakistan Army sitting in the Staff Room at Aitchison College with tears coming from his eyes as he read the names of officers and men in the Indian Army who had been his colleagues just some twenty years before who had been killed fighting the Chinese in their war. Those tears really did prove to me that the world is one and that however much we split it up into countries, into groups, into castes, into clans and into classes, it will always remain one and we diminish ourselves the moment we forget that.

About this time, that old friend who had brought me to see Bulganin and Kruschev being received by Nehru in the Red Fort in Delhi way back in 1959, and who is now in his nineties, asked me for a particular piece which I had written in our Church magazine here when I had come back and he remembered it from about ten years before, so I cut it out and gave it to him and even as I read it now I find it is not too different from my basic thought all the time. I give it here for what it's worth:

IDEOLOLGY? WHAT'S THAT?

To attempt to explain ideology is to risk idiot-ology.

Communism is the ideology with which most people are familiar. It is accessible both in theory and in history, and was well wrapped-up in a man I knew.

He was the son of a Durham miner. Just five feet tall, he won scholarships to Grammar School, Durham and Oxford where he was seized on by public school oarsmen as the ideal cox for their boat. However, accents and behaviour proved incompatible, and he soon wanted to destroy the social system which forced his parents to live lives so different from the oarsmen's.

It was the 'thirties. Communism was in the air. Was it a way forward? He examined it. Blunt, Burgess, Maclean and Philby were examining it in the other place. All around him students were asserting that human beings should be treated equally and given the same chances in life. It seemed self-evident but when he asked himself the question, "Why should everybody be treated the same?" no clear answer would come because he could see with his own eyes that while many men and women were honest and hardworking, others were dishonest and lazy; some were generous, others mean; some civic-spirited, others selfish; some lackadaisical, others power-hungry. Why should he regard them all as worthy of the same treatment? About this time his conversion to Christianity gave him the answer. He suddenly saw that if he regarded every single one of them as a child of a loving God, then he would have a powerful reason for treating them all equally.

But Communism said there was no God. It dawned on him that there was a fatal flaw in Communism. He was also beginning to see how Communists actually behaved.

Even so, he had to acknowledge that many sincere intelligent people belonged to Communism and could not be shifted from their allegiance. They had been taken over by an idea which they believed would take over the world. He began to understand the power of ideology and saw how even limited ideologies like Nazism and Fascism could take over whole countries. As the 'thirties progressed, he struggled to articulate what he felt for miners, oarsmen and humanity worldwide.

The nations were stumbling towards war when in May 1939 he wrote:

> Three great tasks confront this generation:
>
> - to keep the peace and make it permanent;
> - to make the wealth and work of the world available to all and for the exploitation of none, and
> - with peace and prosperity as our servants and not our masters, to build a new world, create a new culture and change the age of gold into the Golden Age.

The nations did stumble into war in September 1939 but he never gave up his struggle to impart a Christian ideology to everybody he met. He died recently at ninety-one, leaving behind a permanent challenge to us all. That's ideology. St. Mary's passes on his challenge in the certainty that God can give to everyone the part they have to play in these great tasks, and the power to play it.

* * * * *

The trouble, I've realised, in recording a memoir for the family is that almost every tiny item could have a whole chapter to itself so I'll spill out now a few ridiculously trivial little things that come to mind lest they get forgotten altogether.

In Uganda, at a certain time of the year, if you had a very bright light and if the climate was exactly correct, certain insects flew up suddenly from their hiding places and fluttered about like tiny butterflies in the air and the local children and adults ran about catching them in mid-air and eating them on the spot, taking them out of the air straight into their mouths and eating them. I remember looking down from the balcony of our house in Kampala and seeing all our servants rush out of the house because the security light had suddenly come on and in this very bright light all these little insects had come buzzing around, absolutely busy, and there were our servants buzzing about even more busily grabbing them and eating them before they got lost!

Another very odd feeling I had was when I heard on a radio broadcast that there was a possibility that the Grand National racecourse at Aintree was going to be closed down because the owner was selling it and there wouldn't be any more Grand National races run. My goodness, I felt the end of the world was about to come – that there was a collapse of civilisation – because I'd grown up with the wonderful name 'Tipperary Tim', nothing else in my head, Tipperary Tim had won the Grand National. When I checked up I did find that Tipperary Tim won the Grand National in 1928 and was the only horse to finish out of forty-six that started.

Another sudden memory was of a rather nasty but very superior lady who made a joke to her other lady friends about another lady who had put up some wonderful wallpaper on her drawing room wall and got them all to see it, without realising that this wallpaper was the same as in the loo at the Savoy. Oh dear, that was a stroke of bitterness which I didn't like but, in fairness to that same lady, when I left the house, having tutored her children for some time, she almost broke down at the motorcar and said, "Goodbye, Mr Mullen, and thank you very much for being so kind to the children."

A moment of wonder was turning over in bed on my holidays from teaching in my very first job and hearing again on the radio that Ireland had left the Commonwealth. That really took me by surprise and I didn't know for quite a while how it would affect us.

Also connected with my time as a schoolboy was the very interesting news that in the same town of Waterford, in the Ursuline Convent, a girl of my own age (later to become a well-known writer called Dervla Murphy), had stood to attention in the middle of the playground at eleven o'clock one morning while all the other children were playing around her; she stood quite still because she knew that at that moment the last living member of a certain group of IRA men was being executed in Dublin.

I remember also a colleague who came to work with me in my first teaching post, who said he had been teaching in Jerusalem and I knew that the old boy of the school I went to, called Dick Easton, who was famous for his ill deeds, had also been a schoolmaster in Jerusalem, so I asked this newcomer whether he had ever come across Dick Easton. He took a pace back, blanched, held out his hands and said, "My God, that fellow! He's left a 'wake of foam' behind him all through the Middle East!"

I also remember a friend I had in Dublin who took immense trouble to raise the standard of what was expected of foreign students back in the 'fifties and 'sixties. He actually managed to get the Nigerian Students' Union in Dublin to hold their annual Anniversary Meeting in Dublin's best hotel rather than in the small place where they had been holding them before. He did this simply by going along to the manager of the hotel, asking him to arrange it and making sure the Press were there to cover the event. All these Nigerian students turned up in bow-ties and it was a wonderful occasion, quite different from what had been happening to foreign students in Ireland before.

There was also Tito Gobbi, the great Italian tenor, giving a master class to a lady who wasn't very good at acting but was a great singer. She wanted to act this particular scene in which she had to sing a 'High C', but what was happening was that she was giving a little squeak at the 'High C' point, so focused was she on the acting that she forgot the singing! He stopped her and said, "My dear, when you have a problem in life, the very worst thing you can do is to run up to it, touch it and then run away. No – stop, come up to it slowly, somehow get up above it and come down upon it and then you will find everything falls into place." She did just that and it worked.

I remember a clergyman friend who was elevated to become a bishop, being teased about it by his friends for some time and one of them said, "How does it feel, Charlie, now that you are a bishop?" "Oh!" he said, "I'm dealing with a whole host of new sins – mostly presumptuous ones."

Another event which amused me at the time, was in Lahore when it turned out that Promilla was pregnant. She didn't know she was pregnant at first but I was having all sorts of pains in my tummy. I went along to see the doctor and after he had done a lot of investigation – this, that and the other – he finally said, "No, you're not pregnant but I suspect your wife might be; you had better send her to me." It turned out to be true!

Another wonderful occasion was once in the Highlands of Scotland when we were on holiday staying in someone else's house, and Cherry, aged about six, discovered a jerry under one of the beds, dragged it out, held it up and said, "What an enormous teacup!"

An English colleague, when I went to teach in Devon, told me how he had been caught in the very early stages of the war and put into a prison camp in Germany, right in the centre of the country, far away from action of any kind, with a lot of Irish Guards who were also caught in the same operation. They more or less spent the whole war far away in the centre of Germany; very pleasant countryside but no hope of escaping unfortunately, and there was nothing really to do with the war until one day – a lovely summer's day with a clear sky – two aeroplanes hove into sight; one was German, one was English and they were chasing each other round the sky trying to shoot one another down. Finally the English plane shot the German down and, of course, all the prisoners in the camp who were now out and watching this, cheered and clapped and roared, but the German guards quickly turned their guns on them and told them to stop. In the silence that followed, everybody saw that the German pilot who had bailed out was going to come down and pass through the one tiny white cloud that was in that whole blue sky, and my English colleague said, "While I watched it I heard a big Irish brogue behind me say, 'Well, may his parachute catch on that cloud and may he hang there forever'."

Another unexpected wakening in the middle of the night came about when we had a little puppy who was so young my wife was very worried that she may miss her mother, so she let her sleep on top of a blanket beneath which she had put a clock with the idea that the ticking of the clock would somehow or other come through the blanket resembling the sound of the mother's heart and the little puppy would feel happy and comfortable and sleep well. Indeed she did... until the alarm went off! You can imagine what happened with one puppy, two adults and one alarm clock jumping about in the bedroom!

A moving experience was to find in the Vice-Regal Cathedral in Delhi that the paintings inside the dome had been done by my wife's uncle and one of the cherubs in it had the face of his wife, which is a tradition in art I understand, and that his portrayal of St. Thomas contained his own face because, of course, the family name was Thomas. That was very moving to see, especially since it was right beside the centre of Government in India, Rajtrapati Bhavan, in the capital city.

Another amusing memory of Lahore comes to mind in that the students of the University marched right down the Mall one afternoon, shouting against the government for some reason or the other. One of the British Council officers saw them coming and retreated to the British Council office but he was unable to get in because the door was locked so he stood against the wall and sure enough a group of students peeled off and came across the road straight for him, right up to him. He was terrified, but they said, "Excuse us, Sir, but could you give us a lecture on Romeo and Juliet next Thursday?"

It was at Douglas Seton's funeral that I began to realise how life can be rounded-off in a very satisfactory manner, a very happy way. I had known Douglas from when I was three years of age and he was probably twenty, and I had grown up around Holycross Church in the village of Holycross in Ireland. His father had been the huntsman, his sister was the whipper-in of the local hounds, his mother played the harmonium in our church and he himself had been to the school I later went to, and he went off to be a veterinary surgeon and joined the Royal Army Veterinary Corps.

In addition to fighting in various wars, he spent a lot of time on the North-West-Frontier of India as it was in those undivided days, later of Pakistan. I was asked to speak at his funeral and, looking out the various things I thought I might say to the younger people at that service (for Douglas was deep in his nineties), I came across the very simple things of our lives:

That he and his sister, Eileen, had driven themselves from home to school in a pony and trap, got to the school, unharnessed the pony, let it graze while they were in school and when school was over, harnessed up the animal again, got into the trap and drove home. It sounds wonderful on a nice summer day with the sun shining but in winter time with frost and snow and maybe both the wheels of the trap and the hooves of the pony slipping and sliding, it was far from pleasant and then, of course, ordinary heavy showers of rain betimes with no cover.

But these were normal things and there was no such thing as a telephone to let your parents know that you were going to be late or that you had been held up because some accident had happened to the pony. Also, there was no electricity to light up the place in the early morning in the winter when you were getting ready to go – you had to have an oil lamp or some sort of lantern, which you took out with you to the stables.

All these things had happened around us at home and to us they seemed perfectly normal. They were very physical things of course, and there were all sorts of local country people who understood them to help us with them. The great thing in the country was that in a funny kind of way you never were alone – even a total stranger was your friend when trouble started. Thus it had gone on like this.

As I thought back over the times that Douglas had come home on leave and I had perhaps been back home from school and we met, and Eileen (his sister) who had married and gone off to Zambia, as it became, (in those days Northern Rhodesia), we were able to see how before the brother and sister and I ever left Ireland, we were well used to the political conflicts, the different parties and the relationship with England. Douglas was often asked, for instance, why, as an Irishman, he joined the British Army.

The other thing that often happened was the difference between Roman Catholic and Protestant, which was quite severe, but we had learned to negotiate all those things because we were friends with our neighbours and this friendship with the local people around us and their friendship with us, saw us through many difficulties; for example, when the Black and Tans were in Ireland those people who were Protestant would take their own Catholic friends into their houses and protect them and those people who were Roman Catholics would take their Protestant friends into their houses and protect them from the IRA, so there was an ability to understand that while there were very fierce religious, political and social differences in the world, the business of life really was to negotiate between them until you could bring them closer together and this is exactly why both Douglas and Eileen were so successful in their lives – one in the heart of Asia and the other in the heart of Africa – and I can honestly say that I myself, following on, found my life really very easy in Pakistan, India, Sri Lanka and in Africa, Uganda. The people were just friendly, which was what counted, and we all had things to do together because we all had a purpose in the fields of medicine, education and general development.

And then I remember thinking of when Douglas came back to England to be one of the veterinary judges of horses – as to whether they were fit to race or not, he went to various racecourses judging them – and me having left Ireland at a time when the very name 'Tipperary Tim' was still on the tongues of local people ten years after that horse had won the Grand National, and here I was now, retired and within comfortable walking distance of the Derby Racecourse at Epsom.

This sort of link with the country and with horses in particular was a very simple joy for us all. Indeed, as I write this, my granddaughter is going to spend her very first day learning how to sit on a pony while the pony wanders about the place. I hope she will enjoy it.

The church in which Douglas's Memorial service was held was called Holycross, the same name as that little church in Ireland where we had all been and where his father had taken up the collection. I can still see him because he had a moustache and, as a very small child, moustaches were quite fascinating and, while his mother was playing the harmonium and his sister was singing in the choir alongside my mother and father, there was this sense of family. There were very few other families because there weren't many Protestants in that part of the world in those days; we were probably twenty to thirty at the most in that church.

Also that church gave us some kind of sense of stability in that Sunday was a day when you did in fact remember God – we didn't know who God was, what God was, or where God was, but you knew he was God – and Sunday was for him. You knew also that while other people didn't talk about it they felt the same, or you imagined they felt the same, so this was a great stabiliser in all our lives wherever we went afterwards, to school, university, training college or jobs. In my very first job the school had its own little chapel right in the centre of the quadrangle. This meant that religion was unquestioned; it was just there, the way food was on the table at lunchtime or the way you went to bed at night and slept and got up the next morning, it was a natural, normal thing.

Another useful thing which I believe that country life gave us from the start was a sort of acceptance of rude physical health and an acceptance, too, that you were always getting cuts and bruises – the natural world wasn't very kind to you, and you had to deal with it; trees somehow or other you fell out of and they didn't help you to get back up – you had to look after yourself and couldn't blame the tree. It sounds ridiculous as an adult but that's the effect it had on us as children. I noticed afterwards when playing games or even when teaching boys how to play games, one of the happiest things was that they grew to accept that you do have to take the rough with the smooth, literally, and you can't go complaining to the umpire or referee that someone has hurt you when you have been foolish enough to let yourself get hurt.

I was interested in the reaction of many of those people in the congregation at Douglas's funeral when afterwards they asked me all sorts of questions about his life and life in the country and what had happened, because of course the experiences I mentioned as perfectly normal were quite outside their experiences and very unusual for them; they had never thought of that having happened to him. They had seen a very successful, retired army officer, retired as the Brigadier, as head of the veterinary service in the British Army. Indeed, one of his most onerous tasks he once told me was near his retirement – to go to the Dublin Horse Show and carefully select some 'fine blacks with nice white fluffy hooves to make a good impression as they drew some important carriage up or down the Mall'.

Douglas's niece, Sydney, was also present at that service and she and I were able to share the fact that our mothers had been the rather naughty girls who, in the thirties, just prior to the outbreak of war, had discovered that because electricity had come to the local places they were able, with one switch, to plunge an entire Hunt Ball into darkness! You can imagine what whoops of delight and happiness and worry and anxiety happened when they did that, but it did happen and of course they hastily put the lights back on and I don't think they ever owned up as being the ones who did it, but Sydney and I discovered afterwards that it was indeed they who were guilty.

And so this long family connection, just because we grew up around the same part of the country in Holycross, played a most powerful enlivening part in our lives.

Also in that same area of the country we had grown up with the Pennefeather family and Lionel had been the very first one of that country to crystallise his religious beliefs along the lines of the Oxford Group, as they were in those days, and this gave a rather less comfortable but more trenchant meaning to religion. The way in which it later affected my own life personally is the only reason for mentioning it here.

There is however a very special reason for rather emphasising Holycross Church because my daughter said to me at various times in her very early childhood, things which almost nonplussed me at the time. One of them was when I was unable to keep a promise to her and she looked at me and slightly stamped her foot and said, "Well if you won't do you mustn't say." Another thing she once said was, "It must be a wonderful thing to leave behind you when you die a beautiful thing like a painting or piece of sculpture or something like that." A third thing she said – she was about seven at the time I suppose – was, "Daddy, when you speak, the words come out of your mouth and they go into my ear and I know what you mean. That's a miracle isn't it?" Well, I just had to admit that it was a miracle.

A little while later she said something else, which was, "When you remember something you did, Daddy, you see yourself in the picture doing it but that's impossible because when you were actually doing it you couldn't possibly have seen yourself doing it, could you?" Now, what went through my mind when she said that was that I once had had a very minor accident in the car when somebody drove out of a side road too quickly and hit me behind after I had almost gone past, and I always imagined in my head that I saw that accident very clearly but of course, as Cherry had said, I couldn't possibly have seen it clearly because I was looking ahead down the road and I only imagined what had happened when I was hit by that other car – I felt it but didn't actually see it hit me.

I was posted to Karachi about that time and it happened that we had to host the President of the Royal Society who was in the country on some special scientific visit. I mentioned this to him and he took it very seriously and said, "Yes, that's a problem that we have talked and thought about for many years and we are on the way to solving it," and then he went into some reasonably sensible scientific description of how the dots of memory and the dots of thought and the dots of actual sight could build up into a picture, which logically would have to be filled out by other dots which finally would give you a sort of photograph of the event.

Aged six, Cherry was asked, "What does your Mummy do?"

She replied, "She's a writer."

"Oh, what does she write?" said the teacher.

"I'm not sure. I think she makes the wrong things righter"!

Well, I am very happy to say that one of them definitely will be fulfilled as far as I'm concerned for my daughter and that is the thought that it is a wonderful thing to pass through the world and then, when you die, leave behind something of great beauty and worthwhile. I think she's already done it:

I have on my wall here in our house two pictures – one of the house in which I was actually born, Springfield, just the other side of Holycross from where Glenree, the second house I lived in, was situated. It's a lovely little painting she has done of it. The other painting is larger and it is actually of Holycross Church. It's not simply that these paintings are good likenesses of the actual places themselves – they are – but they couldn't be of anywhere else... they are very good. But, in some magical way they have caught the atmosphere of the place as I remember it.

It's impossible I suppose to know what will work when you are really painting a picture, unless you are a very great artist indeed, but whatever way Cherry has done these two paintings they certainly for me have caught the whole beginning of my life – no question about that whatever. There's not a false stroke in any section, they're absolutely there.

When I tell you that the beginning of our lives, my twin sister and I, in that house called Springfield (a good name to begin life in I

Cherry's painting of Holycross Church

suppose) between us weighed seven-and-a-half pounds and were a whole month premature (my mother said we looked like two little rats), we have much to be grateful for. Apparently, the midwife who delivered us – Nurse Salmon was her name – wrapped us in cotton wool and put us on a board or something in front of a fire in the kitchen and kept us warm so that we lived, and we are still alive so obviously she did a good job.

Anyway, I am very grateful to Nurse Salmon, my mother, my father, the doctor and now, of course, to my daughter for how wonderfully she has captured that place and that church.

And finally – Tipperary's green fields claim our hearts at birth and, go where we may, hold on to them forever.

The family in 2010